Literary Intellectuals

and the

Dissolution of the State

LITERARY INTELLECTUALS

AND THE

DISSOLUTION OF THE STATE

Professionalism and Conformity
in the GDR
SHL
WITHDRAWN

Edited by
Robert von Hallberg

Translated by
Kenneth J. Northcott

The University of Chicago Press
Chicago & London

Robert von Hallberg is professor in the Department of Germanic Languages and Literatures, the Department of English Languages and Literatures, the Department of Comparative Studies in Literature, and the College, at the University of Chicago. He is the author of *Charles Olson: The Scholar's Art* (1978) and *American Poetry and Culture, 1945–1980* (1985). He has edited two previous works published by the University of Chicago Press— *Canons* (1984) and *Politics and Poetic Value* (1987). He is the founding editor of the University of Chicago Phoenix Poets series and also edits the journal *Modernism in Modernity*.

The University of Chicago Press, Chicago 60637
The University of Chicago Press, Ltd., London
© 1996 by The University of Chicago
All rights reserved. Published 1996
Printed in the United States of America
05 04 03 01 00 99 98 97 96   1 2 3 4 5

ISBN: 0-226-86497-9 (cloth)
0-226-86498-7 (paper)

Library of Congress Cataloging-in-Publication Data

von Hallberg, Robert, 1946–
Literary intellectuals and the dissolution of the state :
professionalism and conformity in the GDR / edited by Robert von
Hallberg ; translated by Kenneth J. Northcott.
p.   cm.
Includes bibliographical references and index.
1. Authors, German—Germany (East)—Interviews. 2. Authors,
German—20th century—Interviews. 3. Intellectuals—Germany (East)—
Interviews. 4. Literature and society—Germany (East). 5. Authors,
German—Germany (East)—Political and social views. 6. Germany—
History—Unification, 1990. I. Northcott, Kenneth J. II. Title.
PT3707.V66   1996
830.9'9431—dc20   95-11341
CIP

To the memory of

William Richard von Hallberg

by Gerd Hellerich. I reduced the transcripts by 60 to 70 percent in most instances, and I sent the edited versions to the interviewees for their feedback. The changes they proposed were incorporated into the texts, which were then translated into English. I edited the English versions quite heavily, cutting again and revising for readability. My objective has been to produce a readable text of conversations on particular themes.

Acknowledgments

I began this project quite suddenly, and I was very fortunate to find support for my efforts on short notice from Alan Thomas and Morris Philipson, of the University of Chicago Press, and from the Alexander von Humboldt Foundation and the German American Academic Exchange. I am very grateful for their timely generosity. Colleagues and friends at Chicago have offered criticism of the Introduction and Conclusion to this book; I owe a great deal to the advice of Lawrence Rothfield, Jessica Burstein, and Alan Shapiro. Anke Pinkert, Mila Ganeva, Vreni Naess, and Matthias Konzett assisted with the notes. Stephanie Hawkins and Cecilia Novero helped with the editing of the conversations. I am very grateful to them for their engagement with this project. Andreas and Ele Höfele kept me stocked with clippings from the German press that helped me stay reasonably current with revelations and disagreements.

PART ONE

Introduction

Introduction

What's that: science, research, and historical processes?
In any event they have to write it the way we want it.

A former member of the GDR Politburo,
quoted by Rolf Schneider, *Frühling im Herbst,* 107

On November 9, 1989, the Berlin Wall became a memory. Five weeks later the Communist Party (Sozialistische Einheitspartei Deutschlands, SED), desperate for new life, changed its name to the Party for Democratic Socialism (PDS). On March 18, 1990, free elections were held in the GDR, and the PDS, with only 16 percent of the vote, lost all hope of governing; the Social Democrats, to the surprise of most German intellectuals, won only 22 percent. The real winner, with 41 percent, was the Christian Democratic Party (CDU) of Helmut Kohl, the party that had first called for speedy reunification of the two Germanies. On July 1, 1990, the West German mark became the currency for both Germanies. Three months later the former GDR was incorporated into the Federal Republic of Germany (FRG).

The authoritarian East German state had been expeditiously and bloodlessly dissolved, despite the existence of an enormous and allegedly efficient police apparatus. Although a very few German intellectuals, in the east and west, had spoken seriously of reunification during the year before November 1989 (Martin Walser in "Über Deutschland reden" [1988] and Erich Loest in *Fallhöhe* [1989]), events took everyone by surprise. "For several decades," as Stephen Brockmann recently said, "the very concept, let alone the reality, of reunification had been almost taboo in German intellectual circles."[1] "German intellectuals, left and right," Martin Walser observed in 1988, "are agreed on very little else: the division of Germany is acceptable."[2] Even conservative West German politicians, who were committed to the cause of reunification, seemed for years to use this issue as school prayer is used in the United States: more to gesture loyalty toward a conservative constituency than to prepare for an impending event.[3] The GDR president, Erich Honecker, had said in August 1989 that the Wall would stand for at least another hundred years.[4] No one on either side expected to see reunification happen so soon, and so easily. The failure of anyone to foresee this quick transition indicates that the cold war status quo enforced constraints on even the imaginations of nearly all German intellectuals.

Americans live like Romans, convinced that the state will endure, or rather that its passing, though inevitable, is too remote to contemplate. The permanence of the state is recognized as an illusion by American intellectuals, but the illusion is accepted because radical change at the level of the nation-state is, after two hundred years of stability, unimaginable. In my memory, the most dramatic governmental upheaval was the resignation of Richard Nixon—nothing compared to what Europeans have recently experienced. Intellectuals in America and the Germanies thought they knew the narrow limits of possible change in cold war Europe. They were wrong. After the events of 1989, they lost credibility and are now vulnerable to sharp reproaches. "Hundreds of thousands, masses, that is," according to Martin Walser, "have expressed themselves more truthfully, more exactly, even more correctly than all the intellectuals."[5] It was partly the intellectuals' belief that they knew themselves, knew their roles, and knew just what was expected of them that obscured from their view the full range of political possibility. Speculation about the end of the cold war was not on the intellectual agenda before November 1989. The professional orders of the intellectual life in the Germanies bear some significant responsibility for the constrained political imaginations of intellectuals: this is one of the conclusions that follow from the conversations recorded here.

What price must Germany and its intellectuals now pay for this failure of imagination? What might American intellectuals learn from the German experience about their own responsibility to imagine great and even abrupt social and political change in detail? The point of these questions is not merely that it is embarrassing to be surprised by the unforeseen, but also, and more important, that a constrained imagination of economic, political, and social alternatives can preclude one's participation in the shaping of the future. That is the price now being paid by German intellectuals, the most articulate of whom desired, expected, and predicted the formation of a democratic socialist government in the GDR after 1989. Intellectuals in the east are better off only insofar as they have the West Germans to blame for the conquest of the five new provinces.

On November 8, 1989, Christa Wolf, Stefan Heym, Volker Braun, Christoph Hein, and a number of others issued a call for democratic socialism in the GDR. On the same day Wolf went on East German television to plead with her fellow citizens not to emigrate. Three weeks later she, Braun, and several other writers and intellectuals signed a plea "For Our Country": "We still have the chance as a state with equal rights to all of our neighboring states in Europe to develop a socialistic alternative to the FRG. We can still recall the antifascist and humanistic ideals with which we started."[6] They were very wrong. Now, largely discredited, they must sit on the sidelines. The surprising feature of this statement is its insensitivity to the popular rejection of the Communist Party and socialism in general. The phrase about the antifascist and humanistic ideals of the past is a bold, obtuse effort to retain the clichés of the Communist Party's self-presentation. Wolf, Heym, Braun, and many other intellectuals discredited themselves by completely miscalculating the direction in which democratic processes would lead citizens of the GDR. It must be said too that East German intellectuals were not alone in believing that the voters of the GDR would choose a democratic socialist alternative to the FRG. West German public opinion polls also ineptly gauged the popular will.[7] Günter de Bruyn acknowledged that many East German writers felt betrayed by their very readers—the ones who voted for the CDU.[8] Less than a week before the March 1990 election, Christoph Hein had felt convinced by letters from his readers that there was no gulf between intellectuals and the people.[9] At the end of October 1989 he had told *Der Spiegel* that the intellectuals and the people of the GDR were united in the wish for an improved socialism.[10] Fritz Rudolf Fries spoke bitterly for many East German intellectuals when he said, "The astonishing ability of the masses to exalt themselves, to defend themselves with common sense, and to show all the world that exactly they, who knew the least, now know everything and want everything, is the most lasting lesson of this revolutionary autumn."[11] That is what has cost intellectuals most dearly: not so much that they did not foresee unification as that the popular support for simple annexation was unexpected and dispiriting for intellectuals. Especially in the popular press, German intellectuals have been attacked for a failure of spirit, for not greeting the fall of the GDR with sufficient enthusiasm. The tabloid *Bild-Zeitung,* on the first anniversary of the opening of the Wall, commented that "Germany's intellectuals are standing in the corner. The vast majority of them do not acknowledge this significant day in German history."[12] For them, the more important day was March 18, 1990, when the East German people demonstrated their complete lack of support for any form of socialism. "Never in the history of the Federal Republic," Andreas Huyssen wrote, "has the sense of self-confidence and self-worth of intellectuals been at such a low point."[13]

Since November 1989 many German intellectuals have continued to characterize their loyalties in terms of two unresolved contradictions: that between democratic procedures and a socialist state, and that between socialism and a market economy. Did East German intellectuals from November 4, 1989, until March 18, 1990, even take seriously the existence of a popular political will that might reject socialism, or did they tend to think that intellectuals, especially writers, would largely shape what would be expressed as popular sentiment at the polls? And what does it mean to advocate a socialist state without a planned economy? These questions, implied by the avowals of democratic socialism, the third way, which became common after November 1989, remain entirely open and indicate that German intellectuals have not yet clarified even the terms in which to discuss options. One week after the opening of the Wall, Stefan Heym asked impatiently, "Where, in the devil's name, is the new thinking that is so necessary, so desperately needed? Should we have more socialism—yes or no? And if we say yes, what kind of socialism do we mean? With what percent market economy, what property relations?"[14] Peter Schneider, equally exasperated, said, "I haven't so far been able to determine what people mean by the phrase 'third way.' No one up to now has described in economic terms how you can have both at once: a market economy *and* socialism, the right to work *and* market-based prices."[15] The nearly silent darkness from which these calls came persisted until the questions became, as they now are, moot.

Intellectuals seem to have failed their public by suppressing the issue of reunification. "What our politicians, our media, our literature, our philosophy, and our films were unable to establish," Martin Walser said in December 1989, "this gentle revolution has achieved: the state of things in Germany has become obvious."[16] They seem subsequently to have failed the German public by not producing what they were ill-prepared to produce: an informed and realistic account of the political and economic options open in the fall of 1989. This critique of intellectuals has come from the left as well as the right, and more from the west than the east. Habermas has referred to the "nearly complete lack of innovative, future-oriented ideas" among the organizers of the revolution.[17] Klaus Hartung has noted that the ideas of the opposition (particularly of the Neues Forum) were merely negations, counter-terms of the state practice.[18] The opposition never tried to separate the masses from the system itself, or to put it differently, never wished to govern, only to correct the excesses of the state, and therefore never thought through what it would mean to govern. When the opportunity for the civic movement to take over the government was offered, as Ulrike Poppe observed in January 1990, Bärbel Bohley and other opposition leaders declined in order instead, as Hartung says, to provide the "masses with an alternative program of political engagement."[19] The wish to instruct the masses rather than to govern Hartung rightly considers an intellectual failure, an "effort in political pedagogy."[20] The masses realized, he claims, even in early October 1989 that only the FRG parties would be sufficiently powerful to unseat the GDR state. The critical commentary on the revolution has been powerfully idealist. The oppositional leadership from within the GDR was conceptually too weak to make a real change.

From the founding of the GDR in 1949 until its collapse forty years later, intellectuals, particularly writers, were consistently said by the party to be of great importance to the state. The GDR rested not on wealth, force, or accident, but on a bedrock of ideology. The establishment of a socialist state on German soil was an idea that could claim the epithet "utopian." Whereas the economic strength of the FRG was a kind of display of national integrity, as Thomas Rietzschel remarked, the GDR needed always to legitimate itself through the word, which is one reason writers counted for so much.[21] Also, the GDR never had a critical press; the newspapers were party bulletins. Literary intellectuals, therefore, took over many of the functions of journalism. Their readers expected to find in novels, plays, and poems some expression of the feel of contemporary East German experience, and of the points of strain and controversy in East German society. In a society where information was precious, contemporary literary texts were eagerly purchased and read for social relevance.

Since November 1989 much resentment has been expressed about the privileges once enjoyed by East German writers. The Writers' Union offered some fellowships, helped members to find apartments, directed them and their families to extremely inexpensive vacation resorts, issued interest-free loans, and above all else arranged foreign travel. Writers have felt the sting of the reproaches about privileges, though not quite in the terms in which they have been made. Günter Kunert, who emigrated in 1979, explained that the privilege of being able to travel in the west became a heavy yoke on him, because he knew that it depended to a certain extent upon his good behavior.[22] Although the freedom to travel in the west was a much-coveted privilege before 1989 (travel restrictions on writers and scholars in fact loosened appreciably in the 1980s), and one that set people off from their fellow countrymen and countrywomen, the greatest privilege enjoyed by writers and scholars in East Germany was altogether immaterial: they felt a sense of consequence. And journalists attacking GDR writers after 1989 know well that this is the real object of their attack: the credibility and authority of literary intellectuals.

Writers and even scholars knew themselves to be participants in GDR society and even in the formation of state policy. Some writers of course saw their work as part of the effort to forge a popular commitment to the objectives of the SED, but they are not the writers who mattered most. The critical writers, as they are called, were those who wrote novels, plays, and poems that cast real existing socialism, as it was called, in a critical light. These writers had little reason to think of themselves as pawns of the state; in fact they suffered materially, though only temporarily, because of their criticisms. Some of them conceived of their literary labors as a help to the people of the GDR. Helga Schütz's terms for the way readers commonly understood GDR literature capture the views of many GDR writers as well: "Readers of contemporary literature in the GDR understood texts as aids to life. In letters to me and in conversations they would comment on and extend the texts with their own experiences and stories."[23] Readers might confront in a novel, for instance, contradictions of which they were not yet fully conscious in their own lives. They might see these contradictions differently after reading such a novel, or they might simply feel consoled to read that others had similar difficulties. The books of Christa Wolf, Heiner Müller, Stefan Heym, Volker Braun, Christoph Hein, and others helped to expand the range of political discussion in the public sphere. Their work brought to public expression issues that GDR citizens were formerly comfortable discussing only among friends. What constituted a public sphere in a society without critical journalism? Party meetings, of course, but also public readings of poems and stories, and theatrical performances. This expansion of the public sphere gave readers and writers alike a sense of possible progress. In that sense, and in others too, this critical literature helped to maintain hope within the limits of the GDR state. Many writers felt ethically obligated to their readers in just this way, even if they would not dare call themselves anyone's beacon. Émigrés like Hans Joachim Schädlich argue that the ultimate effect of this critical literature was to stabilize the status quo in the country and postpone the inevitable political expression of popular dissatisfaction.[24]

From an American viewpoint, this account of the literary function as an aid to living (*Lebenshilfe*) is too naive to utter publicly. American or French writers could not possibly reach consensus, as GDR writers have, in any such terms.[25] Built into this notion of literature as an aid to living are an attitude of condescension and a vulnerability to sentimentality that were profoundly important and little examined among GDR writers. They often piously referred to the letters they received from readers (*Leserbriefe*). Christoph Hein, for instance, in March 1990 said that he got so many letters from readers that he didn't trust himself to go away for more than three days at a time.[26] How many photographs one has seen of GDR writers signing books for grateful fans queued up to get a signature or exchange a few words! Wolf's publisher released in 1990 a volume of letters she received in response to two articles on the failures of GDR education published in 1989—with the title *Angepasst oder Mündig* (Fully conformed or come of age?), surely intended to evoke the debate over her novella *Was bleibt* (1990). And the plot of *Was bleibt* (What remains) turns on a public reading to her readers. West European and American writers make no such display of their own (generally smaller) audiences.

The dangerous sentimentality of this aspect of GDR literary life becomes clear when the question of emigration arises. Writers like Wolf often said that they could not in clear conscience emigrate and leave their readers without the human support writers could supply. With justification, the *New York Times* called Wolf "Mother Confessor": "People needed me," she said. "People needed something to give them strength."[27] Critical writers like Wolf stayed and made what compromises had to be made to continue functioning as writers in the GDR (in the case of Wolf, this meant at the least suppressing *Was bleibt,* written in 1979). Wolf's amnesia about her own work for the Stasi from 1959 to 1962 suggests that much more was in fact suppressed. These adjustments to the state were often rationalized by reference to human solidarity rather than to self-interest, as though remaining in the GDR were more a human than a political decision. This sentimentality about being there for one's readers was effortlessly appropriated by acknowledged agents of the state. The former culture minister of the GDR, Dietmar Keller, said: "I acknowledge my guilt. . . . But . . . if one doesn't act, if one bails out, what happens then? What happens to the people?"[28] Many people recognized how self-serving this sentimental rationalization could be. Rolf Schneider shows how easily the same argument could be used by the most ambitious émigrés. Detlef S., Schneider explains, was a true-to-the-line party member and doctor, but in August 1989 he fled the GDR with his family and went to work in an exclusive private clinic in the FRG. How did he describe his own motivation? "If a hundred thousand GDR citizens emigrate to the west, doctors must go too. Otherwise they leave their patients in the lurch." He wanted to serve others, to help where he could, even if that had to be in a private clinic for affluent capitalists.[29]

For literary scholars, as distinguished from writers, the terms had to be rather different. Again, some scholars surely saw their work as a straightforward aid to the SED regime, but no one with whom I spoke expressed such a view. They instead tended to conceive of their work as part of an effort to educate the princes. Literary historians, for example, might demonstrate to the ruling members of the party that the critical literature of Wolf, Braun, and Hein did not truly endanger socialism in Germany, that instead this literature, after its initial reception, became evidence of the party's tolerance, an ornament of the GDR state. The scholars hoped then for a relaxation of censorship standards.

A number of the conversations recorded in this book make for dispiriting reading, exactly because they show how easily intellectuals can agree to compromise the enlightenment ideal of skepticism; writers and scholars, we like to think, are committed to the work of doubt and questioning. A number of talented writers and scholars in the GDR willingly confined their skepticism within what seemed practical boundaries to participate in the literary and scholarly culture of the GDR. After November 1989 many of these intellectuals referred to themselves as utopianists; they characterized, and implicitly excused, their previous efforts as idealistic. Helga Königsdorff's words have been used by dozens of other writers and scholars: "We believed in the possibility of reforming the GDR state from within; in the possibility of coming one step closer to the beautiful utopia."[30] The expatriot Monika Maron has the last word: "What is it that drives people whose profession is thinking to declare that a state with this kind of history, plus a ruined economy and a demoralized population, is the bulwark of their own utopia?"[31] It won't do to dismiss GDR intellectuals like Helga Königsdorf as weak-spirited.

They were engaged advocates of socialism in Germany and of Marxist analysis in scholarly matters. Their stories have a special relevance for Americans now that neo-Marxism has been absorbed into academic literary discourse in the United States. They show how crucial it is that neo-Marxism be pursued strictly as a *critical* method, without any promise of a positive utopia. These writers and scholars explain how well and how ill Marxism served the literary culture of a people who share with American intellectuals the genealogy of German philosophy and historicism. The intellectual traditions of Germany are pervasive in the United States, as they are throughout Europe, and they have rarely been more timely than they are now. Philippe Sollers recently remarked that for thirty years French intellectuals have expressed their ideas in German loan-words, because German is the language of thought.[32] Many of these traditions—philosophical idealism, scientific positivism, and historicism—were formally adopted by American universities like my own in the late nineteenth century. The GDR showed what socialism looks like in an intellectual culture not entirely different, that is, from that of the United States—though the political situations of intellectuals in the two nations diverge greatly. Certain dangers await those who engage their work politically and surrender the countervailing traditions of skepticism and disinterest. This book is not intended as an indictment of politically engaged intellectuals per se, but rather as a collection of cautionary tales about the hazards of engagement.

Literary, philosophical, and pedagogical traditions are not all that German and American intellectuals share. The insistently secular ethos of professionalism has been adopted by both groups. My claim is that the occupational structures of GDR society were particularly elaborate, that among intellectuals professional organizations helped determine what critics and writers thought, said, and did, less by attempting to prevent dissenting thought, discourse, or action than by facilitating disagreement along party-sanctioned or -tolerated lines. It is common to say just the opposite about GDR society: namely, that professional organization was weak, that "professional people tend[ed] to be much less career-minded than in the west," that multiprofessional networks of association were characteristic of GDR society, as John Ardagh argues.[33] The positive or encouraging role of professional intellectual organizations that I am describing was in fact well recognized by writers and intellectuals. Consider Christa Wolf's interview on October 8, 1989, just at the time of the demonstrations marking the celebration of the fortieth anniversary of the GDR, with Gerhard Rein, who told her that the word for "opportunity" and "crisis" were one in Chinese. She replied,

> I'd like to use that word to describe the condition of the GDR. Obviously, I can only speak for myself. But I know from a great many people, I know from all the artists and art institutions, including the theater, the artists' unions, the Academy of Arts, that this great opportunity does exist, that the changes which are needed have the support of large segments of our society. In the past I hardly dared hope that there were still so many people in the GDR who can say: "Yes, I would like to live in this nation, and I would like to help make it a place where I and my children really want to live."[34]

Wolf was at once wrong and representative. The surprise of the next month was rather that so many people were prepared to leave the GDR. When she speaks of "this nation" in October 1989 she means socialist Germany. Had she said that she simply wanted to believe that many East Germans wished to live in a socialist nation, one might sympathize with her; but instead, she claims to know the commitment of "large segments of our society." Consider how she knows what she claims to know. In the second sentence here, she speaks as any westerner might, that is, for herself, her own individual experience. But the third sentence is that of a social analyst grounding observations in representative experience. She turns not to opinion polls, as a westerner might, but to the professional structures of the East German literary intellectual sector: the theaters, the galleries, the unions of artists, and the elite Academy of the Arts. Among these large segments not of GDR society but of GDR intellectuals, there were many who wished to live in a socialist Germany, but these professional organizations in fact kept intellectuals well screened from the truly large segments of GDR society outside these organizations that wanted no part of any socialist experiment, as all intellectuals would learn from the elections of March 1990. These organizations were at once what she thought of as the field of wide knowledge of her society and the screen that kept many intellectuals from understanding how thoroughly socialism had failed in the GDR.

The professional structures for literary intellectuals, writers, and scholars were more intricate in the GDR than they are in the United States or anywhere in Western Europe. Professional relationships were set, not fluid or even very malleable; policy decisions were removed from individuals and given to collective bodies. The most important feature of professional life in the GDR generally was the shadow structure of nearly every sector. Of course the Stasi was the obvious shadow structure. "There was no career decision," Rolf Schneider wrote, "in which the Stasi did not have a say."[35]

But there was a more pervasive double structure to professional organization in the GDR. Parallel to the teaching faculty at the universities, for instance, was the research faculty of the Academy of Sciences. In the GDR, scholarly and literary activity was structured after the Soviet model. For literary scholars, there were two tracks: that of a university career, and that of a research scholar at the Academy of Sciences. Not surprisingly, relations between the two were not close, not collaborative. The first track was narrower and more difficult of access than the second: very few university professors of literature were not party members (I met only one), whereas scholars at the academy's Central Institute for Literary History were scrutinized less closely, exactly because their influence on the public was indirect. In Berlin about forty literary scholars held positions at Humboldt University before November 1989; at the Central Institute nearly two hundred literary scholars were employed.

The most important duplication throughout the society came from the party's construction of its own parallel structures alongside many professional structures. Just before a meeting of the members of the Central Institute for Literary History or the Writers' Union, party members would meet and determine the agenda and outcome of the later meeting. Those who were not party members soon learned that not everything was open for discussion. And alongside the Central Institute was the Central Committee's Academy of the Social Sciences, where the occupants of chairs in aesthetics and literary studies wielded considerable authority within the Central Institute. The Central Committee's academy was able to propose to the Central Institute certain topics and projects for research and publication. More importantly, research projects proposed by working groups of the Central Institute had to be cleared through the Central Committee's academy.

For writers, the options were more constrained: one either belonged to the Writers' Union or was not recognized as a writer. Without official recognition one had difficulty securing permission to publish, and one was required to work at some sort of job in order not to be classified "asocial." There was no shadow institution for the Writers' Union, though a number of writers mentioned to me the way the party meetings before the union meetings effectively covered all that might happen in an open meeting. Kurt Hager was a regular member of the Central Committee and a member too of the Writers' Union, resulting in some shadow effect. At any one time there were typically three or so members of the Writers' Union who also sat on the Central Committee (two or so having as candidates term appointments to the Central Committee). The redundancy I have described is merely the institutional form that comprehensive surveillance took in the GDR. One knew that there was always an overseer, often many. Seldom did one individual take responsibility for oversight and censorship; rather, some collective made the killing decisions about nonconformity, maybe in a committee.

These professional structures—those of the scholars and those of the writers—effectively instituted conformity, as professional structures programatically do. My point here is not that the relevant conformity was exactly of belief (that intellectuals tended to believe in the objectives of the SED because of professional organization), but rather of dissent: intellectuals knew very well where the limits of tolerance would be enforced, first by the relevant professional organization, which might expel any member who crossed the line, and only later by other nonliterary sections of the state apparatus. The constant contact with one's colleagues at meetings and through memoranda helped to hold these boundaries in sight. One surprising lesson that I quickly absorbed from my conversations is that fear of professional difficulties, not of the Stasi, was what enforced conformity. With elaborate professional organizations in place, it just does not take much to control the ideological activity of literary intellectuals. That is a sad truth that deserves consideration by American intellectuals.

Underlying the recent controversy about German intellectuals is a contradiction between transcendental and instrumental intellectuals.[36] Julien Benda's *The Treason of the Intellectuals* (1927), recently republished in Germany, laments the displacement of transcendental intellectuals by their modern counterparts, whom I am calling instrumental intellectuals. German reviewers have used the reissuing of the book to fortify the skeptical assessment of the achievement of GDR intellectuals. Benda's term for intellectuals is "clerks," because his case draws strength from the historical fact that intellectuals long had a sanctuary in the church (and because Benda wanted to affiliate himself with the Catholic Church against Charles Maurras). As he says, "The modern world has made the 'clerk' into a citizen, subject to all the responsibilities of a citizen, and consequently to despise lay passions is far more difficult for him than for his predecessors."[37] The clerks, according to Benda, are those who "put before the world a scale of values in the name of philosophical reflection, or who are willing to be considered as such" (*TI,* 134).

Chief among the lay passions they resist is the will to political power. Benda understood that in 1927 Europe was expressing such extreme nationalist sentiments that another terrible war would soon become inevitable (*TI,* 183). The scandal he exposed was that intellectuals were participating in the formation of these sentiments instead of maintaining an alternative perspective. They had displaced traditional measures of value in favor of immediate contemporary utility. "Literary critics," for instance, "inquire far less whether a work is beautiful than whether it expresses 'the present' aspirations of 'the contemporary soul'" (*TI,* 101–2). Why did clerks become realists, in Benda's terms? "First of all," he answers, "I see the interests of their careers" (*TI,* 162). When clerks became citizens, they had to make their own way; like doctors and lawyers, they set professional paths. Benda was astute in seeing the professional impulse as capable of corrupting intellectuals. "It may be said today that every French writer who desires wide fame (which means every writer endowed with the real temperament of a man of letters) also desires inevitably to play a political part" (*TI,* 163). The proper function of clerks, Benda argues, is to maintain standards of truth and justice that do not depend upon the material considerations of wealth and power that govern politics.

Benda's English-speaking readers immediately recognize his indebtedness to Matthew Arnold, whose arguments for disinterestedness and the free play of the intelligence are restated by Benda.[38] In 1864 Arnold felt the attractions of an intelligence unaffiliated with any political party (Benda dates the onset of the phenomena he criticizes in France to roughly 1875 [*TI,* 162]). Well before 1927 Arnold seemed to British and American intellectuals a figure from another era altogether. Benda too is a voice from the distant past, but that voice had real force in 1927, and now in Germany it has again. The modern intellectual, more so now than in 1927, can hardly avoid being instrumental to the operation of social institutions that exercise political power and social control, and writers like Arnold and Benda deliberately appeal to the bad conscience of modern intellectuals. Edward Said has argued, following Gramsci, that "culture serves authority, and ultimately the national State, . . . because it is affirmative, positive, and persuasive."[39] Literary intellectuals have responded to the political significance of their work by delimiting the range of writing that properly constitutes literature. Said continues: "In acting entirely within this domain, then, the literary critic effectively confirms the culture and the society enforcing those restrictions; this confirmation acts to strengthen the civil and political societies whose fabric is the culture itself."[40] Said sees that modern literary critics are so strongly debarred from any transcendent perspective that merely by operating in their institutional context, regardless of what they write, they affirm the legitimacy of the political and social status quo.

Between the transcendental intellectual, whom Benda located in the clerisy, and the thoroughly complicitous instrumental intellectual of our era lies a great middle ground where allegiances can be qualified and complicity delimited. In the GDR, literary intellectuals tended to accept their legitimating role to participate in the formation or improvement of a socialist state on German soil. They did so as professionals. When they are now reproached for not having sufficiently resisted the force of the GDR state, one often hears in reply, "Who resisted more than I?" West German critics now effectively bring GDR writers and scholars before an ethical bar. What is noteworthy is that individual corruptibility is not the point, despite the ethical cast of the charges; the question is that of intellectuals as a professional group. Did they live up to the expectations others have of intellectuals? The answer of most GDR intellectuals is that they did what their colleagues did. The level of political skepticism among literary professionals may have been low, but that is a fact of history and no evidence of ethical failure. One lesson of this controversy is that no matter how fully professionalized and secularized literary intellectuals may become in a particular institutional setting, they never entirely leave behind the norms of the transcendental intellectual. Durkheim said that "as professors, we have duties which are not those of merchants."[41] Benda's clerks remain a ghostly presence even in Germany, where they stand for ideals disavowed by modern instrumental intellectuals. It can be plausibly objected that this memory of transcendental intellectuals derives as much from idealizing and politically motivated discourse about intellectuals as from any actual avatars of the transcendental ideal. My argument here, though, takes for granted the derivation of this memory in order to concentrate rather on its consequences. Ideals have lives of their own.

On the face of it my distinction between transcendental and instrumental intellectuals coincides exactly with Gramsci's distinction between traditional and organic intellectuals. The trouble with Gramsci's construction is that these different intellectuals confront each other as opposed classes do, and the traditional intellectuals are inevitably consigned to the dustbin of history. In one sense there is no escaping this historical narrative, as I've suggested: we are all instrumental intellectuals now; but in another sense the historical explanation is greatly misleading. The traditional or transcendental intellectual has disappeared only as a social group, but not as an idea, not as an ideological force, as the career of Benda's book demonstrates. To use Bruce Robbins's term, this idealist intellectual has become part of the "professional unconscious."[42] The question is always how that memory will influence instrumental intellectuals in new historical circumstances to orient their work less exclusively toward the interests of this "new class" and more broadly on the long-term interest of the larger public. The memory of transcendental intellectuals survives too among the public at large, which is why East German literary intellectuals are now regarded so skeptically in the West. Instrumental intellectuals are expected by the public not to step free of their historical predecessors, the transcendental intellectuals, but to absorb their office somehow into that of a modern instrumental intellectual.

Stanley Fish constructs the distinction between transcendental and instrumental intellectuals generally in terms of antiprofessionalism and professionalism, and there is no more stiffly dichotomized view of the problem. The professionalism of contemporary intellectuals is so fully established, according to Fish, that no other option remains. Antiprofessionalism is wholly misleading by this account because it invokes impossible standards: "I define anti-professionalism as any attitude or argument that enforces a distinction between professional labors on the one hand and the identification and promotion of what is true or valuable on the other."[43] An argument for the superiority of any nonprofessional ideal over professional practice counts as this purely ideological (in the sense of perpetrating false consciousness) antiprofessionalism, as he sees it. But whence, then, a critical perspective on professional labors? Eventually Fish narrows his capacious definition of antiprofessionalism (without acknowledging the revision as correction) to admit the possibility of criticism. "My argument," he later writes, "is that a practice cannot (or should not) be criticized *because* it is professional" (*D,* 242; emphasis in original). Fish sees what he calls antiprofessionalism as a screen for self-interest, and the professional by this account is the one led by ideals:

"To be a professional is to think of oneself as motivated by something larger than marketplace conditions—by, for instance, a regard for justice or for the sanctity of human life or for the best that has been thought and said—even as that larger something is itself given shape and being by the very market conditions it supposedly transcends" (*D*, 177). (Fish tries to induct even Matthew Arnold into the professional legion!) He claims against Donald Davie that antiprofessionalism "derives from a militantly ahistorical view of literary study," but the fact is rather that antiprofessionalism refuses to surrender the memory of transcendental intellectuals (*D*, 205).

Fish believes that it would be healthy to expunge the memory of transcendental intellectuals once and for all, were that only possible, because that memory, or antiprofessionalism,

> urges impossible goals (the breaking free or bypassing of the professional network) and therefore has the consequence of making people ashamed of what they are doing. The psychological distress that marks this profession, the fact that so many of its members exist in a shamefaced relationship with the machinery that enables their labors, is in part attributable, I think, to literary anti-professionalism, which is, as a form of professional behavior, almost always damaging. (*D*, 211–12)

Fish does not see memory as influencing the actual work instrumental intellectuals produce; his concern is with the adverse psychological effects of guilt. His message is simply: no shame. What he will not concede is that relatively few historical processes are entirely metamorphic, that most are sedimentary. What he calls "a historically conditioned consciousness" is one absolutely constrained by contemporary conditions, a consciousness with no usable access to memory (*D*, 245). My argument is rather that the memory of transcendental intellectuals does actually encourage particular practices that might otherwise be discouraged, and that instrumental intellectuals are often free to resist conformity to the standardized practices of their fellow professionals, though that resistance may well entail sacrifices, material and otherwise. My hope is that the stories in this book will encourage some of my colleagues to weigh heavily the costs entailed by a professionalism without the memory of transcendental intellectuals.

More than any other people the Germans have shown the world the dangers of nationalism in the twentieth century. One can hardly speak of nationalism without calling to mind the German example. This issue is known in Germany as simply "the German question." Not surprisingly German intellectuals since 1945 have deliberately cultivated skepticism about nationalism. "The word Germany," Helga Schütz wrote in December 1989, "is hard to get across my lips; it produces a furry feeling in the mouth."[44] She used to wish, she confessed, to be a foreigner, perhaps a Frenchwoman. Günter Grass, the most articulate critic of reunification, has said that he too, like the French, fears a larger, stronger Germany; one of the preconditions of the Holocaust was a "strong, unified Germany," a population held together by nationalist ideology.[45] He argued unsuccessfully for a confederation of the fifteen provinces of East and West Germany. Looking at a map of Europe before and after 1989, one wants to speak of a new German nation being born out of reunification, but that is exactly what did not happen. Many intellectuals favored the abandonment of the constitutions of the East and West German states and a new constitutional convention for the founding of a new nation. Instead, the FRG, with the support of the electorate, expeditiously annexed the former GDR territory without any changes to the Basic Law.[46] Germans refused in 1990 to take the occasion to reconsider the nature of a German nation. There is little popular support for self-reflection about nationhood in Germany.

After 1945 nationalist ideology seemed altogether discredited by the preceding twelve years. After 1949 the socialist state repressed nationalist ideology in the GDR in ways that were consistent with Soviet sponsorship of the new nation and with the explicit repudiation of the National Socialist ideology of 1933–45. In the FRG, nationalism was discouraged less forthrightly, but still effectively. The West Germans more than the East Germans were asked to accept the consequences of Nazi nationalism.[47] The result seems to have been a repression of most forms of patriotic expression and most arguments on behalf of German national identity. I remember a West German poster of the mid 1980s advertising a party allegiance (I forget which one) in the European Parliament elections: a young, obviously German teenager was scripted to be saying that she is glad to live in Europe. She was understood, though, to be affirming the existence of West Germany within a NATO and Common Market Europe—"I am glad to live in West Germany"—but that could not be said openly. West Germans, especially of the left-center, subsumed feelings of national well-being in a European complacency, whereas East Germans were encouraged by the state to subsume their feelings of national identity within the international socialist struggle. Helga Schütz's desire to carry a French passport is a kind of commonplace of German intellectuals, east and west. (It should be remembered too that German artists envious of being French or Italian were common long before 1945.) It is clear now that both systems repressed feelings that are now being vented in attacks on foreign-born residents of Germany, east and west.

The violence of German national ardor became clear in July 1990, when the West Germans won the World Soccer Cup; and on July 1, 1990, reunification was effectively realized on West German terms by the introduction of the deutsche mark in the GDR. This was a muscle-flexing moment for Germany. The newspapers carried stories of beatings of foreign-looking residents, particularly of East Germany. Later the attacks increased dramatically in the west as well. Both former East and West Germans recognize that they must now live through a period of racist brutality, partly because of the previous suppression of nationalist sentiments, partly because of the way capitalism is understood to have trounced socialism and won the cold war. For about a half-hour the night of the soccer championship, I was on a subway in Berlin. A handful of youngish people, conspicuously drunk and raucous, treated us to chants, songs, and slurs before, out of eagerness to beat someone, they began punching one another, and the train was emptied.[48]

Intellectuals of the east and west of course feel outraged by this new violence—and not only intellectuals. But a new brutality has also emerged in the terms of intellectual debate and discourse, and this too follows, to some extent, from repressed nationalism. Less than a month before the conversion of the currency, West German critics launched a severe attack on the literary and political authority of the former GDR's most renowned writer, Christa Wolf. This was widely understood as a campaign by the West German literary establishment against East German writers generally. The west was making it clear that East German writers would have a much harder time in the book trade after reunification. East German authors would not be allowed to speak for the national culture of reunified Germany; Christa Wolf and the critical writers like her could not be the conscience of the new nation.

The severe criticism that met Wolf's *Was bleibt* when it appeared in June 1990 had much to do with the dates "June–July 1979/November 1989" affixed to the last page. This plainly autobiographical story about being under Stasi surveillance was the first of her books to appear after the opening of the Wall, and so, according to the editors of *Der Spiegel,* the first to be reviewed without the customary bonus for GDR writers that West German reviewers were formerly inclined to give Wolf and the other critical writers of the GDR.[49] One of Ulrich Greiner's charges against her in *Die Zeit* is that she published the book only when she could do so without risk to herself: it would have taken courage in 1979 to publish a story sharply critical of the GDR as a police state, where innocent people were routinely under surveillance and incarcerated young women could expect to be sterilized after complaining about kidney pain. She could have published this indictment in the FRG then, though Greiner acknowledges that that would have entailed the loss of her state-sanctioned authority in the GDR and might even have required her emigration.[50] But to publish it in 1990 demonstrates, he argues, a lack of sensitivity to the feelings of those whose lives were truly damaged by the GDR state, and this point has become even sharper since it was made, as the revelation of Stasi outrages has grown steadily more impressive.[51] Hellmuth Karasek, editor of *Der Spiegel,* charged that she had no public response to the Stasi in 1979: "Christa Wolf did not leave the Party in which she was a candidate for the Central Committee. Nor did she leave the state that without cause had placed her in a state of panic; not once did she withhold her friendship from that state."[52]

It won't do to accuse Christa Wolf of conformism or complicity with the GDR state, because she has worried over her conformity in her novels. Cassandra's self-knowledge is not hers alone: "Which should they bet on: my inclination to conform with those in power, or my craving for knowledge. . . . I, the seeress, was owned by the palace."[53] Wolf treats this issue as both personal and literary: to what extent has she herself conformed as a writer to continue her work? This is a question that directly parallels the familiar one about the capacity of Germans to conform to totalitarian regimes. In *Kindheitsmuster* (Patterns of childhood, hereafter abbreviated as *PC*) (1976) she refers, on one hand, to the "bliss of conformity" felt by ordinary Germans wearing uniforms (*PC,* 43) and, on the other, to the widely excusing sense that no one can step free of complicity: "It may be impossible to be alive today without becoming implicated in the crime."[54] This self-reflexiveness is constant in Wolf's writing, so much so that even she occasionally feels annoyed by her need for it: "Woe to our time," the narrator of *Kindheitsmuster* says, "which forces the writer to exhibit the wound of his own crime before he is allowed to describe other people's wounds."[55] Self-criticism has ossified into a conventional self-protection for postwar German writers.

Wolf has been clear all along about her inclination to make peace with the GDR authorities: "I don't see myself as an outsider," she remarked in 1979, "and don't want to become one."[56] East German writers, she continued, "have common, collectively formulated goals, and do not defend any esoteric ideals, a great number of people identify with these ideas. This is because they are not simply objectives we have invented ourselves but are taken from society and the demands it makes on itself" (*FD*, 86). The urging of the state makes itself felt among critics as well as writers, Gerhard Wolf noted: "Our critics are constantly under pressure, consciously or unconsciously, to proclaim solemn ideological allegiances" (*FD*, 106). The surprise is that writers like Wolf, as her language here suggests, appreciated that pressure from the needs of the people and their representative, the party. Her husband regrets the critics' lack of autonomy, but they both thought that the engagement of the writers was something precious to protect.

Most of the people interviewed in this book felt that Christa Wolf was quite unfairly attacked by the critics of the West German feuilletons: standards of expression and behavior were invoked against her that had no currency in the GDR before 1989; she was not the most conformist of GDR writers, far from it; she had been very highly praised not at all long before in the pages of these same publications. Also, the most eminent critic from these journals, Marcel Reich-Ranicki, unjustly claimed that Wolf had withdrawn her name from a petition in 1976 protesting the expatriation of Wolf Biermann. She apparently did nothing of the kind, though Reich-Ranicki's allegations were part of the campaign against her in 1990.[57] Despite such unfairness, though, there is a sense in which Wolf is the one writer who has deliberately asked to have her work examined in the full glare of the moment. In 1973 she asserted, as engaged writers must, that the ultimate test of a literary work "is really whether you get a sense of it speaking to one's time" (*FD*, 14). Twelve years later she complicated this by saying that the role of writers is not to reflect their time so much as to instill in their readers a particular sense of the age and society (*FD*, 74). The role of literature is "to articulate a sense of the world and of life which stimulates the reader's individual development, self-discovery and creative desire and helps to develop what is best described in the good old-fashioned word 'personality'" (*FD*, 79). How different is this from Lenin's patronizing notion of artists as the engineers of the soul? Writers don't reflect their times; they help their readers become some timely versions of their best selves. In a period of historical change, such a writer could ask for nothing else than to have her relationship to a past time judged by the new criteria of the present, because she had always avowed her attunement to her contemporaries and their moment.

Frank Schirrmacher focused his critique in particular on Wolf's tendency to view the emigration of her compatriots as an irrational reflex, a psychological refusal to live the more austere life outside Western consumer society.[58] As late as November 8, 1989, as he says, Wolf pleaded with her compatriots on television, radio, and in the press, "Stay home, stay with us!" A week earlier she had propagandized for remaining in the GDR in similarly conventional terms: the GDR was the democratic socialist alternative to the FRG, the state that needed to be rescued.[59] Hers was the counsel of patience, but the revolutionary act that brought the GDR to its end was in fact emigration. Wolf's work looks conservative and mindful of the status quo when one understands, as everyone did after November 1989, that the flight of East Germans to the west was the single act that produced a revolution in this authoritarian socialist country. Wolf, like many intellectuals, east and west, did not wish to see the GDR dissolve into the FRG. On August 31, 1989, just two months before the effects of the revolutionary moment would be achieved, Wolf said that she desired a stable GDR.[60] As Thomas Rietzschel noted, the attitude of East German writers generally toward the GDR revolution was ambivalent from the beginning.[61] Wolf's critics have gone further in suggesting that she was fully implicated in the state apparatus of the GDR, whereas in *Was bleibt* she explicitly calls the state surveillance agents "messengers from the other."[62] Critics have reminded readers that in 1968 Wolf defended the Soviet invasion of Czechoslovakia, and they have insinuated that there was very little distance between Wolf and the center of state power.[63] Hellmuth Karasek retells the anecdote about Honecker's ignorance of the brutal police response to demonstrators at the fortieth anniversary celebration of the GDR in October 1989. Honecker claimed that he only learned of the police actions when Wolf telephoned him to complain about the detention of her daughter.[64] When Wolf wrote about her efforts to find her daughter then, she referred to the unresponsive, Kafkaesque police bureaucracy, without mention of a call to Honecker.[65]

In October 1991 the research for this book seemed complete, and the shape of the book was obvious. The interviews gave a good sense of the intentions and objectives of a large number of writers and scholars. One had from them an understanding of the institutionalized literary life of the GDR. The book began with the most established, complicitous writers and moved toward more critical ones. From these interviews the importance of a literary generational shift emerged gradually, until the young writers of the Prenzlauer Berg scene of the 1980s had their say. This was really the fitting conclusion to the book: those young writers seemed in October 1991 to have successfully stepped free of the burden of complicity with which older writers had to come to terms after 1989. They had achieved this freedom at some cost, but they had chosen to remain independent of the professional structures of the literary world of the GDR. They had founded an alternative public and circumvented the restrictions of the state apparatus more by inventiveness than conspiracy. Beyond that, they had managed to apply to the specific details of their lives on a Stalinist island some of the thought that in Western Europe and the United States seemed most current: "Our slogan then was, the Stasi is an informational structure that extends through the entire society. We were all influenced by French structuralism. And for us, the Stasi was one structure among many structures."[66] This ideology seemed at once resourceful and engaging in that these writers drew upon thinkers who were known in the United States through an elaborate apparatus of publications, conferences, and so on. Sascha Anderson and Rainer Schedlinski—the major disseminators of French theory—made do with small pamphlets from the Merve Press in West Berlin. What in the United States is extremely academic and professional seemed in Prenzlauer Berg more like a naked encounter with the thought of our time.

Nonetheless there were features of this application of French thought that appeared instantly problematic to me. One of these was the cultivation of indifference, then as now an extreme reaction against the tendencies of the engaged generation of Biermann and Braun. These young writers wanted so badly to be beyond ideology that they would repeat, it seemed, by habit, "It's all the same to me"—at moments when I could feel no indifference. What I didn't fully realize was the service such indifference could provide. "Indifference about the Stasi," Sascha said, "was necessary in order to work with each other without mistrust." Now it has become obvious, as it was not in 1990, who stood to be hurt by mistrust.[67] Sascha might claim, with Michel Foucault and Anthony Giddens on his side, that comprehensive surveillance is a condition of modernity.[68] Before they were exposed as informants, Sascha and Schedlinski disavowed conspiratorial activity and admitted having spoken often with the Stasi. Conspiracy is an antiquated mode: modernity demands the free flow of information and the observability of everyone. An American could not but hear in this a grotesque version of the beyond-ideology cold warriors of the 1950s—than which nothing was more ideological. To gauge properly the importance of such writers as Bataille, Barthes, Lyotard, Foucault, Guattari, and Deleuze, one must remember that in a totalitarian society access to alternative, not just countervailing, ideas is sharply limited and therefore precious. "Structuralist and poststructuralist theorists . . . provided an alternative to Marxism-Leninism for the Prenzlauer Berg writers," as one apologist put it.[69] One of the questions now is how well this alternative served these writers.

In October 1991, a new literary controversy erupted. The former-GDR exile satirist and songwriter Wolf Biermann charged Sascha Anderson with having been an informant for the Stasi. Like so much about the last few years, this revelation had a schematic and stagey quality that made one suspicious. Biermann and Anderson are similar in one way that matters greatly to cultural politics: neither is adequately accounted for by the term *writer;* they are both *figures.* One can be skeptical or indifferent about their writings and still have no doubt about their importance. Biermann stood for the 1960s generation of the GDR. His forced expatriation in 1976 marked an era. Many expatriations of writers followed, and the cultural policy of the state shifted toward greater tolerance only after the 1979 purges in the Writers' Union. Sascha Anderson was the most conspicuous avant-garde figure of the 1980s, and Biermann understood this perfectly. In his words, "Sascha Anderson was the cool cult-figure of recent years; he was the spirit behind this spiritless little art-population. He also determined tyrannically who and what 'illegal' texts would be printed: that is to say, the Stasi determined this in this farce."[70] Biermann certainly felt generational rivalry and resentment about Sascha. The rivalry is clear when Biermann says that there is more poetry in his own prose than in the "aforesaid little poems of such a crow as Papenfuss-Gorek."[71] Papenfuss-Gorek, unlike Sascha and Biermann, is not a figure but a writer, which among poets is an obvious advantage, and Biermann wants to assert his own writerly authority against that of the most widely respected poet of the Prenzlauer Berg scene. Even as a literary figure, he claims, he's a better poet than the best of *that* generation. Biermann's charges against Sascha, which were first heard at the Frankfurt Book Fair, constituted a surprise with great consequences for the cultural assessment then under way. Frank Schirrmacher, whose acute case against Christa Wolf put him at the head of the skeptical camp of GDR assessors, said, "To imagine that Sascha Anderson, who in many respects was the heir to Wolf Biermann, worked for the secret police destroys one's last beliefs about a genuine, coherent GDR art." The critical writers, or the engaged generation, had already been sidelined by Schirrmacher's own critique of Wolf's *Was bleibt,* but the avant-garde scene of Prenzlauer Berg remained. Once both these camps were discredited, the GDR would have very little evidence left of having recently existed as a literary culture.[72]

My friend Gabriele Dietze of the Rotbuch Verlag (whom I would not have met, if it hadn't been for Sascha) was visiting in Chicago when news of Biermann's accusation came. She was less stunned than I, because Sascha had been suspected before, exactly because he was so very capable of organizing readings, exhibits, and the export of manuscripts and canvases. It was easy to think that he just *had* to be with the Stasi. Then I remembered a young painter from Dresden, seated next to me on a flight from Berlin to Chicago. "You probably know my friend Sascha, from Dresden." "Yes," she said, "everyone knows Sascha; he's slimy." He had been generous and demonstrably open with me, he had helped me greatly by introducing me to many Berlin writers. "He's not a straight-ahead sort of character," she said. We let it lie.

That was September 1990. Once Gabriele Dietze and I had read all the articles and interviews of the autumn of 1991, we agreed that Sascha was being prosecuted in the public media without any evidence being set forth. She thought that Sascha was not effectively defending himself, that he should have said that when he spoke to the Stasi, as he conceded he often did, he was appearing under the force of a subpoena. Iris Radisch also complained in *Die Zeit* in November 1991 that the charges were coming forth and being debated without any evidence.[73] Wolf Biermann seemed to be out to reestablish his own authority (he was surely doing that) against that of the writers of the 1980s scene, which he had missed by being in Hamburg. The issue seemed to be whose generation, and which idea of political engagement, would be allowed to represent the old GDR and survive in the new German literary community. The stakes of this controversy were like those of the Christa Wolf debate. Both controversies displayed an ambitious, rough jockeying for authority in German letters: west versus east; one generation of easterners against another. "Sascha Arschloch [Asshole]," Biermann had called him in the accusatory article in *Die Zeit*. In the streets and in the literary supplements, there has been an obvious coarsening of behavior, and in both contexts one sees expansive ambitions elbowing their way to expression.

Although this impression of the moment was accurate, I still think, it left out more than it included. In January 1992 Iris Radisch published a devastating essay in *Die Zeit* that began, "He lies. . . . " She spoke with a number of people who had seen in their Stasi files the reports that Sascha had filed with the Stasi. Her claim is that not only had he informed on his friends and associates, he had done so ambitiously. The point of the controversy about Sascha and, later, Rainer Schedlinski (who, unlike Sascha, once he had been accused, quickly admitted having been an informant) is that even the avant-garde or alternative Prenzlauer Berg scene was proven to be deeply implicated in the state apparatus. The Stasi even modestly subsidized the publication of Schedlinski's magazine, *Ariadnefabrik;* an American has to remember the CIA's support of the *Partisan Review* in the 1950s. Independent? Counter-professional? Those are the qualities I thought I saw in Prenzlauer Berg. The conclusion to my book looked hopelessly naive in early 1992. I wondered how many others of the dozens of writers and academics I interviewed had also cooperated with the Stasi.[74] I went back to Berlin to speak to some people I had not yet met, and to talk with Sascha again.

What I wanted to know, of course, was Sascha's motivation and intention. According to him the motive was straightforward: he was imprisoned in 1978 for nonpolitical criminal activity, writing 2,300 marks in overdrafts on his checking account ("I was a simple criminal").[75] Agreeing to supply the Stasi with information was a way out of jail, and continued to be a means of staying out of jail, despite illicit activity such as unauthorized performances with bands and exportation of manuscripts and paintings to the west. But beyond that level of motivation Sascha will not go. (Some doubt about his ever having been imprisoned has been expressed, but Adolf Endler and Gabi Dietze have remarked that the prose about prison life in *Brunnen randvoll* argues convincingly against that suspicion.) His laconic responses to the charges ("I don't excuse myself" [October 1991]. *Do you have a bad conscience now?* "There's no bad conscience. There's a very, very discriminating conscience" [January 1992].)[76] and the facts that have emerged are disturbing in that they suggest his collaboration was simply part of the status quo—a kind of inevitable price for the scene itself. He told the Stasi in 1982 that he wanted to change that which could be changed, but "not like some young idealistic hero who shows up in GDR literature."[77]

One of the things that is disturbing about Sascha's reticence about his actions is the sense that any examination of motives, particularly an examination of some deep motive, would be necessarily misleading. Sascha's generation, and still younger writers too, learned to refuse the notion of depth and insist on equanimity or indifference: "To me it's all the same." One finds throughout recent GDR literature a refusal of depth. The narrator of Christoph Hein's *Der fremde Freund* (1982) says quite revealingly, "I don't feel any need to delve into the so-called mysteries of life."[78] One wants to know the extent to which informants acted under duress, as Sascha and Schedlinski have claimed, and the extent of their ambition to be integrated into the state apparatus. Bärbel Bohley has commented on the tone of the informants' reports in her Stasi files: "Many of them read like letters to a friend. . . . The voluntary quality of the collaboration is surprising. The Stasi official was a representative of state power, and the unofficial informant wanted to participate in that power."[79] Sascha's lengthy strategy paper for the Stasi asks that not only his information but also his analytical conclusions and proposals be taken seriously. He explicitly hoped to influence the GDR cultural political policy in 1982.[80]

I have been driven back to the literature of the cold war to make sense of Sascha's story, which is ironic because in 1990 I understood the Prenzlauer Berg scene as a refusal of the dichotomous alignments of the cold war. In particular what now seems instructive is the curious look backward from the late 1950s and early 1960s to the partisanship of the Second World War.

For Americans, though not for West Germans, the willingness of Sascha, Schedlinski, and Helge Novak to deliver to the Stasi upon demand information about their own experiences and their colleagues—places, events, and people they had observed—is not utterly damning. Very few American citizens would be ashamed to answer the questions of FBI agents—even repeatedly. While some of my friends would take pride in refusing to speak to the FBI—would even take pride in being investigated at all—none would be obliged to feel shame at having answered the questions of an agent. Any parallel to the obligations of American citizenry fails right away. There was greater suspicion of the

Stasi among the GDR population than there is of the FBI in the population of the United States, and in Prenzlauer Berg there was actually a taboo against talking with the Stasi. The scene there represented itself as a resistant node of GDR society, though that resistance was intended to be more cultural than political. Sascha and Schedlinski were prominent members of that resistance—and I use that word advisedly. The proper parallel to Sascha's story is that of double agents, not merely of informants. Espionage agents betray foreigners, so they can be patriots, but double agents betray their countrymen and countrywomen, which is why, although fascinating, they are usually despised. Think in particular of those members of the French Resistance who informed on their comrades and thereby betrayed an imagined alternative to occupied Vichy France. The resistance was comprised of those opposed to the illegitimate French state in Vichy. These resisters were stateless because their acts were treasonous under the law. They had to imagine an alternative historical context in which a French state might claim their allegiance, and they did so easily because the occupying force was so abominable. Membership in the resistance did not in itself identify one's positive political allegiance. Insofar as one allowed oneself to become identified with the Prenzlauer Berg scene, one allowed oneself to be known as a cultural resister. Sascha certainly acceded to such preconceptions—altogether misleadingly. When he gave information to the Stasi he was doing what many GDR citizens had done, but there was an added element of betrayal: Prenzlauer Berg was constantly represented as an alternative to the cold war alignments. He looks now like a cynical double agent, and he accepts that. "I have no morality."

Sascha was proud of having turned his back on the Wall, of notably disregarding the alignments of the cold war. After just a few years of the cold war, American writers were similarly eager to break out of that bipolar logic (by the early 1960s the double agent was a particularly intriguing figure in American writing). What Sascha had in fact distanced himself from was the naiveté of those who thought they might pursue the arts as an alternative to the state politics of the GDR.

Richard Stern's 1962 novel, *In Any Case,* tells the story of an American father who tries to clear his son's name of the slander of having been a double agent in the French Resistance. But before doing so, he learns to feel genuine sympathy and attraction to the actual double agent, who arranged for his son's death in Maulthausen. The father of Robert

Curry speaks to a former officer of the Nazi Sicherheitsdienst, who knew the real double agent—also "Robert." Von Klausen tells him that an agent lives

in high tension every other minute. You're consumed by what you're doing. Allegiance is for those who have luxury. It explains why so many sorts of high living are tied up with espionage, counterfeiting, women, smuggling, piracy. You're like a hot, loose wire that can plug in anywhere, if there's someone insulated enough to handle you. . . . I tell you the layman can't take the agent's measure by anything he's known. You'd like me to say that this "Robert" [the actual double agent] was a traitor who sold out colleagues and companions. I won't. And not just because he was of help to us. I also know he helped the Allies, and took risks in both instances. I can't even say he was more loyal to you than to us. Life lived at the speed he lived it is contingent on itself: every day is filled with risk and threat, and there is no time for strict alignment. These are professionals. And they, *we,* are made uneasy by only one thing, amateurs. And rightly. Who knows if your Robert, your son, didn't do more harm acting "straight" than this "Robert" acting—well, as he acted? Whatever his "allegiance."[81]

The agents on both sides comprise a society of managers, not moralists. And in the United States in 1962 one had to see that the postwar society was also one of managers. Pros think of themselves as beyond ideology.[82] What counts for them is product, not motive: how many were helped or harmed? This is Sascha's instrumental way of reckoning too. What the parallel shows is that there can be no hope of getting at the agent's true motivation: the pro knows and needs the thrills of the game and needs too to help those more vulnerable than himself. Ambitious, hedonistic, altruistic, he finds ultimate satisfaction in the acceptance of complexity.

One cannot easily generalize about the effect of the revelations about Sascha Anderson and Rainer Schedlinski within the Prenzlauer Berg scene itself—insofar as it still exists. There are surely those—especially among the very young—who do not censure these now notorious IMs (Inoffizielle Mitarbeitern; nonstaff informants) because the Stasi was an accepted fact of life for them. Those who had no experience of 1968 had that much vaguer an image of an alternative to the Stasi state.[83] Their counterparts, such as Uwe Kolbe, feel that the mere fact that Sascha spoke with the Stasi is enough to discredit him entirely; by this standard, we now know, many others also stand condemned. In between are some interesting cases. Klaus Michael, the one-time director of the Galrev Druckhaus, continued to work with Sascha. However, he grew increasingly skeptical of his colleague and referred to him in public as a criminal type. Michael resigned his post in protest of Sascha's continuing presence at the press in August 1992. Michael's post was offered to Peter Böthig, also an employee at Galrev, who in March 1992 published an essay in *Die Zeit* about the poet Frank Flanzendörfer. Böthig said that it is not altogether out of the question to think that Flanzendörfer's suicide was provoked, presumably by the Stasi. More pointedly: "One cannot yet look beyond the work done by the informants in the literary circles. Soon the relevant documents will be accessible, and then possibly a gruesome scenario will become visible."[84] The implication here is biting because Sascha and Schedlinski were chief among those literary IMs, but also because Flanzendörfer did what they have admitted they could not do: he resisted. Michael and Böthig collaborated on an edition of Flanzendörfer's work, and yet they both were able for some time to collaborate as well with Sascha and Schedlinski. The distinction between literary production and authorial character holds for them. The good work at Galrev needs to be done, and the ethical judgment of Sascha and Schedlinski is another matter—maybe one that can await some other arena. This is a point that is constantly in Sascha's talk about himself: he has an enormous amount of work to do now, and his past efforts should be (and eventually will be) the basis on which he is judged, and so on. As for his personal character: "I have no morality" was an admission he always made freely and now repeats easily. He was asked in January 1992 why he never told his friends about his conversations with the Stasi: "Because I have never been able to speak about myself. I have never spoken about myself."[85] He has been an explicit and self-aware antiessentialist for reasons that now seem surprising: "The quest for a center, above all for the human center, usually ends in the four-hundred year-old [i.e., post-Reformation] cell between witness and perpetrator. You sacrifice yourself again in the figure of a black reflection. And you have yourself just where you wanted to be. You are the center."[86]

Is he so wrong? If one wanted a literature of character, one read the texts of the critical writers, chiefly Christa Wolf. But if one believed rather that art is produced by linguistic orders that have an agency of their own far more interesting than the moral character of one author, one might well prefer writers of the Prenzlauer Berg scene. The intellectual world of Sascha and Schedlinski has not been turned upside down by the revelations. Their references to structuralist and poststructuralist theory, to the Stasi as an informational structure, and so on, are reminders to their readers that their character was never an issue, that the cool of the Prenzlauer Berg aesthetic left no room for moral outrage on the one hand or profound remorse on the other. They have long been in a position to appreciate some of the possible political implications of the intellectual positions they had espoused.

Sascha talks and writes a very postmodern game. Schedlinski does too, as Peter Böthig has shown. The ideas that engage these two poets have great currency and other sorts of utility well beyond the former GDR. To put it simply, are now familiar claims about language experimentation, about language's duplicity or the instability of reference, about the instability of the subject, or about the multiplicity and equivalence of codes or "channels" rendered dubious by their service to spies? In 1982 Sascha straightforwardly claimed as one of the benefits of the Prenzlauer Berg scene that the Stasi should appreciate the fact that the relatively scholarly (*wissenschaftliche*) and theoretical engagement of the writers there was finding an unofficial distribution.[87] We know now also from the Stasi archives that Schedlinski's control officer advised him in 1985 to seek greater currency for his theoretical writing. Within three months a fixed monthly income for Schedlinski was approved by a Stasi commander.[88] Schedlinski still uses the theoretical discourse of the scene to account for, if not in fact to legitimate, the Stasi. Does the example of Sascha Anderson make the old notion of a coherent and integrated self look more attractive? These are questions that bear directly on international controversies about postmodernism. The German experience of literary postmodernism deserves consideration well beyond the now extended German borders. Not that Sascha Anderson and Rainer Schedlinski together discredit literary postmodernism, but they have indeed illuminated some of its dark potential. From the German feuilletons we still hear that one wants to be able to speak of morality and individual responsibility in the case of Sascha. But why, as Peter Böthig asked, "do these words sound so archaic?" Is there a useful place within postmodernist discourse for issues of morality and responsibility, or does the case of Sascha Anderson pull us toward conservative distance from postmodernist discourse?

In January 1993 the Stasi scandal took yet another turn when the internationally renowned dramatist Heiner Müller and Christa Wolf were revealed to have collaborated with the Stasi. Wolf said that she was surprised in May 1992, when she reviewed her Stasi files, to see that she had written reports for the Stasi from 1959 to 1962. She had forgotten not only the substance of her conversations with the Stasi but also that she had had a cover name and filed handwritten reports with the Stasi.[89] "A classic incident of repression that makes me think," she said.[90] It seems unlikely that such eminent writers could have been driven to collaboration with the Stasi by the professional pressures discussed repeatedly in this book, but in 1958 a Stasi informant characterized the young Christa Wolf as very career-oriented, very timid before the opinions of recognized people.[91] "Is Heiner Müller a Sascha Anderson writ large?" one journalist asked. The shocking thing is that even very talented and accomplished writers were corrupted by the desire to have some kind of effect. "'I wanted to achieve something,' Sascha Anderson said in his own defense of his Stasi conversations. . . . 'I wanted to change something.'—'I tried to advise and influence,' Heiner Müller explains today. Advise the Stasi? A confused dream. . . . It concerned literature: 'They needed knowledgeable people who could tell them what was in a text.' The National Prize winner as German teacher for the Stasi—a grotesque picture."[92]

There is a sense in which the Stasi controversy has erased the intellectual culture of the GDR: "After the examination [of the Stasi past] that Jürgen Fuchs is demanding," Frank Schirrmacher wrote, "the literary culture of the GDR may no longer be recognizable."[93] This is true, partly because Schirrmacher and Ulrich Greiner in July 1990 began the assault on the GDR literary culture with the charges against the critical, engaged literature of Christa Wolf and others. The scandal about the Stasi in Prenzlauer Berg effectively eliminated the avowedly disengaged, "indifferent" writing of the younger generation. By January 1992 the two major (and rival) coordinates of the literary culture had been stripped of cultural authority—again, schematically. Although individual writers still have a claim to attention, they are individuals, not representatives of any national cultural vitality. The literary culture is the locus now where the credibility of intellectuals generally is being examined. The terms in which intellectuals in other areas (Fink, for example, briefly the rector of the Humboldt University) are criticized are roughly the same as those that have emerged from the literary debates. The conclusions advocated are categorical: the historian Arnulf Baring has proposed simply closing the doors of the Humboldt University in Berlin or giving it to the Free University in West Berlin.[94] Betrayal is the charge against intellectuals. Benda is republished in 1991, and documents of 1936 are published to show that even the intellectuals of the 1930s were betraying one another:

Walter Janka on Johannes R. Becher and Anna Seghers, Peter Huchel on Becher, Seghers, and Arnold Zweig.[95] The West German press has presented much evidence to suggest that intellectuals are characterized not by otherworldliness, indecisiveness, or obscurity—the basis of the usual jokes about them—but by cowardice and moral duplicity. I do not want to blame some central agency for the campaign against intellectuals; Heiner Müller misleadingly refers to "the Stalinism of the West."[96] Cultural controversies, in which diverse characters participate, have their own dynamic way of channeling attention along a particular path. Once a path has been cut, it becomes clear that the intentions or interests of many people converged on a single objective. The path that has now been cut is toward the establishment of a new Germany without any interference from intellectuals, especially literary intellectuals.

Although there are ugly signs of nationalism in the attacks on foreigners that have been documented in the German and American press, there is still not much reason to fear a wave of nationalism in the German population at large. But among intellectuals the issue of nationalism is being sharply contested. In the summer of 1990 Günter Grass said, "We are witnessing for the first time, that on one hand the people of the FRG in a comforting way are not at all in a nationalistic mood, nor are they inclined to want to settle old accounts. Instead the will to settle up the past is raging in the feuilletons and is directed against GDR writers all together."[97] It is important to notice that the fight over literature has been staged in the feuilletons, not in the academic or strictly literary press, not in the mass media, but in those institutions responsible for the popular representation of intellectual activity. Where the thoughts of intellectuals are broadcast to the nation at large, in *Die Zeit, Der Spiegel,* and the literary supplement to the *Frankfurter Allgemeine Zeitung (FAZ),* the question of the authority of the East German writers is crucial. It was the staff reviewers of these publications, not any independent intellectuals or academics, who initiated the attack on Wolf. The attacks on her and Anderson originated in the feuilletons and have stayed there, apart from more specialized debates occurring in the smaller, focused publications of the intellectual and literary milieus. The controversies have seemed so personal partly because the critical reviewers have been acting on their own rather than expressing the sentiments of an intellectual constituency.

One issue in these debates is whether the national authority of journals such as *Die Zeit, Der Spiegel,* and the *FAZ* will be strengthened or weakened by reunification. As I have suggested, the GDR had a set of literary and intellectual institutions that were quite different from their counterparts in the FRG. Which institutions will speak for the future Germany? This is a question not at all about emerging nationalism, but instead about the mere maintenance of national cultural institutions. These journals generated these controversies; literary intellectuals in the east and the west have been made uncomfortable by them. East Germans have good reason to be wary about the survival of their own literary institutions, since the West Germans are paying the bills, and these controversies are having the obvious effect of reducing to worthlessness the literary achievements of the GDR. By worthlessness I mean to invoke a moral assessment, not an aesthetic one, though the latter is obviously more relevant in terms of literary history. Questions of aesthetic worth are often said to be those which critics and writers ought now to be discussing, and in ways that must seem unduly innocent to American or French literary critics, who for some time have acknowledged the extent to which aesthetic judgments are determined by political consider-ations.[98] But the attacks on Wolf, Anderson, and Biermann have focused on the moral credentials of the authors, much more than on the quality of their literary writing. Frank Schirrmacher says in passing that Wolf is uninteresting in aesthetic terms, but he adduces no evidence for this judgment. Instead he stresses Wolf's alleged lack of integrity.

Ernest Gellner's claim that "cultures now seem to be the natural repositories of political legitimacy" has a bearing on the Literaturstreit.[99] Writers in West Germany, as in the United States, often lament the lack of consequence they feel in the political and social life of the FRG, but these controversies show how deceptive appearances are. The flawed moral stature of East German writers is being made to serve as justifica-tion for the annexation of the former GDR: the writers have been claimed by the national press as the cases that count, regardless of what writers east or west may actually think about the issue.

The paradox is that intellectuals have been so vigorously stripped of authority that they now are greatly conspicuous in the German scene. "Without doubt," Rüdiger Schaper writes, "interest in the fundamental discussions is growing. With political reunification the big questions are coming up once again: about German identity, about the role of intellectuals and of the artist in the state, ultimately about the form of government."[100] On the face of it intellectuals have lost power, yet it is necessary somehow to fight the intellectuals to make a new German state, or to purge the remains of the state the FRG consumed. The authority of the intellectuals must be reduced. The battle in the end may well show them to be much more important than they realized they were. This whole period since 1989 has reminded everyone just how crucial intellectuals, and especially writers, are. In the streets of West Berlin the claims to one's attention are so insistent and have so little to do with writing that one feels the irrelevance there, as in Los Angeles, say, of literary art. Now to learn that a new nation cannot be founded, even in a highly advanced democratic country, without reducing the dissent of the writers—this is a big surprise. Walking the Kudamm, one thinks that writers would be the last ones to be consulted about the formation of a new nation. The truth seems to be that their existence has been a serious challenge to the politically conservative makers of the new Germany.

PART TWO

The
Scholarly
Life

NORBERT KRENZLIN

August 29, 1990, East Berlin

Norbert Krenzlin *(b. 1934) is a professor of aesthetics at the Humboldt University in East Berlin. His first book was a study of the notion of autonomous
literary works in phenomenological literary theory (1979). He later edited a
collection of critical essays on Peter Weiss (1987) and another on theories of
mass culture (1992). He teaches courses in modern philosophy and aesthetics.*

How are the universities responding to reunification?

At the moment we have a few problems. The first problem received
an absolutely classic formulation in the *Spiegel,* and quite an offensive
one too: "Where shall we send the GDR professors?" The problem here
is the reorientation—both necessary and overdue—of the social sciences from an orthodox Marxist Leninism to what I should call pluralism.
The people involved are differently disposed to the problem. It is certainly a question of different generations, but also a question of the
subject. That is to say that the people who are least able to reorient
themselves are the ones at the Humboldt University or at other universities who only taught Marxist Leninism in the Marxist-Leninist department,
the so-called Basic Studies in Social Science—to give it its pretentious
title—we always called it religious studies. These departments have been
dissolved. People who were of the right age were given early retirement,
others were invalided out of the service for health reasons, others were
found other jobs. Of course, even in these departments there were scholars, talented ones, intelligent people, who, for example, studied the history of the labor movement, or theories of society, whose scholarship
should not be lost.

39

The astonishing thing is that there were no witch hunts in the GDR, at least not up to the moment. That's in keeping with the progress of the so-called "soft" revolution up to the moment. That is, you make decisions but you make them quietly. The department of Marxist Leninism is only one example, a serious one of course, but you have the same problem among the philosophers, economists, and lawyers, though remarkably enough not to the same extent in the humanities. In literature, art history, and musicology it's a slightly different thing. Anyone who had to work intensively with contemporary GDR—or even Soviet—art and literature never for a moment imagined that they could be dealing with a healthy world; rather one had to take care not to become schizophrenic. On the one hand you had the official party line, and on the other whatever was said critically about the realities of the GDR in literature and art. That was something different.

Does a professor's membership in the SED play a great part in the reorientation process? The professors were for the most part members, weren't they?

Not every one, but most of them in the social sciences. I was a member myself, and I don't know anyone in the social sciences who wasn't. But the fact was that basically the party groups afforded the opportunity for free discussion, though regrettably without consequences for the public. Remember the party structure: There was the party group, which was then the basic organization, and there you could speak pretty openly. Then came the district party organization of the Humboldt University. Even there you could still risk opening your mouth. But that was it. Any party structure above that immediately punished dissenting speech, if there was any chance of its attracting public attention. Then things got tough.

What role did party membership play in the careers of young scholars?

We never had disputes in the humanities or aesthetics that destroyed careers. The situation was rather different. The present chairman of the Eastern SPD [Social Democratic Party], for example, Wolfgang Thierse, is a student of ours, did research with us, and had been an assistant for a time. Then—and this was more or less a part of the academic career—he went to the Ministry of Culture and worked there, because it was important for him to learn the practical side of things. From there he went—as a result of political differences, but with the agreement of both sides—to the Central Institute for Literary History and worked there. He became a real "closet" scholar.

But he was at the academy?

Oh, yes. He collaborated on Karlheinz Barck's *Historical Dictionary of Aesthetic Concepts*. At the academy you could retreat from the party. Thierse left the practical side of life because of conflicts with Kurt Hager himself.

The GDR managed to afford an academy with about twenty-six thousand employees. What was the academic policy behind this? It was, I assume, like everything else in the society, for the purpose of centralization and exerting some control over creativity. They wiped out jobs that didn't kowtow to centralism. A gigantic bureaucracy kept an eye on scholarship. For example, the annual report on the research: You couldn't just say, "I've written three books and four articles about this and that. Gave six lectures at this or that conference, etc." No, you had to report in detail: what you had gained in knowledge, the relationship of your work to the international level of scholarship, and all that sort of nonsense. A scholar was supposed to explain this stuff to a civil servant—a civil servant who understood nothing about it, but who was there in the academy and whose job it was to keep an eye on things, that is, to judge them politically. Those are simply quixotic acts of monumental stupidity, and disgraceful as well.

Was there a sort of self-censorship in scholarship?

That was, above all, the concern of the writers, but of course of scholars as well. I published a book about Peter Weiss's *Ästhetik des Widerstands* [The aesthetics of resistance]. I came to the conclusion that this book was the swan song of Marx's doctrine of the historic mission of the working class. I put it this way in 1985 with reference to Peter Weiss's novel: "Is it perhaps not true that epochs, societies, or classes that are historically at an end cause their boundless human content—that is, both their real historical contribution to the development of the genre as well as the ideas that have proved utopian in the face of history—to light up once more in a work of art? As far as the history of literature is concerned, there certainly seems to be a tradition of optimistic works written in the final days of an epoch: Homer's *Odyssey* as a reflex of the heroic age; Dante at the end of the Middle Ages; Cervantes, who gave ancient Spain a piece of his mind; and finally, Peter Weiss, when the century is coming to an end and the progressive social forces are faced with the task of reconsideration." I did not write that he was proclaiming the end of the historic mission of the working class and consequently the end of Marxist Leninism or words to that effect; I could not do that, that would not have been published here. I put it differently. The scholar may be able from time to time to change his way of saying something; for the artist that has to be fatal. That is, for example, Christa Wolf's great barrier. Adorno put it very nicely: "The unresolved antagonisms of reality return in works of art as the inherent problems of their form." One result of the unresolved antagonisms of reality is the change of faith into cynicism, from sympathy into sentimentality, from poetry into popular scholarship, from art and literature into a substitute for publicity. It's only the young people, the new generation, who are beginning to free themselves from it.

• • •

How would you characterize the relationship between intellectuals and the general population of the GDR?

When it was all over with socialism, the GDR intellectuals who were politically engaged wanted to force the ordinary people—who were tired of socialism—to dream of a utopia, and they could, in the process, appeal to Günter Grass.[1] But when Günter Grass claims the right to dream for himself and his colleagues in the West, that's something different. He creates art for a pluralistic society, and for him plurality, as an attitude, and democracy, as a social condition, are a matter of course. But when you hear of a pluralist utopia from the mouth of a GDR writer you cannot escape the suspicion that you are present at an attempt to resuscitate the socialist claim to happiness, which failed because it was totalitarian.

Then we come to the really interesting part of the debate that has been carried on, since the "revolution," by intellectuals in East and West Germany, that is, the instrumentalization of the people. The people and the masses are not, in the strict sense, social categories but merely metaphors. And that's the way they are used. For some the people were those who followed the utopian political ideas of the writers with enthusiasm—the ideal readers; for others the people were a principle of reality, if necessary, a rod that beat into the intellectuals what reality really was. The two sides in this discussion threw back at one another the will of the people. The message of the discussion is fatal; it points to the deplorable condition of the social sciences, which were completely helpless in the face of the collapse of actual socialism in the countries of Eastern Europe. That's not surprising as far as the so-called Marxist-Leninist social sciences are concerned: they distinguish themselves by the fact that for a hundred years they have ignored the development of social scientific thinking. But Western social scientific thinking was also helpless, I mean non-Marxist thinking. This social scientific vacuum was the basis on which poets and writers on the arts were able to fight one another so uninhibitedly using the metaphors "the people" and "the masses." There was nothing else available.

As far as the "people" were concerned, GDR writers were naive. They weren't skeptical, they weren't euphoric. They were above all naive, sociologically and from the point of view of the social sciences. Basically they did what the party fooled them into: they claimed to speak for the people. Art and literature were the only things in the GDR that were able to say anything about the reality of actual socialism. For the rest of the media it was taboo. And from this the artists, especially those who were critical, drew their consciousness of self and believed that *they* were the mouthpieces of the people. But that was an illusion. They were naive. They were talking to a small section of the population that was interested in literature and politics. There they did create a sort of authentic public—in contrast to the apparent public of the party. They did create something important, but it was small, and its influence was slight. And then came the festival of the revolution, where everything coalesced: intellectuals and the population, politics and art. That was on Saturday, November 4, 1989, at the great demonstration in Berlin, where a great many people really came together, more than half a million.

What sort of social science should be promoted, in your opinion? What we call empirical sociology in the USA?

That would be the basis. There was also empirical sociology here, but it was essentially kept under lock and key. It never came out into the open, and the results were never discussed publicly. But that would only be the basis. No, in my opinion, it's a matter of social scientific concepts and theories. For example, concepts such as that of industrial mass society. Social thought in the GDR was played out in categories of the class society, and that was unsuitable. The classes did not cease to exist, but class conflict no longer plays the role in world history that Marx accorded it in the nineteenth century. The problems that face us— embedded in global problems—are those of industrial mass society and mass culture. Social scientific thought has not yet come to terms with the collapse of the socialist countries and especially of the GDR.

Would things have been different here, if the social sciences had developed more freely?

No, I wouldn't say that. The social sciences cannot initiate and guide social movements. But they can do their part in creating an adequate consciousness of reality.

And of authority . . .

. . . and of authority, so that altogether a reasonable policy can be constructed. We need the social sciences as an adequate consciousness of a particular social situation and, in this sense, an instrument of social policy. But I don't think that the social sciences will change anything here. That was my last illusion and apparently the illusion cherished by a lot of other intellectuals in the GDR: a hope that under a different leadership, and in somewhat more favorable circumstances, something could have come out of the model of socialism. But it doesn't work, it's a cul-de-sac.

Socialism as a whole?

The development from 1917 onwards. And what we are now experiencing is a return to the process of civilization, and a very painful one. The ulterior motive in the whole thing is that if today we want to cling to the project of socialism—or to put it more modestly, to the thought of emancipation, to the idea of a caring society—then the first step is to remove such projects from Marxist Leninism, that is, from the idea of a historic mission for the working class. That's nonsense. In this sense I find it a cul-de-sac in history.

The idea of personal leadership—Honecker or Ulbricht—was still strong in the GDR.

The worst thing that we had to experience here—that is, for someone who had consciously debated these relationships with himself, who tried to be critically involved here—was the following: sometime about the beginning of 1990, perhaps in March, there was a pronouncement by the public prosecutor that said that people who were under indictment—Honecker, Mittag, Mielke, Stoph, et al.—were perhaps juridically untouchable, because "senility, mental confusion, and refusal to give evidence" were making the public prosecutor's investigation difficult.[2] The idea that one had been ruled for years—and allowed oneself to be ruled—by people who, because of senility, because of mental confusion could not be held legally responsible, that to me is a hard one to live with.

HEINZ-UWE HAUS

August 27, 1990, East Berlin

Heinz-Uwe Haus *(b. 1942) studied at the Institute for Film and Television in Potsdam-Babelsberg in the early 1960s; later he studied drama and German literature and culture. He did his Ph.D. on Brecht at the Humboldt University in 1986. He has worked as an actor and directed productions in Germany, Greece, Turkey, Cyprus, and throughout the United States, where he has also taught as a visitor at such institutions as the universities of Delaware and Kansas, Kenyon College, New York University, and Villanova University. Since 1989 he has been active in Democratic Awakening; he ran unsuccessfully for a parliamentary seat in 1990.*

One often hears intellectuals say that the present moment is depressing. Is this your experience?

I could only wish that the party intellectuals were more depressed. The fact of the matter is that many of them are now fiddling around looking for an alibi, that a lot of them are sulking, because that's the most comfortable way, they think, of coping with their past. There's a nice sentence of Brecht's: "Revolutions take place in cul-de-sacs." The thing that moves these party intellectuals is that communism is not only at an end in reality, but also in their dreams. The crisis for many of them probably consists not so much in the elimination of the GDR, but in the fact that they took part in starting a movement that they cannot follow up without sacrificing what they call their utopia, which was, for them more than any other level of the society, the premise of life in the GDR-Stasi state. Probably everyone who lived in the GDR was more or less trained to fool themselves in everything they did. But anyone who was also professionally involved in hoping for a better world was, in the process, subject to certain temptations to suppress reality. These ladies and gentlemen—official writers, professors, and scholars—found it very easy to work for the Marxist-Leninist apparatus because it positively forces you to bottle up the inconsistency of existence in favor of pure doctrine, or to proclaim, in spirit, the rational and humane direction in which society is moving. It was among the rules of the system that the change from hardship and privileges gave these conformists an inflated sense of self-importance.

They just about managed to raise a cheer when the irksome stick had served its purpose. But they very soon missed the carrot. They've only had a problem with their identity since November 9, 1989. They stylized their own pastoral cure into an identity problem, but no one is able to share it with them. If they'd paid a bit more attention to what the people were saying, if they had stayed closer to the people in their interests, they wouldn't be bitching so much now. If you look at the way people behaved at the Writers' Conference, where the only thing they discussed was their social problems, when they didn't have even one word to say for the writers who had lost their citizenship; where, on the contrary, they sent greetings and thanks for his years of leadership to Herr Kant on his sickbed . . . When you think how this new PEN Club of the GDR acted in Kiel, where [Hans Joachim] Schädlich, one of those who had to leave the GDR, objected to the presence of the acting minister, Herr Höpcke, and this acting minister of culture had his name cleared by Herr Knobloch and other members[1] . . . These people are laboring under an illusion in their dependence on and their relationship to power, where they are scarcely able to hint at their visions and utopias any more but are perplexed that things don't go on in the old way. They had gotten used to one another and had set aside moral criteria and humanistic values. The people suffered long-term harm and deprivation, but at the core they had resisted. They became more inventive than many of the intellectuals who, to this day, would rather have stuck with their 5 percent of the truth—as Stefan Heym once put it.

How is the process of self-purification proceeding now in the intellectual sector?

I think it's ridiculous that the government we've elected to get rid of the GDR in short order is carrying out an intolerable policy of ensuring the maintenance of living standards in the area of scholarship and the universities. At the Humboldt University, the Marxist-Leninist section was split up into respectable-sounding institutes, so that even the most notorious Stalinists could continue teaching. The minister's answer, just before unification, was to appoint roughly an additional 150 professors from the SED cadre, under the guise of rehabilitation! Aside from a very few exceptions (Bahro, von Berg, and about five or six others), a whole mob of social scientists, Marxist-Leninists, will be changed into sociologists, or else other liberal-sounding areas of activity will be invented.[2] And there will be a repetition of what is otherwise happening in reality. I think it is very important that the East German universities be thinned out, not expanded. There are enough assistants, enough freelance workers at the universities, who have both the expertise and the pedagogical and moral resources to take over the positions of existing full professors. The authorities should not be doing the reverse, leaving the old ones there and appointing additional professors from the old cadre. The continuing power of the old apparatus, and the intertwining of interests out of fear and sinecures, makes a self-renovation impossible.

In the area of culture, too, it's the case that after the elections to the Volkskammer, people from the SED party apparatus who had gotten jobs in the theater, one, two, and three years ago, were appointed to leading posts in Berlin. As late as April 15, 1990, a former member, the second secretary of the SED district administration, was promoted to manager of a theater. If you go into the GDR Ministry of Culture, you'll find the former acting minister as head of the department, because there is no head of the main department, and no acting minister any more. And at the same time he has also replaced the other acting minister who has been dismissed, so that now he functions as the head of two departments. The ministry has been reorganized so that there is an additional minister, with his personal adviser, and two secretaries of state; otherwise all that's happened is a shift in administrative titles. Almost the whole apparatus is still there. If you go to another ministry, Health, you'll find exactly the same state of affairs. It's intolerable. For example, no jobs are advertised, not publicly, and the old party apparatus is directing things just as it did before. If you go to GDR television, where 80 percent of the people were members of the SED, you won't find that the personnel managers were dismissed, but rather that they continue to run newly invented offices with their same directives and "socialistic" policy. You can't expect that out of the pool of 20 percent of the people who were not party members, there will be people with enough courage and energy to fight to introduce changes. To introduce, for example, production groups which have to manage without the excessive bureaucracy of the television operation—that was originally subordinated to the security forces of the SED. Television production is no business of the Stasi. So they've got to get rid of the ladies and gentlemen of the Stasi who were in television production and not give them new jobs. That's the problem. You can go where you like and you'll see how, under the flimsy guise of expertise—"and who's to take over the new job if it isn't those who have the experience?"—the old structures are preserved. It's just a repetition of what happened in Germany after 1945.

How bad would it actually be if the situation of 1945 were now to be repeated? The old Nazis didn't rebuild the Nazi system in 1945.

The anxieties, the deformities, the harm caused by the dictatorship—as one of our women writers put it—are so severe that people are not yet in a position to understand fully their democratic rights. In a revolutionary process like the present one, where we cannot expect that the Stalinists will resign of their own accord, the democratic forces have to gain acceptance for the rule of law in a free society, decisively, in an enlightened manner, and by the exercise of legitimate force. A number of professors, for example, must be removed from their jobs. That's a necessary step. It's not revenge, but an act designed to restore normality. We have to remove power from the hands of the people who are left and who make political decisions, among the intellectuals as well. We're not dealing with simple administrative employees. We're also not dealing with a situation in which circumstances really alter these people and force them to behave differently. To "turn around" is not necessarily a negative concept, if you understand by it the creation of objective circumstances so that people understand the need for change. But in the course of a revolutionary process of change like that, we must not forget the moral side of the matter. Up to the moment, none of the academic Stasi informants has resigned voluntarily, no one has gone of his own accord to court, no one has done anything publicly and tried to present the past in such a way as to make it possible, in the future, to create other structures in these areas. People have merely made a 180-degree turn—at best—if they haven't, like the Mafia, managed to secure their positions on the basis of old connections, or managed to throw sand in the works. Anyone who was a paid Stasi officer or informant has to be removed by the new state. Anyone who got paid for crimes has to be removed. Anyone who, in any other way, was so corrupted by the system that he lived like a rat, must be given the opportunity, by circumstances, to develop into a civilized human being. It's not a question of revenge, not a question of persecution. It's a question of clarification, enlightenment, and justice.

We're wasting a great opportunity for intellectual and spiritual renewal. If we were to succeed at renewal in Berlin, the next few years in Europe would also be filled with substance in every respect. For instance, we could deal with the whole question of left and right in politics, of state thinking and normal thinking, the theme of federalism, the problem of security in Europe—namely, the vacuum that arises out of the disappearance of the Warsaw Pact, of a military system that was always concerned with internal oppression and gratification. A new determination of a more global responsibility would also emerge. The North-South hemispherical conflict that transcends political groups could receive stimuli from clarification of some of these issues. We should be thinking for the future and not for the past. If we don't begin this process here, the wounds in this country will become more and more severe. But the process should not be reduced to a polarity of revenge or reconciliation, because the deformities produced by dictatorship penetrated the whole society, and because victims and culprits do not stand in clear opposition to one another.

So you are not of the opinion that the intellectuals should now keep quiet.

Of course the solidarity that arose from the emergency must be kept alive by the intellectuals. But this solidarity cannot be expressed—if I can be concrete—by Heiner Müller. He was always standing on the mountains looking down into the valleys. Of course, it was pleasant and fruitful to hear from Heiner Müller that the GDR was only a part of a great historical process of change. There was a drop of oppositional power in this truth. But it was only an eighth or a tenth of the truth, and people fell upon this tenth of the truth. A year or even three months before the revolution, he was writing poems saying that he would cross the border and travel to Frankfurt am Main, as to a glittering and festering corpse! The many hundreds of thousands who not only had a wall in Germany, but a wall in front of their heads, and in their hearts, and in their city, and their hopes, shortly after they were born, never accepted this sheer historicization of the GDR. They never followed Herr Müller. No, it was the leftist smart set in West Germany and West Berlin and a few intellectuals from the GDR who were ignorant of reality. But it was, and is, nothing that could now be a vision for the concrete future. That's the way it is with their utopia. This utopia was expressed at all times, either as an exaggerated self-satisfaction, or as an object of cultural policy that had to serve the interests of the party and the Stasi.

Is the word "utopia" merely an alibi?

That cannot be emphasized too strongly. It's constantly being talked about by the so-called socialist intellectuals in the FRG. People are irritated and shocked over there. And that gives their companions the chance to keep their utopia, or to set this alibi aside. There has to be a whole new qualification of the concept, because what I have seen, for years, as left and right in this polarization, has less and less influence in concrete politics. Now for the first time utopians are being forced to name realistic notions and goals for society. In the future it's not going to be so easy to say, "The intellectuals are always on the left, art is always on the left." That's a thesis from the age of the class struggle, an invention of the twenties. It derives from blindness to, and overestimation of, the intellectuals. For the intellectuals, it is most comfortable to be as far as possible to the left, but not in relation to a party. If these people have not understood by now how for years they were exploited as useful idiots, then they should—for heaven's sake!—be taken less seriously in the future. I really think these so-called intellectuals are taking liberties in installing themselves so comfortably and then trumpeting about all over the place that the people don't understand them, that we're a people of banana-eaters and VW owners. The intellectuals all had their bananas and their VWs.

You spoke of hope, the hope of resistance? Were you not then surprised on November 9, 1989?

For the people, the only question was that there had to be an end, at some point, of the Soviet occupation. Anyone here who maintains that this came as a surprise to them must never have talked to people who were farmers, or bakers, or fitters, or foresters. The path that so many intellectuals chose for themselves in their imagination was, in reality, a path trodden by people who had a special proximity to power. The GDR provided them with a livelihood in exchange for their opportunistic compliance. Their lifelong illusion was entirely in the hands of the regime. That's why they now conjure up the myth of obstructed independence. They want to wipe out the traces of oppression, fear, and hatred, and conceal their emptiness and failure in the pale light of false thinking. For the majority of people, it was like living under an old feudal system, what I would like to call a stick-and-carrot system. It was not a state based on law, it was not a system of law. They could not sue a public or state institution. Local courts were done away with. When I was fired one day from the *Deutsches Theater* because of anti-Sovietism, because I had used texts in a production that had displeased an ideological committee of the Central Committee, I was only able to continue to have a social existence afterwards because, by mistake, someone had given written confirmation of my anti-Sovietism. They were frightened that the *Bildzeitung* would publish it. It was only later that a compromise was reached, and the notice of dismissal had to be destroyed. Someone had been so free with his rage as to write out the condemnation, otherwise you never got anything in writing. In my case, the order came from above that a compromise was to be reached. This is the sort of relationship that makes people close to the source of power—with their orders and their deformed personal relationships—continue to nurse their illusions about life.

Were you a member of the SED?

No, and I refused every time I was asked. They asked me to join three times, and three times they promised me jobs if I would join, and I didn't. That's the point: no one in this country was forced to become a member of the SED, if he wasn't interested in furthering his career, if he wasn't trying to conceal his inabilities in his chosen field, or his fears about his ability, by taking such a step. Nonparty members were unable to exploit certain functions in this country. For years they refused to give me a teaching post at the university.

That's categorical?

No, in spite of that, some people did succeed in getting a lectureship, but only a very few. But it's not necessary to have a lectureship, it's so silly. You have to be one idea better, one idea faster, and then there are gaps. Of course some people perish, careers are held up, broken—you have to be lucky. I was lucky. No intellectual can use the excuse that he had to become a member. Nobody *had* to do anything here. They all did it voluntarily in order to follow the path of least resistance. That wasn't necessary. There were honorable niches, and there were so many possibilities in this society to remain upright, to some limited and small degree, that this excuse doesn't wash. The people who said that they entered the party in order to improve it from inside . . . all right, there may have been a few, I believe that. Not everyone who was in the party was a rogue, but there were a lot of rogues in it, and there were also upright people in it who tried, to a limited extent, to do something sensible.

How many people in your circle were not members of the SED?

In my academic circle they were all members of the SED. But in my artistic circle things were a bit easier. They were fools, at best, fools for the regime. In theater and television, and I know these well, most of them were not SED. Painters too, none of them were members.

And if they had been in the SED?

They would have received commissions and gotten their passports earlier and been able to travel. But there were also some, the majority, who weren't, and who simply ignored the illusions because of the niche they were in, and because of their work. These are the people who participated in the real intellectual development, who stayed tough, who now have a responsibility to the future. They could have become civil servants in the regime and also have been members of the party. For this reason, it's especially disgusting when intellectuals who conformed to the system present themselves today as though *they* had been handicapped. Of course they were handicapped, but it wasn't necessary for everyone to become a professor. They could have gotten work all over the place and given other people some hope, in the most diverse fields. Teachers play a great part in ordinary schools when they give people hope. They would never have become principals, but they could have become decent physics or biology teachers, and let it be seen by their personalities that they were concerned with the questions of youth and not with prefabricated answers. There was a place in this society for people who didn't want to accept the prescribed brainwashing. Everything else is a lame excuse in order to avoid coming to terms with the past.

EVA MANSKE

August 31, 1991, Munich

Eva Manske (b. 1942) studied American studies, English, and Slavic studies in Leipzig. She is the coauthor of a critical study of the contemporary American novel (1983) and editor of a collection of Whitman's Specimen Days *(1990) and of contemporary American fiction in German translations. In October 1990 she was appointed to a chair in American studies at the University of Leipzig. She now works at the German-American Institute in Freiburg.*

We are both students of American literature. Could you explain how the study of American literature was structured in the GDR?

I did English, American, and Slavic studies in Leipzig. At that time I was studying for a diploma—that is, the equivalent of a master's degree—and there were great opportunities for a university career at that time. Since the sixties, things have changed somewhat. American and English studies later became relevant mainly for the teaching profession. We also had courses of study that made it possible for students to teach English in universities, colleges, and technical colleges—language instruction. We also prepared students for the practice of cultural politics—that was the term then. They could then get a job in publishing, radio, television, or with a newspaper. These possibilities were there, but they were relatively limited. Most students were obliged to become teachers. Language practice played an important role. The question we were always asked was, "Why should a teacher study English and American culture and literature so extensively?" Ours were looked upon as luxury disciplines, and this affected our effectiveness as teachers very negatively.

Our whole course of study was strictly regulated—you've probably heard that from other people. It was almost like being in school. Only a specified number of people could apply, because it was a *numerus clausus* [restricted admissions] discipline. There were always four applicants for every place. And the students knew that when their studies were completed they would have to become teachers. If, in the course of their studies, they decided not to become teachers, they were generally told to give up their studies. Up until the revolution, students studied two main disciplines and always had to take a huge dose of Marxism-Leninism: training in philosophy and political economy and scientific communism. Our demand that we should include English and American philosophy was always turned down. There were more hours devoted to sports than to English and American literature together. Those were absurdities of the prevailing circumstances at that time.

Didn't it depend on the fact that this particular culture was a class enemy?

Yes, it did have something to do with that. The concept at first was that these teachers were language teachers, who communicated the language. The first foreign language in the schools was Russian. The second compulsory language was introduced in seventh grade. That was English or French in most schools. There were a few who did Czech or Polish, but they were peripheral. A larger portion of hours could have been devoted to culture and literature. That didn't happen. The fact that it was the culture and literature of a country that was viewed as an enemy may have played a part. On the other hand, there was a long tradition of the reception of this literature in the GDR. You can see from the publishers' lists that a representative amount of American literature, for example, was published in the GDR in German translation. In the publishers' lists, at least, American literature was understood as part of world culture. Here people were directed, according to the official understanding, to conduct a critical examination, that's to say, with negative emphasis, of American culture. Life was made easier for us by the fact that American literature belongs, for the most part, to world literature. The GDR always strove to be regarded as a land of culture, where the treasures of world culture were communicated. That gave us the chance to make American literature known to a broad reading public. The function of students who were studying to become teachers, to reach other people as disseminators of information, was always regarded by us as a great opportunity. But when I look at the curricula, we were all treated shabbily—the Romanists, the Anglicists, the Americanists—because we weren't seen as having a large role in the tasks facing the schools. English literature, for example, was only taught by German teachers. It was the duty of the German teacher to teach Shakespeare.

• • •

What arguments did you use to sway a publisher to publish an American book?

For every book you needed two or three independent expert opinions. Then the afterword was written and sent in. Sometimes you'd get it back with a comment that it was too long, and often you were asked to rethink one passage or another. But it was possible for an author to say, "No, I'm not going to reconsider it," and that's what happened. It took the courage of one's convictions, because you had to say to yourself, "O.K. perhaps it won't be published." In one case, I did correct something. I had made a selection of Susan Sontag's essays, and I had chosen three from *On Photography*. In the first essay there was a footnote in which she writes that there are no photographs of the Gulag Archipelago, because no photos were taken there. It was never documented photographically. This was returned to me and I was told that they couldn't publish it because the Gulag Archipelago was taboo in the GDR; as far as the officials were concerned it didn't exist. I was also told that it was difficult enough to publish Susan Sontag, and that it would certainly not go through in this form, and wouldn't I think it over. I wrestled with myself for three days and then said, "OK."

In my recommendation to the publisher I always had to say that the authors not only wrote aesthetically important and outstanding literature, but that they reflected a critical view of America; that they presented American life in a convincing manner and that the American way of life was not represented uncritically in the work. Patriotic American books could never appear here. We were dealing with a realistic literature that could be fitted into a realistic or even social-realistic canon. There was, for example, no problem in publishing Dreiser, but T. S. Eliot and Ezra Pound were more difficult. In recent years Ezra Pound was rejected in the GDR simply because of the political position that he adopted, and yet people could still say that he was a very important poet who must be made accessible to our reading public.

So, after the mid seventies, we were able to present a broad spectrum of books. They came out in small editions, of course—five thousand to twenty-five thousand copies, or if it was a second edition, fifty thousand. Those were ridiculously small numbers. Though fifty thousand was all right. In this way you reached an astonishingly broad public. The really big sellers in the GDR were Kerouac with *On the Road,* or Salinger's *Catcher in the Rye.* A lot of people read these books and then lent them to other people. There was a great response to them. That kept us alive. Part of the response to these books was that you were invited to clubs where writers or prospective writers met, and you were asked to talk about tendencies and directions in contemporary American literature. In the discussions that ensued, it turned out that an incredible number of people had read these books, and that some writers had taken them as models for themselves. For many poets, or prospective poets, in the GDR, the beat generation was a model—Ginsberg for instance. What I always found strangely touching was that a man like Charles Bukowski served as a model for a lot of people. It was completely understandable, because he reflected the outsider existence. But there was also great interest in e. e. cummings, Pound, and T. S. Eliot, who were really read by people whom you would not necessarily have expected to read them, who were not students, but just people who were interested and who were gathered in the Kulturbund. They included nurses, doctors, workers, etc. There was great interest. But they had little access.

You said that in your expert opinions you had to say something about humanism. Could you elaborate?

The official position in tackling the cultural problem was that we wanted to communicate a culture that supported humanistic values. Literature that propagated fascism, or was militaristic, was on the Index and wasn't published—and I always supported that. There weren't any cheap heroic novels here, by official policy. People took a very broad view of humanism, they tried to place the individual and his dignity at the very center as something that was indispensable. That made it easy for us, because people said that if we accepted this attitude then we could receive a large part of world literature here, even if we did not agree with certain positions that were taken in these texts. The sentence,"I consider this a work that is based upon fundamental humanistic positions" was one that was very easy to write.

GDR ideology was also very conservative in regard to sexuality.

True enough, that was the case for a long time. Things only changed in the last seven or eight years. Before that there was a definite official prudery, and Henry Miller, for example, could not be published. It wasn't until 1984 that he appeared. He was categorized as "pornography." If you were here at the revolution, when the borders were opened up in November 1989 and GDR citizens could go to the west for the first time, you could have seen—it was one of the comic phenomena—how the men all poured into peep shows, or went to Hamburg to the Reeperbahn [red-light district] and into the sex shops—they had to make up for lost time.

How does conservatism like this respond to the issues raised by feminism?

That played no part here at all. You're talking about a very complicated field. Officially, women had equal rights. That was written into the constitution. They had the same access to education—there were quotas—and we always protested that we were not "quothildes"; that's not the way it should be. For many years it was a fact of life in GDR politics that the quotas had to be maintained for female students, about fifty-fifty. It differed from discipline to discipline. Not so many applied for the sciences. There were also so-called special programs for women, plans for support whereby women received special scholarships; because at the same time, the authorities were promoting families and young marriages, and the young women all got married by eighteen or nineteen and had their first child at twenty.

And were divorced at twenty-two.

That's exactly it. Then the problem was that there they were with two children having to combine the duties of being a mother with their profession, and all this within a system of nonexistent services. The difficulty for women was their career. They could still enter a profession, but a career meant training and then a commitment. It was tricky when you had to take a business trip or work till late at night and then fetch your child from the crèche and go shopping. Although there were equal rights on paper, working brought a lot of big problems for women. The second thing was that equal rights were only guaranteed up to a certain level. Just take a look at the structure as far as management was concerned. It was worse than in the FRG and a lot worse than in the United

States. Women constituted only 4 to 5 percent of tenured lecturers and professors. And they were a great exception. They were mostly without families. Someone like me who has a family was an exception. It was only because my husband was understanding and we worked well together, but in normal circumstances it was very difficult.

Another thought on this: there was only one woman in the whole government—Frau Honecker, the minister for popular education, she was Erich Honecker's wife. In the Politburo, the absolute center of power—where all the decisions were made, from social welfare to the large political questions—there were only two women. And they weren't even full members. They only had an advisory vote. They were two old ladies, seasoned communists, who never appeared on public occasions. They were token females. Otherwise there wasn't a woman to be found at the upper level. Research was done on how many female directors of businesses or combines there were, or how many women were in managerial positions outside of industry. For example, at institutions of higher learning there were one or two, but never more. And there were dozens of institutes of higher learning in the GDR. Women were underrepresented at the managerial level. And this continued down to a certain level of middle managerial positions. Below that, women were very strongly represented. The official women's organization, the DFD [Demokratischer Frauenbund Deutschlands; the democratic women's union of Germany] was an association where people did crochet and knitting and exchanged recipes.

• • •

Do you worry at all about the opportunities for scholarship that are now threatened?

I know that we now lack what we had before and what we found so pleasant; for instance, finding a book for which you would like to write an afterword. Then I knew that I would reach twenty-five thousand people, because the edition always sold out. You would often see someone in the streetcar reading the book you had published yourself. Or you received mail. People wrote about how fantastic they found the book and asked whether I would autograph it. Such things were really nice and they're gone. America and American literature was always a very popular discipline, but it no longer has the same character that it had up to a year and a half ago. But no, on the contrary, you have to say that the revolution was for me a real liberation in a number of ways. We were very regimented because of the number of hours we had to teach. We had to move within a confined space. I couldn't travel. Finally, at the end of 1988, I got the green light and was allowed to leave the GDR.

Were you a member of the SED?
Yes.

And how was that? 1988 was pretty late.
I was in England in 1970 and 1975. It was financially very difficult, and I made two study trips, each for two or three months. Then I once made a reckless political remark in a private conversation. Someone must have reported it. It went as far as the ministry.

What was the remark?
We were talking about the economic problems of the GDR. I said that I felt unable to give people in England or the United States information about the GDR economy. I wasn't an economist, I didn't understand anything about it, and didn't think it was all that wonderful that people should trumpet its praises all over the world. It should be left to the experts to do the talking. So the official reason given was that no one should be allowed to travel abroad who couldn't even give information about the GDR.

Do you think that socialism is fundamentally bankrupt?
It didn't work in any one single country. I actually joined the SED out of conviction, less because I thought the SED was so wonderful than because my grandfather died in Theresienstadt, in the concentration camp. That's part of our family history. And as far as I was concerned, communism was an obligation. He had been a communist, he couldn't have died in vain. For me it was an alternative. I found a lot that was attractive about communism: social equality and justice. Then I noticed that it simply wasn't working.

What did you see as your role before the revolution?
When you received your appointment, you had to declare that you . . . what was the formula again? When you were appointed professor, you had to declare that you would fulfill the duties that society expected from a university teacher. That also implied educating students. It was not just the communication of culture, but an entire education. You were to train socialist teachers, if you want to put it in simplistic terms. Every discipline had its part to play in this, even American studies. We couldn't remove ourselves from the whole context and say that we were only

going to communicate cultural content. So the clear precondition was formulated that there was to be a critical confrontation with American culture, history, society, and literature.

Do you now find a process of self-investigation, a reevaluation of the past, taking place among your colleagues?

I think one should be clear about these things in oneself and find an opportunity to talk about them, without pointing the finger of guilt at one another or saying, "You were more courageous." If someone was more courageous, I take my hat off to him. Or saying, "You were just as cowardly." What good does that do? But from the point of view of the discipline, objectively, this confrontation with history has to take place. We have to develop the capability to mourn the lost opportunities that we should perhaps have grasped, that we should have seen. We *ought* to have seen a lot of things. Was it because we had closed our eyes?

For me, doing American studies meant making my hobby into my profession. I loved teaching at the university, in spite of all the difficulties. I was always allowed to do what I wanted. No one, for instance, ever checked up on me or would have asked, "What are you doing in your lectures or seminars?" It differed from one institution to another. My boss never did that, and, from my very first seminars onwards, I never had to show him my schedule. In the compulsory seminars that we had to hold, I told him that I was doing this and that, but that I was also doing the great writers. I couldn't leave them out, but I was doing what interested me. No one ever sat in on a class and listened to what I was doing and what I was saying, although I knew that a lot of the students did pass it on. But it was something that you liked to do, and you had the feeling that you had achieved something. A temptation was there: you had influence. The literary picture can influence students, and they will pass it on in turn to their students. That was fun. If, for the sake of consistency, I had left the university, where would I have gone? Where could I have worked in a system that worked the way it did? To that extent you were susceptible to making compromises. That's something one should think about: where shouldn't one have made compromises?

MARIANNE STREISAND

August 30, 1991, East Berlin

Marianne Streisand *(b. 1951) studied Germanics and theater arts at the Humboldt University (1971–1976). She joined the staff at the Central Institute in 1976, took her Ph.D. in 1983 with a dissertation on Heiner Müller, and left the Central Institute in 1986 to teach at the Humboldt University. Her research is concentrated in theater history of the late nineteenth and early twentieth centuries.*

What made you decide to go to the university?

I went because, over the long haul, I found work in the Central Institute for Literary History very unsatisfying. It's true that you could carry out your research in complete peace and publish, but there was no contact with living human beings. You could work there for three or five years without any questions, and you could nurse your neuroses in complete peace without ever having a student test whether your arguments were interesting or credible.

In addition, there was the fact that in the group in which I worked—the group for GDR literature—we had problems that were rather political. We published a book called *Werke and Wirkungen* [Works and effects] that was subjected to political criticism here. For the study group, the results of this were very disappointing. We were a group of women—there was one man in it—who had gotten together with an alternative concept. Our intention was for the book to be a combination of reception history and textual analysis of GDR literary texts—and, more precisely, of texts that had played a part in the cultural history of the GDR, for example, *Nachdenken über Christa T.,* by Christa Wolf, or *Ole Bienkopf,* by Erwin Strittmatter, or *Die Aula,* by Hermann Kant. At that time I was still working on *Die Umsiedlerin* [The resettled woman] by Heiner Müller. Those were all texts that, when they appeared, drew a lot of attention from the literary and especially the political public, but which, for the most part, met with sharp rejection from the political and cultural-political side, to the point that some of the authors were expelled from the Writers' Union. You could observe a process that went from strict rejection to a very large measure of admiration and agreement. Ten, fifteen, twenty years later the texts were celebrated as milestones in the history of GDR literature.

At the time, that was very exciting for us, and it also enraged us to see how texts were rejected on a superficially political level, and with scant concern for aesthetic categories. The original documents are stunning. For example, the debates that took place at writers' congresses at the time when the texts were being written . . .

Was it possible for the group to get hold of unpublished documents, readers' reports, for example?

First of all, everything was permitted. No sort of research was forbidden. The question was whether it would then be published. That was when we started having problems. But this is what happened to my text, Heiner Müller's *Die Umsiedlerin,* which was completed in 1961 and provoked very severe consequences. Müller was expelled from the Writers' Union at the time. The director who staged the work lost his director's contract at the theater in Senftenberg and was sent into "production," as it was called at the time. In other words he became a day laborer for a year. The students—it was an amateur production—all had to write statements in which they were made to condemn themselves for taking part in an "anticommunist, antihumanistic, and reactionary piece of trash originating in imperialistic circles." Some of them were expelled from the university. I found these student statements in the archives and was able to make use of them.

The problem began when the book was finished. There were always plans for the whole year at the academy. And when the complete plan was finished—to this day we don't know how that happened—the book attracted notice in the higher regions of the Academy of Sciences, not in our institute, probably in the office of the vice president for social sciences. At that point there were some pretty strong reactions to it. At first it looked as if the book wouldn't appear at all, but then we were instructed to write a second version. In this case it happened that every-thing passed over fairly mildly, because very good and very clever people from our institute, such as Dieter Schlenstedt, put themselves behind it, and we rewrote it very carefully.[1] That's to say, we didn't simply rewrite so that what was black before was white and what was white was black. In the first version we expressed our rage quite vehemently after what we had read in the evaluations, which had in effect condemned the texts. In the second version we attempted to come to a closer understanding of—and to describe more emphatically—why the state had reacted so strongly to these texts, what boundaries of ideological, political, cultural values these works breached. To that extent—and I'm being quite hon-est, I don't mean it opportunistically—the second one is a better piece of scholarship, because we put more energy into it in order to under-stand the other side, not to excuse it, but at least to explain why these books were so strongly rejected.

After that everything went fine as far as the book was concerned. Then we had to deal with other titles that looked at first more harmless: Bruno Apitz's *Nackt unter Wölfen* [Naked among wolves], for example, was included so that we could have a book where the process of recep-tion didn't run from complete rejection to a very large measure of ap-proval.[2] Unfortunately, however, in our research on this text we came upon similar documents, letters and statements from readers claiming that the book had no business being published and would break with the usual political view, as far as the reassessment of fascism was con-cerned. The same thing came out later. But it wasn't such a very problem-atical book.

I was shocked at something else that affected me more than the official processes and accusations. It got to the point where we no longer recognized the leading role of the party. At some point we were through with it. But what developed inside this group of female colleagues, who had at first worked very well together and had been very collegial, was regrettable. For example, one of our initial principles was—and this isn't just a problem experienced by GDR scholars, but an international problem—to try to keep everyone at the same level of information, not to develop a hierarchy of those in the know, where the boss has more information at his or her command than the assistants. But we shared our knowledge and discussed everything that we had read about the subject of reception theory very openly with one another. That was a good sort of cooperation. There was a boss, Inge Münz, who didn't in any way try to establish a hierarchical structure within the group.[3] It was nice working there, and I learned a lot.

How long did it last?

Because of the political processes it lasted much longer than was planned. Altogether it was a project that took four years. After the political problems arose, the group broke up quite vehemently, and enmities developed, because some people immediately accepted the criticism and confessed everything—let themselves be broken at once—and the others tried to pursue the upright course. That was a rather unpleasant experience, seeing how political processes like that could force their way into interpersonal relationships. That was the real shock. And then in addition—because we started with the question of why I went over to the university—I thought that it was completely stupid to keep groups of scholars in the same formation for ten years or more. I am convinced that groups should be dissolved once a project is completed. After that you collect new people for a new project, because in this way you can have exchanges, and debate, and all the things needed for scholarly work—stimulus and competition as well.

• • •

How would you describe the role of authors in the revolution?

The ordinary people made a great deal of use of intellectuals through the medium of literature, because the people did not have the courage or the language to formulate their demands and their criticism. But the people were motivated by concerns that are not part of leftist utopias. I found that interesting. For a lot of people, the high point of our revolution was the great demonstration on November 4 [1989] on the Alexanderplatz that was organized mainly by artists, but also intellectuals. For me that day was the turning point. We weren't standing very near the front when the proclamation was made—Christa Wolf and Heiner Müller and Stefan Heym and Steffi Spira all spoke—but rather fairly far back where the "people" were.[4] It soon became clear to me that the people I was standing among weren't in the least interested in what was being said up at the front. What was being chanted about democratic socialism didn't interest them in the slightest. They were there to express their protest against, their dislike of, the circumstances. They used this demonstration that was organized by artists and didn't organize one of their own. Their demonstration was to go to the west via Hungary. That was a much stronger demonstration than the one that took place on November 4. It was then that I realized the differences that existed. They showed themselves quite clearly once the Wall was opened up. I think that the idea of a democratic socialism was always the intellectuals' utopia.

Did you know that the socialist idea had no support among the people?

That's the big problem we have to grapple with now. I think to a large extent we were practicing self-deception. Or self-gratification. And that's something I didn't realize before November–December 1989 or January 1990. The election results in March 1990 were a rude awakening, to see how we had been living in limited circles and had always been writing for ourselves.

Did you think a few years ago that the last forty years were good for scholarship?

Yes, that was our understanding, and it was a great mistake. It goes still further. I ask myself also whether we didn't, to some extent, help to support the system with the sort of work that we did, in that we tried to extend the limits of tolerance more and more. We were far removed from the real needs of the population. We understood ourselves, more or less, as an opposition. I saw myself in that light, and to some extent I was. But wouldn't it have been productive to establish a real opposition or to join one?

You were on the side of democratic socialism?

Well that's the question; it's difficult. Of course the idea of a more just society will stay in my head until I grow old.

But that doesn't necessarily mean socialism?

That's the big question that I can't easily answer, because the history of this century has shown that, apparently, socialism is not the order of the day. I certainly wouldn't for the world want to lapse back into things as they were before October. We were finished, at the end of our own productivity, too. That's always a yardstick.

In recent years it became more and more problematic and less and less satisfying. It had been clear to me for quite a while that there were great contradictions between the demand for productivity, which was made to us officially—"You have to work, you have to publish, etc."—and practical experience. When I worked I always, with absolute certainty, met with immense difficulties. Either texts didn't arrive or were lying around for a year at the editor's before they were published, then were out of date, etc. I realized that the best you can do is to do nothing, for then, at least, you don't cause any disorder or trouble. But it's hard to cope with that in the long run. This feeling got stronger and stronger. That September—and all the people who were engaged in intellectual work felt this—when the waves of people started traveling through Hungary and Prague and there was silence in the country—it was unbearable. And then finally to be standing at the Gethsemane Church in Berlin and demonstrating against the exodus, that was—frightened as we were—so liberating, it was wonderful.[5]

Were you a party member?

No.

Did you refuse?

I often thought about it, whether I shouldn't join. A lot of people around me honestly believed—it sounds very strange today—that they would have a greater chance of changing the country if they were in the party rather than outside it. That belief really proved to be a great mistake, because the people who were in the party were always made to toe the line again by means of party discipline. Less could happen to you outside the party. People were expelled from the party for political statements or texts, but that was a very severe form of punishment. That's what kept me, time and again, from joining the SED. Nevertheless, it did mean that up to a certain point I was renouncing my career opportunities.

Is it true that the Germanists were more closely watched than people in other disciplines?

Well, yes. In the academy, research into GDR literature was very closely watched. Academy scholars were always in a state of conflict—something that was a sort of "aha" experience for me. Sometimes they had to do jobs on orders from the ministry. Once, for example, we had to write a study of GDR prose. We started debating among ourselves how to write it. Our question was: should we represent the situation as being as harsh as it was, and so use the study to show the state and party leadership what things were like and make the truth a little clearer? Or should we put a veil over the truth? There was an immediate division within the group. Some—out of fear of drawing attention to themselves and having to come to terms with difficulties and suspicion—always worked according to the formula: "Compromise so that we can go on working in peace." That's the harmless-sounding formula that I'd heard as early as my high-school days. I can't listen to it any more.

But the other argument was: "We'll use this opportunity and describe conditions as harshly as we see them." Later, we reached a compromise, but even with the compromise we incurred a whole heap of trouble. For me at least that was an opportunistic solution.

Did you hope two years ago that the state would come to grief?

No, the process only became obvious to me in January 1990, and it was a very painful process. It was a departure from what I had hoped for. I cannot welcome this union or unification process—it is a union— the way things are going at the moment, because I find it undignified, because we are giving up everything that existed here. I want to talk about cultural identity too. A new system of values is becoming generally accepted in place of the old one. That has little to do with a *reciprocal* process of reformation, something that I, and I'm sure many others, had hoped for.

What advantages of life in the GDR, especially as a scholar, stand to be lost now that the GDR has capitulated?

I think that a lot of intellectuals did identify with the state in a very problematic way. Not in the sense that they admired the country, but in the sense that they maintained an active relationship to the country. There was always the feeling that you had to change something here, and that something could be changed, because intellectual work had a fairly high status. For example, the number of letters that you received from readers if you wrote an article in *Sonntag* was quite disproportionate to what you would get for one in *Sinn und Form*.[6] Those are situations that I'm sure do not exist in the Federal Republic. But it is terrible when grown people are fixated on "Papa State" in this manner, because it was a patriarchal relationship. There was a unity and a good understanding among intellectuals. But this was only based on the fact that, somehow or other, you were *anti*. Then, somehow or other, you were right. The real differences that existed between people, between their ways of thinking, their whole beings, were hushed up. In this way, a situation arose where real debate and the ability to be in conflict were

never learned in this country. For the identificatory or patriarchal relationship always smacked of the kindergarten. To that extent, it is unbelievably liberating that it is finally finished. We are now grown-ups who
have got to have it out with one another.

• • •

**How do you feel now when you meet students? Do you feel
excited at having a new task?**

Now, this may sound a little arrogant, but I really don't know of
anything that I have to change fundamentally in my lectures or seminars.
I don't think that I said things before that I can no longer say. The
questions are different when we're talking about GDR literature. But I
conduct seminars from naturalism to Brecht. I see very little necessity
to introduce a totally new concept. I also find it very problematic to call
something scholarship if you are going to say exactly the opposite from
one day to the next. I simply couldn't take such scholarship seriously.

**If, as a scholar, you felt yourself to be in opposition, did you
think that you would teach other people what you were thinking, or did you notice contradictions that others didn't?**

No, rather, I tried to establish in public a way of looking at things
through contradictions. By a series of refined tricks, so the people reading my work could understand what I meant, but so the people who
had to censor it would be too stupid to catch on. We always played this
game. I tried to push the wall in people's heads farther and farther away.

For you yourself?

For myself, but also for those who read it afterwards. To introduce
new, uncommon ways of looking at the history of the GDR or the socialist
movement.

**You talked about refined tricks. How deep is an opposition that
takes the form of game-playing? Your experience with the two
versions of *Werke und Wirkungen* was something different.**

Well, yes, I personally experienced quite a lot of political interference. But that also has to do with the subject. If you are working on
Heiner Müller or on GDR literature, then everything happens much
more vehemently than in the area of theory. I experienced that just last
year. It was Müller's sixtieth birthday. The periodical *Sonntag* wanted a
birthday article.[7] So I tried to relate a text of Walter Benjamin's and a
text of Müller's to one another. Müller has a thesis similar to Benjamin's

on one of the historical philosophical themes, but it reads differently. As early as 1958, he was writing about this different way of viewing history. Well, of course it didn't work. Great uproar at the periodical. Then reproaches that people didn't recognize my authorial stance, etc. I used a procedure that was used increasingly during the past ten years and simply said, "I'm not changing anything more." Simply remained obstinate and said, "All right, then the periodical has nothing; it's not my problem." Of course authors too get annoyed, because you spend a long time sitting and writing a text like that.

The editor at *Sonntag* was very supportive of this article, and it came out. Then there's a nice little anecdote that is *true.* Periodicals were subject to the Department of Agitation and Propaganda in the Central Committee. Joachim Herrmann was in charge.[8] Apparently after he had read the article, he said, "This Heiner Müller is bad enough, but who's this Walter Benjamin?" And it was someone like that who made decisions about what appears in a periodical like *Sonntag.* But it was all right if you were obstinate. It was all right.

You have talked of GDR literature as an arena for the expression of resistance. What would have happened if literature and literary studies had not been in the opposition camp?

That's the question. Perhaps I did manage to get one text or another through, but what does that amount to? What interests me much more is what prevented me from burning these bridges and joining up with church circles and doing subversive work directly. But I think that I— perhaps in a different sense from people who had to make great decisions about the fate of others—perhaps on a smaller scale also bear some guilt. The problem is that there is scarcely any time left to us, in the rapid historical movement as it came about, to come to terms with our own guilt. But I also recognize that it is an unavoidable question.

How much critical self-examination is under way at the university?

At the university we fairly quickly established in my area a departmental council, consisting of three equal parts: students, employees, and university teachers. We formed a committee called "Reappraising the Conflict Situation in This Department." It tries to deal with particular cases from a period when I was not yet there, with the aim of establishing our own political hygiene. I think what we tried to do there is quite a good idea. The real problem will be in discussing the cases where, for example, someone was expelled. To what extent was the individual also guilty, and to what extent was it the fault of the power structures? It's something that everyone has to settle for themselves, but it's also something that should be talked about in public.

The trouble is that now scarcely anyone is ready to do that, because every individual is engaged in a terrific struggle for existence, and a confession of guilt merely creates worse positions from which to start. That stops the process. I don't believe in pressure; I think that if this reevaluation of one's own history does not take place, the energies will develop somewhere else. And I'm frightened of that. That's something that not only concerns intellectuals, but the whole population. I am frightened that there will be a vehement movement to the right in the GDR population.

Are university teachers in a position to determine the future of the university?

That's a big question: who's to decide actually? It's the question that outrages and upsets me the most at the moment. With dismissals too: who decides who's to stay and who's to go? The people who became university teachers and professors were not, in every case—I don't mean in my own specialty, but generally—appointed because they were the better specialists. At least they had to have suitable curricula vitae. Those who rose to the top under the old conditions are at the top now. And they'll stay there. Those who were on the outside before will stay on the outside. That's the way it goes.

The university will only change through structural alterations. There are situations that an outsider cannot begin to imagine. There are no exceptions. The fact is that people who have studied there and subsequently stayed on in their specialty are still there twenty, thirty years afterwards and have never worked in any other institution. That's death to productivity.

In the past, my hope was—but in the past few months I have had to abandon it—that it would be possible to create an atmosphere and a space free from fear, in which these questions of guilt and responsibility could be discussed among ourselves. I think this possibility has been lost, as I've already said, because it's now a question of ensuring your livelihood. At no point do I see even a germ of a real effort to come to terms with this question.

FRANK AND
THERESE HÖRNIGK

September 11, 1990, East Berlin

Frank Hörnigk (b. 1944) is professor of German at the Humboldt University. He specializes in contemporary German literature, particularly the work of Heiner Müller. He edited a selection of Müller's texts with commentary in 1989.

Therese Hörnigk (b. 1942) also specializes in contemporary German literature. She worked at the Central Institute from 1972, when she finished her Ph.D. on Brecht at the Humboldt University, until 1991, when the institute closed. She originally joined Werner Mittenzwei's research group on Weimar culture, and in the mid-1970s she moved to the group devoted to GDR literature. She wrote the first book on Christa Wolf (1989) and worked on GDR literature in general. She now teaches at the Humboldt University.

How long have you been at the academy?

T.H. I came to the Academy of Sciences, to the Central Institute for Literary Studies, in 1972, immediately after I received my doctorate at the Humboldt University. I started working with Professor Mittenzwei on the literature of the Weimar Republic in the Literature Group.[1] Then, in the mid seventies, we founded a group for the history of GDR literature. Two books were written, *Literarisches Leben in der DDR von 1946 bis 1960* [Literary life in the GDR from 1946 to 1960] (1979) and *Werke und Wirkungen* (1987). As a group, we were torn apart by political interference with the second book. I studied German and English language and literature at the university, and my goal was to become a teacher, because when I registered it was not possible for me to register as a diploma student. But there were diploma students who had registered two or three years before. There were special seminars for them, for example, on Kafka, and we could all participate in them, because for students training to become teachers nothing comparable was specifically offered.

F.H. We both studied between 1964 and 1968–69. As far as literature was concerned, for example, the reasons for selecting focal areas of study were extremely various. These areas were related not only to the history of modernism but also to the history of the proletarian, revolutionary literature that evolved in the milieu of postexpressionism. You could discuss social problems that were otherwise taboo by using the medium of literature. That was also true of literature about the founding of the Soviet Union or the October Revolution and its effect upon Germany. This was the source of a really spectacular interest in a certain trend within twentieth-century modernism. At the same time, there was an unheard of fear of Kafka or late bourgeois modernism, as it was then called. Looking at the great realists of the nineteenth century, in a truly European context, a traditional list was reestablished that included writers like Fontane, or even Heinrich and Thomas Mann.[2] The avant-garde, the radical antibourgeois literary and artistic scene, was seen in juxtaposition to this traditional track—of an established bourgeois art—and to that extent was also rated less highly. Then in addition, by way of Lukács, there was the confrontation with a modernism that was, in any case, problematical. That's not to say—and we have to be honest about this— that this literature and this movement were not also constant topics of university education. But it must be admitted that it had a correspondingly lower value. For certain courses of study, for example, students who were going into teaching, it was pretty hard to find the time to bother about such special seminars. But it wasn't primarily a problem of censorship.

T.H. . . . more of a sort of self-censorship, mediated by the fact that someone had considered what topics to offer in a seminar. Most people decided against Kafka and for Willi Bredel.[3] I'm simplifying this a great deal. From the end of the 1950s onwards, you could do something with proletarian-revolutionary literature. Its status was upgraded at that time. But there was still a long time to go before that happened to Kafka. I think it was a problem because people had to confront the fact that, or explain why, they favored this over other literary movements. In the 1960s, modernist literature was, for many students of German at the Humboldt University, only a topic for private reading and not for a real education.

F.H. You see, there are differences in what we remember. I remember Kafka seminars with Hermsdorf.[4]

T.H. You're lucky.

F.H. I went to them. It was in 1964—and that was certainly late enough—that the first volume of Kafka came out in the GDR: the collected stories. Of course we must also take into account the fact that there was a whole area of confrontation with this literature, always under the pretext that this was a totally generalized critique of bourgeois ideologies. That always made it possible to talk policy through the screen of a literary historical introduction, or a critique of a contemporary situation, in which alienation plays or played a part, as in Kafka's works. The way things were banned and the imposition of restrictions were handled sensitively and with subtle differentiations. Restrictions existed, but not just in the sense of a ban, but as neglect or classification. To that extent, what my wife says is true.

T.H. I think that anyone who was involved in the education of students, when faced with complex matters, always had in mind why they should make difficulties for themselves when they might be more effective somewhere else.

F.H. To come back to the case of Kafka again. There was the legendary Kafka conference that Goldstücker organized in 1963 . . .

T.H. . . . in Liblice near Prague.[5]

F.H. . . . that was repeatedly judged to be the nucleus of counterrevolutionary intellectual activity—after the invasion in 1968, years and years afterwards—and it enjoyed a reputation similar to the Petöfi Club's in Budapest in 1956.[6] The Kafka conference and the acceptance of Kafka by the majority of scholars who were represented there, even from the socialist camp, appeared to be proof of the scholars' counterrevolutionary tendency, and Goldstücker as an individual was the subject of such intense criticism that, after 1968, he couldn't live there any longer.

Kafka underwent the opposite process among the readers of the *Partisan Review*. During the war, the editors tried to link modernism and anti-Stalinism. Kafka was the most important figure in the process.

T.H. Kafka was the subject of the Kafka conference, but the real controversy was that socialism had not managed to remove alienation, and Kafka, unlike almost everyone else at the beginning of the century, represents in his work the problem of the individual in modern industrial society. In the face of the statement that only socialist literature, or the system and the literature in the system, had managed to overcome this problem of alienation, there was a closing of the mind to Kafka. In addition, the way Kafka was dealt with in the west functioned here as the justification of the idea that he should not be treated here.

F.H. The socialist or communist youth attacked Nazism with Kafka. For them he served as a witness in their resistance to National Socialism. That is an enormously exciting story of a discovery that could not previously have been perceived in this way, in the reception of his work— even by me. But for the 1930s, for important socialist people, it had extraordinary importance, because it was directed against the canon of a Marxist literary historiography and literary theory dominated by Lukács. To that extent, Kafka and Brecht are opposite poles in a mechanically conceived, antinomian model of "good" and "bad" modernism.

The New York intellectuals' criticism of Stalinism after the war was often articulated in terms of bureaucracy, and Kafka was very apposite to this.

T.H. That's funny. I was just thinking about *Kassandra,* where one of the themes is the problem of an individual's escaping into madness. The body, so to speak, reacts to an environment that is in itself crazy.

F.H. But what you said before, Therese, is very important in this context: the tendency—in this case a poetic image, a metaphor that did not grow out of a socialist social context, but out of a Habsburg-Bohemian-German-Jewish context at the turn of the century, out of a world that is basically capitalistically structured—the tendency to neglect the context in favor of a different description of the horizon. Suddenly Kafka was a witness to a reality that lay outside the world of his experience.

T.H. Perhaps all good literature has that quality,

F.H. Yes, certainly, but in the west he was used not so much as a witness of the destruction of his own circumstances, but as a carrier of criticism of different circumstances, in the antinomian model.

• • •

Back to the question of censorship. Marianne Streisand believes that when *Werke und Wirkungen* was rewritten it was improved. Is that your opinion too?

T.H. If you have a year in which to rewrite a text, it really can't get worse. Whether the originality had a different value is another question. I personally think that the original version had its own value, but at the

telling the authorities), but on the other hand as making clear to readers that there is reason for someone to write in the way they do, or that what is written could mean this or it could mean that. Many of us devoted ourselves to this mediating relationship for a very long time.

F.H. Precisely because of the recognized role and importance of literature as a medium of resistance, up to the time of revolution (and in parentheses we should say that this function was frequently exaggerated), because of the special situation of literature that appeared to be very self-consciously critical, literary scholars as a group of social scientists were left with a rather negative public image. I hardly know a writer who doesn't immediately want to characterize the wretched, opportunistic, and conformist role of literary scholarship.

GDR literary scholarship, like the whole of cultural studies or social studies, very quickly assumed the role of social advocate, or was forced into a role of promoting and representing the state's interests. Here a worldview became scientifically qualified and thus acquired the status of an objective truth. Here the state that was founded on this worldview—and that's exactly what happened—described its own policy as a scientific policy. The GDR never grew tired of talking about socialism's scientific view of the world and the scientific nature of socialist ideology. The state was supposed to have the most complete overview. The social scientists often furnished the proofs of the claim. The orientation and instrumentalization of the social sciences as the predominant science was the dominating fact of literary scholarship in the 1950s. Many people who are still alive, and who are taking the present experience much harder than we are, were ready to instrumentalize their social roles: they had to be advocates for socialism vis-à-vis literature. That penetrated into their language, into their fundamental understanding of literature.

. . .

Were you in the party?
F.H. Yes.

You were both party members. Did you have two different roles, one as party members and one as literary scholars who wanted to extend the limits?
T.H. That's not at all the way I think. A few things that are inherent in the process have been omitted from what my husband has just de-

scribed. There was a latent opposition, within the party, to the crisis of the superstructure. The party's loss of authority is allied to the fact that many of us strongly opposed what the leadership was doing— particularly since Gorbachev, when it became clear that socialist concepts were completely disintegrating and that the GDR leadership was not ready, and not able, to cooperate in the execution of hypotheses and changes to bring about changes in the society. At the very latest, it was from that point on that people in the party tried to gain influence to the extent that a member could. To that extent I see no contradiction.

F.H. But it's a very difficult tale. First of all, the reasons for joining the party were very diverse, even for the two of us. Often enough, they were connected with intellectual problems—at first.

I started out from a very personal point of view. It began in the early sixties. My father lived in the GDR only because he was too weak to leave it. As long as I was little, it was only a question of when we would leave; in that, we were like many in the fifties. I didn't go to the comprehensive high school because my father wasn't a worker. I took the alternative route of adult education, because I wanted to get my *abitur* [terminal degree of the Gymnasium—received about age nineteen]. I went to work in a steelworks, in Saxony, served apprenticeship there, and was able to do my *abitur*. I experienced a different reality in this sort of production. Perhaps that sounds a bit kitschy, but this was the way that it became possible for me to oppose my forceful father, to oppose the established petit bourgeois, wealthy society in which I grew up, and in which I had many advantages. Entering the party as a worker had something to do with protest.

At the time, I had no notion of studying German language and literature. Then came the transition to the university. My father had died, and it was then that I got to know people who made it seem important to me to be in the party. They were very clever people and, first and foremost, people who were also intellectually stimulating for us. Previously, you'd just accepted the presence of people who were in the party in the old milieu, but now suddenly these were intellectually interesting people, with the exception of a few, at the university. People like Mittenzwei, or Christa Wolf, she was also in the party. Well, they were people on whom you were glad to orient yourself.

So you did it, and there was certainly something like a group consciousness in the society that never wanted to identify itself—at least in our concrete living situation—and that had very little to do with the party leadership and the overall party line. I can't remember ever having unreservedly said "yes." The party was always a more concrete space within which you lived, worked, and knew people. The conviction prevailed that, on the one hand, you would have greater opportunities in the party, could exert influence on more important things. There was a completely egotistical component; everyone must say for himself the extent to which vanity and career played a part. But it was at least an intention taken on oath, perhaps an alibi as well, to say that we must change society at the only point at which, in the given circumstances, it could be moved: that is, inside the party.

On the other hand, we were the Eastern version of the generation of 1968. In a different way the idea was to work through the institution: right up to the end, that was always the hope, to promote and develop—by application of intellect, talent, ability, and perseverance—a policy that would coincide with our cultural plans. Early on, we were part of grave and decisive events, disappointments, and disillusions. The 1968 invasion of Czechoslovakia was, for our generation, the first decisive disappointment. For those who were a little older, it was the Twentieth Party Congress and the crushing of the uprising—or, as it was officially known, the counterrevolution—in Hungary.[7] But for us the Czech experience was a disappointment that could be remedied only by accepting a terrible lack of alternatives: "If we don't improve things now, then there are no alternatives. We have to help this society change by using its own resources." That was the contribution. That's what we committed ourselves to, and for that we were criticized—and more. We certainly got into difficulties. But I insist that we were an oppositional force within the party, and the society that went through autumn 1989 fell not least because the grassroots members resisted the leadership. That's got to be said, it may be contested, but it's got to be said.

The majority of people in the GDR would shake their heads over what we're talking about, because it isn't their problem. They deny responsibility for the fact that things were so awful. I have to repeat that over and over again to remind you that we are talking here about a very thin veneer. Seen in this light, it's not a contradiction between membership in the party and scholarship. You had to establish yourself as a critical Marxist, as the representative of a critical theory. It was a question of being good enough to take up and maintain positions, in the name of an "enlightened Marxism," within a doctrinaire Marxist understanding, and wherever possible to assert these positions against a narrow, aggressive, and dogmatic party leadership.

T.H. You could do that even in the choice of the topics you worked on. No one dictated to you whom or what you had to work on. That choice came from your consciousness of conflict and your readiness to live with resistance. And your research topic also served to document your position within the society.

F.H. A decision in favor of Christa Wolf, Heiner Müller, or Volker Braun was also always an expression of a certain approach to social analysis.[8] It always meant that you were also the representative of the idea of an alternative society that emerged from this literature and its circumstances, that you supported it and stood up for it as the projection of possible and real circumstances. For us, it was always a problem to be working in a projection booth with a literature that not only had a dissident character, but also saw itself constructively, as contributing to a utopia, or a better socialism, or at least working towards that. At some point we had to recognize that these hopes were over, perhaps as early as the 1970s—anyway, earlier than people have been saying in the past few months. Reality had overtaken utopia.

You had to have patience. Presumably you asked yourselves not only as citizens, but also as scholars, what was the right measure of patience. Had you accepted too much?

F.H. There lies the truth of the process and the truth of the results. On the one hand, I too think that the intellectuals, including us, failed. That's a responsibility that we have to accept, to say, "We were not strong enough, not analytically, not as agitators, not argumentatively." With few exceptions, no one here managed to express the real crisis of the society with persistence, and no one successfully intensified conflicts. But even the exceptions, people like Biermann or Havemann, who were paradigmatic cases of resistance in the GDR, always had a different socialism in mind and did not intend the end of socialism.[9] We didn't evaluate the actual crisis correctly.

T.H. Excuse me, I feel—looking at things from the end—that it is extraordinarily problematic to come to the conclusion that the intellectuals failed, because there is also the question of who makes such judgments. The "failure of the intellectuals" comes as a reproach from outside. I find that extraordinarily problematic. Seen from the end, it's easy to say, but there are two truths. There are enough people in the FRG, in France, Italy, the USA, who, as leftists, identified themselves with what was happening in Eastern Europe. Events in the East were highly differentiated, in Poland, in Czechoslovakia, the Soviet Union; but they were focused by Western leftists as from a projection booth, for their own alternative ways of thinking. GDR literature, for example, was for many years a theme of this sort. A lot of our colleagues, at least the leftists—if you can make such a sweeping statement—were just as unable as we were to see that the end would come as it has.

F.H. But, Therese, that's not a point at issue between us. All I want—at the risk of receiving false approval—is to avoid doing one thing. We've already talked about it in another context. The fact is that people who have a different perspective, who come from outside, say that the intellectuals failed. The fact that that happens, and that I do not agree with it, should not—because the way they are saying it is wrong—be allowed to bring me to the point of not talking about where the elements or dimensions of the failure lie. My attempt was to consider, in a preliminary way—of course it wasn't the first time; we had thought about it for months—where the possible elements lay in which we had been illogical, and where we did not draw conclusions that were perhaps already apparent at the time. It's hard to formulate criteria for that. One criterion, for example, could be: what alternative forms of human behavior were available in a particular situation at a particular time? While we didn't manage to take a given critical step, we could look and see who did and how.

Could you say that the writers did it better?

F.H. Well, not actually the writers.

T.H. A few.

F.H. But that's too generalized. First of all it wasn't *the* writers who did it, but a few of them, and besides it wasn't only a few writers, but a few intellectuals as well, whom you could compare with us. And there were masses of people who left, who made applications. The first thing they did was the most radical step and, looked at from the point of view of the end, the one that finally led to the collapse. It was their leaving the GDR. I'm thinking about possibly the most important female literary figure, Sarah Kirsch.[10] When she went, none of us despised her for taking the step. We were terribly sad, depressed, and only felt it as a loss . . .

T.H. . . . and described it as such.

F.H. . . . and drew people's attention vehemently to a conflict that was present for us in her action. We understood that from a personal point of view she had to do it, but we also said that she had abandoned her readers. That was something that was strangely therapeutic. We implored Christa Wolf to stay here. The conflict ran right through literature. But going away, not-being-able-to-stand-it-here-any-longer, was not an alternative for many people. Looked at now, at the end, it soon appears that they were all heroes, far-sighted individuals. As far as I'm concerned, Erich Loest, Karl-Heinz Jacobs, or Hans Joachim Schädlich, because they left—and after severe conflicts—are far from being an alternative to the people who stayed here.[11] You could have done more in the GDR, something different; could have lived in a different way, left the institutions. It was certainly also a question of ease and of conformism, of age, not to take such radical steps without turning a hair. The readiness to say "We'll still manage to do something" was always there.

You can, if you like, take the younger generation that really dropped out as an alternative example. My level of experience is different. I'll allow myself to be criticized by my students and at the same time I'll accept it and say, "It's not my business, I can't"—in any case, I couldn't. There isn't *a* group that behaved differently. There was a cross section of society. There are some points that have to be assessed very drastically, points where we perhaps failed, in moral professions and attitudes— that's to say, not ones of which we have to be ashamed of having said, "yes," that's not the case; but there was some degree of solidarity that we did not practice where perhaps we should have. Today, I know, we should have done so.

Solidarity with the young people?

F.H. We were too established for that. I've been teaching at the university for more than twenty years, and I was questioned as a teacher. I had the people in my seminar. That was never the point—I did show solidarity. But it was always solidarity from another perspective. I was also never so close to them that we spoke the same language, so to speak. It would also have been coquettish of me to have tried to do that. The really basic things were to keep quiet, for example, on the matter of Sakharov and opposition in the Soviet Union.[12] We followed that story for years without taking an inner part in it. We were sorry for him. We thought it an indignity for him to be held in Gorky; that's not the question. We built too little upon the moral, intellectual, and political integrity, and the analytical capacity of people like that. We overlooked it, and that's what we have to ask about today. Perhaps there was something like it in the GDR.

Those are the points on which we have to work, but I would generally not accept the idea that any one group in the GDR was in the resistance. There were always individuals who were, and their resistance was powerless. It achieved power for the first time in the fall of 1989. At that point, we stood at their side in different ways and were ourselves a part of the infrastructure of this mass of people that had, finally, asserted itself successfully against the administration, a victory that did not lead to a hangover—that should be clear from the outset. I think that neither of us is talking from an attitude of elegiac reminiscence. I don't want it back. But what we are experiencing now also has something to do with defeat.

T.H. . . . and that belongs in our biography. You can't suddenly turn black into white. You have to stand by your work and your life. You can't stash forty years away in another drawer and start out anew.

SIMONE AND
KARLHEINZ BARCK

September 13, 1990, East Berlin

Simone Barck *(b. 1944) was a research scholar at the Central Institute from 1970 to 1991. She studied Russian and German literary history at the Humboldt University and wrote a doctoral dissertation at the Academy of the Arts on the poet and one-time GDR minister of culture Johannes R. Becher. She specializes in twentieth-century German literature, particularly the literature of German émigrés during the Nazi era. She collaborated with Werner Mittenzwei and others on a study of Georg Lukács in the 1920s. She is coauthor of a two-volume study of German writers in exile during the Nazi era,* Exil in der UdSSR *(1979), which was published in a second edition in 1989 (cultural-political policy in the GDR did not allow the publication of this edition in 1985, when it was completed). In 1983 she edited a collection of papers from a conference on Johannes R. Becher. She is now retired from the Academy of Sciences and a fellow of a special society for historical studies sponsored by the Max Planck Society.*

Karlheinz Barck *(b. 1934) is a member of the research center for literary history sponsored by the Max Planck Society in Berlin. He is a specialist in modern Romance literatures. He joined the academy in 1965 after studying Latin American literature in Rostock, with a dissertation on Ortega y Gasset. In 1968, when the Central Institute for Literary History was founded, he switched from a research group on the Enlightenment under the leadership of Werner Krauss to a new group devoted to literary theory. From the early 1980s he led the literary theory group at the Central Institute. His work on reception theory,* Gesellschaft, Literatur, Lesen *(1973) went through three editions and had great influence in the GDR. He has published the first of a five-volume historical diction-*
ary of aesthetic terms from the eighteenth century to the present. He compiled a

large documentary anthology, Surrealismus in Paris, 1919–1939 *(2d ed., 1990) and coedited a collection of essays on avant-gardes (1979). He edited a selection of writings by Gongora and Argote in 1974 and translated a collection of Rimbaud's poetry (2d ed., 1991). His most recent book is* Poesie und Imagination *(1993). He and Robert Weimann direct the research center for literary history in Berlin.*

Am I right in thinking that there was a consensus about methodology here, that reception theory dominated literary studies and that some methods, for example psychoanalysis, were not pursued?

K.B. With some exceptions, psychoanalysis has not until now played a part in literary studies in the GDR. It is important to stress the fact that there were exceptions because, in our experience, the sciences in the GDR, including literary studies, were often looked at from the outside in an undiscriminating way, as though everything came out of one pot. That's not the case, and it never was. There was always an ideological mainstream, but there were very differentiated positions within that mainstream. The orientation to reception theory or reception aesthetics—from its beginnings in the seventies—was important to all the scholars at the Central Institute and also at the universities. That represented, so to speak, an attempt to put an end to the dominance of the ideologically oriented conception of literature in this country that came from Lukács's aesthetics. That was the point.

Did *Gesellschaft, Literatur, Lesen* [Society, literature, reading] (1973), once established, lose its element of resistance? Or is it going too far to speak of it as a work of resistance?

K.B. You could look at it as that even if, in our circumstances at the time, it was not a pronouncedly political matter. But this was the part it played in the discussion, because of the critiques it received from those who were defending a conservative, traditional view. It was perceived as a proposal to break something up. The provocative effect has somehow been lost. Afterwards there were a great number of attempts to apply the model to the practice of literary studies—for example, *Werke und Wirkungen.*

S.B. Yes, that touches on a very important problem. It seldom happened—because the academy was isolated from teaching, our institute as well—that research scholars and university instructors did things together. Our colleagues at the universities did their thing, and we did ours. And they didn't necessarily coincide. It is a real drawback of our institute, doing no teaching. It was an enclave, if you like, and we could do a lot of things without running into any major difficulties. Our colleagues at the universities, under pressure "from above" to politicize their students, were subjected to a stronger ideological control and dictatorship. From their point of view, we at the academy were in a state of "splendid isolation."

Marianne Streisand left the academy because she had bad experiences with the collective project, *Werke und Wirkungen*.

K.B. That's an interesting phenomenon. Literary studies in this country, like the other social studies that are now called the humanities, are being criticized by the public. Every one of us has to come to terms with the problem. What was our role and the function of our work in the past? The criticism comes from writers, among others. There were constant and violent debates. The one about lyric poetry in the seventies that has, in the meantime, become famous was a frontal attack by writers upon German studies that were established within the system and that ignored the real problems of society—and thus their depiction in literature—or else deliberately suppressed them. There certainly was something like that, something that only now we are perceiving more precisely—that is, that the system had closed up like an oyster in the face of reality, in order to preserve itself, and this had the final effect of reducing the potential for resistance and criticism. In reaction to the constantly increasing crises—1953, 1956, 1968, 1976, Biermann's loss of citizenship, 1980, and finally the beginnings of perestroika—an insidious opportunism started to develop among a lot of scholars. People said to themselves, "For heaven's sake don't rub them the wrong way politically, or else we'll endanger our scholarly work." There was always a row when a certain limit, determined by the system, was overstepped. That was the case with *Werke und Wirkungen,* because there the state's cultural policy and the party's absolute claim to leadership were a matter for debate and were being questioned. At the time, the regime reacted with repression. The book's affront simply consisted of the fact that a few standard works of GDR literature were analyzed from the point of view of their reception and effect. These works had been attacked by the official cultural policy at the time of their publication and then, years later, after the cultural policy had changed, were accepted into the canon. The analysis revealed the lack of principle and the economic objectives of a cultural policy that was simply led by the interests of power politics. Then for almost two years this analysis played a big role in our institute, while party committees were installed, statements were demanded from the leadership of the institute, etc. Guidelines were drawn up by the political authorities on how scholarship was to proceed. Colleagues absorbed the lesson and returned to the agenda. But a fundamental problem is clarified by this case. Really burning problems of our country were raised in literature. When, for its part, literary scholarship posed these problems to itself, the authorities tried to discipline the profession. The result was that scholars, arguing that it wasn't possible to work in a serious and committed way on problems of current literature, withdrew to areas that were apparently less sensitive.

How well did your colleagues live with the restraints on their work?

K.B. The manuscript of *Werke und Wirkungen* was revised in a spirit of intellectual opportunism, with my colleagues thinking, "All right, we'll do it, and we'll still try to get something past them." My colleague, Inge Münz Koenen, who was the leader of the project at that time, said to me once, later, that they really ought not to have done that. Because the revision—although it wasn't really bad—did not of course lead to the book's being better. The first version was much sharper.

S.B. Normally we came up with our own research projects and were able to carry them out. But GDR literature was a different story, simply because there was interference from all sides.

K.B. Among the "scholarly organs" that supervised the study of GDR literature was the Department of Sciences in the Central Committee of the SED and the different scholarly committees. There was, so to speak, a system of scholarly committees that received official legitimation as organs or media of understanding among scholars, but that, of course, had the function of creating ideological coherence and controlling scholars. As far as literary scholarship was concerned there was one such committee, "The Committee for Scholarship in Literature and Art," and this was institutionalized in the Academy of Social Sciences in the Central Committee of the SED, in other words, in the party academy. The chairman was always the person who occupied the Chair of Art and Cultural History in the party academy. For example, until the mid eighties, the chairman was Hans Koch,[1] who had worked on Franz Mehring[2] and who played the role of an ideological high priest for Marxist aesthetics in the GDR. Then, in 1987, he suddenly disappeared under mysterious circumstances and was found, months later, hanging from a tree in the Thuringian Forest, where he had committed suicide.

A reassessment of GDR literary scholarship would almost certainly begin with the question: to what extent was literary scholarship supportive of the state and how oppositional was it?

S.B. Yes, that's obvious. That question comes first and foremost from the corner of the young writers who are of the opinion that established German studies do not pay enough attention to them, a criticism that is justified. The whole so-called subculture of Prenzlauer Berg has not been accepted by scholarship as a legitimate subject of study, it was excluded for clearly political reasons. Officially, from the point of view of the state's ideology, it was not allowed to exist. So among scholars there were fears of contamination. This was a real failure, and we realized it.

Looked at from the area of exile literature, something I have been working on for years, it was recognized here, from the mid eighties on, that research into problems of exile and fascism should not be isolated from one another, as had been the case up to then. They should be united in method as well. The concept of antifascism, for example, even in its relationship to so-called Stalinism (itself only a makeshift concept) has to be newly determined, because those of us who were involved in writing the history of exile literature approached the problem with great hesitation. We didn't take seriously the fact that in the 1930s antifascism had a lot to do with Stalinism or that it was often the case that if someone was against Stalin then he was no longer an antifascist. That's the way things were historically in the discussions that took place in exile. Now we have to rework that on the basis of contemporary sources and document it with autobiographical statements, because it will be important for the whole situation in the GDR after 1945, where a new (or old) concept of antifascism was used and instrumentalized. This concept was used for antifascist literature—that's a current term of ours—but it is not sufficiently separated from others as to its content. The same is true of the problem and concept of Stalinism. How do the emigrants come from Soviet exile—and the camps of the Gulag—to the GDR? As antifascists, but also, apart from a few exceptions, as Stalinists. We never allowed ourselves to present this combination in a precise fashion, but I am also of the opinion that we should work on this in a scholarly fashion and not jump to conclusions and substitute one cliché for another. Up to the moment, we have not seen this so clearly in our own minds, because a lot of documents are only now available to us, internationally as well. What the Soviet Union has now published on concrete everyday Stalinism, how many and what sort of victims there were, has only been documented by sources since 1985. Of course, you could see the outlines of it all as far back as 1956. We, too, understood that the whole sociopsychological dimension of fascism had also been absent here. That's the second thing that affects our field of study.

Are you both of the opinion that German literary scholarship was not sharply oppositional?

S.B. A scholarship of legitimation, we certainly had that.

K.B. I think nothing of the superficial idea of making every scholar—to the extent that he worked in this country—responsible for the system in toto. That's the discussion that's being forced on us in connection with the Christa Wolf affair. Which doesn't mean that there aren't some really critical points there, as far as the behavior of every single individual is concerned. But that's not the way to go about it, because if you do, you'll overdo it. I suppose it's a typically German story, especially regarding the function of literature and thus of literary scholarship as well. The Weimar idea of German classicism that had a historical justification at the time and saw literary figures and intellectuals as the teachers of the nation—in short, Weimar idealism—became a state doctrine here. The status of literature was, on the one hand, enormously enhanced but, on the other, too much was demanded of it.

There's some truth in it when people from the outside say, "The GDR intelligentsia is rather opportunistic and cowardly." As a phenomenological observation that's certainly right, but it still doesn't explain the problem. "The GDR intelligentsia sold its critical spirit for a carefully measured web of privileges." That's not entirely false, but it's also not quite right. From the outside you are only looking at opinion leaders, personalities known to the public, "but you don't see in the dark," to quote Brecht. Of the approximately twenty-five Romance scholars in our institute, two-thirds, for example, had never been to France right up to the revolution. Where were the privileges?

What was my role and that of many others in the conception of ourselves as apostles of the Enlightenment in Stalinism? That question returns. The prevailing attitude was that, in these circumstances, you had to maximize the latitude available to you, and that always implied—and it becomes clearer now—that you were of course also an accomplice. You also have to differentiate attitudes that approached the criminal, even in the case of the literary scholar. We have a case now where, because of the opening up of the files, a colleague in the Akademie Verlag (the publishing house of the academy) has found out that a former leading literary scholar in the GDR, a man of position and authority, obstructed his career for quite wretched ideological reasons. The man in the publishing house then became a gardener. There were cases like that, and they have to be reported. The opportunism that was linked to the complicity of not stating radically enough in our scholarly work what we knew—and we knew practically everything—I always managed to justify for myself because I had an idea of a socialist utopia. A motivation in my work, and what I shall never get rid of, was the critical scholar's search for a different Germany—and the experiences with Werner Krauss, who comes from the German antifascist resistance, played a part in this. This utopia has entered a crisis, but this will not by any means destroy it. I must say that the national problems were never a problem for me. The fact that the GDR, as a state, was a temporary measure, was clear to me. But the other German state was by no means an ideal for me because of that. Socialism was something different, beyond these things. Taking this consideration as a starting point, I still saw the role of apostle of the Enlightenment in Stalinism as justified.

Instead of being educators of the nation, as writers often thought of themselves, literary scholars were the educators of princes.

K.B. Yes, the educators of princes, or as people tried to convince us, the educators of educators, for they always tried to manipulate us as the ideological wardens vis-à-vis the writers. As late as 1989, I can recall meetings where functionaries came from the Central Committee and, already scared, asked what was up, saying how wrongly the writers thought, and that we had to teach them "right thinking." We should, as Brecht, in his argument with Lukács during the expressionism debate, so cogently expressed it, be the aviators who say, "Doves, for example, fly all wrong."

S.B. At the same time we have to say that the role of the writers and the effect of literature in this country are not to be compared with that of scholars and their work. Serious works in the so-called leading scholarly organs were scarcely read by the functionaries. There is a corresponding difference in attitude between writers and scholars.

K.B. But it was clear in the revolutionary period from fall 1989 to spring 1990 that criticism of the writers, and after them the intellectuals, was coming from quite different strata of the population: "You're talking about socialism now, but where were you then? You have absolutely no right to talk about it, because you accepted all the advantages and privileges." Of course that's being blown up in a highly superficial manner in West Germany at the moment. But that's still not the way to explain the phenomenon, because underlying it there is not naiveté, but a cleverly devised, political perfidy, by which the writers were bought by the political powers-that-be, so to speak, through a highly differentiated system of privileges. The point then comes where we have to ask, "Did we like letting ourselves be bought?"

S.B. The scholars also had something like that. The fact that the presiding body of the Academy of Sciences condescended to take a stand about the revolution only very late, and as the last of the institutions, is also related to the fact that among the members of the academy political good behavior was linked with privileges. Of course, there were differences, and I don't want to overstress anything. But you have to call a spade a spade. And of course everyone who stayed here had to adapt themselves, whether they were workers, intellectuals at the university, or writers. It was compulsory. In every society you have to adapt in one way or another, and here you had to adapt to a lot of different things. We did our work throughout the years with this attitude. It was the provision of historical experiences for a socialist system, because we always thought that with a few corrections and repairs things could go on in a totally socialist manner. That was what motivated us to work. People could, for example, make certain historical experiences available, from the period of exile and persecution [1933–1945], that were of use to the topical discussions we had. That was an illusion that we clung to for quite a long time. To the end, as far as I'm concerned.

K.B. That didn't exist in the other socialist countries.

S.B. Then there's the other German element: the two-state system. It was said with justification that there was no Vaclav Havel in the GDR; in Poland too there were comparable personalities. These figures emerged from the confrontations that took place throughout all those decades. Our confrontations with power were slighter because we believed the state's claim to be a better and different German republic. We did not look on the FRG as an alternative, and it still isn't to this day.

Even with only two possibilities, either a Stalinist GDR or a consumer culture, it's not easy for West Germans to understand why you didn't say to yourselves, "The FRG isn't all that bad." But I understand that if you were an intellectual in Poland, you could more easily imagine various possibilities that were different from the existing state.

S.B. In our case it arose from the fact that, since 1949, the threat had always existed that we in the GDR would be swallowed up by the FRG. It was the period of the cold war. These fears weren't so absurd either, and we internalized them completely. Now it's happened, because unfortunately things didn't work out here. But because of that, it's quite different from Czechoslovakia or Poland, where sovereignty was never questioned except by a few crazy exiles in West Germany, who still wanted to have Poland back again. On the diplomatic level and in the popular consciousness there was never any question about it. I can still remember the desperate struggle to gain recognition for the GDR. What a victory we felt when we finally did achieve recognition. And that's all tied up with the fact that we still have a relationship to the state in spite of all the criticism. Somehow or other it's good that we achieved that.

K.B. I'm thinking about it. You've actually dotted the "i." How people managed to put up with a police state like that when in comparison the system in the west would have been the lesser evil. A lot of garbage will still come to light. But I see the following great danger, that a superficial ideologization of these phenomena will proceed under the heading of Stalinism. Perhaps that's only a generational problem. In all the need for reviewing the history of this period, I sense a tendency to suggest that Stalinism and fascism are one and the same thing. And this applies to the role of the Soviets in the GDR camps, Katyn, and all the atrocities that happened under Stalinism and in the name of socialism.[3] I see this being discussed in the FRG on certain sides—not in the interests of discovery and a better organization of society, but in order to divert attention from their own problems. So that people say, "That's so bad we don't need to talk about Nazi things in the Federal Republic any more." I think that here we should be very careful that, as critical intellectuals or scholars, we do not again allow the one to be justified by the other. That was a tendency in the Historians' War. It was Nolte's[4] tendency: "All right, let's finally stop talking about the German past; if we look at it carefully, fascism is really a result of bolshevism."

IRENE SELLE

August 29, 1990, and September 12, 1991, East Berlin

Irene Selle *(b. 1947) worked as a research scholar at the Central Institute. She studied at the Humboldt University from 1965 to 1974 and wrote her dissertation on Louis Aragon. She specializes in modern French literature. In 1987 she edited an anthology of poems and essays from the French Resistance and is the author of a critical study of the resistance. She also edited a selection of Senghor's essays (1991). At the institute she worked in a research group concentrating on twentieth-century French literature and headed by Manfred Naumann, and collaborated on a lexicon of French literature. Her father was the Berlin philosopher and translator Rudolf Schottländer (1900–1988). She is now a translator for Arte Broadcasting in Strassburg.*

You spoke about the 1987 lexicon of French literature edited by Manfred Naumann. Isn't there a special tendency for GDR scholars to produce synthetic works to facilitate reading or teaching directly?

There was a gigantic need for substantial works of reference. Since the ordinary reader was cut off from Western books of this sort, something had to be produced for the domestic market in the GDR. French literature was always sought after. These projects gave us a sort of alibi: we showed the party leadership that we were tied to practice. A lot of colleagues thought this unworthy of the academy. There was, though, in the GDR, a tremendous need to catch up. For example, all the authors who are classics in your country, like Malraux, Gide, Camus, initially had to appear in special editions in the GDR, and you needed an afterword. So a lot of work was needed beforehand. First of all, you had to write an opinion for the publishers as a specialist to answer the question: "Can we print Camus at all?" He was looked upon as a pessimistic, absurd, bourgeois philosopher, an anticommunist. There was a lot more sympathy for Sartre, although he didn't always play along. It was so difficult to

work against the prejudices of the fifties, the period of Stalinism, because they were still lodged in the heads of the people who had to make the decisions. Part of our work was to do something subversive.

I myself had trouble with the publishers. Since 1980, I had been trying to find a publisher for Simone de Beauvoir's essay, *Le deuxième sexe*. Other books of hers had appeared here: the resistance novel *Le sang des autres* and short stories, as well as the first two volumes of her memoirs. Everything that was not politically or ideologically risky had appeared. But the essential work that had brought her international fame and actually started a world movement had not appeared. That meant that you could never consult it. You had to get hold of it from the West, and that took a lot of trouble. Then finally, in December 1989, the book appeared. It was just in that month that a new woman's movement had been formed in the GDR, the Independent Association of Women. They took up a lot of things that were old hat in Western feminism. But the founding ceremony was an event for me, for I felt, "That's something I've fought for, and now it has become a reality." Although the name Simone de Beauvoir was never mentioned, many of her ideas were already present and had become topical again. As I knew the original of *Le deuxième sexe* and also had the West German translation at hand, I often spoke to church groups, where the opposition was formed later on. I did work like this, but I didn't tell the institute, because it wasn't good for my career. But I did it in spite of that. If people wanted me, I went. They weren't so much scholarly activities, more popular scholarship, but we thought that this part of our work was very important.

Did you go to conferences abroad very frequently?

Not to the west, except at the last minute, barely a year before the Wall was opened up. But never during the whole course of my education and the beginning of my scholarly work. That was a big handicap compared with my colleagues, who could show a "cleaner" cadre file to the Stasi. That's also true of scholarly contacts, which are now bearing fruit for them.

How could you demonstrate "cleanliness"?

First of all, by having as few western contacts as possible outside your scholarship. In any case you had to report your scholarly contacts: all letters connected with your discipline passed through a sort of censorship office. The letters that you received from the west were also opened and registered. In addition to this you were to have as few contacts as possible with friends who were not colleagues. And if you did have western connections—and of course there were some family ties—then you had to report them. I have a great many relatives in the west, because my family originally lived in West Berlin. There were still lots of friends from my school days with whom I kept in touch: I wasn't prepared to break these contacts off. And I wasn't a party member.

My father was Rudolf Schottländer, an oppositional spirit in the GDR, who had come from the west. But he had not fulfilled the GDR's expectations that he would be an especially well-behaved propagandist. Quite the contrary. He had become involved with the Protestant Academy, where opposition groups started to form fairly early on. He lectured there (incidentally without being a Christian) from the beginning of the eighties. He talked about a lot of subjects: about Judaism—he was himself a Jew—about being German and Jewish, about democracy, tolerance, Spinoza, and things that aroused people's interest because he treated them in an unorthodox fashion. Of course, the Stasi knew all about it and put pressure on him. So I was not exactly a suitable candidate for a career and travel.

Did you nevertheless manage to get a visa through the academy?

Finally, some higher, fairly secret authority made a decision, but the academy had to apply for it first. In the first place everything had to be secure from a disciplinary point of view. I never figured out who finally made the decision. But things had loosened up in recent years, otherwise I would not have been allowed to travel at the last minute.

Was it difficult for you not being in the party?

You knew what you were doing when you didn't join; that is, that you would never have a career, and that you wouldn't be able to travel to the west. No one bothered me, perhaps because they knew my father's position. On one occasion only they tried to recruit me into the party, and I said quite plainly that it wouldn't work; I couldn't submit to the discipline, if I didn't agree that it was good. I couldn't put up with the lying propaganda in the newspapers. I pointed to my parental home, that my father was a bourgeois humanist—I was happy that this catchphrase occurred to me, because to bear that stamp was still actually morally good—and they accepted it, and there were no further attempts.

• • •

How was your book on the French Resistance viewed by the authorities? On the one hand it treats an antifascist theme, but

on the other it describes literary resistance, something that the authorities might not view favorably.

Yes, that's true enough, but the general estimation was overwhelmingly positive. Only I, myself, felt how topical the book actually was. Contraband poetry, saying something between the lines, was what was practiced everywhere here. But the readers always drew conclusions of this sort; that's why they threw themselves so greedily on Western literature or literature from other ages and countries, so that they could extract something for themselves for the current situation.

Writers were forced into a particular role because of the oppressive regime. They can complain of that now in part. For example, I recently heard Jurek Becker in the Academy of Arts in East Berlin, in a conversation with Christa Wolf and also with literary scholars from the east and the west.[1] Becker has been living for some years in West Berlin, but he said that he had always demanded of himself that his books contain things that were politically critical. Otherwise he could not have accepted himself as a writer, to say nothing of his readers' judgment. It's clear that that's what they expected. The presence of the censor was there. You had to react to it in some way, it didn't matter how. If it was as a conformist party writer then you had fulfilled the norm; or you had to write against it, develop strategies against it. But the censor was always there. You couldn't ignore it.

I've heard it said that the last forty years were a good time for literature. Can you say the same for literary scholarship?

No, certainly not for the humanities as whole, and I also don't know whether the notion "a good time for literature" is right. If you start with the premise that interesting works are produced under pressure, then you can also say that war makes a good time for literature. But that's all very relative. Or did you mean from a material point of view, that writers were secure from the material point of view? That certainly. Artists and musicians as well. That's the welfare society.

And literary scholarship?

Also materially. Not fantastic, but for us literary scholars, as for most people here, there was job security.

• • •

Would you have thought two years ago that the SED would have gotten so few votes in an election?

Yes, I could have imagined that. Of course, I wouldn't have thought that so many people would vote CDU. I think utopia was especially important for the generation that was engaged in reconstruction, the one that was active after the war. They found it hard to separate themselves from the ideals that had, in part, motivated them to put up with a lot and tackle the problems. And it's true that in the time of the cold war the world did look different historically. There was something new to defend, and people were able to see that there were some neo-Nazi tendencies in West Germany. Proof of the failure of socialism was still lacking. We also had the high costs of reparations to the Soviet Union; there were, so to speak, a lot of mitigating circumstances. The historically earlier experience with a planned economy—people were inclined to say that that was a time of childhood diseases. But that whole system was based on false premises: nationally owned property serves more as a brake than a stimulus to initiative, because the individual does not receive proper recognition for his efforts. That all became very obvious in the last ten to fifteen years as the gap between east and west became greater and greater.

But because the majority of people were not allowed to travel, many believed the propaganda—perhaps blindly. Of course everyday life was in total contradiction to the sham information in the newspapers, but many people only started to experience the real shock after the mid eighties and then increasingly, when they visited the west. Actually seeing the difference in standard of living was more effective than television. It was then that people became more and more bitter and envious. Then there was also the nasty feeling that everyone was active in planning the next trip to the west, that was bad. A policy of divide and conquer that became totally absurd. Suddenly people who had relatives in the west—who could entertain them and support them materially over there—were privileged, whereas the members of the party who had previously been respected were not supposed to have contacts in the west and certainly no relatives there. They were the ones who suffered. The deutsche mark made a strong impression upon people's consciousness, more so than ideology, and this travel policy was a slap in the face for ideology. It was totally absurd and became increasingly so.

DOROTHEA
DORNHOF

September 10, 1990, East Berlin

Dorothea Dornhof *(b. 1951) worked as a research scholar at the Central Institute for Literary History from 1977 to 1991 as a member of the research group in German literature of the twentieth century. She also worked in a group concentrated on FRG literature and wrote her dissertation at the Humboldt University on the West German poet Hans Magnus Enzensberger (1983). She edited a selection of Enzensberger's writings in 1988 and has published essays on nineteenth- and twentieth-century German literature, particularly on the representation of women in German culture. She is a fellow of the special research center for literary history sponsored by the Max Planck Society. She and Petra Boden are collaborating on a history of the discipline of German studies from 1945 to 1989.*

How long have you been at the academy?

I've been working since 1977 at the Central Institute for Literary History, in a section that deals with twentieth-century German-language literature. At first, I worked in a section concerned with theoretical and methodological questions, an interphilological area. Today all the sections have been disbanded, and we have planned projects that we hope the Academic Council in Bonn will financially support, not within the framework of an institutional community in the academy, but rather as individual groups that will be financed somehow or other for two or three years. That's quite a different sort of existence from what we have led up to the moment. We had worked on a big project on the now   99 very topical postwar period—from 1945 to 1949—before the separate German states were founded—on the journals, the publishing houses, and American, English, and French occupation policy. The book was already being produced in the Akademie Verlag, and now we have been told that it will not appear, because the press cannot finance anything. It's a bit sad because we spent five years on this project. Our great scholarly advantage was that we had long periods for thorough, intensive, and solid research without having to rush about pursuing this or that development or having to adapt ourselves to this or that new trend. But there was also a disadvantage, I must admit, for I often lacked any thrust towards innovation. We knew when we were working on a project that we had a publisher, at least we frequently did, or else that it would be presented to the public in a different form, but there was always the possibility of going on working and, in spite of that, it was somehow unsatisfying. That is the ambivalence of being socially secure in scholarship: on the one hand, you had a lot of space to work thoroughly and do solid research, while, on the other, a lot of it was just deadening. I mean it didn't demand original thought. You could write down the old stuff for the tenth time and just give it a new accent.

What role did feminism play in scholarship?

In the late seventies and eighties, feminism was regarded as a four-letter word, as hostility towards men. A feminist was considered an unsatisfied woman who made her own lack of satisfaction the theme of her scholarship.

But didn't your colleagues trust you sufficiently to ask about feminism?

Absolutely not. No, everyone had his or her own little private niche where they did their research and worked on their topic, sometimes for more than twenty years, and had no interest at all in developments in the field. That was the generation of those who had been academically socialized here. I belong to it too, although I came into it in the seventies. Those who grew up with Marxism since the fifties have, I think, very little flexibility of thought—base and superstructure, literature and society—these are relatively simplistic mechanisms for treating literary and cultural processes. If my colleagues had to start thinking about things from a psychoanalytical point of view, or if they had to get away from these standard concepts, it would be incredibly difficult for them. The development of philosophy and literary theory in Western Europe was seriously engaged in our institute, but feminism simply remained on the outside. I was the only one who took it up. As far as the dominant branches were concerned, academic development in the institute was in the hands of men, though of course male colleagues did write interesting books.

There was a skeptical attitude here toward the theoretical challenge of feminism, because feminism questioned fundamental concepts of our thought (the concepts of subjectivity and objectivity), and that wasn't right. The problem here was that we thought of ourselves as Marxist literary scholars and knew that, in the institute, Marxism was totally ideologized and primitivized.

It was also difficult to publish anything on feminism. Right up to the end, "Women's Studies" was occupied by women who were sociological apologists, who were working for the Central Committee of the party. They had to conduct investigations to show how fantastically well the relationship between motherhood and working and child-raising—the old patriarchal pattern, in other words—functioned in the GDR, and how wonderfully well the emancipation of women was progressing under that system. That was called "feminist research." In 1964 a council was established on "The Woman under Socialism." It developed further, at the Institute for Sociology, into a separate study group whose research established the myth of the complete and victorious emancipation of women.

When you had difficulty making your colleagues understand the seriousness of feminism, were you still working with the theorists?

No, I'd already left. By then I was with the group working on FRG literature. We had a great deal of flexibility; we could decide for ourselves what research themes we wanted to pursue. The framework was very broad. It was predetermined by a research group for the social sciences, partly by the Central Committee, but in very general terms. It was something like "Trends in Cultural Development under Capitalism." You could do all sorts of things. I often intended to work on women's literature, but that was simply not accepted: it was "fashionable" and "feministic." My boss, who was a woman, wasn't open to the topic either. She once said, "You're only doing that because you are having problems with your husband." That was the level on which we often operated.

Do you see direct methodological consequences of the division of Germany?

The point of departure for us was the émigrés, who returned from tremendously diverse places of exile, but only certain exiles were effective here, namely those who had been in Moscow like Georg Lukács, for example, or Alfred Kurella, who wasn't a scholar, but became a party cultural politician.[1] They introduced into the GDR a debate that took place in exile, about realism and expressionism, the famous Brecht-Lukács debate. This is the only way to understand the very vehement debasement of modernism, which was labeled "decadence" at the time, the debate on formalism that took place here in 1951. I was born in 1951 and would never have had access to Kafka or Joyce if it hadn't been for the fact that my father was a Slavist and also got books from the west through private contacts. You couldn't get Kafka and Joyce here in the library or the bookstores. At first the universities and the academy were still staffed by bourgeois professors, because there weren't any others available who could be called Marxists—they had to be created. We simply didn't have a Lukács, and Kurella and Alexander Abusch (*Irrweg einer Nation,* 1946) were in the Central Committee or the Politburo.[2] In the antifascist, democratic, revolutionary phase (1945–1949) there were some very erudite bourgeois academics at the University of Leipzig who played a big part in the discussions about the development of Marxist literary studies: the linguist, Theodor Frings, who continued the Scherer school's positivist tradition of the unity of language and literary studies; and Hermann August Korff, who was oriented towards intellectual history (*The Spirit of the Age of Goethe*). Important changes took place in Leipzig at the end of the forties with the appointment of the Romanist, Werner Krauss, and the historian, Walter Markov.[3] Krauss had been arrested in 1942 for active participation in the resistance movement together with other members of the Schulze-Boysen–Harnack group (Die Rote Kapelle) and was condemned to death.[4] On the basis of a cleverly written expert psychiatric opinion, the death sentence was commuted in 1944 to five years in the penitentiary. In prison, he wrote the novel *PLN, Die Passion der halykonischen Seele* and the book on Gratian's doctrine of life[5]—outstanding evidence of intellectual work and the will to resist National Socialist power. In Leipzig, Krauss laid the foundations of the development of Marxist classical studies in the GDR and entered into a massive fight with the tradition of the history of ideas and positivism in literary history, for example in his long article "Literary History as a Historical Commission" ("Literaturgeschichte als geschichtlicher Auftrag") [1951]. Also, Hans Mayer and Ernst Bloch were in Leipzig, people who could not, in the view of the party at that time, be so unambiguously classified as Marxists.[6] Alfred Kantorowicz was then in Berlin.[7] He had been an émigré in France and Spain and then became director of the Heinrich Mann archive in the GDR, and he also gave lectures at the Humboldt University. People like Bloch and Mayer left their marks on a generation of students, who in their turn went on to teach in universities.

But then the reserves grew scantier and scantier. That's what I meant earlier when I was talking about the teachers: the quality of the training grew weaker. The good scholars were all driven out at that time, and that was also a tragedy for our society, that it simply couldn't stand scholars who thought differently, who had not totally adapted; and that it worked, both by propaganda and ideology, for as long as it took to drive them out of the country. I regret very much that I never had teachers like that at the university. "Society" and "literature" here formed a sort of derivative structure. And to this was added, in the fifties, the rising conception of history: the idea that history is always the history of the ascent and progress of humanity, and that the highest stage is socialism, in which we are living. This was simply the way literature was classified, as a rising line: Enlightenment-classicism. Romanticism was designated as decadent or reactionary. That's why romanticism made such a huge comeback in the seventies, not by way of literary studies, but by way of authors: Christa Wolf, Günter de Bruyn. They tried to bring romanticism back into play through their literary texts.

If literary modernism was suppressed, I imagine that the materiality of language as a literary theme did not play a large role in academic criticism.

That's right, it scarcely played a role at all. Texts were reflections of a reality and evaluated according to the extent to which they reflected or portrayed the reality, a concept that people already had in their heads about a notion of life being like this or that. That was the way literature was analyzed—partly with very philosophical constructs of the appropriation of human history, or with the nineteenth-century pathetic concept of realism. After 1945, a pedagogical concept dominated, because people assumed that the population was so corrupted by the pernicious fascist ideology—as people referred to it at the time—that they had to be educated. And the education used was German classicism. The beautiful, the good, the true: this was a totally ideological understanding of humanism. The people were to be purified by literature, by art, by humanist thought.

Can you say that certain methods of literary study were excluded in 1948 and later, or that things were structured so that certain methods were ruled out?

That's true of the period up to the end of the sixties. There was no discussion of methods at that time. For us, the only way of looking at literature was sociological. It was somewhat more sustained, more historical, and more solid among the Romanists than it was among the Germanists, where it was often very schematic, and where there was a division of literature into bourgeois, nonbourgeois, and proletarian—although, strangely enough, proletarian literature wasn't acceptable at first to the socialist society either. But then real discussions of method only emerged when, in the mid or late seventies, different approaches became clearer. I have always been very sorry—and on this point I was not aggressive enough—that certain developments, like psychoanalytical criticism, or even structuralism, were so little known to us from primary and secondary texts. It's a pity, and I don't think we can catch up. Because the border was always closed, and only a few colleagues could travel, and only a few had friends who sent them books, it was always left to chance as to what you would receive. From our point of view, it was always very difficult to get an overview of developments in international scholarship and research. There were prejudices at the university—that we at the academy were a bit more elite and had such a lot of time. We did have more time for research, and the people at the university had to do more teaching. But there was very little readiness among university scholars to introduce the things that we had published into their teaching.

I've heard that Germanists were less free than scholars in other fields at the university. Was this the case at the academy?

It wasn't true for all the Germanists, only for those who were involved with contemporary literature. I was in the same area as Marianne Streisand, and I'm sure she's told you the story of the book *Werke und Wirkungen*. It was a terrible experience for me, because I had to play along. I was a party member; I was one of the party leaders in the institute, and we had some good people in the leadership. As far as I was concerned, the party was not some great nebulous fetish, but rather people who called themselves comrades and with whom I worked. And they were critical, open-minded people willing to make changes. We at the institute tried with the help of the party leadership to avert the worst effects of the cultural policy that affected us too, and we were supposed to implement it regarding GDR literature. We always tried to act as a sort of buffer. But among the problems with this book was the fact that, in order to ensure its publication, it had to contain self-criticism. So the editor engaged in self-criticism, and she did it very cleverly. By that I mean she did not engage in self-criticism, but she said that when she began to write the book, it was a different period, one of high hopes for a democratization of literary and cultural processes. There were two years between the two versions of the book. Conditions had hardened, grown more severe; they were just worse. There was no longer any hope that the cultural processes would be democratized. People ought simply to have said, "What we are doing here is unworthy of our discipline." Except that probably the state would then just have closed our institute.

This was really what we always feared, that they really did have the power to do anything they liked with us: chuck anyone out, close the whole institute. A director's fear is especially repugnant: "Now we have to criticize this, although perhaps it really isn't all that bad, but we have to act as though it is, just to save our whole institute's work." This repulsive employing of tactics and strategy certainly helped the system last as long as it did, because everyone thought in the same way. There were a lot of people who were certainly very, very critical, but they all employed tactics so as to avoid becoming part of the opposition, to avoid confrontation. Confrontation always troubled us. When sometimes we confronted people at the highest levels of the party, there would be a control commission that wanted to discuss things with us for weeks and then evaluate us. Those are the circumstances that you really can't render convincingly to anybody, but that, as an individual who thinks rationally, you had to put up with. And when you're in the middle of this there are no alternatives: either you're in it and play the game and try to get the best out of the game that you can, or you get out completely. I didn't really want to get out completely, I didn't see that I had any chance to. So you tried to make the best you could out of the general misery, anyway to try to be a halfway decent person, but you weren't always successful. Today it's as though I'm telling a fairy tale. Now it's all over, and I can't imagine that things were once like that.

Did you believe that the party would introduce significant reforms?

From 1985 onwards the attitude of the SED leadership to Gorbachev was so negative, so unreceptive, and so lacking in solidarity that it was obvious that the leadership had no interest in reforms. But where the forces of change were to come from was completely unclear to me: they weren't in the Politburo; I didn't see them among the intellectuals; and I also didn't see them in the working class. I never believed that they would appear in the street, never! But there were people who said, "We've come to the end here, it's all over; I don't want to go on." They had no political plans or motivations, they simply left, fed up; they didn't want to go on. Then of course the ones who were politically motivated came along. They took to the streets, in the Leipzig demonstrations, and here in Berlin on November 4th—that was a lovely demonstration. And then it just turned around. The citizens' movement that started so bravely, so courageously, to help prepare the changes and the masses, to mobilize people for it, they were overrun by the mass of the population who simply wanted to live better; I don't want to denigrate that, it's a legitimate need.

One shouldn't judge intellectuals harshly. The controversy about Christa Wolf is so unspeakable: it was egged on by parlor liberals in the west, who say, "You should have done more. Christa Wolf kept quiet." That's simply unreasonable. Yes, Christa Wolf, just like a lot of others, and like me too, kept quiet about certain things, all right. The great majority of people in the country had no other choice. There were a few who opened their mouths and they went to prison, or were shoved off to the west, or lost their citizenship, like Wolf Biermann. I have great respect for these people. I wasn't that courageous. Christa Wolf didn't do it either; the majority of people didn't. I think you have to look at the mentality, the structures, and the forms of existence; and you can't do that from the outside. The people who are passing these judgments now didn't live here. After the Biermann affair, Christa Wolf did retreat in silence because she was desperate, because she had noticed that intellectuals were no longer needed by the state; they could become martyrs—but that wasn't her style—or they could leave.[8] And so she withdrew, in silence, to write her books. That's perfectly legitimate. No one has the right to pass judgment on that.

I think the attacks on the academy are like those on Christa Wolf:

the sweeping judgments that we were all SED writers, completely undifferentiated, and that we were all supporters of the system. One should oppose a stupid and sweeping criticism like this. Either people have read our books, the ones that were written in the institute, or they haven't. Or people have read the project proposals that have now been prepared for the commission in Bonn, or they haven't. We are self-critical about the topics we're working on, about what's going on at the moment.

Everybody helped support the system. That's where the guilt is, if we are talking of guilt. But to different degrees: in the sense that many had a greater share because they were in higher positions, and others had a smaller one because they were right at the bottom, simply collaborators; then simply some who worked for the Stasi. No phoenix will rise from the ashes; it's the old people with their old guilt, as it was after 1945. Ninety percent of the German people helped support the Nazi system, were onlookers, or turned a blind eye, and they had to help build up the new society. But there were no new people at that time, neither here nor in the FRG. It was the people who had cheered Hitler, who denounced the Jews—that's who these people were. And now, once again, we are dealing with people who, at the very least, kept their mouths shut; that's still probably the very least. Then there are some who denounced others; that has to be proved, beyond mere assertion.

The different posture of writers and intellectuals in other East-bloc countries, such as Poland, is striking.

KOR in Poland was an organization of intellectuals and workers. Among the intellectuals, there was always a traditional link to the working class, and that was simply not the case in Germany. Our intellectuals always kept their distance from what people called "the people," from the vital needs and problems of most people in this country. I have to include myself among them. I also have little contact with workers, with minor clerical workers. My friends are all intellectuals and there's a consensus there, though with differences, and there are similar conditions of life, similar privileges, similar worries, desires, and wishes. But it is not comparable with what the majority of people in this country thought, felt, hoped, and wished for. That's why we were so shocked at the election results on March 18 [1990]. You simply can't imagine how shocked we were; we really thought that the SPD would win the election.

What were the greatest drawbacks that you had to put up with in order to work with the system?

That you really felt that you lacked the courage to have a showdown with the leadership when you really should have done that. This is a question that I can answer quite concretely. There was a very nasty case in May 1989. A colleague of mine did not go to vote, and that was a political crime: a party member had to vote. He didn't want to leave the party, but the people at the top wanted to expel him, if we didn't bring an action against him. He lives here in a small ward quite close to me, and his roof was supposed to be repaired, but it wasn't. The ward's plans were manipulated to show that all the roofs had been repaired. He had discovered that someone was guilty of manipulation and told the party secretary in his ward that he wasn't going to vote, because someone was guilty of manipulation. His roof had not been repaired . . . a story drawn from his own experience, terse and to the point. Our party leadership had to work on this. We were ordered, by these criminal party officials, to impose a political punishment on him because of his behavior in not going to the polls. I thought, "That can't be true." But I had to learn that it was a party member's duty to go to the polls. I went to the polls too, but I crossed everything out. That was what I did. I went into the polling booth—that was not the usual thing, for the booths were only there as a piece of scenery, but I went in—and crossed all the names out. It didn't have any effect, but it was an inner salving of my bad conscience. In the case of this party member, I thought, "This is where you stop playing along, it can't be true." But in spite of that, I did go along, because I said to myself, "He doesn't want to leave the party."

In the meanwhile he has been rehabilitated. He got the most lenient punishment from us. There are three party punishments: a rebuke, a reprimand, and expulsion; so we gave him the lightest punishment, but nevertheless we did it. I was very ashamed to be going along with it. I make absolutely no excuses. The circumstances were outrageous, and there was little room to maneuver for people who felt differently; you could only be consistent and leave the party, but that was very hard for me to do because I saw no alternative. Where was there to go? As far as my working situation was concerned, it would not have been possible to do something totally outside, like working free-lance. Or I could have swept the streets or taken in sewing, but I couldn't have worked at the institute any longer. It was clearly a matter of life and death. For anyone who was in the party that's the way it was. I probably should have left the party much earlier.

But there is an intellectual tradition to think skeptically, to express oneself independently and to be ready to quarrel with the prince. But that's more true of a writer perhaps than a scholar.

I think that's a myth from the time of the Enlightenment: that the intellectual is critical, responsible for society—speaks against society— like Diderot, for example, who even then had gotten to the point where he could see through this role and look ironically at the pointlessness of it. I think that you should not renounce criticism and skepticism, but you should be under no illusions about what an intellectual's conscience can achieve. Christa Wolf and other writers in the GDR became, so to speak, the conscience of a nation, because we did not have a democratic public. In contrast to us at the academy, they had a relatively autonomous status, because we were employees, really government employees. The fact that writers could assume this conscience- or medium-function is connected to the system's strange bureaucratic-administrative, and perhaps also feudal, societal structures. It was a regression to pre-capitalist times. I don't think this can be compared with the role that intellectuals have assumed in Western Europe or America.

PETRA BODEN

September 4, 1990, East Berlin

Petra Boden *(b. 1954) studied and wrote her dissertation at the Humboldt University on the Germanist Julius Petersen (1984). She began work in 1983 as a research scholar at the Central Institute for Literary History. At the institute she worked in a research group devoted to German literature from 1830 to 1871 under the leadership of Rainer Rosenberg. She is now a fellow of the research center for literary history sponsored by the Max Planck Society. She and Dorothea Dornhof are collaborating in a study of the political contexts of German literary scholarship in the years shortly after World War II.*

Is there tension between the staff of the Central Institute for Literary History and the literature faculty of the Humboldt University?

Yes, there is. I can't tell exactly what the origin of the fight was, but there are animosities between the two. Probably a part of the reason is that the conditions of work are different. The university professors and scholars say, "We can't do research; our time is completely taken up with teaching"; whereas the academy is removed from and out of touch with reality, beyond good and evil, and can go on with its research without having to bother about teaching and practicality. But that also hurts it. This is the level at which there are tensions. Since I've been at the institute, and all the while that I was at the university, there has never been any cooperation, or if there was, it was as minimal as possible. When I went to the academy it was a move, so to speak, into the Realm of the Privileged.

You said that in Berlin there are about three times as many scholars employed by the institute as there are at the university. Why are there so few students at the university?

It all has to do with the fact that people have always tried to plan the number of students on the basis of a foreseeable need. People tried
to say, "We need so many teachers and so many Germanists, literary

scholars, who will enter the publishing houses or the cultural sphere," and that was the basis on which they limited the numbers of students. The crazy thing is that criteria had to be created for the way people were chosen to study, for example, German language and literature. Since the collapse of the GDR, people know what sort of criteria these were—what the effect was of letting people who had shown themselves to be well-behaved, nontroublemaking students into these disciplines and giving them a place at a university. Still, there are more people with a critical intelligence in the humanities than in the sciences, but they are few and far between. You couldn't be a rebel if you wanted to go into one of those disciplines, because you would later emerge from it into the public arena, where behavior that was critical of culture or society was not to your advantage.

Is it true that the literary scholars were not particularly active in the construction of a new ideology?

People have said, for example, that the disciplines that were least relevant to ideology were the languages, ancient history, and German studies. Is that what you mean?

Yes.

All I can do is laugh, for I'd really like to know what the others did. I don't find it at all embarrassing to say that German literary history was a discipline that had relevance to ideology. That was its job. The texts that we produced which were supposed to form people's view of the world, regulating the literary heritage or selecting the literary heritage—that was ideology. You can't just hide and say that we had nothing to do with the whole ideological mess. You can't do it.

Did you do it self-consciously, hopefully?

Yes, as far as I'm concerned, I'd say that was the case. I'm not ashamed at having claimed to see something in literature that Dieter Schlenstedt expressed very well when he said that literature was a society's expertise. If I did see my job as creating a worldview—the way you approach it is quite another story—then it was something like a social duty: to reflect literature in such a way as to see what it shared with other things that still had to be put in order in society, things that had to be set in motion or kept alive, like justice, social equality, and that sort of thing. I don't feel ashamed to say that I pursued my scholarship as something that was relevant to ideology and still saw something in it that was useful and hopeful. The fact that inflated claims for literature were made and that we thought we were important in a way that we couldn't possibly be are other stories. But we weren't aware of that.

How can one differentiate between supporting a state's ideology and constructing an ideology of resistance? Which ideology did you hope to support?

Precisely that of resistance. But that's what's crazy, and I'm not the only one today who can't draw up a concise account of where we started from. In the institute, we always worked on the premise that we were there to be questioned by politicians and that people had to turn to us for advice. The fact that our everyday experience was that nobody gave a damn about what we were doing led to deep depression and individual crises: you felt useless in this society; you were simply ignored both in your hopes and in your sphere of influence. That's a different experience. I think that the atmosphere was dominated by a malaise of this sort until the advent of Gorbachev in 1984. He took the humanists in his own country seriously, and that encouraged us. He suggested that one could have an impulse towards enlightenment, that we were competent to see through social structures to perceive the way those structures functioned, and that we could see the point at which something needed to be changed. I still haven't reached the point where I can say, "That won't work." I still hope it could be possible, a pedagogical concept of this sort. You'll start laughing immediately—the west has shown that it doesn't have to work, that things are regulated differently.

Personally, I am trying to understand that we don't have a chance like that any more, and probably never did. That it was all simply an illusion that we did have one. This illusion was what disciplined us and kept us in our niche. We thought that at some point it would become clear—and here I come back to the beginning of your question: "Perhaps," we thought, "it's still possible to exert an influence somehow, if we can gain some breathing space for ourselves and write certain texts."

Wasn't it also true that the literary scholars were taken seriously by the state, because people in the Central Committee hoped that the state would then be supported by them?

That all has to do with the fact that people thought that by influencing social thinking, by creating greater awareness, they could support this society and keep it alive. That's what one of my colleagues reduced to the concept of "Hegel-Marxism." While you change or correct awareness, existence can be maintained and advanced. That's a principle that goes from theory into practice. Actually it's the other way around. We should have learned that from Marx. You made the distinction between a resistance that corrects and one that wants to topple things. What we laid claim to was a corrective resistance. That was the subversive element that kept us going in our work. I laid a special claim to this as a stimulus, because I was working on realism, to unmask the ludicrousness of the conception of realism, and it was fun trying to do this. What finally emerged was very amusing and very funny; the only stupid thing about it was that the work wasn't even really begun. History simply overtook me. "The subversive element" could serve as a label for the whole professional group. That's also what made people feel good.

It was a game with very strange mechanisms and an area of activity that became larger and larger as the years passed. Of course it had its limits; you couldn't go beyond the prescribed area. You could sun yourself, within the confines of this area, in your intellect and your critical consciousness; and you could talk about it and feel free. I would tell my friends outside the academy about the things we discussed at our meetings, and they could hardly believe me. We were locked into a large space and that was our playground. The way the critical intelligentsia was disciplined served as a model. We could go to America, or to West Germany or West Berlin, and we were very happy about that. That's the story of privileges, that such a strange independent self-consciousness was communicated to us as privilege. The crazy thing was that it worked. I can still remember the times last year when the wave of people fleeing began. Endless debates had taken place beforehand, ever since Gorbachev came to power. These only gave rise to crises and mild explosions at the academy, and at the university too, as far as I could make out. Suddenly everyone realized that our whole effort, to educate and to enlighten, to motivate and to talk, was totally useless. History follows quite different patterns, and people simply run away. At some point we noticed that people simply had no need of us.

You wouldn't have thought that?

No. We really took ourselves very seriously, especially we young people. People like the director of our institute, Manfred Naumann,[1] or his contemporaries, who had come through quite different political crises in the 1950s, had a much more serene relationship to these things and probably didn't take their role as seriously as the young people did. But the people of my generation grew up with ideology, and we thought that ideology was very important. Individually, everyone certainly had a different idea of it, but night after night, we would sit and debate and work ourselves up. As far as we were concerned, there was nothing more important in the discussions than the decisions being made in the Politburo that we were getting worked up about. Now that the whole structure is collapsing, you can suddenly see how silly it all was. This makes a harsh inroad into your personal life. You acquire a strange relationship to your own past and to what you used to call your identity. I still can't laugh properly. Perhaps in two or three years' time I'll be able to do so again. The decisive point came as early as September or October 1989 when we learned that we had nothing to say. The great demonstrations that took place—for example, the one on November 4, 1989—were eye-opening experiences for me. That was so crazy. When the demonstration, with all the announcements, speeches, etc. was taking place, I thought, "Now we who prepared the knowledge ought to go straight up to the microphone and say so." Instead, we stood by mute. Quite different people were doing the talking.

Do you think that socialism simply ran out of steam?

This type of socialism, yes. It destroyed itself. Perhaps we should be happy that that's the way it turned out. Because the GDR is only one among many. Things went relatively well for the GDR, whatever the reasons. But when I think about countries like Bulgaria or Romania or Poland, or even the Soviet Union, what was bottled up there in secret and never became public and now starts exploding. . . . Of course you have to relativize the terror. The slap in the face that we're getting now is probably not so bad if you compare it with Third World hunger and drought and exploitation. But this practical, so-called real socialism destroyed itself, and it's a good thing it did. The bad thing about it is that there's no opportunity to try it again. The so-called third way that we always had, that was a product of the minds of the intellectuals. We have to understand that no one wanted to go along with it any longer.

And that seems a shame?

Of course I think it's a shame.

But you still believe in a utopian socialism?

That's a question of conscience. At the moment this utopia, this hope, is not in the least decisive for me. It used to be, but I, at least, can no longer be enraptured by it. Nonetheless I still can't bring myself to say that it's over for good. If I try to think a bit further I get back into my old ways, where I start thinking that there is always something that needs to be put in order in a society.

What role did the Stasi play in the fall of the GDR?

It would be too feeble to say that it was the Stasi that brought about the fall of the GDR. The Stasi was a sort of abscess within the system, something that grew out of the system of necessity, when at some point it became necessary to keep a total watch on this society, when a consciousness arose that it could always explode again. There's a man who lives in our building who was formerly employed by the Stasi. Recently he has suddenly started saying, "The people, they chose freedom." I said to him that if the people hadn't run away in June, July, and August by the hundreds of thousands, we would still be sitting here and brooding and churning around in our own mud. He said that I was making a great mistake. Because the results of the Stasi's investigations—however much they served to cover things up—nevertheless made it known that if people didn't go away the country would explode. It was already at the boiling point. One area didn't know what another was doing. To that extent, the danger was relatively mild, but when the explosion did come it showed what had been there.

· · ·

If the money were there to allow the academy to continue to function, what would you personally do? Would you work on something totally different from what you imagined you would a year ago?

Actually no, because I always did things that were unacceptable. But in the same breath, I also have to say that I was not a victim. I always wanted to study the history of scholarship.

Do you think that the discipline has its own history that goes on with or without socialism?

Yes, that's really crazy. There is a notable continuity in the history of German studies, and this is only now becoming clear to me, as I read the personal letters of scholars in archives. I'm not yet at the point where I can describe succinctly how the mechanisms function, but I've often burst out laughing when I've been reading these letters between leading Germanists of the past. I used to believe that the history of method explains much more than it actually does. But the fact that certain features of the history of German studies turn upon quite personal matters—that Professor X couldn't stand Professor Y, because Professor Y once insulted his wife—this I would never have guessed. It was also partly a question of sympathy and opportunism: who was going to get which chair, and at what levels that was decided. A whole series of lights lit up for me as I read these letters. People who already know these unpublished works will laugh at my naive belief that the decisions about what happened were made in the realm of ideology and methodology. I think it's an unwritten book, a new description of the history and context of these institutions in conjunction with the history of the individuals involved, the lives of scholars, and the history of methods—the whole structure of relationships. I also don't know whether the story can be told at all, whether it could be completed.

You knew at once, as you were reading the files, that the same thing was happening in the Federal Republic as in the GDR.

And how it was happening, in the time around 1945. But the criteria of development in the (later) GDR were quite different, and they were not developed by scholars. I think you can assume when decisions were made about appointments to chairs, or about the canon of literary history before the founding of the GDR, that other reasons played a part—and possibly other criteria—that had far more to do with the discipline than in the GDR. Because in the GDR the question of who had what chair was decided by how opportunistic he had been. Or what grade he had gotten in the Marxism-Leninism exam.[2] If you were good you got an appointment somewhere. The people who made the final decision were not the most competent people in the discipline. The institute made appointments, or arranged for an appointment, or wanted an appointment, but whether someone in particular was actually appointed or not was ultimately the decision of the Ministry of State Security. That's what was so stupid. I was lucky—and I came across this just recently, when I was talking to my boss about it—for the fact was, when I started at the academy I was married to a state's attorney. I was divorced a year later, but I think they decided that a woman who was married to a state's attorney and had written her dissertation on the history of fascism in her discipline and who was also a party member could not be a troublemaker. That wasn't a problem. I had always thought that I was appointed because I had written such a good dissertation. I really had to laugh when it became clear what had actually happened.

Any history of GDR literary scholarship will be first and foremost concerned with the institute. If you're involved in writing this history you would have to name the Stasi collaborators. You'd have to throw them out.

That would be difficult. That's the really painful part of the story. I'd be glad to write about the ones that I know of at the moment, but there are people we don't know about. We still don't know who the actual Stasi people in the institute were. We were very easy on our masters. In the factories the fur really flew. There were actual physical assaults when it became clear who the informers were.

Did you doubt the presence of informers?

No, we had already named the people, and we were very reserved in our attitude toward them. They also weren't in a very strong position; people had already guessed that it could be him or her. The suspicion was there. It was simply that nothing happened. There were two of our colleagues who were Slavists who were involved, and it was known in the institute that they were collaborators with the Stasi.

Is that already clear?

It's as clear as it is unclear. In *Sonntag,* our cultural periodical, there was an article that appeared when I was abroad by someone who is still working in the field, about Slavic studies in the GDR—namely, at the academy—and about two people who were not mentioned by name, but it was clear to all of us who was meant. This article was photocopied by a young colleague and put up on the bulletin board in the institute. The people involved, who knew exactly that they were the ones it referred to, walked past with their heads held high. Nothing at all was done. We are really wimps in the academy. It's a powerless institution. For that reason, the whole thing should be dissolved. The encrustations are so impenetrable that there's no point in it.

CHRISTA EBERT

September 2, 1990, East Berlin

Christa Ebert *(b. 1947) was a research scholar at the Central Institute. Her specialty is modern Russian literature, particularly Russian symbolist writing in the late nineteenth and early twentieth centuries. She worked in a research group concentrated on Russian literature from 1917 to 1985. She is the author of a critical study of modern Russian novels,* Symbolismus in Russland *(1988). In 1992 she edited one anthology of Russian symbolist poetry and another of symbolist prose. She is now professor of Slavics at the new University at Frankfurt/ Oder.*

Was the revolution a great surprise to you?

No, it was expected. If only because the Soviet Union and perestroika had shown for years what was not functioning in the system. Everyone could figure it out at the same time, all the Soviet failures applied to us, admittedly on a smaller scale; people involved with the economy had seen it coming even earlier. Among intellectuals, of course, you can still kid yourself, because you are living in a relatively secure space. For us at the academy, the conditions of work were absolutely ideal. You could go on kidding yourself for a long time that things weren't all that bad. The people working in factories, constantly experiencing economic failures, had been saying long before that they were surprised the whole thing still functioned.

Where did people say this to you?

Privately, of course, but also within the institute and even within the party. I myself was not a party member, but I know from other colleagues that they brought such things up and expressed them in party meetings and called in economic experts who told them quite clearly that everything was actually finished and that they really didn't know how the system was to go on. But those were all things that could not be published. A lot was talked about, even in certain public committees, roughly from the time perestroika began.

As a Russian scholar, I was immediately concerned with the history of perestroika and noticed in my own life what was happening here. Slavists acquired a function that we had not had before, or rather we imposed it upon ourselves. We informed people about perestroika. Not me personally so much, because I do turn-of-the-century, not present-day literature. But colleagues who were directly involved with the theme of current Soviet literature traveled around as lecturers. The same thing took place everywhere: a ten-minute talk about literature, and immediately afterwards a talk about what was happening in the Soviet Union at the moment; that was what interested the people. Then my colleagues simply told people what was in the Russian newspapers. From the Soviet newspapers and periodicals we knew a lot more than the people here did, because nothing appeared in the GDR press about perestroika. We had a lot to do in recent years keeping people who were interested informed.

But of course there were always difficulties; if you wanted to publish something, an article or something that had anything to do with perestroika—even the word itself was taboo—the article was rejected. *Neues Deutschland,* the party newspaper, wouldn't even accept reviews from us any longer. Or else they were so distorted by editorial revision that the authors took them back and said, "We're not going to write for *ND* any more." Before 1985 there had been a great demand for reviews of Soviet literature.

I heard that the journal *Sputnik,* the "Red Reader's Digest," in Allen Ginsberg's phrase, was banned, and that the House of Soviet Culture became a meeting place for oppositional gatherings.

Yes, yes. Previously the House of Soviet Culture had never evoked any interest, but in recent years it was terrifically popular. This was when Slavic studies had really good things to do. They showed films there; new Soviet films were taken out of the cinemas here. Of course for this reason people became very interested in them. At the same time, in the institute there were no limitations. On the contrary, our activities were supported. The limitations were always imposed from the outside.

What do you mean by "the outside"?

The "outside" means the directorate of the academy. The party secretary who was responsible for the whole academy was a personal guest in our study group, simply because he wanted to teach us how to deal with perestroika. That had never happened before. He was careful about it. Actually, he said that he wanted to inform himself about how research was being carried on within the framework of perestroika, and we put all the difficulties on the table: the fact that we couldn't do research because we had no access to certain materials and archives, and that we couldn't publish, and that the *ND, his* paper, was making difficulties. He promised to help, but at the same time he emphasized that perhaps the editors were right and it was a question of content. In any case, we continued to be regarded with the greatest mistrust by the directorate of the academy, that is, by the party.

Was the party always mistrustful like that, or only after 1985?

It apparently increased with perestroika. They were people who didn't have wills of their own, they only reacted to criticism from other places. For example, there was an Institute for Social Sciences in the Central Committee of the SED, and an Institute for Literary History, a parallel institute to ours. They were then changed into an Academy of Social Sciences, and they censored us ideologically. For all practical purposes, they were our reviewers, and when they complained about something the leadership of our academy sat up and took notice. The party was, after all, as it was everywhere in the state, the actual executive committee. The leadership of the academy would not of its own accord have been interested in suppressing anything here, but whenever criticism and complaints came from the party or some other outside agency, it reacted immediately, afraid that it would be permitting ideological errors. I should think that this was the way it happened, and not that some severe individual at the academy tried to suppress everything. That probably wasn't the case.

Whether it was always that way I can't really judge properly, but I think it probably was. The pressure from the party was stronger after 1985. It was especially noticeable in Slavic studies. It was almost impossible to study something like symbolism ten years ago. I had great difficulties in getting a theme like that approved at all. It's a literary approach that didn't fit in with their point of view: aestheticism, etc., that was something that we weren't supposed to get involved with. But I never wanted to work on contemporary literature, because I knew that there would either be constant trouble, or I would have had to follow the ideological guidelines. I wasn't prepared to do that. After I'd overcome the initial difficulties, there were no more limitations. Better aestheticism than perestroika, that was the catch phrase.

Was your theme actually rejected? By the group leader in the institute?

You can't actually say it was rejected. The leader of the research group didn't welcome the theme, of course. But I can't say that anything was absolutely forbidden me, not at all; but there were attempts to talk me out of it: "Wouldn't it be better if you did something else?" I began work on the theme with an edition of short stories. Then we had to fight against the difficulties at the publisher's. The publisher had offered me the edition but was afraid there would be objections from the Ministry of Culture. There were no problems. I don't know really what the reason for that was. It may mean that in general—and I think that is the case—there was more fear than necessary. People could have probably done more in a lot of areas than they actually dared to. A lot was simply not tried.

In what way has your work developed methodologically away from the institute's point of view?

I had planned, before everything happened here, to write a volume of studies on literary circles and salons at the turn of the century. It was not to have had such a strong sociological bent, but was to describe the atmosphere of the salons and how different mind-sets came together in certain circles; how poets, artists, painters, philosophers, etc. met and exchanged views, and what went on there that was afterwards found, at least in part, in texts. I simply wanted to describe it as a cultural phenomenon, a special sort of cultural life that was very distinctive at the turn of the century and which—and this is our thesis as well—laid the foundation for the intellectual culture of the whole century. That's to say that all the important things that have played a part in Russia, in the Soviet Union, in this century were conceived intellectually at this time. It was a situation where everything was still open, people didn't know in what direction the country would develop. It was the age of utopias, and for that reason we wanted to tie our project in with utopian thought; we wanted to show how utopian thought has changed in this century.

Salon literature is actually a current theme. In Prenzlauer Berg, private apartments were the forum, even though Stasi informants were present. That idea of such a literary culture goes back to fin de siècle salon culture.

In recent years it was of course a matter of self-protection for people to withdraw into private circles, as for all practical purposes the whole of GDR society did. Intellectual life, if indeed anything of the sort existed—and of course there was some—took place in private circles and no longer in institutions.

We had meetings of our research group, and nothing very constructive took place there. You were paid to attend—after all you were employed there—but if we wanted to do something seriously we met at home. Once a month I met regularly with two colleagues, usually at my house, and we were going to write a book together on Russian culture before the end of the century. We had thought out a plan and we are still profiting from it. And for years a small group of friends met once a week in a pub, really, in the middle of the city. Thursday was the day for meeting, and anyone who wanted to could come along. It was a very nice arrangement: you met people there and we discussed everything under the sun. I'm sure that there was someone from the Stasi present. You didn't expect anything else when a group like that met, especially regularly—it can't be kept secret. It lasted for seven years, but now it's been interrupted because the pub has been remodeled, and, in any case, people don't have time at the moment. Most of them are active in political organizations and hardly ever come to our regular table.

· · ·

How would you describe, in the abstract, your role as a scholar?

To communicate and preserve literary culture—in fact a rather conservative idea of the profession. I am not one of those who, following fashionable trends, want to establish the fact that cultural and other values are in the process of dissolution. There has always been culture, and, as I believe, there always will be, somewhere. It doesn't always have to materialize, but as a spiritual substance it will always be there, and there will always have to be people who will carry it on, no matter how popular or effective it is at the moment.

In your opinion, does culture have its own value, aside from its use?

I believe in the existence of spiritual values that are simply there, and that are of course always instrumentalized, in different ages; but that are present as substance, and which can, with our help, perhaps be made more visible, no matter how much demand there is for them at the moment. I believe too that they should simply be carried forward and not lost, because I believe that to be a condition of human existence. Human existence without culture is unimaginable, no matter what you call it.

How did you arrive at this idea of your function? Most of your colleagues thought rather of what effect their work could have within the immediate political culture.

Yes, the superficially topical. What I said to you just now was of course always valid, but from time to time I have also used topical forms of expression. Five years ago I was concerned with fighting taboos, fighting canons. When I got interested in symbolism it was, first and foremost, a protest against the current doctrine of socialistic realism. Symbolism—that meant propagating the freedom of the individual in the realm of aesthetics, just as in life, and introducing it as an idea into the society here by means of this subject. It was a totally concrete topical interest.

At the moment we are faced with the difficulty—I am too—that we have to reorient ourselves, because we have lost our enemy. Suddenly there were no more taboos to write against. But that was a false conclusion, as soon became apparent. What I'm writing against now is the general tendency to destroy culture. That's not an ideological or a political enemy any more, but a general process that is threatening the whole of civilization. In any case I never regarded it as so superficially ideological and political, but as a way of life. I didn't like what was preached and molded here—with all the nonsense about leveling and collectivization. The accent would certainly have been different a few years ago, but otherwise my idea of my function is the same.

What sort of influence did the theoreticians in the academy have on their colleagues?

Well, actually, in the institute they were the only ones who tried to create a methodological consciousness and develop theories, but of course on a Marxist basis. They are all Marxists: left-wing, committed

Marxists. Not orthodox Marxists, but people who want to create a Marxist apparatus. They always tried to shape things progressively. For that reason they got involved in certain conflicts with official policy. Some even had a consciousness of mission. They believed that if you proved certain things scientifically, the cultural politicians would accept them. They believed that by means of this concept—let's call it an Enlightenment concept—you could affect the cultural policies of the country. To some extent they gave information to the Central Committee about trends in literary scholarship, because they believed that the committee should know what was going on. But they did defend new literary phenomena like the work of Volker Braun. They actually played a large part in the cultural or cultural-political life of the country.

BRIGITTE
BURMEISTER

June 6, 1990, East Berlin

In 1967 **Brigitte Burmeister** *(b. 1940) came to the Institute for Romance Languages and Literatures, which was later absorbed into the Central Institute for Literary History. She had studied Romance languages and literatures in Leipzig when the influence of Werner Krauss was still strong there. In 1983 she published a critical study of the French* nouveau roman, *left the institute, and began a second career as a novelist. Her first novel,* Anders oder vom Aufenhalt in der Fremde *(1987), was very well received and understood as a Stasi novel. She has translated the work of Alain Corbin and Pierre Bergounioux. In 1989 a collection of her shorter prose texts,* Im Angebot, *appeared.*

When did you come to the Berlin Academy of Sciences?

It was 1967 when I came to what was then the Institute for Romance Languages and Literatures, headed by a student of Krauss. Werner Krauss was the most celebrated Romance scholar in the GDR. His intellectual heritage was still on hand in, among other things, the form of a very distinguished study group that was working on the French Enlightenment. The main focus of Romance eighteenth-century studies initiated there by Krauss was the so-called Minores, Enlightenment figures of the second and third rank, who were subsequently forgotten, rightly or wrongly, but who played an important role in their century, and in any case ought to be studied, if you want to understand how an intellectual movement like the French Enlightenment functioned. And this group began, at the time when I joined it, to prepare a book that was a long, long time in production, a great fat volume on the French Enlightenment for the use of teachers, students, and other people who were interested in it. It went back to Krauss's effort to understand the intellectual and literary thought of the time, and also to explain its genesis from the political conditions, the view of the world that had preceded it, and the socioeconomic structure: all in all, a materialistic approach to history. I wrote two articles for this volume.

That was the first time I was in the academy. It was very pleasant but also difficult at first, but then increasingly just a pleasant way of learning: working together with people who were already specialists in a whole area instead of working alone and writing on a prescribed theme, writing texts that owed a lot to a collective process of understanding. That was my very first important experience of working in a collective. But the positive side of it that I am emphasizing now was accompanied by a sort of ponderousness and a relationship to time that bothered me: it was as if you had all the time in the world to sit down and work on a project like that. It took us almost two years to come up with the outline, because the idea was that the people who were responsible for the individual chapters should be bound, almost by oath, to a common central idea—through discussion, discussion, discussion—so that the collective approach should remain evident throughout all the individual contributions. This was colossally difficult and only succeeded to a certain point and was, in any case—I'm firmly convinced—something that could have been successfully achieved with far less effort. Anyway, since you were at the academy and since the academy treats its associates as employees—they had a monthly salary and lifetime tenure—the ambience of the academy encouraged the department to approach such things with great care and thought. That in itself got on my nerves a bit, but as I remember and also as I experienced it at the time, the advantages outweighed the disadvantages, because it was a very thorough and solid piece of work that we did: a piece of the German scholarly tradition, specialized, in that someone worked for ten or twenty years on a period—and really knew almost everything about it after that—so that this portion of German scholarship was combined with a Marxist historiographical approach and was interesting in that you were actually occupied with something relevant, making your contribution to the understanding of emancipatory movements and correcting certain attitudes to the French Enlightenment.

How large were the editions?

I reckon the first edition must have been about ten thousand. But you must be careful how you treat this information, because I really don't know exactly any more. Paperback editions were always relatively large. Our book was considered a popular scientific one. It was written with a view to a wider dissemination, and to that extent it was different from other books that appeared, for example, in the academy's Literature and Society series. They were planned differently from the beginning, with editions of three thousand to a maximum of five thousand. This popular learning didn't go any farther than to teachers in high schools. They certainly didn't think that working men would read it, or some minor party functionary, who was serving an apprenticeship.

Was the book critical of the party?

Yes, in this very cautious sense. I think that it itself was almost an Enlightenment critique; that is, it was tactical, and written in such a way—which is certainly problematic—that people who already held the same attitude about the need to criticize dogmatism understood it, but that it was not understood by those who were to be held responsible or those who, because they had the power, had been indoctrinated from childhood. We never attacked them frontally.

Were you in the party?

No, I was never in the party. I did actually make an application in 1973 after the putsch in Chile—not a written one—but I told my colleagues who were in the party, "All right, I'll set all my objections aside; all that matters now is that we strengthen the ranks." I was very lucky: they didn't accept me. Somehow there was something wrong with the percentages; there were already enough women and too many intellectuals in the party. Besides, they said that I should reexamine my decision. I did that, and didn't join.

What is your response to the criticism that intellectuals in the GDR distanced themselves too much from the workers?

The intellectuals and the workers have different interests. These differences became clearly apparent in November, or—at the latest—December 1989. In any case, they cut right across intellectual circles and right across the people. There were those who wanted—and for a long time believed and hoped—that the GDR could be reformed. And there were those who said, "Let's live the way they do in West Germany, because things work well there; there's prosperity and freedom there."

How many friends did you have who were in the second group?

Among my friends, no one. That's just the way it was, I really always went around with people who thought the way I did. I wasn't that aware of it for a long time. I mean, there were enough differences; we often quarreled. In spite of that, it turned out that you moved in relatively homogeneous groups, and these groups determined, to a large extent, your own view of the world and also your idea of what most of the GDR citizens were thinking. I assumed that, whatever this perverted socialism actually did do, it made good Social Democrats out of the inhabitants of the GDR. The elections of March 1990 taught me something different, and now I am very, very careful, and I think this caution is right. The GDR is very varied. People don't believe that because it makes such a uniform and gray impression. When you approach from outside, everything looks the same, but the people are very different, quite astonishingly so.

In the West we often hear that as an intellectual you are bound to think skeptically, to believe nothing, to doubt everything; that is our tradition and our duty. Was there a lack of skepticism here?

At home, or in the institute, or in our study groups, we said just what we thought, but as soon as someone came along whom we didn't know, or when we had to consider how we should write something for the public, a sort of inner censorship started up for well-founded, and also exaggerated, reasons of caution. Well-founded caution was, "If I want to achieve something then I have to make compromises," but this attitude stopped many people from recognizing, and exceeding, the amount of leeway that they may have had.

I have also noticed that skepticism and the breaking down of prejudices was also associated, in the writers of the Enlightenment, with very firm ideals and convictions, and with illusions. That was true here too. Socialism was a sort of substitute for religion, a secularized religion: that it would be possible to establish communities that had a solidarity, where one individual is another's brother—truly and not just in the realm of ideas—and that Marxism would provide the instrumentalities that would allow you to recognize conditions so that you could change and reform them appropriately.

I want to talk about oppression. Up to now all that I've heard from your colleagues is, "I was afraid my book wouldn't be published, I was censored"; but no one has said, "I was afraid of landing in jail." Didn't people think about that?

Certainly, some did. I think Rudolf Bahro must have taken that into account. He can't have been so unrealistic that he didn't take the risk into account. Anyone who has had the experience of having sentences deleted (Volker Braun, for example; or Christa Wolf, with *Kassandra,* could tell some tales about that) certainly wasn't frightened of ending up in jail—and if they were, I'd think it absurd. You had things to fear from a quite different angle. An example: in 1968, we had an illegal study group in which we read forbidden texts, and we held seminars with friends in West Berlin in order to school ourselves. Our goal was to find those points in the contradictions that existed in our society where we could, and should, take some practical action. It didn't get that far, because acquaintances in Leipzig were arrested, and we dissolved the study group immediately. That was because we were afraid of jail. We burned materials, put books into storage, spent weeks discussing how we would make our statements agree in the interrogations we expected to be subjected to, etc., etc. We knew what was in store for us.

But it didn't come to that?

No. My husband and I were very lucky; we weren't even called as witnesses, as other friends of ours were. Later one of the people who was arrested said that it was quite clear to him why we weren't. Our acquaintances in Leipzig had prepared a "flight from the Republic"—as it was called—and unbeknownst to me, I was a part of it, because I sent off some fictitious telegrams. That was the crucial point for the Stasi: not the study group, but, "Where did these people from the west come from who were helping with the escape? Where are their contacts? Where is their headquarters?" We were under surveillance for a whole summer, and I have to gather from the fact that they didn't arrest us that they decided we were not the place.

And you weren't.

No. I sent telegrams, and while I was doing so I thought, "I don't want to know what it's all about." I always thought that it was just the study group that was the problem. We didn't notice that we were under surveillance. The people who were arrested told us later, after they had been released, that our apartments were certainly bugged. Perhaps that was our good luck. So we are also glad that one day we shall have access to the Stasi files.

I wonder what part jail played in people's oppressing themselves, and I assume little.

For me it played quite a part, from the moment that I and others said, "We have to do something to change this society." After 1968. We knew at that time that such attempts were dangerous; you had to play it carefully. And when it became publicly dangerous, then we simply gave up. But when I was writing, I really never worried about jail. Then I told myself that the worst that could happen would be that it might not be printed.

If the consequences were so minor—that in the worst case a book would not be published—why didn't intellectuals try more frequently to go one step farther?

It all depended on what you were working on. If you were working on Goethe or Walther von der Vogelweide, that wasn't a problem. But if you were working as a historian on the history of the Soviet Union, then you said to yourself: "There are certain things that I cannot write, for the mere fact that I write them will create difficulties for me in my institute, in the party, long before the work is published. It will cause difficulties for me in my profession; there will be disciplinary difficulties." There certainly were. It didn't matter so much for us as Romance scholars because we were relatively protected by our field. You could take more liberties there than where the risk of a direct confrontation with prevailing opinions in the party was much nearer at hand— contemporary history or economics, a whole range of areas. There I think the fear was much stronger and much better founded. But I have to say that in every case there is a lack of the courage of your convictions if you don't put feelers out to see how far you can go.

You admit that?

I would maintain that—in differing doses for myself and for all the people whom I know—we were unduly anxious, and disciplined, and willing to come to terms with prevailing conditions. We lacked the experience to know that we could be different. It's not as though we once had the experience and then had it taken away from us: we never had it. There was a tiny beginning in Czechoslovakia, but this was put down so violently that it was, of course, a kind of shock. People said to themselves: "The consequences would be just the same here, the Soviet Union won't allow us to . . . only when the whole world situation changes and when the counterpart to state socialism is not only imperialism but other countries as well with a different conception of socialism." That was always our starting point: that there were reform wings in all the communist parties—with the possible exception of Romania—that's to say, people, even if they stay completely in the background, who were waiting for the chance or the hour to strike. Gorbachev came out of the depths of space, so to speak.

Do you think that intellectuals are facing a period of self-examination?

I think they *should* be facing one, but I think that it will be de facto far smaller than the situation invites, if not demands. Because there are other ways of doing it. Among other things, it's connected with the style of German reunification. Criteria like competence in your field, experience that can be used in the rapid production of efficient structures, now often appear to be more important than the question of how someone behaved before. There are certainly a few points that are intolerable. For instance, when it comes out that someone was for years a paid informant for the Stasi, then he certainly can't be tolerated to perform most functions. But for the most part, reality consists of much more differentiated and even simpler cases—perhaps someone was blackmailed, or had never worked for the Stasi, but had imposed an authoritarian or intolerant style of management and caused suffering to other people in this way. That was certainly the case with many managers, down to the schools. There I think it would be necessary to talk to those who were involved—the schoolchildren, the parents, and the employees—about replacing people like that. But there are a lot of concerns where the situation is simply no longer suited to that sort of action, because the whole existence of the enterprise is in the balance, even if the new director is still the same as the old one. In any case, it's a fact that many people from the old management level have maneuvered themselves into new posts, and are, for example, now on the board of a corporation. In the institutes, too, there were people like that: people who were loyal servants and ideologues under the old system, and are now the ideologues of the infant democracy. If they weren't too bad, and if there's no one to say, "You have to be responsible for my having lost my job before, for my being forbidden to carry on my profession," in cases like that, some action will certainly be taken, but it's difficult, especially for the person who was sacrificed, because he has to fight to see that his old oppressor disappears. A few can manage it, but a lot of others would say, "What's the point now?"

Should you and your colleagues have asked what literary scholars might have been able to do?

Yes, just in the interests of our concern with our past. Looking back, I see it in my case roughly as follows: when I was no longer working on the eighteenth century, but on the modern period, my colleague Karlheinz Barck and I, as Romance scholars, administered the theory of modernism, so to speak. We were both in a special position, in that we were both trying, with great difficulty, to introduce and make known for the very first time in the GDR something of French thought of the sixties, so that Marxist literary theory could do something productive with these approaches. We had our hands full; we weren't in a particularly good position as far as our material went. For instance I could never go to France to buy books. It was all very complicated, and, given these adversities, we did a relatively reasonable job on figures of thought in Marxist aesthetics—I mean reflection theory and a whole series of main doctrinal pillars—that could easily be questioned with the help of the positive application of other theories. We did this very happily and agreed more forcefully in our private communications than in the ones we published. But even there, I think, there was no mistaking what we were up to. The readers understood exactly what was meant, who was criticizing what. I know of no one in my immediate circle who was a daring thinker, but you can see the effect of the attitude that you described earlier—namely, of watchful skepticism—that people were not prepared to go on perpetuating nonsense that they recognized as such. But the means were relatively gentle. You also have to take note of the fact that the readership here reacted to even mild tones. For example, one of the reproaches to be leveled at GDR literature is that it worked to a large extent with allusions, between the lines. Perhaps so, but almost everyone here understood.

Did you yourself have problems with the censors?

Once in an afterword to Saint-Exupéry I had a sentence deleted and a few words were called quite severely into question, but I defended them, and I put the lost sentence back when I was reading the proofs in the hope that only the typesetter would read it.[1] But I was mistaken: it was deleted again. My experiences in this respect were pretty harmless.

When I wrote my first novel, I thought: "Either it will be published or it won't. The censors won't have a long discussion about it." It took a long time before they came to a decision and announced it. They gave permission for publication. The novel's criticism of our situation lies, perhaps, in a process that is a sort of distancing: to have someone tell the story who is a completely loyal subordinate who gets caught up in a crisis and becomes—and fundamentally this is something quite unbelievable—an artist, i.e., his so-called diaries become a novel. And this protagonist is described so vaguely that the suspicion quickly arose—for a time I had it too—that he might be an employee of the Stasi. That was the way the novel was read in the FRG.

My concern was describing a structure that I consider largely relevant, not only in our society: namely, that a large part of the population is involved in processing data from sensually perceptible reality in such a way that it can surface somehow—in reports or in series of numbers—as a reflection of reality and become managed material in a number of different institutions. An employee of this sort who, as he insists, feels good doing this work and does what he is told, is confronted with the fact that reality changes overnight if you really expose yourself to it, if the same incident that is processed statistically, bureaucratically, or however on your desk day in day out, confronts you in your own life. Then he doesn't recognize it. That is the fictional exaggeration and, at the same time, my criticism of the naive assumption that it is an easy matter to change the world into language. It is an enormous adventure and often something bad as well, if you think of bureaucracy for example. My own suspicion that the "hero" could be a member of the Stasi came about through a verbal association. This character is very lonely, looks out of the window, "observes" a lot. In French the word is *"observer"*—"observe"—and "observe" is a security service term. Then I said to myself, "This bastard is a member of the Stasi." And I fought against this suspicion for a long time, but finally gave up. I grew to like the character more and more as I went on writing.

KLAUS MICHAEL

September 7, 1990, East Berlin

Klaus Michael *(b. 1958; pseud. Michael Thulin) was a research associate and a doctoral candidate in modern German literature at the Central Institute for Literary History from 1987 to 1991. He was a member of the research group on twentieth-century German literature. His specialty is Weimar culture: expressionism, Dada, and the Neue Sachlichkeit (New Objectivity). He wrote a doctoral dissertation on the early film and media criticism of Siegfried Kracauer. As Michael Thulin, he wrote poems and essays for such unofficial journals as* schaden, verwendung, *and* Ariadnefabrik. *From 1990 to 1992 he worked with Sascha Anderson, Rainer Schedlinski, and others at Galrev Verlag, resigning as chief in protest against the continuing presence of Sascha Anderson at the press. He edited the anthology* Vogel oder Käfig Sein: Kunst und Literatur aus unabhängigen Zeitschriften der DDR 1979 bis 1989 *(1992) and, with Peter Böthig,* MachtSpiele: Literatur und Staatssicherheit *(1993).*

Are you still at the Academy of Sciences?

Yes, but it's a paradoxical situation. Meanwhile people are taking the pictures down from the walls. Punctually on October 3, 1990, when Germany is reunited, the academy will be dissolved. The GDR is in the process of abolishing itself and its institutions. One of these is the academy, where I have been employed since 1987.

The academy was founded as a place alongside the universities, which were concerned with training and teaching, to allow people to pursue basic research. The founders belonged to a generation that had gone through the war and the postwar period and had consciously sought out the GDR as a country. They thought of the academy as a platform from which they could set the switches for society. Anyone who—as an "idea man"—had not left for the west came into the academy: Robert Weimann, Manfred Naumann, Werner Mittenzwei, Sylvia Schlenstedt, et al.[1] And it was perfectly natural for that generation to assume positions of leadership in the party and in the state.

The fact that this great beginning developed, in some scientific areas, into an institution for the plagiarism of western patents, or, in some of the humanistic disciplines, into a factory for the legitimation of ideologies is quite another matter.

What ideological role did the institute play in literature?

I think the institute had, for the most part, two tasks. One was the usual basic research: the publication of dictionaries, lexicons, studies in the history of literature, and the production of editions, like the editions of the works of Wieland, Herder, Büchner, Herwegh, and Brecht.[2] The other was the function of a think tank for cultural policy: preliminary studies and internal contributions to discussions for party conferences, writers' conventions, and cultural conferences.

However, one thing is certain, the Academy of Sciences was not the elite school of the GDR. The party had its own universities for this purpose and its own Academy of Social Sciences in the Central Committee. Nevertheless, there were a lot of direct guidelines. They came from the cultural division of the Central Committee, or from the Academy of Social Sciences. In cases like this, a Frau Ursula Ragwitz of the Central Committee of the SED would be announced, and half the institute sprang to attention.[3] I remember that I came into contact with her for a brief time, quite by accident. One day, the telephone rang, and it was she, summoning one of the professors to the telephone. Since I didn't know the woman and was surprised at her tone of voice, I hung up on her twice. A few days later, I was given some coaching in who's who in GDR cultural policy. There was a visible and an invisible power structure, codified and noncodified hierarchies. Political instructions were the job of the latter: instructions were transmitted—almost exclusively—orally through party channels. Nonparty members were just as much affected by them, but they had no insight into the way decisions were made.

Of course the ideological structures were not public, though they were visible as staff structures. Ninety percent of all my colleagues were members of the party, although many of them were opposed to it; and there were also members of the Stasi, as there were in every state institution. The chief personnel officers were the only ones who made decisions about your professional future and journeys to the west, but they were not independent in their decisions.

The visible and invisible control of the individual functioned in a similar manner. It differed widely according to the focus of the professors' research and their political convictions. There were scholars who took their ideological duty just as seriously as their research and saw to it that instructions were also carried out. This led, for example, to a book on the influence of GDR literature, *Werke und Wirkungen,* being rewritten by the research group for GDR literature three times, because the reigning political premises had changed.

You never intended to join the party?

Why? There was simply no reason to. I had all the wrong qualifications for a GDR career. My father was a clergyman, I had relatives in the west, I hadn't been in the army. I was banned from giving readings at the beginning of the eighties, had trouble with the Stasi, collaborated with the peace movement, had the wrong friends and acquaintances at the end of the eighties. . . . It would actually have been senseless, even the orthodox comrades would not have believed me.

Nevertheless, even as a nonmember of the party I had to appear at the party apprenticeship meetings in the institute. After two or three times, I didn't go back. Nobody ever asked about it. The ideological instructions were already beginning to break down at that time. Interestingly enough, these events almost became a tribunal in the course of the last year. The strict requirements for topics and books of instruction were thrown overboard, and we began a review of Stalinism, with contemporary witness too: the triumphal progress of Stalinism in Eastern Europe, the repressive cultural policies after the formalism debate in 1951, the workers' revolt of June 17, 1953—in the language of the GDR, that was always shunted off as a "counterrevolutionary putsch."

What career could you have made for yourself without being a party member?

You made a career in the GDR by accepting political repression. You fulfilled the demands in the hope that your opportunism would pay off at some point. If you didn't want to do that, you had to be ready to accept a kink in your career. That's what would have happened to me. If the GDR had gone on, I probably wouldn't have become eligible to travel abroad until the end of my life.

When you traveled abroad, you were never just a private person, but always a representative of GDR research and the current state institution—whatever that happened to be—as well. Thus you had a precisely defined foreign policy task assigned you and had to sign an agreement before you set out on your trip. This meant that you had to behave in certain ways controlled by the Stasi. Personal letters to the west had to be reported with the name of the addressee and the contents; you had to write travel reports; minutes had to be written on your contacts with people in the west; professional correspondence had to be presented for approval; money earned by lectures given, or articles published, in the west had to be surrendered; you had to break with your relatives in the west, any sort of contact with them was forbidden; etc., etc.

My career would have been to get a university appointment in an East-bloc country after ten years and perhaps pay one visit to the west after another ten years. In other words, no career at all.

• • •

Is the artistic scene itself more important for your generation than the writing of poems, one by one?

The poems of my generation were always concerned with establishing communication with other people. The texts always related to an interlocutor or a concrete situation that needed to be broken up. Of course in the early eighties no one thought that poems could be lasting. There was also no possibility of writing books. This opportunity has only existed for about three years, with this series in the Aufbau Verlag that's being published by Gerhard Wolf.

In the early eighties, the literary scene was more important. You could find everything there that wasn't otherwise to be found. It was a fascinating microcosm within society. It was a substitute public, with its own periodicals, readings, and exhibitions in which you got to know new people: authors, painters, musicians, women. This was where you tried things out and developed your own style. Here too you could find people who supported you in legal and financial matters. You got tips about apartments that were empty. And it was here that the first contacts with the west were made.

The scene was not an idea, it was always very concrete; but it did not emerge from the attitude of one artistic group, or from a particular literary trend. It constituted everyday life in East Berlin: a closely woven network of social contacts and literary subcommunication. Any new arrival in Berlin who didn't have a regular job or who wasn't at home in the state institutions as an author ended up in Prenzlauer Berg sooner or later. That was automatic.

Within this subculture, then, there were different "scenes" and trends. Among the literati, it was the way you handled language that determined what group you belonged to. Looking back, no one belonged to a "scene," that's simply how it was. If you ask one of the authors directly, he would deny that he had any connection with a "scene" at all. Yet there were distinctions. In the first place there were those who handled language quite uncritically and articulated general political and moral states. Most of them were to be found in the care of the church. Then there were the authors who wrote critiques of language, who were also differentiated according to their poetic approach. There were semantic processes in the works of Stefan Döring, Leonhard Lorek, and Bert Papenfuss-Gorek; the metaphorical handling of language in the works of Sascha Anderson and Andreas Koziol; and textual recycling processes in the works of Jan Faktor, Thomas Rösler, and others.[4] The literary culture was so many-faceted that it would be worth writing a large work about it simply as a historical factor.

Will formerly suppressed books now appear, and how will they alter things?

Of course a lot will come out now. There are piles of manuscripts in people's drawers. Now that the possibility of publishing books exists, we shall see some longer texts: treatises, short stories, novels. In the small-scale periodicals that appeared in the past few years, you had to submit short texts because they couldn't be reproduced by machine. The individual numbers were all typed by hand on a typewriter: five times seven copies represented thirty-five copies of an edition. It was only later that we had electronic typewriters and computers. You simply couldn't produce an edition of five hundred copies. The upper limit was probably about one hundred, but to do that the typewriter or the computer had to clatter along day after day, making an unbearable racket. You were forced to write a certain form of text, simply because of the technical limitation of the periodical medium, or rather the stapled book edition; that's what explains the predominance of lyric poetry.

Was there actually a dogma as far as lyric poetry was concerned? What was expected of the lyric poets?

The role of the literary intelligentsia was constantly overestimated. The reasons for that are historical, because in the Soviet Union—and in the Slavic area as a whole—the intellectual and the writer is something like a prophet, a teacher and enlightener, or a popular leader. The writer has a cultural mission; and, at least in the Slavic area, the intellectual, whether he's at home in the samizdat or the state, fulfills this mission. In the postsocialist history of the states of the Eastern bloc, the overestimation of the word has continued in a system that is dependent upon words. Indeed the main task of ideology consists in simulating reality: there is a constant pressure to produce a second and better reality and to sell this as something real.

It was expected that the person who was publicly involved with words would not question this simulated reality. If anything was expected of the writer, that's what it was. And there were at least two generations of authors who kept to this agreement and said nothing. Above and beyond this, it was of course expected that the poet would support socialism and the politics of the GDR with their texts. During the so-called lyric-wave at the end of the sixties, it was indeed the case that poets like Kunert, Braun, Mickel, Kirsch, Endler, and others met these expectations, not because they were forced to, but voluntarily. That was the period of the Vietnam War and the student movement, the period of the Third World and of great hopes in Marx, Mao, and Lenin. Because of this, a particular image of the poet and concept of poetry developed in the minds of GDR politicians. It's clear that the author and his literature were anything but autonomous. For literature, the example was the simple, clear, almost functional language of Brecht. Literature went about its business mimetically, not imaginatively; it was realistic and scarcely influenced by modernism.

The great surprise came at the beginning of the 1980s when a new generation of poets appeared on the scene demanding autonomy. Because people had no idea of European modernism, no one had any experience in dealing with this sort of literature. For this reason, the aesthetic breach of the rules was originally interpreted as a political breach, and poets were treated, as a precaution, as criminals.

Underlying this was a primitive notion of literature and the structure of human consciousness. The party theoreticians thought quite seriously that they were dealing with a sort of black box that had to be filled up with the right contents. If one of the contents was not "right," you only needed to exchange it for something else. This was the reason for the overestimation of propaganda and the attempt to enlist literature as well.

**I assume that a playful sort of lyric poetry or writing would not
have suited that at all.**

That was not intended. In the cultural theoreticians' limited understanding, literature could only serve two functions, a political one and
an illustrative one. If the one could not be traced back to the other, it was
excluded from the beginning. It even got to the point where publishers'
readers, Germanists, and literary scholars couldn't handle the linguisti-
cally critical, playful, procedural poetry of the last ten years. Even Volker
Braun had his problems with it, although he used to read Rimbaud and
the classical modernists. He didn't really understand what Bert Papenfuss-Gorek wrote either, although for a time he was in almost daily
contact with him. In a big essay on Rimbaud, in 1985, he dismissed the
new literature as pubescent verbal garbage. Afterwards he did apologize
to Elke Erb, but his first statement was published, the second wasn't.

**The term "pubescent" suggests the role that generational con-
flict plays in GDR culture. This seems an ingredient too in the
recent controversy over** *Was bleibt.*

Of course, Wolf was a member of the generation who thought that
the structures of the GDR could be reformed by working from the inside
to the outside. As far as I know, she was in the Central Committee for a
time, in her younger days.

Yes, in the late 1960s.

All right, that wasn't necessary. I think you've got to allow her the
right that other people have to make her own personal decisions—and
her own mistakes. If you can reproach this generation of writers with
anything, then it is that they allowed themselves to be partly corrupted
and repressed. There were always exceptions, but the majority accepted
intellectual repression along with the benefits given them by the state.
The most embarrassing thing, from my point of view, were the diatribes
that were directed against those people who went to the west in 1976
and afterwards—first and foremost by the head of the Writers' Union,
Hermann Kant.

PART THREE

The

Literary

Life

HERMANN KANT

August 28, 1990, East Berlin

__Hermann Kant__ (b. 1926) is the author of a number of best-selling novels. He was a soldier during the Second World War and held as a prisoner in Polish prisoner-of-war camps from 1945 to 1948. In Warsaw he joined the antifascist movement. When he returned to Germany he studied German literature at the Humboldt University. He has received virtually all of the literary prizes awarded in the GDR. He was president of the Writers' Union from 1978 to 1989. After 1989 he was widely regarded as one of the functionaries who had special responsibility for the persecution of writers in the GDR. His most successful novel, Die Aula, *appeared in 1965;* Der Aufenthalt *appeared in 1977, and* Der dritte Nagel *in 1981. He published his autobiography,* Abspann, *in 1991, and received quite critical reviews. In 1992 his collaboration with the Stasi was exposed.*

You were president of the Writers' Union for the past decade. Can you tell me what role the union played?

I think it played a very significant role, not only in the realm of literature, but generally for the whole GDR society. At first—when I wasn't even part of it and didn't even exist as a writer, but when the union was already active—this was due to the importance of the people who had founded it, the most famous people in the country: Anna Seghers, Arnold Zweig, Ludwig Renn, Johannes R. Becher, Bertolt Brecht.[1] The names should be enough, but those were the people who founded the union and supported it later. The union initially had more of a symbolic significance—in the sense that here was a place where the old antifascist literature had gathered again. It changed after that as new writers joined. But where, in what other union, would you have had once again such a world-famous group of people?

143

When I joined the union in 1960, it had become a professional union. It did not enjoy the same reputation as it had in the early years. In the early years it contained, so to speak, a ministerial group and a writers' group. In the intervening period it had become a union for everybody. Then we began asking a few questions that had not been touched upon up to that time—for example, the question of travel. If people ask me what I think was the most important thing that happened while I was at the union, I would say that we gradually made it a matter of course for writers to get passports—and I have to say that it was above all because of my initiative and my persistence that this happened. Of course, other people took it amiss that we had managed to get this through. It's obvious, and I understand perfectly well why. In their eyes it was a privilege that we had, and everyone would have liked to have had the same privilege. But we couldn't give it up simply because other people didn't have it. We were always of the opinion that we could show by our example that it would be OK, that the state wouldn't lose by it, but rather would profit from it. And you can make that into a general principle. But it was very late before it came to that.

The importance of the union grew more and more because we introduced changes in cultural policy. In part we broadened, increasingly, an idiotic narrowness of cultural views and the view of what was publishable. The union is responsible for the fact that a certain cosmopolitanism, so to speak, developed in publishing here. It wasn't other people. It was, above all, people in the union—that also includes publishers—who caused literature to be brought into the country. But that's old hat. And the union's conferences always produced progress in the general consciousness. The people here knew that to be absolutely true. On days when there were writers' conventions, people didn't get their *Neues Deutschland.* That meant no national newspaper, because the speeches and discussions—my speech was always carried in toto—were printed there. On those days there was something in the papers that was otherwise never to be found there. The critical tone of the convention was something that people waited for here, the relatively self-assured attitude of all the participants—all that.

Wasn't there a danger that the writers would be occupied too exclusively with the relationship of literature and politics?

Literary figures in all the socialist countries played this sort of role, sometimes more successfully, sometimes less. The danger of being and acting politically instead of literarily was of course a big one for everybody. Havel, for instance, is a politician, and—in the meantime—he has quite logically become a president. In his case it's particularly marked, but that doesn't mean that he has given up having a literary mind. But now he's become a politician. And I think that's a very interesting product of our situation. Of course we were a various group. Our union was considered more loyal to the state than others. I'll tell you something. I've frequently heard very harsh criticism of the union from a number of different sides, but I always said, whenever possible, that we were faced with the alternatives of either being as unimportant as the Czech union—which never recovered after August 1968 and consisted of a small group of not very important people who produced no literature—or we could be as all-powerful as the Soviet Writers' Union, but that meant building our own empire. We do very well here with the GDR union.

Roughly how many members of the union were there?

There was originally a rank of "candidate" that was only recently abolished. If I count everyone, members and candidates, we were close to a thousand strong.

I assume that writers, in general, supported the state. Is that true?

If you mean that the majority of writers were for a GDR, for a socialist state, you can readily say that. If you get a little more concrete and ask whether they were for *this* GDR and for a socialist state like this one, then it's a lot more difficult. One day we'll be able to read all about it and determine the truth. That's where scholars are important, and I'd like to say something to them as well.

If you were to draw a graph of criticism in the history of the union meeting, it would, for as long as I have known it, be a constantly and inexorably *rising* curve of critical attitude. We had in the Berlin union, for example, the institution of what were called panel discussions. Leading people were always invited to them, secretaries of the area administration or people like that, sometimes people from the Politburo. No one was ever let off the hook. For them, these were always moments of truth. The writers were not afraid to come forward with their critical and urgent questions. That's to say, the picture that was accepted at the time—of the servility of yes-men—had nothing to do with reality. The fact that the books written by these people were not always characterized by such an aggressively questioning attitude is another matter. That also has to do, to some degree, with opportunism, with wanting to earn money, and with the fearfulness of the publishers and people of that sort. That's quite another matter. But meetings of the Writers' Union were disliked by political officers and were, at best, to be avoided. I will prove this to you in a word. At one of the last staff meetings of the Berlin publishing house, where all the Berlin newspapers are published, there was a large party meeting at which the acting leader of the Central Committee's Agitation Department appeared. He listened to the discussion for a time and then, at some point, angrily shouted out the lovely sentence, "We aren't in the Writers' Union, you know!" That's a sentence for which I am very thankful, but it expresses precisely how the Writers' Union was regarded in these circles.

Doesn't a Writers' Union of this sort run the danger of promoting agreement where diversity is needed?

If you're looking for the source of a lot of agreements, you shouldn't be looking towards the union. The union was not very influential as far as theory was concerned. You should be looking at the literature in this field that was significant in this country, starting with Rilla, Reimann, and Bloch, until you reach Lukács, who was the summit for us.[2] We all learned from Lukács. The union had too little influence in this field for my taste.

Can you tell me how someone became a member?

Anyone who felt that he or she should join the union had to make an application, in which the most important thing was to be able to point to the publication of at least two books. That's to say, fiction writers needed two volumes, novels or something of the sort. In the case of lyric poets, of course, the proportions were quite different. In other words, you already had to be able to prove that you were a writer before you could be accepted into the Writers' Union.

Secondly, you needed people to vouch for you, that's to say, references from two people. At least one had to be a writer, and the second could be someone outside the union, but had to have something to do with the literary business, say a radio editor. Then you submitted this with the usual accompanying papers—a curriculum vitae and things like that—and made the application to the area administration. That then had to be confirmed by the committee. Once a month, we looked at the documents that had been collected by the area administrations and had the right to object, and we made use of this right a great deal. It's true that we also had the right to admit someone to the union against the will, if you like, of the area administrations, but we scarcely ever exercised this right. But we did use the right to reject someone very often, because, in the first place, the union was very attractive because it afforded the opportunity to travel. We had a large travel department of our own in the union that did nothing else but take care of passport business for the members. If, in other countries, a dowry played a large part in a marriage, in our case this part was played by the access to a passport.

We actually never had a case where someone applied who was not acceptable to us politically. That actually never happened. I can't remember anything like that. We shall certainly come to the story of people who were expelled, but in my time there was never a question of refusal of *admission* for political reasons.

Do you mean that not all members of the union were members of the party?

Good Lord, no. It was about fifty-fifty, and that's still a very high number.

Over the years a number of writers, especially younger writers, emigrated. Is that true?

Among the people who left in the last few years were some who were not so young, but were in the age range of Becker, Loest, or Seyppel, that's to say, over fifty.[3] In the case of some people I had no idea that they were members, because among the very young there was an attitude of reluctance towards the union. The people from Prenzlauer Berg wanted to have nothing to do with the Writers' Union—that was their declared program—they didn't want to join, didn't want to correspond with it, didn't want to enter into discussions with it, they wanted nothing at all to do with us. The reason was that we were part of an establishment, and they were opposed to establishment of any kind.

When Biermann talks about the family aspect of GDR literary and political culture, does it mean that the elite group among whom he counted himself was so small?

Yes; now listen. It's a good thing to stay with the question of the role of the union when we're dealing with this question. There, too, you've got to pay attention to what I'm going to say now. We managed to achieve a very high official reputation in this country, and that was hardly understood by anybody abroad and was then only seen as being suspicious. But we were ourselves always suspicious and remained suspi-

cious. That's what's so comical about the whole thing. We were always
very lovey-dovey, and the authorities always kept an eye on us: "What's
going on now?" the politicians would ask. Always. Of course that's all
connected with the profession of writer, and, to that extent, I have to
say that the case where a writer is a total supporter of his state is very
rare. He is, if he's worth his salt at all, at one and the same time a fellow
who is not entirely reliable, because he's always thinking thoughts that
go far far beyond what is desirable. That's to say, a writer is someone
who thinks about things. That's his profession. The fundamental question
for him is, "What would happen if . . . ?" The fundamental issue for the
party is, "The way things are is the way things ought to be." These two
positions are only partially reconcilable, so that Biermann's statement
hits the nail on the head. We were, in some way, total enemies, and
yet—well not exactly familiar—but we knew one another.

I'd like to use another image to express that. Once, in the fifties,
early on when I was doing a lot of political journalism, I'd just started
publishing a few stories. I was at the University of Münster in West
Germany. I had been invited by the the Socialist Student Society of
Germany for a discussion. I was walking through the university with the
very left-wing leader of this small group. There were, I think, eleven
members of the group in the whole university. Very seldom, but now
and again, he greeted someone and exchanged a word with them and
would then say, "That was someone from the Christian Student Society"
or "from the CDU," or "That's the old liberal here." And at some point
I said to him, "I really think it's great that you greet one another in such
a friendly way"—it was a time when political differences were very great.
"Yes," he said, "but it's really not difficult. As political thinkers we are
an increasingly small group, so that we actually constitute a group ourselves." It was something like that, if not quite so sharp. The writers, for
all their diversity and their frequent enmities, were all linked in the eyes
of authority by a common suspicion. I thought for a time that it might
pass and that you could get rid of this sort of mistrust. But you can't.
The more closely I came into contact with what was called the party
leadership—people from the Politburo too—the more clearly I noticed
that they simply thought differently, and that they were always anxious:
"What are they up to now?" I had a whole lot to do with Hager, who
was the man in charge of our field and a powerful man.[4] At one congress,
I had made a lot of notes in my notebook, as I always did, and he had
seen me doing it. At the end of one day, after I had made the closing

address, he said, "Ah, and now you'll write all that down in your black book." It was a sentence from the black heart of a suspicious man. The black book wasn't simply black in color, it was a black book. What was most interesting to me, and I noticed it, was his tone of voice and the look he gave me, and later I understood: it was the look and the tone of voice that people used when they were talking about us, and it was the way that they looked upon us. That's what Biermann meant.

What price did the union pay for the high reputation that it enjoyed?

The price was that we often entered into a dangerously narrow alliance with the leaders of the state. Or, let's say, that *I* had to. Look, I don't want to describe myself as a tragic figure, not at all, because I entered into these alliances for the sake of the union, and I could only get something for my colleagues if I was accepted. That's to say, I tried to make it possible for the people from whom I wanted something for the union to see me as someone who would not upset them. Of course, that's a matter that, as soon as it's no longer necessary, becomes the subject of general opprobrium. At that moment, you are suddenly nothing but the person who was with *them*. But people forget, of course, that I was often with *them* on behalf of other people, and that I would have achieved nothing for others if *they* had been suspicious of me. All right, that's the way it is. But I know that, in part, it's stupid and unjust.

On the other hand, no one made me do it. To put it quite clearly, I always did everything quite voluntarily. I saw my role as that of someone who had the chance of creating a position for a literary society in a socialist country; one that had never been achieved up to that time. I knew that, I saw that. I knew, too, that it meant that I had to see that people listened to me.

All right, I was fully conscious of what I was doing. But on one point I never made a concession. I never wrote anything literary in order to be able to do this. My literature was my literature. I never allowed myself to be talked into anything. Of course it's natural—and there's no pretending it's not—for there to be a natural controlling authority within the individual when you live like that. That's quite clear. Yet, if I may be allowed to point to someone else here—you can check up on it—I was very happy when, about two years ago, a well-known West German public affairs man had a long interview with me, parts of which appeared afterwards in the *Frankfurter Rundschau*. He said, "You are unusual to the extent that it is not only in the GDR that you are an important and well-known writer. That's relatively rare, at least in a so pronouncedly political sense." That's true, it was a rare thing. When I look around among my colleagues, they were either pronouncedly literary people with little interest in politics, or vice versa. But then you sometimes have idiotic ambitions. Mine was to be able to do both and to be both. I used to say to myself, now and again—I said it in the course of any number of quarrels—"If the union is to be what we want it to be, you cannot have a weakling in the post running it, you can't have a literary nobody, because the powers-that-be won't listen to a literary nobody." One of the reasons why they listened to me was that people had told them that I was not an unimportant author. And that gave me more power in my position.

Were you, as a literary figure, a different person from who you were as a functionary?

I wouldn't go so far as to say that. I tried to describe that in an essay, where I portrayed myself as the servant of two masters. It didn't get to the point where the political functionary would, so to speak, have spit at the author on paper, or where the author would have stuck out his tongue at the functionary. No, I tried to achieve the strange feat of being both at once. And I think that to some extent I managed it. If you like, I was not exactly an average functionary, and I wasn't exactly an average author either, precisely because of this combination. Among the functionaries in the Central Committee I was, naturally, the writer. When I was elected to the Central Committee, they bled a little internally. . . . They had a few writers, but the ones they had didn't make trouble any more; let's put it that mildly. And now here was someone who made trouble all the time and who was known. I feel a bit comical, pointing this out myself, but I was an author in this country who had the reputation of being someone who had something to say, who had a critical way of thinking that you didn't find everywhere, especially not in public life, not in the newspapers; but being critical was almost a motto for me. I gave a girl an "A" in the *Die Aula* because she said, "but." That was actually the catchword for my writing, not to let the word "but" disappear from people's vocabulary in this country, something that certain people would have loved to have done—a whole lot of people. Saying "but" was very troublesome. I set store by this "but." That is—if you like—something quite different from *opposition*. You can look for the "but" in my books.

I sometimes wished that people would look again at what made people fight for those books. It was only mentioned in passing in the reviews. If I tell you that when the volume of stories called *Bronzezeit* was announced—and it was the same with *Der dritte Nagel*—one winter people stood in line on the Spandauerstrasse for an hour and a half, in subzero weather, before the books came into the store. That was how long the line was. They did it because they hoped that this was another book in which something had been written about this "but."

How can you reconcile this "but" with the pedagogical function of literature?

You can only arrive at the "but" if you don't believe in the pedagogical function of literature. I have always looked at the function of literature as something quite different. For instance, in the famous decades-long dispute in this country about whether literature was the *conscience* of the nation, I always said: "No, we are apparently not the conscience, because no one can monopolize conscience, and you cannot ascribe conscience to a group. And the group cannot arrogate it to itself. But now we are apparently the *memory,* we are the people's memory. We do not forget what takes place and what doesn't appear in the annals." You can, of course, get to the "but" from *this* position, or you can stay with the "but," or it is only through this position that a "but" is possible. To come back once more to my relationship with my fellow functionaries, they knew the word "but" too, of course. "He's really a good chap, but . . ." You always have to say "but."

Do you think that GDR literature was critical enough?

No, I don't think so. At the moment they stand there as people who never ever said "but." At the moment they are represented by different sources as simple yes-men, as simple beneficiaries, as privileged people, whatever. The Christa Wolf dispute is symptomatic of the whole thing. Facts that were in front of everyone's eyes for decades are simply no longer valid. I don't know whether you read my conversation in *Der Spiegel.* That was three weeks ago. I picked a quarrel with the editors and asked what had gotten into them to start something like this with Christa Wolf of all people. For an extraordinary number of people, innumerable people—and among them many young people—Christa Wolf was an authority to whom they clung. That's what the writer could be here. The people from *Der Spiegel* said, "Yes, yes, she did help people here and there." That's not the point. The point is that Christa Wolf was in innumerable small communities, held readings at church functions, up and down the country, and talked with the people. She didn't incite them, but she *listened* to them. At the moment of course that doesn't count. At the moment you have to have suffered, you have to point to some periods in prison, or something of that sort. That's entirely understandable. Even the mere assertion that you were always in opposition, as I now sometimes hear from our new members of parliament, who were, nevertheless, professors under Honecker—if they hadn't been relatively well behaved they wouldn't have been professors. That's what really distinguishes the literary figures from the scholars. They could become writers without being well-behaved characters, but they couldn't become professors at the university without being well behaved. So the same people proudly go on bearing the title and maintain that for twenty years they were constantly kicking against the pricks. Now, it may be that the linings of their pockets are worn out because they kept clenching their fists in them. I don't know. But the sort of division of people that is being made at the moment, into those who opposed the old regime—the unjust regime, as it's now known in the new treaty— and on the other side a few beneficiaries, among whom are all the writers, this division is absolute nonsense. Of course there were some people among the writers who adapted; there are money-grubbers there too—pompous asses and vain brats and I don't know what. But when you add up the whole of GDR literature, I have to say that it didn't play too bad a part in all those years. You'll find in it what you'll look for in vain elsewhere. And the "but" wasn't only my "but."

What were the difficulties you had to overcome in order to go on working with the state system?

The greatest difficulty, or shall we say, the price you had to pay was having to forget a lot of the ambition that drives a writer, because you had to use your powers for quite different things. I'm still of an age when you ponder things like that. I have applied a lot of the mental energy that would have been of use to my writing to a pile of other things. But no one demanded that I do so. I'll come back later to this degree of free will. Let me repeat so that there shall be no mistake: I came back to this country from prison camp with very clear aims. I came back from four years in Poland and had not only seen what we did there. I was, so to speak, almost at the very center of fascist horror. I sat down once more in the former ghetto, in the midst of the desert that everyone knows from pictures. I never again wanted to belong to a people from whom other people hid. That was my quite basic aim. Either I had to hide myself, or the others hid themselves when I came. I wanted to rid myself of this lunatic relationship, and I believed that I had found some way of doing that in the socialist idea, because I was together with Poles and Jews in Poland. The common means of communication, the bridge, was socialist conviction.

In the course of time, however, it has transpired that—because of their power—the socialists here have forgotten what they, just as honestly as I, I presume, had nursed as an intention. What I recognize clearly in the sum of my life is a commonplace that the whole world has known for a long time, something no one wants to believe, but that is true. The most dangerous thing in politics is that you have power. Whenever it's impossible for you to cry "but," it turns into something bad. There are no characters so good and so noble that they can be left alone with power. There are no such people.

Did you as an independent writer earn enough money from your books?

As far as that went, we were, according to other people, unique in the whole world. With 80 percent of the Writers' Union freelance—that is, living only on the earnings from their books—we were quite alone. In France there are eight or nine writers living entirely from their literature without having another job. I don't know how it is in England, certainly not better, probably worse. In the USA there are a few more, if we take the size of the country into account. But no one achieves the percentage that the GDR did. I am the notorious inventor of the phrase "Reading-country: GDR." It deserved the title. People read like crazy here. An average novel never sold less than thirty thousand copies. Never. That means that—because you received one mark per copy for the book— you were assured of thirty thousand marks. Besides this, there was a contractual system that functioned in the following way: you expressed to your publisher an intention that you backed up with an outline. If the publisher liked it you signed a contract, and you received at once a quarter of the total sum that you expected to receive. You received the second quarter when you delivered the manuscript. That, too, was money you were certain of. So that half of the honorarium was assured. You didn't have to pay it back. If the publisher then said, "No, we're not going to do it," that was his bad luck. The author lived on half of the money. If it was published, the third quarter was paid when the license to print was obtained, and the fourth quarter was paid according to the level of the sales. That means that even a weak author had plenty of time. If he had completed a book, he could go on working on his next book, supported by his earnings, even if the original book was not a great success.

For us in the union it was a problem—this may sound comical to you—persuading the young people not to go freelance. They always arrived, their education behind them, with their *abitur* and their military service completed, and they'd just started to work as an engineer somewhere; they'd written a book or a volume of poems, and now wanted to work freelance. They could do so without more ado. With the contractual arrangement they could ensure their livelihood. And incidentally there was sufficient demand for writers. They could write firm histories, etc. Literature presupposes a certain level of experience—if you disregard a lot of exceptions in lyric poetry and a very few in drama—that they simply could not have, and that they could then no longer acquire. If they stopped being engineers, they stopped being a certain sort of citizen. That was the danger. And that was bound to express itself in a certain literary anemia. That was the problem: the way to freelance writing was too easy.

That's all over now. Now even authors as well known and experienced as the ones I see around me have to concern themselves with reordering their financial needs, among other things, finding part-time employment at the age of fifty or sixty in order to have some financial security. Freelance writing only functioned against a background of those huge editions. It's not as though it stopped at thirty thousand, but a novel that was even relatively reputable could achieve an edition of eighty or a hundred thousand. God knows I'm far from being alone with my record-selling *Die Aula*. All right, *Die Aula* is still a record because, as a book about conditions in the GDR, it has sold just over one million copies, in a land where there are fifteen million readers.

In the future the GDR will not be a land of readers. You'll probably notice that it's hard for me to talk of an unjust state, when it made possible a literary production of that order—and not just my books. Foreign authors were just as much in demand. All that has to do with the particular situation of the GDR. It is also, in part, the perverse fruit from a garden that was enclosed by a very high wall. People simply brought the world to themselves by reading, if they couldn't reach it by train or airplane.

RAINER KIRSCH

August 31, 1990, East Berlin

Rainer Kirsch *(b. 1934) is a well-respected poet who has been known as something of an aesthete by comparison with his contemporaries. After studying at the Johannes R. Becher Institute, he refused to accept a diploma in 1965 and became a freelance writer. The appearance of his play,* Heinrich Schlachthands Höllenfahrt, *led to his expulsion from the party in 1973. He has written a wide range of books, stories, fairy tales, critical essays, and poems and published two selections of Russian poetry—by Mayakovsky (1980) and Mandelstam (1992). Among his best-known books are* Ausflug machen *(poems, 1979),* Kunst in Mark Brandenburg *(poems, 1988), and* Amt des Dichters *(essays, 1979). In 1990 he was elected president of the Writers' Union to replace Hermann Kant. It was hoped that he would have greater credibility than Kant did, but the West German government disappointed Kirsch and others by refusing to give financial support to the union. Kirsch presided over its dissolution.*

You have been elected the new president of the Writers' Union. What do you think the new Writers' Union should do now that it didn't do before?

The only thing the Writers' Union can do is dissolve itself. Yes, we did want to renew it. What's the point of such a union? One, to represent professional interests. That's always important, perhaps more important now than before. And then it is a place for literary contact, where the country's authors can meet and talk about literature if they want to. But a union of this sort cannot exist simply on the fees of its members. It needs some sort of funding, which we had from the state but that has now been canceled. That's to say, a political decision was made: the artists' unions are not worth being renewed. People don't want to discuss *155* this politically, so they just cut off the money. It's pretty ridiculous to tell us that money isn't available. They've got 4.5 billion marks for the army that hasn't anything to defend any more, but they don't have 1.5 or 2 million for us—1 million would have done.

How solidly were the authors behind the idea of renewing and continuing the Writers' Union?

The people who created so-called socialism, those groups of leading people, had a remarkable respect for literature, they took it seriously. For that reason they also kept an eye on literature; they censored it. A lot of people died under Stalin. They were considered dangerous people, but you only consider someone dangerous if you think he's important. No one was done to death in the GDR, but the idea that literature was important—for society, for the education of society as they see it—this idea persisted. As a result, authors were more or less respected as people. We didn't have any newspapers in the country. What they called "newspapers" were the Politburo's court newspapers, and artists were—and later on, in fact, even more so—a social power group, a small one, but they were one that could articulate itself, that actually articulated the questions and the state of mind of the people in the country. That's how they were looked upon, and in fact the people regarded them positively, just as the leaders sometimes regarded them positively, but always mistrustfully, and sometimes negatively.

So if there is this pressure and supervision by the state, a sort of super-father who sits up there and is sometimes kind and sometimes angry, sometimes lets you publish, sometimes not, then there is a natural solidarity—but not of all the authors. There were courtiers, you know, people who put "party" on their cards and tried to do what they wanted. But the good authors were solid. Yes, there was a solidarity of this sort among the good people. A union of this sort would have been a place to preserve a solidarity like that. The new board that's been elected is quite different from the old one.

How would you describe the role of literature in the present circumstances?

A writer is a man who reflects, if he's a good writer. Relatively early we started not to care what the people up top said about the way literature ought to look. Or socialist realism: no one was interested in that after 1965, not even the party writers. The good people's concept was: you write literature the way it has to be. If you happen to be in the privileged position of being able to articulate something, because of your abilities, your mind, your talent, then you have a duty: you're working for German national literature. You also have a job to do in society. At least that's how I understood my work, and so did my friends. You have a duty toward society, namely, to help people live, not by getting rid of the system—at that time no one wanted to do that—but by articulating and analyzing circumstances directly or indirectly.

Ten or fifteen years ago one often heard about the educational function of literature. Did this sort of idea play any role in your work?

There are two sides to the word "education." You can understand education as indoctrination: you know something better. But you can also understand education as something like an enlightenment, as something like offering people thoughts, ways of behavior. That's my way of putting it. If I do something—this is more true of an essay than of a narrative or a poem, but there too—let's say I have a thesis, then I feel obligated by courtesy to advance all the arguments against this thesis that occur to me. It's possible that they don't all occur to me, but at least the ones that do. In so doing the whole thing becomes a thought-offering to the reader. That—if you use it positively—is also education, because I am showing the reader that if you have a thesis you don't simply beat someone over the head with it, but you consider it and say "but," and then you say "yes, indeed, but," and "indeed," and "however," and "given that," and "on the other hand." This going round and round a thought—to present everything you know about it—well, that's the positive conception of education, that's my conception, and it's Mickel's or Dieckmann's conception, or the Saxon school's conception.[1] You make thought-offerings, and then people can take them or leave them. That's something quite different from indoctrination, which says, "That's the way it is, and you have to believe it." Then, of course, indoctrination can achieve exactly the opposite effect: namely, a lack of readiness to think, and also an inability to feel. Even if an indoctrinator does say something right for once, it won't be believed because he's lied seven times, even though now he's telling the truth.

Do notions of literature as resistance or as legitimation of the status quo have no meaning for you?

There are two sides to that, like most things in this world. Pascal says, "Yes, if you have two contradictory opinions about a thing, you don't have to choose the middle way, but you must attack it from both ends." The one thing is thinking through a situation and describing it. That's a very abstract way of putting it. That's what happens in literature: you find a lucid analysis in an essay, but these analyses are also implicit in poems and in prose. That's how you help people, when they find that their situation has been articulated. That's a step towards more freedom in my opinion. For if you're simply angry, mad, insulted, humiliated, that is, you have feelings, then you have less freedom than if you have opinions—you don't have to accept them—but from an articulate opinion you get a suggestion of how to think, or one way to think.

The other point is, "Qui scribe, scribe pour le roi des Prusses"—"Who writes, writes for the king of Prussia"—what Frederick the Great is once supposed to have said. Someone reported to him that someone had written something bad, disparaging. He didn't care: who writes, writes for the king of Prussia. That's to say—and that's what people reproach us with now—the better someone wrote, the more he contributed to the prestige of the system. However, if you push the thought further it becomes totally absurd. For then it turns out that the ones who have written well have stabilized the system, and the ones who have done a botched-up job and produced bad literature have harmed the system. Using the same logic you can say, "We had a fairly bad shoe industry, but if the head of a shoe factory made good shoes he strengthened the system, and if he made bad ones he weakened it." So the one who made bad shoes was the resistance fighter, except that people had to suffer in his bad shoes.

The word "resistance" has now taken on a meaning that prevents my even uttering it. There was resistance in all the good literature, certainly there was. In spite of everything that was said and spread as propaganda there, I have to write the truth and—the truth is not sufficient in itself—I have to create literature. This is resisting in the face of demands that are alien to literature, demands that call on you either to lie or to institute an inner censorship. The word "resisting"—I don't know whether it can be translated—means something different from "resistance." By "resistance," we understand direct political action. That is, you go out into the street and say, "Honecker must resign," or, "The Politburo consists of fools." If writers had done this—and that's what people are now demanding we should have done—then they had only one alternative, and that was to go to the west; but then people here would no longer have had access to them. All the people in the west, perhaps with the exception of the complete right-wingers, always said: "Stay there as long as you can. You have to work there in the GDR, you are irreplaceable. If everyone leaves, then the people haven't got you any longer"—like a minister. The Protestant church here said, "You're a minister, you have to work here in your parish." They even made an agreement with the church in the west: if a minister left the GDR, he could not become a minister over there, because he had left his parish. Now if you take away the Christian aspect of the whole thing, I too have regarded an author's position in this way, and the people also looked on it in this light.

Whenever someone I thought a lot of emigrated, I always accepted it, because if you can't go on writing here then you have to leave. A writer has to go to the place where he can work. I was able to work here, others couldn't. As far as I was concerned, I didn't reproach them. I went on visiting the ones who were my friends, when I was able to travel to the west. But that was my experience, you have to work here. And the public here understood it in this way too. Ah yes, now I'm coming to the point, that wasn't just a personal decision because it put so-and-so many people in the position of taking a stand, of saying something was or wasn't right. If a woman with a great reputation like Christa Wolf, if she had gone, she would have left behind a readership—not a readership in the commercial sense but in the intellectual-spiritual sense—she would have left a readership for whom she was a comfort and a help. She would have forced all her colleagues here to ask the question: "Was it right for Christa to leave, or was it not right? Do I have to leave now because she's gone?" The responsibility for a step like that was not purely individual.

T. S. Eliot spoke of an "aesthetic sanction": because Dante created a masterpiece out of his beliefs, those beliefs acquire a special validity on account of this.

Yes, that's right. Now, the political conditions in Dante's time were also pretty terrible, and you can glean that from the *Inferno* and the *Purgatorio*. But you are right, subsequently—people perhaps didn't think that way in those days, in systems like those—at least the time was such to produce these important literary works. He was not beaten to death, and somehow he managed to write. That too was not contrary to our intention. No one wanted to get rid of this system, although as people got older they saw that it was irreparable. Every book that appeared, that had some sensible things to say and contained something aesthetically valuable, was a piece—people argued—where reason could crystallize, and this was allowed, was again a step in the right direction. Ours were piecemeal tactics. They also worked in part. Nonetheless, while people were forcing this liberalism in gradual steps they were adding to the state's prestige.

What did you imagine as an alternative to this state?

Did people seek alternatives? People did think within this framework. Otherwise we were working for German national literature. No serious person thought there were two literatures. The official thesis was that there were two. But we said, "No, there's only one, but there is good and bad if you want to talk about two literatures."

Today I would place the accent rather differently. There are special features within this one German literature, simply because of our different knowledge and experience. I can already see the danger that these special features will be discarded, simply by discarding the authors, putting them in a position where they can no longer write. In our case it is unusual economic mechanisms and also ideology that put people in a position like that. If you come from the west you can smile at what goes on in the *Frankfurter Allgemeine* or in *Die Zeit* and say: "My dear friends, there are always wicked or nasty journalists who make their mark by articulating hatred. You just have to put up with it." That's all well and good. We would, too. We put up with invective and hatred before. But what you read there appeals to a potential for obedience among people who were always accustomed to reading between the lines in the newspaper—the smallest hints were important. Now they read the attacks on GDR literature and are convinced that that is the new line, and they act accordingly, including booksellers, people who give money or who do not give it. To that extent what I have called ideology has a relevance to the market, because authors, who even in normal circumstances have a hard time of it, now in different conditions, where the reading public isn't waiting for the next book, are up against another market restriction, a sort of brokerage. These are the things that secure the system. Why should a bookseller invite an East German writer to give a reading? Why should the state give him or her a prize?

Are you talking about the controversy over *Was bleibt?*

That was what got me on to it, but that is only the significant point in a way of thinking that intends, perhaps, to go along with the spirit of the time. It began with the defamation or the pejorative use of the term "intellectuals." TV commentators started this about December 1989 or January 1990. It continued with a remarkable decision that a lot of people all made at the same time: namely, that the rules of European civilization do not hold good for contacts with GDR artists. For example, it is a journalistic rule that you must write the truth, but people have consistently written—over and over again—that every member of the Writers' Union received a monthly salary. It's absolute nonsense. There wasn't anything of the sort. There were individual grants for individual works just as there are in other countries.

The rules of common courtesy were later suspended—namely, at the time of the controversy about Christa Wolf. People used expressions like "ghost," like "her real-socialist soul should go to hell." That means wishing a person were dead, nothing short of that. It's an old atavistic death-wish: your opponent ought to be dead. "They spray the deadly poison of socialism"—you can scarcely go further than that. But that's what you can read in civilized newspapers.

Now I find in this—I'm fifty-six now—remarkable parallels right down to the individual formulations: "The intellectuals have separated themselves from the people"—Zhdanov.[2] How often have I heard that! When I was still in the party, when I was expelled: "You intellectuals have separated yourselves from the people." Then a wonderful formula: "The writers complain." Today that means they talk about a state of affairs that the Western partner doesn't acknowledge. He says, "Oh! you're complaining again instead of being an optimist." Again, what does Zhdanov say? "The writer has to look towards the future optimistically; and if conditions today are not bright, then he must depict what they could be like, he has to be an optimist." Word-for-word repetition of old formulas, point-by-point repetition of old practices. A work of literature is not criticized for the extent to which it is a work of art, but rather for its view of the world and the political opinion that lies behind it. If that's not enough, the work is criticized according to the writer's—be it man or woman—political actions, imagined or actual. "She did that, now she's writing that . . ." Then there's no more need to read what has been written. "He did that": the work's already beneath contempt, and literature is condemned.

Take Zhdanov—he was a bad man of course, he killed people, I know. If you were to hear his remarks today, you'd say, "That's terrible, what he said." Yet that is precisely the way Western critics talk. Zhdanov was, at least in one point, more cunning. That was the official ideology of so-called Marxist literary criticism. An author's personal political views and his intellectual affiliation with the party have nothing to do with the criticism of his work. I was always called Balzac. Balzac was a royalist, but he portrayed the bourgeoisie of his time faithfully, and I don't give a damn whether he was a royalist or not. But they don't manage to muster even this little bit of truth, though Zhdanov had it.

How would you describe the literary advantages of GDR authors?

It was perhaps a bit characteristic of working here that we took our time. Again this is connected with the peculiarity of this society: people waited for the books because other attractions were lacking. But there was also the need, and then it became a habit, to work with precision, also out of an attitude of defense against the state. They were watching all the time, so I had to be able to answer for every sentence. I took that in with my mother's milk. I simply couldn't afford to overlook any laxness. That's the point. And after all, that is something positive: permitting no laxness and preferring to give up this opportunity, and the next, of earning something, and preferring to create a text that will survive for ten or twenty years.

When you had written something, did you have to go to the censorship authorities?

That's right. But as I said at the beginning, censorship functioned this way: the censor said to the publishing house—for example, in the case of a volume of poems—"This and this poem have to be taken out." Or, "this passage." And then they negotiated. Possibly they did sacrifice a poem, but then they said, "And now the others will appear." But they never printed a change that I had not accepted. A text was always printed the way I wanted it to be, or it wasn't printed. There was no interference with the text against any author's will. That's part of copyright law; that's how it was before.

The good people then said, "All right, it won't be printed." Certain journals in the west still offered an opportunity to publish, and then it came out there. But that was one of the strengths of professionalism. If the text is any good, it will still be good in ten years' time. Incidentally there were a lot of texts that were published five or ten years later— some of mine as well. And if it wasn't that good then it wasn't such a bad thing for it not to be published; in fact you might be glad, because then you're not held accountable for it. There were similar mechanisms in history as well, in all sorts of times, without state censorship.

State censorship was one thing, and the other was inner censorship; in other words, you saved the state censor work by anticipatory obedience. One of the most important tasks of all the good people here was to overcome repeatedly this inner censor. Because here I am sitting and writing, and as I'm writing a sentence, the inner censor says, "That won't pass." Now I have to decide whether the sentence is essential to the work. If so, it has to stand; it doesn't matter whether it's published or not. If you do this for a time, you break yourself of the habit of listening to an inner censor, because you learn to formulate something so that it is good and you can answer for it, so that it hits the target as well as possible. My contention is that the real merit of the people here is that they repeatedly overcame this inner censor, and when you've done that for a while, state censorship doesn't matter any more. Then the only thing that matters is the consistency of the text, which is part of its verisimilitude.

Isn't it controversial in the GDR to talk of the survival of literature? You mentioned the minister who has a duty to pastoral traditions, and to whom this duty is more important than contemporary political reality.

What the Protestant church here said to its ministers was something quite different. That was the point: "We have to concern ourselves with the care of souls. You are a sort of authority for people. They can ask your advice, you can comfort them. You have to take a position on this reality. You have to live in the present. You apply the old ideals to the present, not by stating that they're already present, but by stating that they are important: that's how you help people."

I don't think that that is the main impetus in writing, but it is one. Another is ambition. An actor wants to play well, a painter wants to paint well. You're always betting on posterity: namely, I'm doing it so well that it will survive. There are two components there: personal ambition, the vanity of not wanting to be forgotten; but also it is a service to people if I do it so well. Then, from a statistical point of view I have helped more people. That's the good old German choirmaster tradition. Whether there will be any people at all who want to receive it, of course, you don't know. You hope there will be, you bet on it as Pascal did on God. Pascal said that you simply can't know if there is a God; you can only bet there's one. Because I'm an atheist, I shall bet on my readers.

KARL MICKEL

February 16, 1991, East Berlin

Karl Mickel *(b. 1935) is a poet, translator, and playwright of Kirsch's genera-tion. He has been much more directly political than Kirsch. His early books of poetry include* Lobverse & Beschimpfungen *(1963) and* Vita nova mea/Mein neues Leben *(1966). He coedited with Adolf Endler the anthology* In diesem besseren Land *(1966), which was interpreted by official literary critics as at-tacking the principles of socialist realism and initiated the big "Lyrik debate" in 1966–67. In 1983 he received the National Prize, third class (III. Klasse). In 1986 he became a member of the Academy of the Arts. Since 1978 he has been teaching the recitation of verse at the Drama Institute in Berlin. His other books include* Studien an Goethe *(1968),* Nausikaa *(play, 1968),* Eisenzeit *(poetry, 1975),* Gelehretenrepublik *(essays, 1976), and* Lachmunds Freunde *(novel, 1991). His collected poems, essays, plays, a novel, an opera for radio, and a film screenplay have recently been published in six volumes (1990–93).*

What role will Marxism play here in the next few years?

Certainly anything that begins with "M" will not have an easy time of it. Such a panic has arisen that you can hardly utter a quiet and sensible word. The best thing about Marx was his analytical approach. For a long time now, it hasn't been possible to do history, sociology, any of the hu-manities, without including Marx's analytical and satirical approach in your way of thinking. It either happens consciously or unconsciously, and in this way Marx will survive and continue to exert an influence.

But not as a hope for a new society?

The first thing I see in Marx is an analysis of the status quo. But that is seen not as a state, but as a tendency, or more precisely as the changing of tendencies. Marx then makes a certain prognosis based on an analysis of this interplay. Of course, new tendencies and new material change the prognosis as well.

Has the role of Marxism changed in the last fifty years?

The theoretical level of what was proclaimed as Marxist philosophy was "vulgar economy." "Vulgar economy," the phrase that Marx invented for bourgeois economists, had repercussions for his imitators. It was often the same in teaching: students only got to know original literature in excerpts. The editions were there, no one was denied the right to read the whole text, but only extracts and key sentences were asked for. Most teaching was done on the basis of—secondary literature is too kind an expression—quaternary or octonary literature. I haven't spent any time with all that nonsense in the past few years. When I was younger I used to get annoyed by it. "Let no one complain about what is malicious, for that's what's powerful, whatever people tell you" (Goethe).

What do you make of the current talk of utopia?

The word "utopia" is excessive, but no one imagines that reality has hauled in the black utopias and that the black utopias have become reality. Ninety percent of the world's population, 4.5 billion people, are starving or living on the edge of starvation. Isn't that a black utopia that has become a reality? Has there ever been such a gross difference between prosperity and destitution in the history of the world? Isn't the weapons technology that has been developed and used—although everybody knows what devastating effects it has—a black utopia that has been realized?

But there's not much talk in the GDR of "black utopia."

That's right, because it was so obviously and ubiquitously realized in the past decades that it had disappeared from sight. Anyone who uses the word "utopia" has to define what concept he has in mind. The apocalyptic writings, the great negative social utopias, have not been integrated into the concept. I'm fifty-five years old now. When I was young, I could go swimming in the Elbe; twenty years ago, I could bathe in the Müggelsee over there. Now you can scarcely skate any more; dust dulls your skate blades in a very short time. Fifteen years ago the forests were still standing; we can say that we were there.

The socialist countries did little for the environment; it's imperiled by capitalism too, that's true, but under capitalism—with the press and other institutions—one can fight against the poisoning of the environment.

Environment is a euphemistic expression. We should say "destruction of the biosphere." The process has moved significantly towards a culmination in the last fifteen or twenty years. But the present situation is the consequence of two hundred years of industrial society. The countries that called themselves socialist latched on to and competed with the industrial societies seventy years ago. They imitated capitalism, and did it badly. They too have become part of the two-hundred-year history of industrialization. But what were the conditions under which this took place? Now people in the Soviet Union are discussing whether the collectivization of agriculture was the right thing. Hitler was at the door; that was plain then. The gigantic and backward land, if it wanted to survive, had to achieve the original accumulation of capital and the Industrial Revolution in two decades. These were revolutions for which England had needed three centuries, and North America two. The Russian way certainly wasn't the best, but without forced industrialization and the hasty collectivization of agriculture the Soviet Union would have had neither tanks nor their drivers to send against Hitler. For it was the farmers in their *kolkhozy* who learned on their tractors how to smash Hitler's troops under their caterpillar tracks.[1]

Does the demand that literature and art serve the purposes of enlightenment appeal to you?

You use the word "enlightenment" in the typological sense. I usually use it in the historical sense. Of course they are related. Up until a short time ago, I thought that the European Enlightenment had ended with Hegel, when dialectical thinking superseded compartmentalized thinking. Now I think that the European Enlightenment is ending today.

Philosophical thinking has become fashionable. People no longer think in concepts. The theoretical level descends to the practical level. The nineteenth century still maintained a distance between theory and practice. Reality that was contrary to reason was, according to Hegel, bad for reality. At that time, clarity of thought was always set up as a corrective for miserable practice. Nineteenth-century practice prepared, for example, the death of the forests today. The gap between theory and practice is closing in an obscurantist, shamanistic way. Even in heads that entertain noble thoughts.

What are the important consequences of state pressure on intellectuals?

A government that forbids its intellectuals to read Kafka programs its own end. You can't put pressure on the humanities and expect that, at the same time, a really high level of scientific and technological achievement will emerge. Time and again, laymen decided what book each specialist might read. The case could be instructive: all over the world, a deficit of humanist theory is confronted by a surplus of technological interest. We ought to put it to the test and see whether we do not euphorically transfigure the level of the sciences, and whether the discrepancy—even if it is not the result of state repression—causes permanent damage. It is then remarkable that this pressure had a destructive effect upon the stability of the country. In the long run it did not have a destructive effect on the arts; it produced a paradoxical effect. Let's stick to the example of Kafka. Of course, I managed to get copies of Kafka, but it was a nuisance getting them (the books had to be smuggled in, or you had to raid those parts of the library that were off limits). So I first read E. T. A. Hoffmann and had the leisure to ascertain Kafka's prehistory. That's the way aesthetic-historical thought is evoked.

You think that the pressure of the GDR regime on the arts was actually not bad?

I try to differentiate. The demands that were made were for the most part simply idiotic. Until quite late in the sixties, we were urgently required to create works that would so enchant the workers that they would increase productivity on the day after reading. But everyone could ignore this nonsense insofar as he was working for the sake of art and not for prizes, orders, and decorations. Being good and being praised are often two different things, not only in the GDR. Every modern society uses its means to be hostile to art.

GDR writers certainly experienced their own importance. In West Germany and in the USA it is certainly not the case that an artist or a writer has this experience.

That's probably true. Authors seldom suffered from feelings of inferiority here. The citizens of the GDR read a lot of good things, because there was a lack of bad stuff as well. The price of books is part of cultural policy. Books were subsidized. Students could buy volumes of the classics for five marks, or Reclam paperbacks for two to four marks, and they could build up a library early on.

Ulbricht—to put it in somewhat exaggerated form—was the high school teacher on the throne: the physiognomical likeness to [Emil] Jannings's Professor Unrath (in the Dietrich film, *The Blue Angel*) was astonishing. The sentence "There must be Art" is part of political skillfulness. The maxim comes out of the German labor movement, from social democracy. German printers were highly educated people. In my younger years, I was standing next to a typesetter who was able to judge the books that he was setting, and who, of his own accord, paid attention to the aesthetics of the book. A German metalworker or woodworker who was a member of a union had a solid personal library, eighty to a hundred volumes. That was a lot for that time. The educated German craftsman—and there were such people before 1933. The traditions were adopted here, but they were trivialized. The noble aim that every East German citizen should have his Goethe not only in the bookcase, but in his head as well, was reduced to the simple formula, "Faust's last words proclaim the GDR." It often took me a whole semester to make clear to my students that this is a lot of nonsense, and that they had to start to open their eyes and read what was actually written. But even the classical bourgeois literary studies of the nineteenth century had already simplified Goethe and made him tedious. Platitudes, too, have their traditions.

Is there actually a process of self-examination going on at the moment?

With every line that you write you are interrogating yourself and the world. If you had to do that outside your writing as well, your poetic existence would be unsuccessful anyway, because what someone writes down and doesn't toss into the wastepaper basket is his clearest thinking.

In your opinion the mistakes lie not so much in the intellectual arena as in the literary or the political?

At the beginning of *Dichtung und Wahrheit,* Goethe says, "Anyone born ten years earlier or ten years later, could, as far as his education and his effect on the outside world are concerned, have been a completely different person." I experienced 1945, and I experienced 1990. I had, and still have, the opportunity to experience, observe, and represent the beginning and the end of a great social experiment. Pascal says that being a human being begins at the point when the generic example is brought, for the first time, into confusion by reason, and that is generally not the case before a person has reached the age of twenty. Each particular personal experience takes place in its own particular historical field. The poets who are about thirty now grew up behind the Wall. They experienced the pain of the world in their own persons exclusively, in the form of the repression practiced by the state here. They are being broken of this illusion now. My generation had to leave the illusions of 1945 behind. That was no small task, for at first it really seemed as though a society could emerge from a need that was fairly justly distributed, a society that would spare its members the day-in, day-out struggle for the fundamental necessities of life, that is, a society that would inaugurate freedom from earning a living. The fact of social mobility also yielded, in addition, palpably pleasant consequences. Under the old system, I would never have been able to go to the university, but then at the university I was required not to apply what I had learned about social analysis from Marx to domestic customs and traditions. I was in high school from 1949 to 1953. At that time, the old high school teachers were still teaching—Nazis too. Three pupils out of thirty came from working-class homes and of course we were oppressed. If I wanted to get a B, I had to do A work. Later on, officially socialist-oriented teachers repressed the teenagers' independent or otherwise unruly thoughts. My children survived that. Things like that teach you to be skeptical. And this skepticism is, I think, specific to a particular generation. It is the root of my aestheticism, which, banished into strict art forms, was able to flourish and reach a just verdict.

RENATE FEYL

February 18, 1991, East Berlin

Renate Feyl (b. 1944) studied philosophy and since 1970 has lived in Berlin. Among her novels are Bau mir eine Brücke *(1972),* Idylle mit Professor *(1986), and* Ausharren im Paradies *(1992). In 1981 she published* Der lautlose Aufbruch: Frauen in der Wissenschaft. *She published another historical examination of sexist resistance to educated women,* Sein ist der Weib, denken der Mann *(1991).*

It is not immediately apparent why the Writers' Union was such an important institution.

So many people called themselves writers here, but they were merely literary functionaries. We who wrote were the exceptions. You've always got to bear in mind the fact that literature was an administrative business. People like Henninger, who was also a member of the Writers' Union, were only the chief administrators.[1] Every head reader, every head of a publishing house, was a member of the Writers' Union. At the end it had become a ridiculous organization.

Is it true that the main advantage of membership was the possibility of travel?

The role of the union did change considerably in the course of its existence. At first it was a forum for meeting, a chance to talk to one another, to discuss problems in your work. Then in 1961, when the Wall was built, the union was important insofar as there was no real public in the country. The newspapers were subject to total censorship. They only contained reports of successes and permanent untruths. Everybody experienced a different reality from what was reflected in the newspapers, so that the union was a small form of publicity behind closed doors. A lot of people had hoped that their colleagues would show solidarity when a book was forbidden. This happened now and again. From the beginning of the seventies, the union became more and more of a travel agency. If you got an invitation to give a reading or a talk abroad, you went to the union, and the union checked up to see whether you could go or not. It was a selection process and was subject to political evaluation.

I could see that because I was never in the party, and so no one was able to force me to obey party discipline. For that reason, I wasn't allowed to travel at first. When I received an invitation to the Hoechst Club in Frankfurt am Main, they told me directly that there were some former Harvard students there, and I had just written *Bilder ohne Rahmen* [Pictures without frames], a series of conversations with descendants of famous German scientists.[2] Some of them were members of the club, and I was told straight out: "You're not going there to talk with them. Hermann Kant hasn't been there yet, and he's the one who's sent first, to sniff out the atmosphere, and, if it isn't anticommunist, then we'll think about whether you can go there or not." That's a bit of unwritten history that we experienced. The Executive Committee of the Writers' Union, of course, had quite different opportunities for travel from those available to an ordinary member. You also have to realize that the union was filled predominantly with members of the SED. They still had a party committee and supported their own people especially. If you had a license—say, in a Western publishing house—it was harder to reject you, because the GDR wanted to earn money from royalties. The more editions you had in the west, the more the copyright bureau was able to fulfill its hard currency plan: we received our payments in East German money, whereas the state received payment in foreign currency. The cry for foreign currency grew louder and louder in the mid seventies. As we now know, they had sold the whole country to get foreign currency. The art treasures, morality, ideology, everything sold. People who didn't have a Western publisher behind them had very poor chances of traveling. The authorities simply refused, or didn't respond to applications to travel.

Later, at the beginning of the eighties, there was the so-called passport, or visa: a six-month or a full-year visa. Incidentally, the members of the Academy of the Arts generally had a full-year visa, that was simply a part of their function. They didn't need to go to the union and apply for a full-year visa; it was part of the honor of being a member of the Academy of the Arts. The state tried to differentiate the bestowal of privileges, because privileges were an instrument of power. In this way—by staggering privileges—they tried to prevent any sort of solidarity from arising among writers. There were writers who had a so-called permanent visa. That was the greatest of good fortune. They could go back and forth, with or without their families. A large number of privileged writers and state bigwigs had one of the full-year visas; at the end, it was understood that they would have one, even if nothing was said about it.

They were allowed to travel with their families?

I can't say for certain now that they could, but I know colleagues who traveled abroad with their families. Then there were some who did not get passports from the Writers' Union, but from another institution. There was a mishmash in the union. The union was of no use to the serious writer who didn't want to travel but wanted to write books, because the union was not a publisher. If it had been a publisher it would have had a really interesting and important function. Then there was a third point that made the union attractive: fellowships. Today, anyone who never had a fellowship from the union during all those years is a person of special integrity. He or she doesn't need to say "thank you" to anyone. That's an especially good feeling. But there are a whole lot of writers who regularly had fellowships. There was a fellowship committee that made decisions according to social requirements. But we also know that the Executive Committee, together with Herr [Klaus] Höpcke—who was the person in the Ministry of Culture responsible for book-publication permits [i.e., for censorship policy]—set the limits on editions.[3] The people on the Executive Committee had no material needs, and yet, in spite of that, we know that fellowships also flowed in their direction. It was just that the Executive Committee was not controlled by the fellowships committee of the union. That was the way the whole state operated.

No one could control the Politburo either. They could do what they wanted. All this was done under the pretext that this was the most democratic country in German history. It was an edifice of lies and deception. A lot of people had been aware for many years of this prison of lies in which we were forced to live and turned away from it all and took a different path in literature, the inner path that lay beyond all prescription. Those were writers who had a great reputation in their own country and who were thanked for not illustrating the prescribed themes—for example, the history of the GDR. For the state ideologists wanted to establish an independent national feeling here. And for that they needed the necessary literature. Anyone who wrote that literature earned a lot of money, received national prizes, got all the decorations and fame as well. The fame that a few GDR colleagues also enjoyed abroad was created here by the party. But that's another story. The party arranged for anyone who made an appearance in support of them to receive the appropriate publicity. That was a really diabolical mechanism. Whether or not these people could write didn't matter. They were the representatives of official socialist literature. In spite of their large editions, they did not have the fundamental importance that emanates from the word, and that is important for a dictatorship—and that can undermine a dictatorship.

There were also writers who quite consciously went their own way and who wrote for years under the harshest conditions of a market economy and had to live by it. They got no fellowships, no state funding, no large editions. They were only published so that the authorities could say to foreign countries that "the GDR is a free country." A few writers were published to serve as an alibi. It was a very difficult mechanism. In principle, this is the way it worked. Everyone, no matter at what level, felt the prescribed dualism in which we had to live: being, on the one hand, a private person who thinks, feels, and talks, as he feels within himself; and being, on the other, an official person who has to watch out when he says something in public, who has to be afraid that, if he says something wrong, he'll have difficulties, or even possibly be sent to prison. It didn't matter whether he was in the party or not. The population of the GDR is very devoted to those who wrote the many courageous words that were spoken at readings. At the end, all we had left were conversations in the form of readings, because the media was subject to censorship. For ten years, I wasn't able to publish anything in a newspaper. That was closed to me. So we used readings to produce a bit of publicity, and that has not been forgotten.

That was a very undignified situation for the individual. And that's my thesis: that suddenly a consensus arose from within, that this undignified system, this prison of lies, should be burst open. That's how the events of October came about. Everyone took part in them: a party member helped to topple the Politburo just as much as an admitted dissident. It was actually a deeply felt consensus, which came out of the people. Forty years is long enough to have to live like that. For that reason the explosion was a peaceful one because everyone thought the same. Everybody felt this contradiction, this dualism, and everyone said: "We have to shake this off. We have nothing more to lose. We no longer want to live the way we used to." You can't go on living against the truth for forty years. Your strength runs out. That's how the events of October and November came about.

Who are the writers who preserved their integrity?

Well, there are a lot of them; for example, Günter de Bruyn, Heinz Czechowski, Juri Koch, Horst Drescher; a whole lot of writers from Halle; Erich Loest, from Leipzig—but he was forced out later.[4] He wrote a very courageous book, *Es geht seinen Gang* [It goes on]. There are people who quite consistently went their own way. The dissidents who have been made famous by the East were state-recognized dissidents with a full-year visa or a permanent visa. They all had privileges, whereas someone like Lutz Rathenow[5] was able to set foot on Western soil for the first time only after the collapse of the Wall. He simply wasn't a state-recognized dissident. You also have to realize that a whole lot of writers earned a lot of money because of the partition of Germany. Of course today they regret that the Wall is gone. They all have to come to terms with that themselves. I'm talking about those writers in the country who tried to create a public in the face of the lack of a public and who tried over and over again, completely individualistically and subjectively and in full knowledge of the risk, to say what they thought. Think of the former GDR as an aquarium. The surface of the water is perfectly motionless and quiet, but beneath this surface, beneath what is official, there was an immense, diverse life. Today the trade union libraries in the factories are for the most part in shreds; but formerly they had libraries, and they invited writers, because for once they wanted to listen to a different way of thinking. People would come after work simply to listen to someone who would spread a little bit of inner feeling, who said what he thought, who had the courage to do that. It was courageous too to say those things in closed meetings.

Do you recognize actual advantages in the GDR literary system?

You could work without being under pressure from the market. In fact publishers would say to us, "Write slowly, save the woods, don't use so much paper, write something fundamental." This wasn't due to virtue but to necessity, because there was a constant lack of paper. That's why a lot of publishers took two to three years to produce a book. So you were able to go into archives and libraries, make yourself knowledgeable, do precise research—something that's important for historical themes and for which the West German readers were grateful.

If you were writing a book slowly, was that also because your personal overhead was low?

Yes, if you were paying thirty-eight marks for two rooms or ninety-eight marks for a four-room apartment, then you could afford to write slowly. The rents were extremely low, but the deterioration of East German buildings was very far advanced, as we are now seeing. The cost of living for an author, without special needs, was manageable. You could manage for two years, and if perhaps you got a new edition of an old title, you could manage to live. But you still needed a lot of idealism, because you always saw that the state bigwigs got an edition of one hundred thousand for novels and books that the state wanted. I came out with a first edition of ten thousand; that was the normal figure. The books were gone in four or five days, and then two years later—according to plan—there was another edition.

What happened to the books that were not wanted by the state?

In my case, it was difficult when the literary policeman, Höpcke, banned a book of mine, the satire *Unser aller Mann* [The man for all of us], with the observation, "We can't use laughter like this at the moment." I had some hard years then. Nobody showed any solidarity with me—on the contrary. Expert opinions were sought on this book. One of the experts and Höpcke himself are still on the Central Committee of PEN to this day and pretend to know nothing about censorship measures. But I think the time will come when questions will be asked.

How will that happen?

I am one of the very few GDR writers who do not mourn the loss of a socialist utopia. For this reason I left the PEN Central Committee a week ago, because I said to myself that the eighty members want to leave everything as it was. I am pleading for the dissolution and reconstitution of the committee. Censors, expert witnesses, former Stalinists, and the people who published hymns to Mielke and his Chekists are all on the committee.[6] We have to beware that these people do not pretend to have been the defenders of intellectual freedom in the old GDR system: they did too little to oppose the state-ordered censorship. I can't remember that it ever passed a resolution against the decisions of Hager, or Joachim Herrmann, a member of the Politburo responsible for ideology and literature.[7] Their ideological verdicts and the censorship measures that they ordered hastened the intellectual desolation in the country. When people today say that the GDR-PEN was more active in foreign policy than in domestic affairs, that's true enough; but I can't recall that they ever passed a resolution against Afghanistan. It's the same party group getting together now as it was then. The party group always met before conferences and discussions. But there has to be a radical discussion about the past everywhere, and that includes the PEN Central Committee.

The disappointment expressed by GDR intellectuals now sets them at odds with the feelings of working-class GDR citizens.

You have to remember that the overwhelming majority of people here were imprisoned. My mother was not allowed to go to the funeral of her mother in Stuttgart in 1968. She didn't even get an answer from the state committee as to why they had refused her a visa. Six months later her father died in Stuttgart. She applied again and wasn't allowed to go to his funeral either. Half a year later my mother died of sorrow: she couldn't take it spiritually. Yes, and I grew up hearing the claim that this was the most humanistic system that history had produced and absolutely the acme of human development. A woman like my mother took, of course, a different view of socialism from that of a lot of privileged writers who had an annual visa and could travel back and forth after 1961. You mustn't forget: people here had different experiences of socialism. Some had resisted the Wall, some had leaned on it. Now that it's gone, both groups have lost their security.

• • •

Have women in the intellectual fields been more affected by unemployment?

Women in the scholarly professions were mainly involved in the lower echelons. The man, as the boss, belonged to the advance guard of the spirit, and the woman, as his assistant, to the infantry. Take the social science areas, today they are called the humanities. They were evaluated and dissolved because they fulfilled, first and foremost, not a scientific but a propagandistic function. It was precisely in these areas of the social sciences that women were employed, because they were supposed to be able to function better than other people on account of their social dependency. So in these areas women were preferred as associates. Now these areas are being dissolved, and it's like everywhere else: first the associate goes and finally the boss, so the women go first and finally the man as the boss. In addition there is the fact that the whole middle management of scholarship was predominantly male. They had possibilities, through the party, of traveling abroad to take part in foreign conferences; they had international contacts. This wasn't possible for their associates in subordinate positions. An associate in a scholarly institute could not correspond with America without her boss's permission, let alone publish something in a Western periodical. She couldn't just get up and go to an international conference. That was something that enhanced your prestige, and the boss wangled it for himself. If anybody went, then it was the boss. Women in scholarship were overwhelmingly in the service area, and there were far too many employees in that area. Now the whole area is being dissolved, and women are the first to go.

What can be expected from women authors now? Have they been especially affected by the revolution?

Yes, it affects women authors in particular. It doesn't affect me, because I always had themes that I sought in German history and not in GDR reality. Long before the revolution, I began a novel about the downfall of the GDR on the level of a family. Fortunately my books are not written in the language that used to be written here. The lifeless, arid, written-out journalistic German does not, in my estimation, belong in literature. I consciously opposed it with a different language that was reminiscent of the old German vocabulary, which is much more sensual and full of images than the current profanation that we experience every day as language. To this extent, literature was always a force in the art of language, in the diversity of language, in the wealth of images in language.

I began this new novel with the same inner feeling with which I ended it: that is, that the individual stands for nothing in socialism, and that the practice of socialism is inhuman and profoundly contemptuous of humanity. I knew that something like this would not be published. That's why I didn't sign a contract in the GDR period, although I was offered one. But it was an offer that involved censorship. They said, "You complete the work, and we'll decide what we'll publish and what we won't." I couldn't accept something like that after my experiences of forbidden satire.

It's difficult for female authors who didn't have a publisher, or whose publisher was in the process of being liquidated here, and who did not find their own language and their own view of the world, but for whom it was enough to depict what was there, or what was asked for. Or for women writers who consciously accepted the prescribed view of the world as a wall against which they could scratch themselves and in front of which they could start their honeymoon with the censor. The motive for a lot of people was, "Where there's a prohibition, write against it." That's the way you could be totally creative under repression, by always struggling against prohibition, against the censor, and that always garnered the unofficial respect and recognition of the readers. That's the way you make a name for yourself when there is no freedom. Now suddenly the taboo is no longer there, now we have been released into freedom and we have to reorient ourselves, and, for many people, that came as such a surprise that they are still almost speechlessly confronting the historical events. They are still looking.

Do GDR authors, though, have a special subject now?

The experience with a dictatorship is something you can introduce into literature. For the German-speaking area too, and especially for anyone who has lived here under a dictatorship for forty years. That's something that only the former inhabitants of the GDR know. That's something you can make the most of: the intellectual damage that dictatorship does, how it warps the individual, how it demeans one, how it makes one into a hero or a liar, how it forces one to make compromises. All those are themes for great literature that has a significance far beyond the narrow boundaries of the GDR. When the library of the Writers' Union was broken up in the summer, I got a few books that I had never seen before—because I had not been aware of them—about scientific communism, about the picture of the personality up to the year 2000, about the strategies of scientific socialism, etc. At the time, I quite consciously refused to pay any attention to all the works of our state philosophers, because I knew that they did not agree with what I felt and with reality: the books are simply ideological embellishments and prescribed success reports. Those works are now going into the archives. Future historians will use them to find out what life felt like. But that will be another lie. We, as authors, therefore, have to cling to the unwritten truth that represents the true history and so contribute to the necessary coming to terms with the past. What is unsaid and unpublished that determines the actually existent everyday life under socialism has to be made public in order to describe the dictatorship with its repulsive effects on man, nature, the economy, and morality. This process of the destruction of the individual has to be shown, the evils of socialism have to be demonstrated ad hominem. This is a very big task for literature, and it has to mature, it can't come about tomorrow. It will take years, but it will come.

RICHARD PIETRASS

February 11, 1991, West Berlin

Richard Pietrass (b. 1946) studied clinical psychology at the Humboldt University from 1968 to 1972. He is a poet and translator who edits a well-known literary magazine, Litfass. From 1975 to 1978 he edited the poetry section of the magazine Temperamente; from 1977 to 1979 he edited the series Poesiealbum. He has published several volumes of poetry: Notausgang (1980); Freiheitsmuseum (1982); Spielball (1987); a volume of selected poems, Was mir zum Glück fehlt (1989); and Weltkind (1990).

You were in the Writers' Union. What advantages did that provide you?

First of all, I could engage in a certain kind of communication. There were simple opportunities to see colleagues there from time to time. Even if it was incidental, you could discuss something, make a date, and also have an argument there and then. There were phases too when the meetings were extremely spirited. I remember the Biermann affair and the last weeks before the collapse of the GDR, when—under the pressure of the mass exodus via Hungary and Czechoslovakia—the grassroots members of the union demanded that an open letter be sent to the government demanding that the authorities change their disastrous attitude. The leaders of the union tried to block this demand. The party members, in particular, knew what the attitude would be and tried to calm things down.

In addition to the guard members' meetings there were genre-specific gatherings. The dramatists met, the detective story writers, the translators. There was also a lyric poetry committee, but that was always coming into political conflict with the union functionaries. It was dissolved on several occasions and not re-formed for a long time. If we were able to do anything in the union, I guess we got some promising things started. Unfortunately, it just as often came to blows.

The last thing to mention is the social component. For instance, the union was in a position to give out fellowships that were decided on by a committee. In the ten years that I was a member, I applied once for one of these fellowships and got it. Incidentally, I only applied because someone had given me the tip that there was still some money there, which would otherwise go begging. At that time my ambition was still to live by my own efforts.

How much money was involved?

One thousand marks a month for a year: that corresponded to the average income in the GDR. I felt as if money had been showered on me, and I tried to save some for later. There was also a social committee. This took care, for example, of colleagues who had fallen on hard times because of illness or other circumstances beyond their control and was able to help them out. In addition to that, there were health spas and working and recreational retreats in establishments that belonged either to the union or the trade unions—fringe benefits that, like summer camps for children, were otherwise given to the workers by their own firms. The union also tried to help in questions of housing—with varying success.

I should also mention what has been described as the main privilege of writers and artists: towards the end, the union's main function was that of a travel agency that got you passports and visas. With the exception of a few people who had permanent passports, you always had to make an application. For example, if you were invited to give a reading in Vienna, that had to be decided on by the central secretariat of the union and, behind the scenes, by the Stasi. About four out of five of my applications were granted, and at the end even about nine out of ten. Rejections came if the person sending the invitation was politically unacceptable or if the general political climate was disturbed. Of course, the invitee's position, or the extent to which you were currently being tolerated, also played a decisive role. I can remember four of my applications being rejected. All in all, not a very dignified process, but I had learned to live with it and thought that there were more important things in life.

To what extent is it possible to talk of the union's independence?

Not at all. Even in our area, the SED took care to stay in control—as inconspicuously as possible, but often enough in a quite brutally public fashion. This control function that they called a "leading role" revealed itself by the fact that, among other things, the party group always met immediately prior to the members' meeting or the official start of the conference. As the self-appointed advance guard, they rehearsed the meeting in advance; they discussed what problems could arise and how they could, should, and would be faced so as to avoid their being given a dangerous emphasis, and also to see that they were diverted and channeled in the way they wanted. As one who didn't belong to any party—and still doesn't—I found this rigged game highly unsatisfactory and paternalistic.

You spoke of the liberalization of travel. Did that only affect writers?

Not only. A general liberalization began in the second half of the eighties. The number of those who then had the opportunity to visit their relatives in the west—admittedly for strictly defined, but sometimes carelessly scrutinized, family reasons—soon ran into millions. I think there were four or five million. That already marked substantial progress, even if it was questionable progress, because it excluded those who had no relatives and those who had access to so-called secret information. Five years previously, the number of approvals was on the order of one hundred thousand. So you see it had multiplied, and I think that it would have gone on getting larger, though the hopes that the government attached to these steps were not fulfilled. The total number of dissatisfied people did not grow smaller. For the very few it was enough that they could travel to the west; most people wanted to live like their relatives.

What advantages did intellectuals, especially writers, have in working in the GDR?

It may sound paradoxical, but the main advantage was the imperfection of the system. Willy-nilly, it provided us with a real task: to press ahead with improvements. Thus the deficiencies became a challenge, a productive incentive. The lack of personal freedoms spurred you on to contribute to the general emancipation. The fact that there was no press worthy of the name gave critical literature the chance to compensate for it, and so gain in significance. This admittedly abnormal situation gave us writers a feeling of importance. That's something that intellectuals in the West do not experience. There you need best sellers that are created by advertising. Here it was enough if there were a few unpleasant truths in a book for it to make its way.

Did you really believe in an ideal socialism?

No, but in the idea of a more just society. I thought it would be more just if the distinctions between rich and poor were not so great, if there were a redistribution of wealth. At the end this system was pretty ineffective, but it was pleasant not to see any beggars and to have hardly anyone to envy.

Did you think that your work would lead to a more just society?

Yes, I did entertain the feeling that we could get closer to it. I wanted to make my little contribution.

How would you describe that?

In my poems—not in every one of them; I'm looking at them as a whole—I constantly deal with the overcoming of taboos, I mean with a larger breathing space, more room for movement and action: an increase in freedom. In several of my poems, I take a stand for the individual, the underdog, who is in danger of being pushed to the very edge of society. In our collective society, it was important not to disregard him and to defend his dignity. The recognition that everyone has a right to happiness is already an effort on behalf of justice.

It's difficult for me to understand how you could believe in a just society when so little justice was to be seen. So much of life here was under surveillance that justice hardly seems to have been an issue.

You mustn't paint yourself a false picture. We weren't constantly aware of feelings of injustice that had been suffered, or of a lack of the rule of law. We only came up against them from time to time. In between, we lived as people do in other countries, had happy experiences, a normal life. It was similar with the limits of our own potential for development. We human beings have the gift of forgetting injustice and unhappiness, of repressing it, or making everything seem relative. The latter seems important to me, because it forces you to look in two directions. And in this way, you become conscious of the fact that while many people live under a luckier star, there are worse dictatorships. Because of that, you learn how to make a realistic evaluation of your own situation.

And then there was the belief that the system could be reformed, the possibility of improving it step by step. The majority of intellectuals were—like me—opposed to getting rid of it, but supported efforts to democratize it gradually.

What future do you see for GDR writers?

The majority of us will have to accept our new insignificance. Only a fraction of us will continue to play roles comparable to the ones we've had until now. Most of us will be forced to look for steady jobs to make a living. A very few will find one.

About the function of literature: the pedagogical role of literature was actually unimportant for your generation?

That literature has to be an instrument of popular education, the pedagogical handmaiden of politics, was an idea espoused by communist politicians. I think that literature has, or can have, different functions that nevertheless go beyond mere entertainment or mere work with language. What seems important to me is to reach the feelings of the individual, to sensitize him and help him, quite subtly, evaluate his own existence. After all, we do also learn directly from life, through our social contacts, to evaluate our situation. But not everyone is communicative, and a lot of people expand their knowledge of other people's lives by reading, enhanced by form, style, and original thought. That would be the existential side of literature. Its effect: identification and polarization.

Then I see another point of view: that it is an addition to historiography. For example, if you read Dickens's novels, you learn a lot about the England of the nineteenth century. In addition to this documentary and social historical aspect, there is also the moral authority: when literature performs the office of judge and evaluates the deeds and misdeeds of rulers and the ruled, recent ones and those of the distant past. If writers look into the future, they assume the role of prophet and give Cassandra-like warnings. They do not always preach to deaf ears. If the poet's arrows are skillfully cut, they go farther beneath the skin than the journalist's, even if the latter does reach more people.

If you live in a society in which literature is so important, are you not constantly tempted to make compromises and avert your eyes from the terrible things to continue working?

You're right. But that's not only true of literature. Everyone who did his job, and who looked at one thing and not another, behaved like that. I, too, averted my eyes from a lot of things, but at least I pointed a finger at others. Anyone who wanted to take on all the evils at once would have blocked himself, would have been unable to say anything convincing and would probably have succumbed, in the conflict, as someone who had run politically amok. That's probably what most people thought. Some, like Günter de Bruyn and Christoph Hein, opposed the censor, while someone else might write against a taboo but say that something else was "not his topic." Anyone who wanted to remain a writer had to preserve the minimal conditions for his or her work somehow or other. Only the absolute moralist did not weigh things that way, and went straight to prison. The moralist should certainly be admired for courage, but it wasn't absolutely necessary to go behind bars in order to create an effect. The zone of decency began before that.

• • •

Is it difficult for you personally to know which direction your work should now take?

Yes. For one thing, I lack inner peace. I haven't recovered my balance since autumn 1989. I prefer to write from a sovereign attitude, from an insight that I have gained into conditions. On the other hand, I feel a lack of competence vis-à-vis my West German colleagues. I first have to find my way around in the new circumstances, unless I want to write about my own uncertainty. Then I can begin right away. But if I don't want to express uncertainty, then I have to go on keeping quiet. I've been quiet for a year and a half. I refuse to continue simply doing my duty as a writer. They can't con me into a new form of state and order me to go on writing, smiling all the while. I refuse to do that. Reunification came too quickly. My silence is my caesura, the deserted no-man's-land of conflicting feelings.

HELGA SCHUBERT

September 18, 1990, Neu Meteln

Helga Schubert *(b. 1940) is a fiction writer whose most recent book is* Judas-frauen *(1990), a collection of stories and sketches based on women who denounced their friends and neighbors during the Nazi era. She joined the Writers' Union in 1975. Before 1977 she worked as a psychotherapist and medical psychologist. Her first collection of stories,* Lauter Leben, *appeared in the GDR in 1975; another collection,* Das verbotene Zimmer, *appeared in 1984; and in 1985,* Anna kann Deutsch: Geschichten von Frauen. *She has also written radio plays, children's books, and journalism. She lives with her husband in Berlin and Neu Meteln.*

Were you a member of the Writers' Union?

Yes, I was a candidate for the Writers' Union in 1975 and have been a member since 1976, under the sponsorship of both Sarah Kirsch and the Aufbau Verlag. You always had to have two sponsors.

What were the advantages of membership?

It had two advantages for me when I joined. I was still employed full-time, and it was compulsory for us to work. I was between marriages, and I simply couldn't have stopped working. I'm a psychologist. You couldn't just hand in your notice and say, "Now I'm a writer." Membership in the Writers' Union gave you the advantage of receiving a tax identification number. That gave you permission to work freelance.

That was the first advantage. The second was that, at the end of the seventies, candidates and members of the Writers' Union could apply to take a study or business trip to the West and the Federal Republic. More and more frequently since 1978, I was allowed to have a passport with an exit visa in it. Those were the two advantages for me.

Was it also possible to get money from the union?

No. Well, in principle there was a way. The union suggested to me, for example, that I should take up a special study at the Leipzig Institute for Literature that would have given me a three-year scholarship, or a different scholarship for a year. Or they would have given me a fellow-ship if I didn't earn anything, and if I'd applied for it, but they didn't suggest that to me. There was a special development committee. But I didn't apply, so I never got any money from the Writers' Union.

For two years now there has been provision for our old age. That's actually a third advantage. When I reached pensionable age, I would have received a larger pension than ordinary workers, but that was of no consequence to me because I had worked so long in the hospital and had always been in a supplementary old age pension plan there. So the pension that I received later, I earned because of my own contribu-tions, and, for this reason, the provision for my old age through the Writers' Union, though very pleasant, was not of consequence because I would have gotten it anyway. That's why I was also ready to forego it.

Do you think that any sort of relationship existed between pro-fessional structure and literature?

Yes, Herr State had a greater measure of control over us because of the professional structure; it was a control over graduated privileges. You were given more privileges, or you were given fewer, and you knew what level of privileges you were at. The privileges could take the form of receiving an exit visa for a week or one for ten years. You also knew which colleague had which privileges, and you knew what your own were. So that by means of this bestowal of privileges—a direct result of the Wall—the state had an influence on the attitude of writers.

And part of what a writer offers for publication is an attitude. That's to say, not only what one says in the media, in public, in readings, but also in what one offers for publication: one's attitude affects all that one writes. Because he has to ask himself, "Will I be able to publish this at all, within this state, if I want to hang on to my privileges?" It's a bit like Skinner and the rats. It affects everyone. It's like a veil that's thrown over you, and you know for certain that you live in the system. Whether you agree or not. But first and foremost, you are an object within the system.

Everyone had to decide for themselves to what extent they were subjects, and how far to try to exploit it, or to break through it or leave it. You could always leave the system. I could have left at any time after 1978, when I was first allowed to travel to the west. I could simply have stayed in the west. Other colleagues could even live over there and travel back and forth, like Jurek Becker or Monika Maron. There were even certain colleagues here who could travel back and forth with ease. But they all arranged it for themselves. And, I think, they were all clear about the fact that they felt some degree of gratitude to a misanthropic state for allowing them to do that, while, at the same time, knowing that it was basically a violation of human rights. But you were thankful that you were allowed to get out. It was a schizophrenic situation, and all the more so for intellectuals, who actually ought not to have accepted a dependence of this sort. If you wanted to remain here you had to accept this dependence, because otherwise you would have been sent away, as Biermann was.

In your opinion do intellectuals, and writers especially, have a duty to achieve independence?

Yes, of course, they must always regard the system in which they live in a critical—not a destructive but a skeptical—way. I firmly believe that. It is very difficult to do this in a dictatorship, because the state controls this criticism. It criticizes the criticism, and with much greater effect than in a democracy. In a democracy, the state would also like to be loved, but it does not regulate writers directly. That takes place through the market. That means that you can escape control more easily in a democracy. And a democratic state cannot disburse privileges in the same way a dictatorship can.

Did your generation write too uncritically?

Well now, I would have to think about those in my generation whom I take very seriously. I think that those who stayed in the GDR were, in a certain sense, not such strong opponents of the GDR, or else they kept quiet. Volker Braun belongs to my generation, and he is a convinced communist. He wrote critically, but with reference to the implementation of the communist idea. Jurek Becker, too, wrote critically—he's of my generation too. But he always criticized the implementation. Those who found the system basically dishonest either kept quiet or left the system.

I found the system basically dishonest; I'm not a communist. But in spite of that, I didn't write a fundamental criticism of the GDR system. I thought about the system the way Huxley and Orwell did. It would have been impossible to publish anything profoundly critical within the system, because what was published was controlled. I don't think that we in the GDR wrote critically enough if we stayed here. Someone like Monika Maron who criticized the system couldn't publish here. Independence from the state is a basic presupposition of art. You have to confront it.

But she was able to publish in the west, and so could you.

I did that too. Since 1975, I've published all my books in the west first. Of my three most important books, only the first was published in the GDR. It contained laconic, critical stories that actually only covered marginal phenomena. The real criticism of the system that appeared in my book *Das verbotene Zimmer*—that's where I treated earlier party positions ironically—has still not been published in the GDR.

Permission to publish that in the west . . .

That I got. I waited nine months for permission. I am the first GDR writer who received official permission to publish a book first in the west, and I had to accept the conditions that were imposed upon me. The most important condition was that the GDR should receive all the money from the west, and I would receive 1:1 in our currency—and that was worth nothing. I was allowed to change a small amount, not into western currency, but into purchase vouchers for the Inter-shops [consumer shops for goods purchasable only with western currency]. I was not allowed to sell the rights for the GDR. The GDR publisher was able to negotiate with me directly, because otherwise they would have had to pay the western publisher with western money. They allowed the book to be published abroad, outside the boundaries of the GDR, and they profited by it themselves. But they could be sure that the book would not enter the GDR, because books from the west were not admitted here.

And did the GDR authorities read the book?

No, they didn't even read it. They only said that they would allow it to be published abroad if I accepted all the conditions. I received a literary prize, the Fallada Prize, in the Federal Republic for *Das verbotene Zimmer*—it was about my generation—for the book with the greatest politicosocial commitment written in the German-speaking region. I accepted the prize and then applied for permission to travel to West Germany to receive it. I wasn't given permission, and it was then that the censorship authorities read the book for the first time and said that if I refused the prize, they would publish the book in the GDR. They wouldn't include certain stories: "Über die Partei" [About the party] isn't there; and "Mildernder Umstand" [Mitigating circumstance]—that's a death penalty for writing—isn't there; and "Ansichtskarten" [Picture post-cards] isn't there either, that's a story about people who leave and are always sending picture postcards. But if I accepted the prize, then I might as well stay in the west. In other words, they threatened me with expulsion if I accepted the prize. Faced with this blackmail, I refused the prize. The book immediately appeared in the GDR, and I received the Heinrich Mann Prize, awarded by the Academy of the Arts. Unambiguous black-mail. And then the academy said that they had no idea I had received the Fallada prize, and it had no connection with that, but the Heinrich Mann Prize was awarded simply on the basis of my work. But I don't know, I'm suspicious. I can't judge, because they all lied all the time. You don't know what are tactics and what are lies. I was never able to get to the bottom of it properly.

• • •

The controversy about *Was bleibt* raises the question of complicity.

I have asked myself the question, "Was I in part responsible for this dictatorship's being able to last so long in East Germany?" Formally, I can begin by saying that I had no part in it. As far as external features are concerned, I can state that I was never a member of the SED, never worked for the Stasi, and rejected any cooperation of this sort that was offered me. As far as external things go, I can say I never supported the system. I also never spoke differently from the way I thought. I didn't work in any opposition group. I never protested publicly. I never went on hunger strike. I never did any sabotage. I didn't protect the system, but I didn't try to topple it either. I didn't found a party, no leaflets. . . . I didn't remain silent, but I only voiced my criticism in approved internal groups. That's to say, I did express my opinion in the Writers' Union, and it was known. I also voted in 1979 against the expulsion of colleagues. At a public meeting, twenty people out of four hundred voted against expulsion. In 1979 it was a question of whether colleagues were to be expelled—Stefan Heym was one, then Rolf Schneider, Klaus Schlesinger, Seyppel, and Adolf Endler—in a public vote of the Berlin regional union.[1] I voted no. But I only expressed my opinion in those groups that were officially sanctioned. I also tried to gain support for my position—at the beginning. Later on, I didn't try any more because I knew that the SED always ensured that it had an absolute majority among the membership. That's to say that more than half of the members of the Berlin Writers' Union were members of the SED, and for that reason they were always able to discuss everything beforehand. There was a party group in the Writers' Union. They could discuss everything: candidates, resolutions, agenda. And when I found that out, I knew that any motion you made would only be symbolic and could never be passed because they were already organized against it.

But my part in the stabilization of the dictatorship consisted, as I look back on it, in my functioning as an alibi for the state, because I took advantage of the chance to travel and went abroad too. I worked twice in American universities and was a guest in other universities in Europe. I constantly met with marked surprise on the part of other scholars who always said, "You are actually a person who is not afraid, and you are someone who has a sense of humor. If people like you can live in that society, it can't be all that bad." And if you then said, "I'm just a court jester. It's part of the game in a dictatorship to keep court jesters, just to show that jests are possible. I'm fully aware of this role." Then they would say, "The very fact that you say that you're a court jester means that you are somewhat distanced from the role, and distance from a role means that you have freedom, and to have freedom means that things aren't so bad in a dictatorship." People often said to me, "But you're quite normal, are there others like you?" "Yes," I would reply, "there are others." And I said, "I'm a quite typical GDR woman. I can only do this because I fulfill my function in society."

But not a typical GDR writer?

I'm a quite atypical GDR writer. But that's because I never felt as though I belonged to the group of writers who played the game. I always oriented myself towards those who had gone to the west. I oriented myself on Monika Maron or on the work of Hans Joachim Schädlich. I always oriented myself on the people who really knew how to express their opinion. My colleagues were different. That's only now becoming clear to me, while we are talking. I didn't orient myself towards West German, Austrian, or Swiss colleagues but always towards former GDR people who had gone to the west. I felt as though I belonged to that group, although I have no close contacts with them and have never met them. Monika Maron and I met in January, but we have very infrequent contacts too. So I have almost no personal contacts with other writers, because I look upon writers as mirrors, and I am myself a mirror. My mirror does not want to be reflected in another mirror; one is enough.

We were forced to be close to Christa Wolf, because it was she who brought us to Neu Meteln. She and Gerhard lived across the way, and they asked us whether we would like to buy this house. Then after the houses were destroyed by fire, the contact ceased. That's something that fascinated me, but it was something that gave me a strange feeling. And I paid the penalty. She described me in *Sommerstück,* and that is precisely what I always wanted to avoid—being described by other writers—when I alone want to describe my world. But that was an experience that can happen to anybody. The publishers said it happened to Ingeborg Bachmann with Max Frisch.[2] You have to keep your own world at a distance from other writers.

You said that you were an exception . . .

Now, this year, several hundred people voted against me in the union. At the beginning of 1990 I made a motion that the SED (which meanwhile had become the PDS) should not hold its meetings in the Writers' Union any more, that they should go to the areas where they live. I said I regarded the Writers' Union as a cover organization for the SED, and I demanded that it should no longer meet there. We want a professional organization, and we only want to get together for professional reasons and not, as before, as a party group. I no longer intend, now that it's over, to be terrorized by them. But they all voted against it; they wanted the SED to go on meeting there. I also moved that we should collect our own passports and buy our own tickets—the Writers' Union used to buy our tickets—that we should do all this ourselves. We should go to the embassies and get our own visas—you still needed a visa at that time. Surely we could get our own visas stamped in our passports, we didn't need a Germanist with a doctorate to do that for us, I said. And we should give up our old age pension and not be treated better than the workers. Finally I was the only one against about four hundred.

It was then, at the beginning of 1990, that it became quite clear to me that the others had not been hypocritical. For years I thought that they just didn't trust themselves and were hypocritical when they kept their mouths shut. In the meantime I have learned that they really did take a different view of things than I did. I was very bitter when I realized that I had been so alone. I'm not reproaching my colleagues: it was my own naiveté, because I had no personal contact with them, and I overestimated their criticism of the system. That's apparent now.

I didn't really think carefully enough about which of the GDR writers who stayed here were good, because I wasn't sufficiently interested in the literature that was produced here—I have to be honest about that—because I was very distrustful of what was allowed to be published here. It couldn't be good—that was what I thought—because the state permits it. It can only be good if it asks fundamental questions about the system. I always thought that if a particular individual were really good then he would live in the west. I had a great contempt for all the people who lived here, myself included. And for years, I didn't want to live here any more. I tried to persuade my husband to leave. But I didn't succeed. He was far more hopeful than I was that the system would fall, and so he said that he'd stay. I thought, "I can't live all my life under a dictatorship, that won't work."

And so, at the end, I was no longer in any way identified with my surroundings here. I also stopped working as a psychologist in the counseling center in 1987, and, from that time on, I lived here totally unidentified with the country. Then I taught for two three-month periods in the USA. I was delighted at every reading I gave that took me outside the country. In literature I concentrated entirely upon the past. It was a question of getting out of the present. I did research in the court records of the Nazi period. In *Judasfrauen*, I tried to get out of my current existence and move back into what I was thinking about, what I was reading. I only identified with those people who lived outside the country, so that basically I was here only in body. That was my strategy for staying here from 1985 onwards perhaps. So that for me, what happened here is a terrific relief. It's the end of a nightmare for me. Since that time I haven't had any more thoughts of suicide, and my life has been reorganized in a completely positive way.

What role did historical material play in GDR literature in the past?

First of all, historical material is basically dangerous because it leads you out of a hermetically sealed present and makes it possible to compare the status quo with something else. That was the great opportunity for GDR literature: making comparisons by presenting historical facts. Not only having people from the past speak like people of today—that was done in comedies—but also by giving exact descriptions of earlier times so that, all at once, you notice that there are power structures that are similar or that can be overcome. In one way or another it is possible to diminish the authority of the present by describing historical facts. That's what I find to be the most essential thing.

That's why I think that, in a society in which people do not feel oppressed, the danger exists that they will become ahistorical. There was a lot that we were not allowed to compare—Nazism and Stalinism, for example. In a closed meeting, Stefan Hermlin demanded the death penalty for people who wanted to make such a comparison. That shows that heroes, and wonderful societies, and everything that we now have are fundamentally unique, and that every recourse to history is something that must be regarded with the utmost suspicion. For this reason it was an act of courage for every writer who stayed in the GDR to have recourse to history. There's always the hint, "Dear people, your time is limited; you are not unique."

• • •

Is it now time for writers to examine themselves?

I was very afraid of the dictatorship, and now I see this fear of all-embracing control was justified. But, in some circumstances, I also overestimated the danger. What I would now want to examine is whether I magnified the danger so that I shouldn't do *more* against it. The question I ask myself is not, "The values have all collapsed, how could it also happen that my values collapsed?" My problem is, "Where could you have said something earlier?" or, "Should you have gotten out earlier?" But that too is not the main problem. I don't think that now is a time of self-examination, because those who really supported the system have to show, in retrospect, that it wasn't as bad as all that and that they always did their best. Hermann Kant—I've just read this in a prepublication copy of *Konkret*—tries to say that he was always trying to educate the princes, Honecker and the others. That's a form of coming to terms: you did do the best you could, and so forth. The people like me who are now delighted that it's all over will get to the point where we will not write about the past so much. For the first time I will really write entirely about the present: namely, what is happening now as the systems are changing. I'm terribly interested in that.

Was the writer's relationship to the state a generational issue?

I always thought very carefully about what the risk was and then kept the risk very small, not because I was afraid, but as a result of calculating the risk. Yes, it was fear. These young people lived in attics in Prenzlauer Berg and thought: "Gee, I still haven't got anything. If I really go to prison now and get myself expelled, I can live a few streets away in West Berlin. If I'm famous enough perhaps I can get a passport and go back and forth, and then they won't arrest me but they'll throw me out." They were much more uninhibited. They also didn't have older children. I had a son who was at the university and a husband who was a professor there. I always thought, I'm doing my husband harm. The concerns that I, as a grown woman, had were different, because I went on working in my profession. I would have lost my job at the clinic. I would have done harm to my husband and my son and that would have meant everything . . .

. . . that was too much.

Well, perhaps it wasn't too much. I often think that it was good for me to stay here. I am a very spontaneous person. If I had been all on my own, perhaps I'd have taken some risks and I would have developed differently. This way it's better for me.

Better than being a single woman?

If I'd lived as a single woman, I would not have stayed here. Then I wouldn't have had all these experiences here. I'm thankful for that. One would never have experienced the relief of knowing what it's like when a dictatorship comes to an end, and when there are a million people on the street. And I was one of those who called for the demonstration. A week before November 4, 1989, I and four thousand other people in the Erlöserkirche (Church of the Redeemer)—there were two thousand people outside—took part in calling for the demonstration. At that time, it was still illegal. But I must say, I saw what it means when hundreds of thousands of people are on the streets. Staying here wasn't all in vain after all. There would have been one less than a million.

Do you think that the difference between your generation and the generation of the Prenzlauer Berg people has something to do with relationships to your fathers?

Uwe Kolbe and Papenfuss-Gorek, very good people, had fathers who were very close to the system here, or who even held positions of power, and there was Thomas Brasch as well. [Brasch's book] *Vor den Vätern sterben die Söhne* [The sons die before their fathers]—that was their attitude: you're powerful, and we kick the bucket. Or Katja Lange-Müller. Her mother is Inge Lange, the Politburo candidate. Very good people. Monika Maron is not the natural daughter of the minister of the interior, but she's still his stepdaughter. She didn't live in Prenzlauer Berg, but she counts as one of them. One practically counts as an insider because of one's family, and if you are opposed to the state you are at the same time against your father, and that's yet another power. My generation grew up more or less without fathers. Our fathers were soldiers, and, from the beginning, they were despised by the whole world as German soldiers. For a time they were even called fascist soldiers, a fascist army, even if they hadn't been in the SA or the SS. My father, for instance, was not in the SS, but he was in the SA and was also a student leader in the National Socialist Student Union. I also had to say to myself, "I am the daughter of a National Socialist jurist," and thus I had, so to speak, two different objects. I couldn't associate the state with my father, whom I didn't know. The people from Prenzlauer Berg, however, could identify their fathers with the state, and they knew both of them very very well. Because of this they were able to concentrate much harder. Many people in my generation had quite different objects, and it was impossible to identify National Socialism with Stalinism. That taboo was so strong, both in yourself and also objectively, that it provided a good precondition for writing, because as a result of it you were always forced to differentiate. But you couldn't really confront authority and your father, because he wasn't alive. And that also led to a glorification. Because I was fundamentally opposed to such glorification, I was only really able to confront Stalinism, because I didn't know the other.

You've said that you didn't have any friends who had a positive attitude toward the GDR state, but I can name many writers who did not wish for the state to fall.

Well, Christa Wolf brought us here to this village, visited us, asked us over. The initiative came from her, and I felt very honored by her interest. Otherwise I would never have approached her, because I looked up to her so respectfully—on her pedestal. And if I hadn't approached her, I wouldn't have unmasked her in the way I did. In my eyes she unmasked herself. I'd rather not elaborate on that in this interview. But I succeeded because of the proximity that she created; otherwise I would never have known it. I knew of course that she was a candidate for the Central Committee of the SED. I knew that she had always been a member of the SED and continued even after the fall of Honecker. I never regarded her as a dissident but as a significant writer, and it was only when I got close to her that I noticed that she was not writing a basic criticism of the system, and so, as far as I was concerned, she was on the other side.

She had positive feelings towards the state.

Well, she educated the princes. She talked to Honecker and then obtained the release of one person or another. That's a completely different attitude from asking yourself, "Isn't it really terrible for anyone who has done nothing to be in political detention?" and then to go to the world and say that. I mean, I didn't do it either. I'm not making a moral criticism of her. I simply took as a starting point your question about what writers might be thinking who had positive feelings towards the state. I am convinced she was only exploiting it, but on a different level and with other assumptions. In that sense, I do not consider her an intellectual—that's my assessment. Possibly she is more pragmatic, much more pragmatic than I, and because of that she is not really an *artist*. I make a distinction between writer and artist. Someone who writes essays can possibly be for me someone who sums up other people's thoughts, but artists are people who really expose themselves to reality and make their own summaries of it. She is not like that, because she is psychologically so stable that she does not constantly have to reassure herself by looking at reality, but can take other people's thoughts and, in spite of that, is not remote from reality herself. For that reason she is more of an essayist than an artist, and for that reason I found her less interesting when I got to know her.

· · ·

Can you describe the danger that arises for literature when newspapers become party bulletins?

There is a single danger, and that is didacticism—propaganda perhaps even more strongly than didacticism, but that's the direction it goes in. I looked on that as a temptation to which one may not succumb. In the GDR, things were organized in such a way that writers could apply for a postal number through the Writers' Union. Then you received permission from the postal customs authorities to receive books. The person sending the books from the west did not have to write the number on the package, because in any case every package was opened, and they could see that so-and-so was allowed to receive books. This led to my receiving books for other people and forwarding them. If I'm a writer and communicate something to my fellow citizens that they are not allowed to read in the newspapers, but which I can get hold of because of the privileges I enjoy—either by traveling or by importing books that they are not allowed to read—then, to all intents and purposes, I turn myself into a state-licensed disseminator of information.

If I now introduce Greek mythology and feminism into my *Kassandra,* as Christa Wolf then did, it is, for a lot of people, as if those were their own thoughts. But the fact that there's a collection of more than one hundred books on feminist literary scholarship was something the readers on the Alexanderplatz did not know. As a writer, you can be tempted to present what you've read as your own thoughts. At some point, you stopped making lists of references. Because people are not in a position to compare and do not have access to the whole spectrum of world scholarship, you could, as a GDR writer, create the impression that these were your own ideas that you were writing, and not just summaries. That's the second danger. And then, by means of the controlled criticism you could communicate to the reader the feeling of achievement that, on page thirty-one in the third paragraph, there was a critical sentence that would never have been found in the newspaper, and that the writer is so fantastically courageous that he feels confident enough to say it and risks putting his head into a noose. But the fact was that it was, of course, all calculated criticism . . . and then many readers' terrible disappointment: "Oh, so that wasn't narrated in a roundabout way, that was really the only criticism, and the writer is, in fact, really positively inclined towards the state." In this way a lot of GDR residents were disappointed after the so-called revolution and said the writers were not on their side as they had always thought they were.

The danger consists then of writers being held in too great esteem when they are only writing superficially.

Yes, yes. That's what I was saying. You may be superficially educated, but you are still the one-eyed man in the kingdom of the blind. But the people here were not blind, they had merely been forcibly blindfolded. Their ears were not stopped, because they could always listen to the radio. They could learn about things. But western newspapers could only be imported on your person. However, people increasingly followed discussions on television—you could watch the Bundestag sessions in West Germany. So people were already very well informed. A dictatorship tries, in any case, to bring about a coarsening of art, and also a coarsening in the reception of art. I'm absolutely convinced of that. What's happening now is not a coarsening of people by the market, but a differentiation of the satisfaction of their needs and of their needs themselves. That I find human. A development in differentiation is always a development towards a greater humanity.

CHRISTOPH HEIN

February 16, 1991, East Berlin

Christoph Hein *(b. 1944) is a very well-known playwright and novelist. He began working in the theater as a director's assistant in 1961 and later (1967– 71) studied dramaturgy in Leipzig and Berlin. Beginning in 1971 he worked as dramaturge and then in 1973 as house dramatist at the Volksbühne in Berlin. He left that theater in 1979 because fifteen of his pieces were not performed. In 1982 he published the novella* Der fremde Freund *and received the Heinrich Mann award of the Academy of the Arts. In 1983 his play* Die wahre Geschichte des Ah Q *was very well received by audiences and ignored by the GDR press. The novel* Horns Ende *appeared in 1985. In 1987 he held a much discussed talk against censorship at the Writers' Union congress. He is well known for his critical essays, which are collected in* Als Kind habe ich Stalin gesehen *(1989). In 1989 another novel,* Der Tangospieler, *appeared. On November 4, 1989, Hein spoke with Christa Wolf, Stefan Heym, and others at the mass demonstration at Alexanderplatz. His most recent novel is* Das Napoleon-Spiel *(1993). In 1994 he published* Exekutions eines Kalbes und andere Erzählungen.

I've just read your *Kein Seeweg nach Indien* [No passage to India] (1990), which I understood as a parable about the GDR as a utopian experiment.

The parable doesn't appeal to me all that much. In the piece you're talking about, I was asked by *Time* magazine to write something about GDR literature, and when I started it turned out to be journalistic rubbish. So then I thought, "I'll write a story that tells something about it," but—and that was the deeper reason—I thought that perhaps this is the proper cloak for it. The Columbus story can, perhaps, explain to the Americans something of what went on here, without its just being explained by the Wall, or the Stasi, or blood and force—the sort of patter that can explain anything, the Third World and things far removed that one has nothing to do with. There were things at work here that can't be explained just by blood and the Stasi. The story is meant as an aid to understanding, not a parable in the usual sense.

Is it not an analysis of circumstances in the former GDR?

But underlying your question there is a suggestion that, because of censorship in the GDR, authors wrote, or had to write, differently so as to get by the censor and publish. I certainly don't exclude that. But I think the important literature in the GDR is independent of that. *Kassandra,* for example. If Christa Wolf were to write it today, I do not think that she would write it differently, except that she is now ten years older. But the text came about independently of the GDR censors. Certainly there are a few—perhaps quite a number—of my own works that I would not have written, if there had been no GDR. One of the reasons for that is that I lived here. Life, the environment, and the political milieu are reflected in one's work. It's been the same for millennia. Even in Shakespeare I can prove certain things about the way England was governed. When he suddenly starts to write comedies, there are reasons for that in a change of policy. That's quite normal.

I do not think that I would change my works in any way, if I were to write them today. I am very sure that there's not a sentence there that would not have been written by me if there had been no censor, or that there's a sentence I wrote because there was one. When I was writing I was on my own. There was no censorship. That only began later when I took the work to the publisher and he needed to get permission to print it. But I was not ready to let the censor come on to my desk or into my head, so that even as I was writing I was thinking about censorship. Anyone who does that has, to all intents and purposes, already lost out and should, basically, be looking for another profession. It won't work in this one.

Many writers speak of an inner censor, which is why I was asking earlier about indirect literary genres, such as the parable.

I think that's a great problem and one that really existed. I tried to resist it, for I was of the opinion that if I did this I would indirectly be reacting to censorship, and my work would once again be determined by that censorship. It might mean that I could write some outrageous sentence because there is censorship. That seemed to me disastrous. I tried to avoid the two dangers that arise from censorship, not only not bowing to censorship—that doesn't take much; you don't do that—but also not writing something simply to provoke the censor. Anyway the bans came on their own. The fact was that censorship itself could only begin after the work was complete. Then I tried to set the area of my own productivity completely free from it. I was relatively unconcerned about how long it took for a piece or a book to appear. It usually took a few years, up to ten. A colleague of mine had to wait for twenty years until a piece of his appeared. That's the way it was. But I tried not to let this enter into my work.

I would like to return to the Columbus story, because the discovery of the New World might well be related to utopian socialist aspirations. GDR intellectuals often say now that they believed that the system could be improved, and in that sense they were utopians.

Yes, to that extent, I was a utopian. That's got nothing to do with the GDR. The GDR was certainly not a better world, but I cling to the idea now, as I did then, that humanity has got to work at making this a better world. It has no other choice; otherwise it will sink into barbarism. And quickly. The Enlightenment is already 250–300 years old. It has practically failed. If I abandon the idea of the Enlightenment, then we'll have barbarism the day after tomorrow. Utopia is not necessarily something that can be achieved, but it is a spur that may strengthen us a bit in our work. If I'm satisfied with things as they are, there'll be a relapse.

This is exactly what we experienced in the GDR. The state didn't die in the fall of 1989. It died earlier, because there was a total standstill and political equilibrium. People were satisfied. There were no innovations, not political, nor economic, nor—well, least of all—any cultural ones. There were no changes any more. That was the end. The moment a human community is satisfied with something, it's the end. A big corporation that doesn't innovate any more will be dead tomorrow. That's just as true of society and the state as it is of individuals. I couldn't work if I weren't dreaming about something.

Yes, but the opposite of utopianism need not be complacency. On the contrary, we may ask whether utopianism and idealism helped GDR intellectuals to be more patient with things as they were than they might have been if they had been more skeptical.

I understand what you mean, but I simply don't accept it, because a utopia that is not skeptical is not a utopia. It's just a lot of nonsense.

All right then, what does skepticism mean to writers and intellectuals?

What I said it does. I can't speak generally for writers and intellectuals in the GDR. Different people reacted very differently, just as they do in every country in the world. I think that the idea that I can have utopias without being critical of the existing society is impossible—or extremely foolish. I don't understand your objection. For me, utopia is an antiworld to the existing world. If I don't open up an antiworld, I leave the existing one untouched. To that extent, a skeptical attitude would be one that is fundamentally utopian. It tries to negate something that exists because it believes that there is something beyond it that cannot be reached, (that) would be really utopian, or else that can be reached but not be identical with what exists.

Did the intellectuals in the GDR, in the past few years, hope more for reform than for a revolution?

I can't answer for the intellectuals in the GDR.

And for yourself?

As far as I was concerned, it was over in 1968. When Prague was invaded there was no more hope of reform in this society. I believe that 1968 was the last time reform was possible. Gorbachev's reform in 1985 simply came too late. That's his catastrophe: he came twenty years too late. In 1985 there was no consensus for reform among the population of the socialist states. At that time they didn't want reform, they wanted an end. In 1968, there was still a consensus in all the socialist countries in favor of reform; there was a majority for reform. When the tanks appeared in Wenceslas Square, that was gone.[1]

The shock of 1968 was of course not the first, but it was the decisive one for all the socialist countries. Here once again was the great chance. It came from one of the socialist countries, not from outside. That was very important. Everything pointed to its being able to work. It could only be stopped by force.

So you believed twenty years ago that the state would collapse?

That the end would come as quickly as it did? No, I didn't foresee that. I was afraid the whole time that it would end in violence. The fact that it happened with so little violence, and so quickly, seems almost like a miracle to me. It's not necessarily a sign of the strength of the countermovement, but it does show how rotten the system was. I heard in a speech that the reason was that the real power of the state itself, the Stasi, etc., no longer believed in it. They had lost sight of the idea. In this way they paralyzed themselves. They had no goal. The counter-movement had a goal, but they, on the other hand, no longer had one.

Do you think it was an advantage for the GDR intellectuals to have been needed in society?

No, I spoke in detail about that at the Writers' Congress in 1987, in my speech about censorship. I drew attention to the dangers of this being "needed," for the significance that writers enjoyed was excessive. It was wrongly weighted. It also wasn't good for literature. I saw the danger and spoke about it then, and I feel much better now that these false poems are gone and literature has the weight it deserves: a smaller one—there's no question of that. There was also a substitute function that literature had to fulfill. I was always opposed to that, but the readers wanted it, because there were no newspapers. To give into that meant betraying literature, and that is a dilemma from which it is difficult to escape. But the writers and intellectuals did, more or less, manage to do their work during the past eight decades, and they paid the price. It was often quite a high one, if you think of Bulgakov.[2] To that extent they were significant and important, and there were a few functions that they could fulfill, and so these seven or eight decades of intellectual work were not entirely in vain. But it's not finished. Intellectuals worldwide still have a few jobs to do.

Can you explain this danger of "being needed" in more detail?

If you accept the role completely, what emerges is certainly not literature. That was one of the reasons why I kept on giving warnings at that time. For what you get then is something that is to be accepted morally and something that is good, but it is not literature. Literature and morality are two different concerns. There are outstanding writers who were morally worthless, and there are authors who were morally valuable individuals but who were no good as writers.

Where does this urge for morality come from?

I imagine that it has something to do with the nation. There are nations that place the highest value on morality and others that do not take it so seriously. The Germans place a very high value on it. For years

I thought that the positive hero was a GDR foible. I was very amused when I noticed that the West German readers were also saying, "What's happened to the positive?" Germans want something positive. There are other nations that don't have the need of it. The great Russian literature does without it entirely, and so does the French. In great American literature, too, it's not all that important if something is positive or not. The Germans, on the other hand, have a penchant for edifying literature. They hold it in high regard. It's very strange. The Germans always pick these passages out of the works of the great German writers. Just look at what the Germans like and revere in Goethe. Goethe is not an edifying writer, but there are passages in his works that are edifying. They don't qualify as great literature. The fact that, when looked at in the totality of his works, Goethe is a completely different, almost destructive, writer can be suppressed. Where is Shakespeare positive and edifying? Quite the contrary! The Germans want to have a moral literature.

There was a pressure from the populace that placed the writer on a pedestal. A pedestal is a terrible place to sit. You can't work there any longer. People wanted a figure like Christa Wolf, an identity figure. That wasn't possible in politics. The figures that the state put up were rejected, so they got themselves a writer. That's something that's really dreadful.

· · ·

Do you see a process of self-examination taking place among your colleagues?

I think the process is taking place, both privately and publicly, in a very lively fashion. That's normal too. When something comes to an end, whether it's a state, a society, or a family during a divorce, people take another look. There are huge mutual reproaches, and perhaps people think things over again for themselves. That's the way people end things—by taking another look back at them.

Is it important for the discussion to take place in public?

Yes, it is important. A state is a public concern, in contrast to a marriage. Another question would be in what form it takes place, but as with a divorce, good manners are sacrificed. Sounding rougher or false notes is part of the whole thing. That's normal.

Did you find the controversy about Christa Wolf disturbing?

No, it didn't disturb me. As I said, it's part of the whole thing, and journalists have their own rules of the game. The artistic director of a

West German theater wrote an amusing article in the *Süddeutsche Zeitung:* Christa Wolf had been overestimated for years, for decades, and she is being punished for that now. But it is clear that that wasn't Christa Wolf's problem, but the critics' problem, and that's something both strange and funny. But it is also completely normal.

You have said that artists and intellectuals should have reacted to the changes with a readiness to take risks and not with depression and fear, but you still see a lot of fear and depression, don't you?

Yes, but I make a distinction there. I fully understand that a large part of the population is depressed at the moment. The atmosphere in the GDR is extremely dangerous now; it is frightening. I have just read in *Der Spiegel* that the workers' consciousness is turning to reform. They are transfiguring the old GDR. A consciousness is arising—in the provinces more so than in Berlin—that people are longing for the old days, when there was a lot wrong, but when you had a place to live, and a job, and everything was secure—and now all these insecurities. I have the fullest understanding for these insecurities and these depressions.

I maintain only that intellectuals have no right to depression. An intellectual should regard a feeling of insecurity as an opportunity. I understand everyone who needs security. But an intellectual should know that security is something deadly and should also see in it an opportunity that is part of scholarly work or simply of thought as a whole. What I mean is: I say something just so as to be able immediately to call it into question. I do my own work in order to call it into question and don't just rub my belly and say how wonderful everything is. That is a very antiintellectual attitude.

You often said that you regarded your work as a chronicle. Is it a disadvantage for the chronicler not to be able easily to take up a firm position? You present a theme simply as it is, not as you would like it to be.

I think that the precise description of a condition has a tremendous revolutionary and explosive power within it. I once said, "The beloved who has been abandoned mourns a world in which there is no happiness, and in that there is already the dynamite for a new world." That is to say: the precise description of a condition is almost unbearable. Those were my experiences in the old GDR. It was not the description of a more beautiful world but the unembellished description of the existing one that made them angry. That was the explosive, and it did perhaps effect some change. But perhaps you understand something different by the term "chronicler" than I do. Brecht praises Homer a lot. He said that he was an outstanding chronicler. Even today you could, with Homer's help, put together a meal and carry it off, just as it was done in Homer's own day. It is his precision that he praises.

What you mean by "chronicle" has little to do with the precision that you see and hear on the street. When you talk about Kafka . . .

No, it does have something to do with it. There are sentences in Kafka where I know exactly that he has overheard them. I can prove it to you. Four years ago we published a book entitled *Kafkas amtliche Schriften* [Kafka's official writings]. Those are the things he wrote when he was working for the insurance institute. You would be astonished how congruent these official writings, this office junk, are with his literary work. It is totally turned around, reduced to absurdity. But you hear this same rubbish in the military. He just gives it one more turn of the screw and makes it funny, but this is everyday military nonsense. And if you add just a touch more it becomes extremely funny. That's military rubbish, the training of fighters, completely normal. That's the rubbish that goes round and round the whole world over. That has nothing to do with America. That's why it was a worldwide success, because this rubbish is perpetrated on every barrack-square in the world. I really recommend Kafka's official writings. You see where his imagination comes from, how it's stimulated really from the office. He is the great man of this century, who recognized that the office is the dwelling place of the twentieth-century individual. Our secure home is the office. Kafka is the prophet of this attitude. That's the chronicler's precision.

KERSTIN HENSEL

February 14, 1991, East Berlin

Kerstin Hensel *(b. 1961) is a poet and fiction writer who, after working as a nurse, studied at the Johannes R. Becher Institute in Leipzig from 1983 to 1986. Her first collection of poems was entitled* Stilleben mit Zukunft *(1988). She has also published radio plays and dramatic pieces, as well as a book of stories,* Hallimarsch *(1989). In 1990 she published* Schlaraffenzucht, *another collection of poems. In 1991 she published a novel,* Auditorium panopticum, *and another volume of poems,* Gewitterfront. *Her most recent book is* Angestaut: Aus meinem Sudelbuch *(1993).*

Do you think that readers in the GDR are in some ways more earnest than they are in the FRG?

Yes, I think they are. My texts are mainly specific to the GDR. I always took the trouble to make them more all-embracing, concerned with things that are common to the whole of humanity, or with things that are general and take place in social orders. In spite of this, people in the GDR—because they have different knowledge and different experiences—reacted differently to the texts. For example, it's much harder for the FRG reader to decode certain poetic images, or to come to terms with metaphors or with allegories. These literary means of communicating, not an inability to communicate, were present to a much larger degree in the GDR than in the FRG. Especially in lyric poetry, far more than in prose. It all has to do with the traditions that people espoused after 1945, and things were quite different in West Germany.

How would you describe the two traditions?

Let's start with lyric poetry. In the GDR the tradition in lyric poetry was Brecht. But Brecht himself espoused certain classical traditions. There were a lot of teachers in the GDR—Franz Fühmann, Georg Maurer.[1] They formed circles around them, and within these circles they tried to mediate the tradition. Mainly but not only German traditions; also traditions of world literature. In the meanwhile in West Germany things took a different course after 1945. There was a strong movement afoot to isolate yourself from, and reject, all traditions; or rather there was a strong concentration on American traditions, mainly in prose, but also in lyric poetry. Of course that had its effect.

That's experimental literature?

Yes, first of all literature that goes in the direction of pop art. But also in lyric poetry: no poetic lines are written any more, only hacked-up lines and words set down alongside each other, something that emerges not from experimental lyric poetry but from a blurring of values. I mean that poetic verses are no longer written, but just a lot of stuff all higgledy-piggledy. There are also exceptions, like Enzensberger and Grass.[2] I'm talking about the average lyric poetry.

How was it that more attention was paid here to old forms, and how do you account for the emphasis on humanism in the cultural policies of the GDR?

I assume that it started with the presence of the different occupation powers, and the fact that we, as the GDR—at the latest when the Wall was built—were sealed off. We were in an insular situation, so that there was absolutely no temptation to allow American pop art to come streaming in. Whether that's a good thing or a bad thing, I won't say. That's simply how it was. The humanism that was always being summoned up by the cultural policies is right and is not right. I don't have to tell you about the degenerations that emerged from these policies. The fundamentals were already there, thanks to Fühmann and Maurer, for example.

Were you disappointed that things went so badly wrong with the GDR?

Yes, of course, but the disappointment cannot be explained so easily. For example, the disappointment that socialist ideas—no, that has a nasty aftertaste. . . . Let's say, rather, ideas of humanistic progress, that there is no poverty, no hunger, all the things that are fundamentally human—

that they have all disappeared, with a single blow. We now have to start again at the point where the Middle Ages ended. The only things I can praise now are little things, daily amenities, that suddenly there's good wine. That's fine, but it's no yardstick.

Did you hope that the GDR state could be improved?

I did hope so, yes, but I didn't believe it. The signs indicated that it wasn't possible. There was never an actual time when the ideas expressed by artists could ever become a reality. Because, previously, the GDR did all that it possibly could—in a helpless and clueless manner—to make the population into consumers, and to orient them towards fashions rather than values. In this point the two systems weren't any different. Only in the form. People didn't listen to what artists said about living values then. Even at the time of the revolution, they only did so for brief moments, and then they were gone again.

Did you know that intellectuals did not speak for working people?

That was the case earlier too. Intellectuals covered up by saying that they were doing it for the people. But that was soon over. There was a sort of time, after 1945, when there was a true feeling of "we." That soon passed when people noticed that the split between intellectuals and the people was getting bigger and bigger.

What was the most difficult feature of GDR life to accept in order to go on working in the system and hoping for improvement? Was it the Stasi?

I was never affected by the Stasi, but I know a lot of others were. That may have been accidental. I never bothered about whether there were any files on me either. I wasn't afraid, because I can't write if I'm afraid. I cut myself off, out of self-protection. You couldn't live in this state without loving it, and I didn't love it and accept it in the form that it took in the last few years. I also know nobody who was living with their eyes open who accepted it. That's the way it was. We made our islands, we were groups, and we had our thoughts. We were at home in the worlds of thought, and we only observed with astonishment what was taking place among the leadership. But other people were affected more directly than I.

• • •

I noticed that Luchterhand has produced a deluxe edition of *Schlaraffenzucht.* **Is it a new idea to produce works in such small editions?**

Previously—and that was the great advantage of the GDR readership—you could publish an edition of lyric poetry that only ran to three thousand, and it was sold out at once. It didn't appear in the bookshops at all; it was immediately out of print. Now the publisher needs three or four years to get rid of an edition of one thousand. That's painful, but I have no more illusions as far as the sales of my books are concerned, because I'm not a popular author and never will be one and don't want to be one. The publisher will always only be able to "afford" me, he'll never make any money out of me. I have to live with that. In the GDR there was quite a different attitude toward reading. There you were heard, accepted; that's almost all gone.

Is that regrettable?

Yes, it's regrettable on all sides, but there are reasons for it. The readers cannot be gone, and yet it appears as if they are gone. I haven't gotten to the bottom of the causes. In the past six months, I haven't been able to sell a single copy of my volume of stories through the Mitteldeutscher Verlag. Where have the people gone who would earlier have bought it? Other people are asking the same question. A lot of booksellers won't accept any GDR books. They refuse to offer books from former East German publishers. That's the majority of bookstores and the largest ones. What are you to do?

Why the embargo?

It's no longer the done thing. A lot of the large book concerns, like Bertelsmann, have taken over these bookstores, and they won't sell any GDR publishers. These books are no longer to be seen, and they are piled up in the stockrooms.

Do you think that the literary culture of the GDR won't survive?

First of all there's a wave of Luddism now.[3] That may last for years. Perhaps in fifty years' time people will find out what was important in it. In my view, if you talk about twentieth-century literature, you have to talk about GDR literature. That's the way it will be, if everything doesn't collapse.

The clichés in the west run to the effect that people in the GDR took more time to think, that life was slower, literature could be enjoyed.

That's true enough. We were a much smaller country. Nothing that was thought was lost to it. But at the same time there should be no illusions about the size of the circle of readers. It was not very large. But the word had a meaning, and painting, too, had greater emphasis. The state too is always afraid of words and of poets and artists. That's why everything was so carefully watched, more so than scholarship.

And promoted.

And promoted, both together, but at the same time this promotion and the privileges . . . that's all so childish. For you see, I don't even have a telephone. I lived for years in the cellars of condemned houses. Not a sign of privileges. Other classes of the population had far more privileges: doctors, engineers, craftsmen. It was just that the writers appeared in public, and that was why everything changed so quickly.

Were you a member of the union?

Yes.

Were you allowed to travel?

A short while before the revolution I was allowed to travel to Austria. But only because I was invited to a competition. Otherwise, no.

Is FRG literature different in technique or in terms of style from the literature of the former GDR?

Yes, I think so. Without simplifying things you could say that in lyric poetry, the GDR has a great qualitative advantage, whereas in prose it's quite different. The stronger prose writers lived in West Germany. We didn't have any people like Böll and Grass.

What about women's literature in the GDR?

There were women writers who said that they were producing women's literature. But it was not as marked in the GDR as in West Germany, or other Western countries, where there were whole organizations of women. There were other problems here that were much more important. But there were hints of this in documentary literature, in the form of reports, authentic reports, and literature that was breaking taboos, like women's themes or alcoholism or homosexuality. That all counted as women's literature. It was almost exclusively women who produced it.

HANS JOACHIM SCHÄDLICH

September 10, 1990, West Berlin

Hans Joachim Schädlich *(b. 1935) studied literature at the Humboldt University in 1954, then moved to Leipzig to study German linguistics from 1956 to 1959. He worked from 1959 to 1976 as a research associate in phonology at the Academy of Sciences. After signing a petition protesting the expatriation of Wolf Biermann in 1976, he lost his position at the academy. He then published his first book of stories,* Versuchte Nähe, *with a West German press. It was very well received, and he was then declared an enemy of the state. He tried to work as a translator but soon expatriated to West Germany in 1977. He published a novel,* Tallhover, *in 1986, and his most recent novel is* Schott *(1992).*

Were you previously at the academy?

Yes, but not in literary studies. I did start to study literature once, in East Berlin, in 1954, and I gave it up after two years, because the sort of literary studies that we were offered were mostly—not only—an ideological campaign. They were always wanting to teach us the rules of writing, the way it was practiced by the proletarian-revolutionary writers in Germany in the twenties and thirties, and they made a direct connection between that time, for example, the League of Revolutionary Proletarian Writers, and the GDR socialist writers.[1] To some extent they were the same people, for example Willi Bredel, Hans Marchwitza, and whatever all their names were, and I was terribly bored by the whole thing.[2] I tried, and perhaps it was a childish attempt, to look for certain verifiable or objectifiable principles. But there weren't any. Perhaps there really aren't any, but I didn't want to hear about them in this form. Then I began my studies again in Leipzig, Germanic studies too, but the linguistic branch of Germanics. I was a very good boy and studied Gothic, and Old High German, and Middle High German, and later on

213

German grammar, dialectology, and things like that. That was at least, so to speak, objectifiable, on the basis of the text.

Nonideological?

Nonideological—it's nothing to do with ideology.

So that's why you ended up in . . .

Phonology.

In 1975 or so, GDR writers spoke about a pedagogical role for literature. Nobody talked about literature as an investigation of language . . .

. . . among other things.

I wonder whether style and language were regarded as simply formalism.

There was a time in GDR history, or literary history, but later, perhaps it started just around the middle of the 1970s, when the official bureaucracy stopped making formal objections. They did object to innovations in literature as so-called formalism, but that was very much earlier. About the middle of the 1970s, that stopped, and they permitted a greater number of formal possibilities. But the whole subject is also interesting from another point of view, apart from the fact that all these people ascribed a role or a function or a task to literature in the GDR. I don't share that either. At the beginning of 1990 I and some other people organized a conference in West Berlin, and we also invited GDR authors to come to that—it wasn't very long after November 1989—since they had been liberated in that sense, but they were conscious of it. Each of them, in different ways, had lost their subject matter, and a lot of them said: so now what? A few of them, for example, Adolf Endler or Elke Erb said, "All right, then we can turn our attention more to the formal side of things." It was very odd. They had no perspectives on the future. On the one hand they said, "We must occupy ourselves with the past," and on the other, "We can occupy ourselves more with literature as such"—though I don't really know exactly what they meant by that. They meant form and language.

And previously you weren't allowed to do that?

You could, but it often got lost in the demand for function that was made of you or that you wanted to fulfill yourself. Literature always had a sort of enlightening pedagogical function. This discussion is being continued today with GDR writers in the Federal Republic, but, of course, within the Federal Republic there are a number of different views. There are very enthusiastic proponents of a view that literature has, from the outset, a specific task to perform. This always ends up in some sort of idea of bettering the world or improving society or sensitizing the reader's ability to perceive, etc., etc. I have also gotten into discussions like this, because I said literature has no task to fulfill at all. Literature— what is it anyway? It may be some sort of organism, if that's the way you understand it, that gives someone a job to do, and I'd heard enough about that, about the job. In fact there is a formulation by Lenin, and this is what communist literary studies and literary criticism have always appealed to, or rather it is by Stalin, I made a mistake, and this statement says: "Writers are the engineers of the human soul." You can translate this into triviality as well: they are the manipulators of human consciousness. That's what they wanted. And I said, "No, literature does not have a job to do. It gives no commissions, and I will not recognize the right of anyone, or any office, to give literature a job to do, like some homework exercise."

Would you have thought that in 1976 too?

In principle, yes. I didn't say it in the GDR, because I didn't have any opportunity to say it. I was not part of literary society—I don't mean in the sense of a literary association, but of the society of literature—I wasn't. Nobody asked me either. I wasn't anybody at all, nothing at all. I might have been able to say it in my kitchen or in a bar, but apart from that no one was interested. At that time, I also didn't set myself any exercises. I saw my job as describing something. That was the job, description. Nothing else. The nature of the description—that was how I imagined it—was determined by the object and the totally individual characteristics of the person writing, who is also not a blank sheet of paper. The writer is formed by his education and his experiences and the description will also be formed to correspond to the way he has been formed. My first idea was always the text; the description of something is determined by the object. That was the task: description.

Today, I have come a long way from that. I no longer believe that the task is description. That seems to me now to be a very elementary stage of the work. Today I think rather—but not in the sense of an exercise but rather in the sense of a game—that it is important for me simply to say things, not necessarily in a flat realistic sense. Of course there are people who say: "Here, pay attention, don't you have any sense of responsibility?" But I say to myself, I am always responsible for what I do, that's my responsibility to myself. I have to answer to myself for what I do, but not to other people. If you want to exaggerate you could say: the demands made of writers by readers are totally without interest. They can throw what has been written away if they don't like it, that's their right after all. I am not in the least interested any more in what people say. That's not pride or arrogance but a reflection on the autonomy of writing. If you're asked at a reading or a discussion, then what you are asked is chance anyway. Then I often say, if I'm annoyed, "Imagine I'm dead, then you can't ask me any questions either." Then they may say, "Yes, perhaps I'll buy this book, perhaps not, and when I have bought it and am reading it, then I'll burn it." Be my guest. You need— and this is connected with the question of the function of literature—you also need an autonomy of the writer, not just of the concept of literature. The very worst thing for me is things or books that try to capture the taste of a particular audience at a particular time, so that they are ten centimeters ahead of the audience and can tell them what they enjoy. That's really boring. All right, if that's what they like, it's OK, but I'm not interested in that.

Let me tell you about a strange episode. I was giving a reading once in New York, in the German House at NYU, and there were some very nice people there, really nice, but helpless too, for of course someone immediately asked the question, "What does what you have written mean, and above all, what were you thinking about when you were writing it?" I was quite embarrassed and about to make a polite verbal escape, when a man spoke up—a physicist—and said, "I think I can say something about that." Oh, was I relieved, someone jumps in and does my work for me. And he said, "I'd just like to tell you a little story. An accused man is standing before a judge. The judge says, 'Prisoner, what did you really think when you were committing this deed?' And the accused says, 'Actually, nothing at all.' The judge insists on his question: 'But you must have been thinking about something when you were doing it.' The prisoner thinks it over for a bit and then says, 'Hm, if I think about it for a time, then I have to say that I thought: well, well, well.'" So this man saved me from embarrassment, for after that the lady who had originally asked me the question didn't ask any more. But we haven't talked about your question?

Yes, but I'd like to understand better your sense of the autonomy of literature.

I do not understand this idea of the autonomy of literature as some sort of fiction or as a sectarian matter but as a general condition for a free literature. At the end there were only a very few young authors in the GDR who had asserted that, in any case, they had no connection with the state or the bureaucracy, and a few older ones who, while insisting on literature's right to self-determination, still clung to the idea that they were important and stood by the state. Franz Fühmann was a very important author who moved in this second direction, but he died a short time ago. There are others, for example, Günter de Bruyn or Elke Erb or Fritz Rudolf Fries.[3] Others, who were opposed to this state doctrine either on literary or political grounds, have all left the GDR over the years. A lot. To say "goodbye" is the strictest expression of a literary and intellectual autonomy.

The idea of autonomy was opposed to the doctrine of the state, and for most people it was also opposed to their own understanding of their role in this comic society, for they were often in principle socialistically or communistically oriented, but not necessarily happy with what was being offered as socialism or communism. For them this meant an interference in public affairs. That could always only happen if you yourself had the idea that you had a task to do.

This touches on the whole discussion around Christa Wolf, which I don't care about in principle. I merely see it as a symptom. Christa Wolf is only one name, for which you could substitute another. But there were people—now I'm imputing the best subjective will and the best subjective belief—who took offense at the imperfections of a society, with which, in the ideal case, they would have gladly identified. Their literary interference, which they practiced as ersatz psychologists, so to speak, had as its aim the improvement of existing conditions. There's a beautiful book by Karel Capek called *The War with the Newts.*[4] In this book, which is written very ironically, someone founds a moderately progressive party within the framework of the existing laws. That was actually Christa Wolf and company's party. They didn't really question the existing laws, but they wanted to achieve moderate progress within the framework of the existing laws. You could say that. But of course what I am saying is polemical and ironic. People like that also saw themselves as the tutors of princes, you *could* say as the tutors of dictators, but, and I add this as well, there is a huge difference between educating a dictatorship and rejecting it. That's their dilemma.

Did you see this difference as early as 1976?

Yes, actually a bit earlier. You know, I recall a little story that's relevant here. It's about the difference between improving dictatorship and rejecting it. I have a friend. He maintains that he spoke to Adolf Hitler during World War II. He didn't, but he believes he did, and he said to me, "I said to Herr Hitler, 'Herr Hitler, the extermination of the Jews is a mistake.'" And Hitler is supposed to have replied, "Why?" And my friend says that he said to him, "Because it doesn't look good." He didn't say, "Because it is a crime against humanity," he didn't say that, he merely said, "Because it doesn't look good." This story reminds me of the current discussion about these writers, Christa Wolf and company, who saw themselves as the tutors of princes, who were actually in agreement with the idea of communism and with communist society, but who discovered certain things that didn't look good.

For example?

Oh, a lot. Well, for example, the repression of the fascist past in the GDR, or the suppression of freedom of travel, or censorship, or the lack of means of existence, or the lack of a free press. They saw all this and decided that it didn't look good. But they didn't go so far as to say, "Even if all these shortcomings are eliminated, the dictatorship still has to go." They didn't say that. They only wrote about it, wrote that things would be better if they weren't like that, or they talked to the leaders personally. They said, "Don't you think it looks bad if so many writers are leaving?" It *didn't* look good. Speaking polemically, they wanted a communist society, that would be better than the one there was, but they didn't understand that you can't have such a thing. There is no such thing as a good dictatorship, I don't believe in such a thing. This seems to me to be the kernel of the debate that is going on now about Christa Wolf and other writers.

How did the writers deal with the imprisonment of their colleagues? A number of younger writers were imprisoned in the late 1970s and early 1980s, weren't they?

There were some older people doing time too; for example, Erich Loest. He's already an oldish man, he did eight years.

What for?

What for? They didn't connect it directly with his literary work, but indirectly they did. There were articles in the penal code that were as flexible as rubber: for subversive incitement, for illegal contact with the west, for degradation of leading representatives of the state, all that sort of thing. The article that was most frequently used was called "subversive incitement." That can mean anything. In the early years of the GDR people were condemned for making a joke about Walter Ulbricht. That was two things at once, degradation of a leading personality and subversive incitement. Yes, there were older people in prison too. But what you were really asking was whether there was solidarity within the GDR with the people who had been sent to prison. Yes. Mostly on the part of people like Franz Fühmann, for example, I know that. Franz Fühmann cared about people like that. I don't know about writers who identified with the state. I also don't know about others, who played the role of critical mediators or who adopted a position of critical identification with the state, because their actions were not made known officially, they couldn't be made known, because then the people who supported the people in prison would have been in danger themselves. I really only know about Franz Fühmann, who, for example, stood up for an author called Frank Wolf Matthies.[5] Matthies was in jail, and Fühmann took up his cause. Wherever possible there were internal petitions by other writers to the heads of the state, but nothing is known about that. Actually it's a shame, for the effect would have been all the greater if it had been known publicly.

Was it simply human fear that kept writers from protesting in public against the acts of the state?

Everyone is a bit of a coward.

Or did it have to do with their not wanting to lose the public status of a writer in GDR society?

Perhaps it was both. Unfortunately you can't check it out. You don't know what Anna Seghers was thinking. It may be that both things played a part, that she wanted to save herself as a writer who still wanted to write or say something and at the same time—even if that were not what she would have wanted—was personally so afraid that she didn't do or say anything. The rumor is that Anna Seghers did have some relevant experiences while she was in exile in Mexico. It's said that the Stalinist secret service in Mexico was supposed to assassinate her by involving her in a serious car accident. She did get injured in it. People maintain that she was so traumatized by this experience that she never said another word against the party, or said or did anything against the interests of the state in the GDR. That may be, but you can't prove it.

Incidentally, the State Security Service also used this method. There's the former GDR writer Reiner Kunze, who lives near Passau. He said that before he moved to the Federal Republic he was warned by the Stasi. He said people from the Stasi had told him to keep his trap shut in the west, that there were fatal traffic accidents in the Federal Republic as well. I'm sure he too was living in the Federal Republic with the sense of a threat hanging over him, because it was already known—and now we know it with greater certainty—that the Stasi did operate in the Federal Republic.

Recently he said that the German intellectuals' real fatherland was ideology and systematic thought.

Yes, unfortunately. Writers should look for their fatherland—if that word has any meaning at all—or rather their homeland in language. Your homeland is language, not your country, and not ideology.

Were the utopian hopes of GDR intellectuals simply ideology?

Many intellectuals in the GDR put up with the state, because they had a utopia that corresponded verbally with the dictatorship's alleged utopia. They had, so to speak, the same utopia. They only differed in the conceptions of the way in which the utopia was to be realized. That is, they had no really deep motivation for being opposed to the state in some way, because its appearance, in principle, was verbally like the promise of their own utopia. Most of them could only express themselves as critics of the realization of a common utopia and not as the possessors of a contrary plan, a totally different utopia, which would lead this utopia *ad absurdum,* because it had already been led *ad absurdum* by reality. Then, after November 1989, there was this strange appeal by various intellectuals and writers—"For Our Country" was what the thing was called—for the GDR in the sense of a communist society better than this. That wasn't an alternative, it was a variation, and I wasn't surprised that no one was interested in listening to it. Especially because one of the last dictators, Herr Krenz, even emerged as one of the signers of the declaration.[6] This meant that the declaration wasn't worth the paper it was written on.

Many GDR writers who dreamed of a communist utopia also justified the GDR as a state, because they were convinced that it was an antifascist state. In any case they could point to the fact that many of the communist leaders were antifascists, they had been in Nazi concentration camps or in the penitentiary, etc. And then they stopped thinking, at this point already. It can't be bad—they had to believe—if people head up this state who were in jail under Hitler. But these former antifascists, who were themselves communists and who founded a new dictatorship, a communist dictatorship, misused antifascism in my view, more or less as a label for the justification of their own power in the face of the people and of the dumb-smart writers. As far as I can see this whole thing was not thought through, because people should have seen that it simply wasn't enough to be an antifascist. Antifascists built up a dictatorship themselves, a communist one, which in the means it used differed very little from the means used by a fascist dictatorship. There's a proverb in German that says, "Age is no protection against stupidity." You could adapt this by saying, "The antifascist state of mind is no protection against dictatorship," and the alternative to fascism was, for many people, in the GDR.

It's strange that the options could seem so narrow: fascism or GDR-type communism; that the neighboring Federal Republic seemed no alternative.

Yes, you're right. They had to learn that too. When the GDR was functioning more or less decently, and the majority of the people were going along with it, even though they had the Federal Republic in front of their very eyes, there was still—and we don't know any numbers—but I think it was a huge number of people, who didn't want that system in the GDR, who thought of a different, a free order. Now you could ask why the GDR lasted so long. A difficult question. There are several reasons.

You already mentioned one reason: the Nazi period was used as an excuse.

Exactly, as justification.

Can one say that the intellectuals would have tolerated less, if recent German history had been less extreme? A more moderate alternative to fascism, something short of state socialism, would have also been more attractive.

Sure, I think you're right, yes, definitely. It was a flight from a bad conscience that the people had as a result of the Nazi past. It was a comfortable basis for the communists, although they developed dictatorial power from the beginning, which was in the course of time an additional reason for the relative stability of conditions in the east. In the final analysis, if you look at it from the point of view of 1990, there hasn't been the least attempt to form or practice democratic consciousness in the east of Germany since 1933. You could say that from 1933 to 1989—that's almost sixty years—a more or less unbroken tradition of a society that's not free. That's tough. But at the same time you mustn't forget that from the beginning there were people in the GDR (even when it was the Soviet Occupation Zone) who did, of course, recognize this and opposed it or left the country. The GDR has about sixteen million inhabitants today, and in the course of the postwar period almost three million inhabitants fled from East Germany. That's not a small number if you add to that the fact that after 1961 you always took your life in your hands if you fled.

A concept that played a role after 1945 has been taken up again—the idea of the fellow traveler. It's hard to pinpoint this concept. As far as I'm concerned it contains a mixture of opposition and collaboration. The mixture differs in every case. In the case of a lot of people the measure of opposition was greater than the measure of collaboration, but in the case of others the measure of collaboration was greater than the measure of opposition. In the long run everyone who did not leave the country was—to take the extreme point of view—a fellow traveler, with a greater or smaller share of opposition and collaboration in each individual case.

That's true for me too. As long as I lived in the GDR I must also have been a fellow traveler. I never belonged to the party, I wasn't a proponent of this policy but just an individual who went along and, it's true, with an interesting admixture of rejection and participation. It couldn't be any other way simply because you were living there. Yesterday, I met an emigrant from Hungary who's living in Australia now, a man called Leslie Bodi. He is a Germanist in Melbourne. He had a tough life. As a Jew he was in a Nazi concentration camp, and as an anticommunist in a communist prison in Hungary after 1945. He fled to Australia in 1956. He said to me, "Everyone who lives in a system like that has a share in it, everyone. You've bought a share, and everyone who lives there is a shareholder. You can't sell the share because you think there's going to be a recession, no one will buy it, you have it for life. You can only tear it up and leave the corporation." But in the words of Leslie Bodi, that means that everyone bears a certain measure of common guilt, everyone is to a certain extent jointly responsible for the fact that such an order continues to exist for as long as it continues to exist. It's interesting, no one wants to hear that. I have thought long and hard about it, because someone like me who left the GDR thirteen years ago is naturally easily inclined to say, "I had nothing to do with it." But I lived there from the beginning, as a child in fact, but also as an adult, and when I left I was already forty-two years old, so I must have held a share too. That's why, and I thought about this quite a long time ago and said so, I have to regard myself up to the time I left, or at least up to a certain point before I left, as a fellow traveler. Of course I would be happy to claim that in my case the degree of opposition was larger than the degree of collaboration. Again, that's only human.

Anyway, since I've been gone I no longer own a share. When I tore up my share and left, I was freed from being a fellow traveler, and that's thirteen years ago. I think that justifies people like that—ones who left thirteen or fourteen years ago and who on the other hand know what the circumstances are—to address the matter in this way everywhere they go. Above all, also to address the fact—and I'm only talking about writers—that there were a lot who stayed there to the bitter end. Good, they can claim that they were living in the inner opposition, had nothing more to do with the state, like Adolf Endler, or that they did have something to do with the state, but most of them did not make a real break with the system. Nowadays there are often discussions with reference to the GDR that compare the immediate post-World War II period with the present. There are people, especially among the West German left, who say, "You can't compare the two." I don't mean the regimes, but the times. But there's an inaccuracy in this objection. What people really want to say is, "That's not the same," and they say, "You can't compare it." The comparison can become meaningless, of course, but after all I can compare a book with a wineglass; I can. The comparison wouldn't be productive, but you can compare the social and political situation after 1945 and now, and the comparison is not meaningless. There are certain identical characteristics. After 1945 and again now there is—and we have already discussed this—a reluctance to face the immediate past and to describe one's own personal part in the existence of such a state. That can be guilt or not. Guilt is after all another qualification of behavior. In the first place it could arise if someone said, "I did participate in this way and that." That would be what most people would like to keep quiet. It gets to the point where different parties and views would like best to destroy the files of the State Security Service, so that they wouldn't need to analyze the past. If you can imagine someone saying in 1945, "We want to destroy the Nazi party files," it's unthinkable. But in comparison there is a tendency, both then and now, not to talk about one's own part in the affair.

Because they are so afraid.

Yes, because they are ashamed or because they're afraid. Life has to go on, nobody wants to admit guilt, otherwise he won't get a job, or he'll be disqualified as an intellectual or a writer, etc.

What is to be lost if one looks at one's own past in such a way as to notice one's own guilt?

For me it means, when you apply it to a whole society, to a quarter of the population, it means, if you don't analyze the past and do not describe the part played by different individuals and social groups, then the result is an abstract danger, namely that history of this sort will repeat itself. But there is also a quite concrete danger, namely that of a mendacious society, of a society that rests on lies, on a lack of the ability to trust, and, in my view, that is not a good basis for the development of a democracy, a pluralistic, open society. That's the worst thing about it.

Are there particular consequences for authors?

They are in danger of losing their language or becoming sheer liars. That is not literature. If you gloss over everything that took place, then it is easy for people to lie. You are responsible to nobody for your own words; or else somebody who bears this conflict within himself and is aware of things, but still doesn't have the courage to say it aloud, can be throttled by it, he can't do anything more.

The danger of "going along" is there for writers in parliamentary democracies as well as in dictatorships.

In a dictatorship you don't have the chance to say something. Speaking out in dictatorial circumstances often means that you may very easily lose your means of livelihood or end up in prison. There are also fellow travelers in a parliamentary democracy, but you can always speak out against them, and you don't have to go in fear of being locked up or losing your post as a professor. Perhaps you have to be afraid of getting into conflicts with your colleagues or the president of the university or the academy, but you put up with that. You don't have to leave the USA because you hold different opinions from the ruling party. It's often only a question of suffering some discomforts or losing certain people's respect, not actually the destruction of the society or putting your livelihood in danger, at least that's what I've learned here. There are tough fights, for example, in PEN. I took part in a discussion recently where there was only one topic, and that topic was—actually it isn't a German word but we use it—*Zivilcourage* [civil courage]. I don't know if you have the word?

We speak more often of "civil disobedience."

Civil disobedience takes into account—as the word is understood in German—violation of the law. To have *Zivilcourage* does not necessarily mean that you violate the law, if you demonstrate *Zivilcourage*. It can of course lead to people violating the law. *Zivilcourage* means the following: the public utterance of a personal conviction regardless of the consequences that this may have for the individual, regardless of possible eventual personal disadvantages for the individual who publicly expresses his view.

Do you think that the Germans lack *Zivilcourage?*

No, actually I don't. It's also a way of behaving that has a history. I have the impression that in the Federal Republic—because of developments in the postwar period and because of postwar history—the people have quite a lot of *Zivilcourage,* and in the GDR too for the last few years. Since the mid 1980s I think I've observed an increase in *Zivilcourage*. But I know that the West Germans had too little, before. I have the impression that they have learned a lot. Through their postwar experience of democracy, they have become, so to speak, fresher—that is, they are more self-confident. That doesn't mean of course that one sees *Zivilcourage* very often. I can imagine that the bulk of the people would rather take it easy and say, "Hm, what business is it of mine?" But very often I find that people are really courageous, in civil life, in the sense of the public utterance of a point of view that is not necessarily so widely accepted or which has opponents.

Have you noticed this among GDR writers?

Yes, I have noticed it there too. There's been a division. There are indeed a lot of GDR writers who were attached to the old order. For them *Zivilcourage* consisted of defending their order, but they didn't need a lot of courage to do this, because they were after all legitimized by power. Another group that formed a sort of center didn't say anything for or against; they also didn't show a great deal of courage. Then there was a third group, one that did show courage, and this can be divided up again. The larger part of this group has gone, and the smaller part stayed and fought it out. But you can count them on the fingers of two hands.

You began your life as a writer in West Germany long ago. What is the outlook now for former East German writers who will have to make the transition to another literary milieu?

It's really difficult for younger people who have worked critically in the GDR, who didn't get a chance there, who are poor and who are also not known here, and who are now exposed to the free book market and stand there like children. For them it's really difficult.

I notice that the young writers from Prenzlauer Berg are not depressed.

Yes, they're not depressed. The people who are actually depressed are the people who came to terms with the GDR state. They ought to be depressed, in my opinion. They have really got to think things over, keep quiet, start working, and then perhaps they can start again, or perhaps not.

They don't look good at the moment.

No, *they* don't look good at the moment.

REINER KUNZE

February 8, 1991, Passau

Reiner Kunze (b. 1933) is a very well-known poet and prose writer who expatriated to West Germany in 1977. He studied philosophy and journalism at the University of Leipzig from 1951 to 1955, where he then taught until 1959. He left the university because of "unacceptable conditions." He was recognized as a freelance writer and translator in 1962. Since 1955 he has published a number of volumes of poetry—such as Widmungen *(1963),* Sensible Wege *(1969),* zimmerlautstärke *(1977),* Auf eigene Hoffnung *(1981),* Eines jeden einziges Leben *(1986)—several of which have found a particularly large readership. In August 1968 he protested the invasion of Czechoslovakia by giving up his membership in the SED. His 1976 collection of prose sketches,* The Wonderful Years, *was a best-seller in the West, so much so that in October 1976 the Writers' Union expelled Kunze, which meant practically a ban on all publication. In April 1977, in the wake of Biermann's expatriation, Kunze received a long-term visa to West Germany and moved to Bavaria. He has received literary awards in Czechoslovakia, Austria, Sweden, and West Germany. His work has been widely translated. In 1990 he published a selection of documents from his Stasi file which exposed some prominent figures as informants. He lives with his wife near Passau in Bavaria. He and his wife have done numerous translations of Czechoslovakian writers.*

In *Deckname "Lyrik"* you quote a Professor W. commenting on *Die wunderbaren Jahren:* "The simple, easily remembered language leads us to suppose that the author expects the book to be quite effective especially among young readers." I think he's reversing things.

[Laughing] I think so too.

You were influenced by young people. Did you write the book in the role of a father?

The daughter who appears throughout the book is not identified with our own daughter. A lot of daughters went into this character, just as a lot of fathers went into the character of the father. At that time there were a lot of young people who visited us, from all over the GDR, simply because they felt the need to talk. They hoped that people would listen to them here. There were so many that I often had to make my escape from their conversation in order to get any work done at all. So a lot of young people's experiences went into the book. There's a prose piece in the book called "Element." It's about a young man who wants to go on vacation in the Tatras and keeps getting arrested because people think he wants to go to Berlin to the International Festival.[1] I listened to a whole lot of stories like that. The same thing happened to a lot of different young people, so that this story is just as much invented as not.

I've talked to a few young writers and assume that those who were born in the sixties have far fewer illusions about politics. Do you assume that young people wanted to have less to do with politics?

Maybe yes, maybe no. And your premise that we older people had illusions . . . yes, I'll admit it's true, but I would like to differentiate it a bit.

If I may talk about myself, I come from a working-class family without books. In 1945, after the war, we were selected as the new high school cadres. We were to populate the secondary schools and go on to the university so that we could preserve and support the regime. The only thing was that we didn't see what we had been chosen to do. It was suggested to us at the time that what was happening was the opposite of what the National Socialists did; and that was what we wanted, that was the hope for mankind. We were, I was, brought up in this faith—please don't take it in a religious sense—and I was very isolated, because from the age of fourteen on, I lived almost exclusively in boarding schools.

How long people hung on to these illusions and hopes differed greatly. At the beginning, I didn't want to admit that for years people had been lying to me either; but when I finally understood, I drew the obvious conclusions and started quite early to face the music. I don't know whether by any chance you read the extracts from the files—in *Die Zeit,* number 44, last year—that the Stasi had kept on me during the years I was studying. You can see from them when the process of disillusionment set in and at what point I became conscious of the fact that I was the victim of an illusion. That was back at the end of the fifties. There are colleagues my own age who were by nature more skeptical and noticed what was happening earlier than I did, and there were colleagues who noticed it and repressed it—right up to the present, and they're still repressing it. It's the same, I think, with the younger generation. There are some totally upright people whom I know, who for as long as I've known them, and to this very day, have taken up a position against the regime; and there are those who have gone along with it.

Did the younger generation's point of view oblige you to adopt a different sort of writing in your new book?

No, not all. I wrote the book because I was convinced that it would not be published. That is, I did it without looking outside, or feeling that I had to win over a lot of young people, or write so that young people would understand. Either you write what you have to write, as precisely as possible, as simply as precision will permit, and as honestly as you can, or no literature is created. Everything else is outside of any sort of literary intention.

You say that you write as honestly as possible; how does that jibe with writing between the lines?

I never did that. It's something I can't do. If I wrote a story, I didn't write it so that I could write between the lines, but because I had the idea for the story. That's why it ended up as a story, and not because I wanted to deceive the censor.

So you didn't have any attachment to the pedagogical conception of literature in the GDR?

No, that was never an aspect of my work. Wait a moment, I have to qualify that: up to the age of twenty or twenty-two—I studied journalism among other things—those were *the* aspects of my work. Only, I hadn't yet produced any *literature*.

In *Die wunderbaren Jahren* you wrote about conformism among the students. But what about among the writers? When you were deprived of your citizenship, did you experience conformism or solidarity?

One day, when we were still living in the GDR, and proceedings were initiated against me for contempt of court, I received a remittance from Stefan Heym. He had collected money so that I could pay the fine. That was an act of solidarity. When there was just a minute possibility that a selection of my writings might appear in the GDR, namely in 1973—that was the selection of poems *Brief mit blauem Siegel,* which appeared from Reclam—Stefan Hermlin did what he could to see that the book appeared. That was an act of solidarity. When I was expelled from the Writers' Union, Jurek Becker came to see us in Greiz and declared that, though he did not agree with my ideas, he condemned my expulsion. My colleague Wulf Kirsten in Weimar always showed his solidarity—a very good lyric poet, a completely upright colleague.[2] In *Deckname "Lyrik,"* I talk about the fact that at one meeting almost all writers avoided talking to me. Wulf Kirsten was the one who always sat at my table. Günter de Bruyn was always a good colleague.[3] Without making a lot of fuss about it—I only learned of it afterwards— Franz Fühmann showed his solidarity as a colleague. But these are examples covering a span of fifteen years. The majority of colleagues did not show their solidarity, and a few of them did us a great deal of harm.

What kind of harm?

For example, when I made a public appearance—here in the FRG, when we were already living here—they supported and initiated precisely those calumnies that suited the Stasi's book. Hermann Kant behaved particularly disgracefully in this connection.

When he was talking to me, Kant said that he regretted his behavior in the Biermann case, and that he had always tried to be the mediator between the authorities and the writers to foster tolerance among the authorities and improve the circumstances of writers.

He wouldn't be human if he didn't do a good deed now and again. But you cannot get rid of the damage done by someone who damages other people by saying that he also did some good. The real question is: "Why did you do so much evil if you also did some good? Why did that have to be?"

If one wishes to understand compromises, one needs to consider the importance of literature in the GDR.

Do you mean for the official policy?

Not only.

You really have to distinguish between its importance for the readers and for the people in power. The former had need of *literature,* the others of pseudoliterature.

Was literature important to the readers as a safety valve?

I wouldn't call it a safety valve. It was more in the interest of the people in power to have a safety valve, at least for some of them. Let me give you an example: I was once giving a reading in Leipzig to a few hundred spokesmen of the Catholic student organizations from all over the GDR. Because we knew there would be at least two people working for the Stasi present at each reading, and because the political situation was particularly complicated, I had put together a program that would create the least possible danger for the organizers. I began with a poem that is one of the most harmless poems I've written. It's called "Cycling," and it really does deal with traveling by bicycle. The poem begins like this: "Turn off into the woods." I say the words "turn off," and the students start clapping, clapping wildly. I was so surprised that for the moment I didn't understand why they were clapping. I started again, and again . . . I couldn't get past the first word. It was only at the third attempt that I was able to go on reading. That wasn't a safety valve, but by their applause they showed one another what they were feeling and thinking. The applause was more important to them, much more important than the whole reading. That's nothing to do with being a safety valve. On the contrary, it is really a mutual charging up, condensing a pressure, not lessening it.

On the one hand, it's nice for the writer that people react immediately . . .

And on the other hand—that's what you wanted to suggest—it's not good for a writer. It's not a reaction to a work of art but a diversion of the work of art into politics—as far as possible according to a *particular* attitude. What actually constitutes the experience of art is misplaced as a result.

What is it like for you to work in the FRG? Readers don't react so sharply here.

In normal circumstances, wherever you are, there are only a few people for whom poetry is a vital necessity, either here or there. If you discount the nonliterary reaction, then as far as my work and my readers are concerned, there's no difference between being here or over there.

Not even in quantity. There's no way I can handle all the invitations I get to give readings. The people who ask existential questions turn to me more than they did over there—that's understandable—because over there you couldn't avoid day-to-day politics, the ideological iron fist, something that people don't need to do here. But here there are so-and-so many other points of view on life: for example, a certain surfeit of stimulation, a superficiality in life, a need to be entertained. And one day there arises a moment of inner emptiness and you ask yourself, "Why am I living, what is life?" Again, it is young people who ask these questions earlier than others, who go on living out of a sort of habit.

• • •

In the press, the writers who stayed behind, who tried to improve the system, are now being characterized as fellow travelers.

That's very complicated. Whoever still believed, had believed for decades, that human happiness was to be achieved under that system either had to suppress a terrible lot of things, or had to close his eyes to a lot of things; or he didn't want to go on thinking. I can understand that it was too hard for a lot of people to bear the consequences that they would have had to have borne, if they had drawn the obvious conclusions from what they had seen or what they had recognized. The terror did not have to affect the writers themselves; it could also be that it affected their families, their children. I think you have to take each individual's case into consideration separately.

Is the time ripe for that?

As far as self-analysis goes, certainly. There's no way around it. But for some of my older colleagues their whole life's commitment is at stake, and that makes a *public* discussion unacceptable to them.

The fear of a market economy also has a bearing on writers' unwillingness to see their own mistakes publicly displayed.

But no one who wants to appear in public with a new book is spared the debate with themselves. In that case you can only withdraw and accept the fact that you won't publish a new book for five or ten years, and that then you'll present something that's carefully thought out and honest to the core.

At the moment that's not what's happening.

No, it's not happening. The externalities that affect the whole economy are simply pushed into the foreground and take precedence.

Was the GDR a state founded on the rule of law, where there were limits to threatening actions, in contrast, for example, to Solzhenitsyn's experiences?

The GDR was not a state founded on the rule of law. But there is in Germany, and especially in Prussia, a sense of exactness. Essentially everything is more orderly, more bureaucratic, and there is a certain security attached to that. There were fewer possibilities for the individual to be cruel. In the Soviet Union, people disappeared to Siberia in hundreds of thousands. It wasn't as easy in the GDR. Besides, there was the fact that the Western public was right on the doorstep. People couldn't do a lot of the things they would have liked to. As we now know, people would have liked to execute clergymen in Berlin: even the intention is a fearful one. But in the end they didn't give the word. It was connected with the fact that we could also be deprived of our citizenship. If I had lived somewhere in Vladivostock, it wouldn't have been like that. The crimes that the regime committed in the GDR were committed *within* the individual. To that extent the state was much more total and much more cunning in its grasp on the individual. It went for the individual's soul.

The young writers of Prenzlauer Berg showed how this exactitude could be exploited: for example, readings could take place in private homes and the public could be admitted . . .

I'll bet the Stasi was there.

Yes, but they didn't try to make their meetings conspiratorial. A few informants even admitted passing on information. Apparently it wasn't all that bad, because there was little to hide.

If they knew about it, then it wasn't so bad. When I had to read through the twelve volumes of my files in order to write *Deckname "Lyrik,"* I came across the following example. I was invited to an apartment—just among friends—and that evening I was absolutely certain that there were only people there who knew each other and who vouched for each other. I related so many details about other people! And there they all are—in my Stasi files. Even in this small group there was someone who was, coldly and systematically, sounding out the group, and—as I learned from the reports of the Stasi itself, not from informants—there was already an "operative action" in process against this group. All of those who were there were singled out for arrest. Because the state was so thoroughly organized, it was well-nigh impossible even to have a small public gathering in which there wasn't somebody working for the Stasi.

Reading through your files was a surprise for you?

It was a nasty surprise, because I kept reproaching myself, "How could you have said all that at the time?" I wanted to encourage them; I wanted to give them facts that would give them strength.

• • •

Some months ago, you said that the fatherland of German intellectuals was ideology. Is that as true of West Germany as of East?

Yes.

Why is that?

Perhaps it's connected to our intellectual tradition. As far as our way of thinking goes, we come, on the one hand, so much from Kant and Hegel and so little from Claudius and Hölderlin; and, on the other, we are very Protestant-oriented, and that too of course leaves an ideological imprint on our thought. Together these forces can have a devastating effect. We are lacking a bit of . . . [Elisabeth Kunze, Reiner's wife, whispers in the background, "Slavic mentality"]. These peoples' tradition, for example the Czechs', is determined by a completely different development. Over there, custom, myths, folk-poetry kept the vernacular alive for two hundred years, even though German (from 1620, after the Battle of Weissenberg) had become the official language.

What part did skepticism play among GDR writers? Did intellectuals feel a duty to think skeptically and use language differently?

There is an ideologized skepticism that is actually an antiskepticism. You have to be skeptical about everything that does not accord with your own view of the world, with your own ideology. Popper's skepticism is different: you have to be skeptical and exclude everything that is not in accordance with truth. Unfortunately you come across this sort of skepticism less frequently. But perhaps not only in Germany.

In the States professional intellectuals do sense a duty to say "no," or "yes, but."

. . . before you've found out that you can say "yes." Then you have to say "yes," too.

Do you have to? You can.

No, when a fact is proven to be a fact, and human intellect is no longer in a position to cast doubt on it, then I *have* to say, "yes," then I *may* not only say, "possibly," even if it costs me my life.

KATJA
LANGE-MÜLLER

September 13, 1990, West Berlin

Katja Lange-Müller *(b. 1951) served an apprenticeship as a typesetter and later worked for a number of years as a nurse in a psychiatric clinic. From 1979 to 1982 she studied at the Johannes R. Becher Institute. She grew up in the milieu of the political leadership in the GDR. Her mother, Ingeburg Lange (b. 1927), became a candidate of the Central Committee in 1963, and of the Politburo in 1973, when she became secretary for women's affairs. She had studied at the party academy and later became a professor of social science there. In 1983 Katja lived in Mongolia, and soon after returning she left the GDR in 1984 to live in West Berlin. Her first volume of stories,* Wehleid: wie im Leben, *appeared in 1986, for which she won the Ingeborg Bachmann Prize.* Kaspar Hauser: Die Feigheit vorm Freund *appeared in 1988.*

Your first book was published in West Berlin?

All my books have only been published in the west.

Does that mean that you had difficulties starting a career as a writer in East Berlin?

No, I wasn't a writer in East Berlin. I don't even have an *abitur.* I learned ordinary trades. I learned typesetting and some other aspects of printing technology. Later on, I worked as a nurse: first as an assistant nurse, and then I did specialized nursing and worked for a long time in psychiatric wards. Seven years. I started writing very late. I never felt in the GDR that I had been defamed as a writer, because I didn't consider myself a writer. I had written much too little. I also had contacts with a publisher in East Berlin. It was clear then that my texts weren't suited to them. I didn't write for publication—not at the beginning—but rather, I would say, in a broader sense, for therapeutic reasons. I had an enormously difficult job in the locked female ward, and in geriatric psychiatry. I simply had to come to terms with the pressures of experience. At the beginning this was, for me, the function of writing. And in spite of that, from the very beginning, I was writing satirical texts. I regard myself as a satirist.

Your decision to come over here—was that totally unrelated to your writing?

It didn't have much to do with it. I was previously in Outer Mongolia, outside the European cultural orbit and outside all of the juridical regulations and norms that I had experienced in life. I couldn't go back. If you let a canary out of its cage for just an hour, then it's happy to get back into its cage, but if it's outside longer . . . it won't work any more. Somehow, I just couldn't go back to those structures.

What was the worst thing about them?

That was very personal. The very worst thing was that my mother was a member of the government, and I couldn't see eye to eye with her—even as a child. I lived my life more or less for myself, but because she was in such a high position, I was, no matter what situation I found myself in, always this person's daughter. I simply wanted to be myself. That's more a personal than a political reason, but it's tied in with circumstances as they were in the GDR at the time. Thomas Brasch's father, Monika Maron's stepfather, all these sons and daughters of political authorities either became actors or writers.[1] That must have something to do with the structures.

When you were in East Berlin did you have any contacts with writers?

Of course. You can say that in the GDR everybody really knew everybody else. Everything was very like a family—actually too much like a family. That too was something that no longer appealed to me.

And here in West Berlin you have anonymity?

Yes. Here it doesn't matter in the least. It also doesn't matter how you earn your money. As people in Berlin say, "Beers that have been ordered are drunk and paid for." How you got the money, whether as a pipefitter or a writer, basically doesn't matter at all. The role of culture, art, and literature is neither under- nor overestimated; well, under- rather than over-. But I prefer that. If you were any sort of artist in the GDR, you could easily find yourself in the position of being the conscience of the nation, and that doesn't appeal to me in the least. I have a completely subjective—almost existential—access to what I write. I neither wanted to do censored social criticism, nor did I want to do counseling. What that all means or is, and how you can go about it, and how little is really achieved by taking away from people—individuals— the responsibility for their own lives, even if it's done with the best of intentions . . . I learned in psychiatry that that doesn't work. It's true of all forms of help-syndrome, even when they originate in writing or politics. In the final analysis, the individual's responsibility is not enhanced, but hampered.

Hampered in what way?

Individuals are constantly in a situation in which decisions are made for them, in which their opinions are formulated for them. If literature formulates people's opinions, so to speak, then, as far as I'm concerned, it has missed its mark, and its effect is the wrong one.

Let's pursue the question of the role of literature. The didactic notion of literature as the educator of the nation or, to take the other view, as the educator of princes . . .

. . . critic of princes—and educator of princes. All right. I think you can see from my other answers that I consider the pedagogical function of literature as something inimical to literature. As far as I'm concerned, no literature is created in this way. I don't know a single book that I like, that I really like, that has been created in this way. The closest would be Charles Dickens, because he really was a philanthropist. He also certainly had—well—a pedagogical effect; whether he had pedagogical intentions, I don't know. I think he did. But he is almost the only one; and possibly the early humanists, the really early honest ones. I grant them that, and I accept them as such. For they really had the chance, and they lived in a social environment where they could do it. If it works, if it can really function, then you can do that; it doesn't matter whether literature that is of great or little value is produced in the process. But I think that literature has long since lost this function, in Europe on the eve of the twenty-first century.

It occurred to me that very few GDR authors of Christa Wolf's generation have talked about language or style. In *Was bleibt*, Wolf writes, on the first page, about a new language. I think that what she intended by that is a clean language, uncontaminated by ideology.

But the phrase "clean language," the concept itself, annoys me. I'm all for a dirty language, if it's good—just as much, perhaps more so.

When I hear the concept "clean language" I immediately think of laundry detergent.

Do you think I'm interpreting Wolf wrongly?

No, I think that's what she means. And that's the best thing about her, and what I think has helped. Why? The whole GDR seemed to me in recent years to be like a great Protestant church. Starting with all the candles. What Christa Wolf has, thank heaven—and that's the best thing about her—is pietistic thought in her head. That's an offshoot of a remnant of bourgeois humanism in the Protestant church. But it is horribly Protestant. It is so orderly, and so opposed to pleasure. It's so simple, and I've never found that life is like that. I just don't think everything works like that.

I assume from your stories you find Kafka important.

No, I don't find him important. As is the case with all great comedians, his material is very existential. But I'm quite certain that Kafka was not understood by many people in the GDR, because you don't joke about such things. Kleist was understood no better for what he is, because he was taken too seriously. Ambrose Bierce was also not understood. You're not allowed to think things like that. You don't make jokes about such things, like Kafka in *Der Hungerkünstler* or *Bericht an eine Akademie*—that was understood—the thing with the monkeys, that was comprehensible. But when what is comic becomes really great and goes beyond satire to become world literature, then the material it consists of is very existential and, of course, very bitter. But in spite of this, I think that Kafka has always been regarded as a very sad author and more as a victim who is defending himself. I didn't see him in that light. And even, who is Gregor Samsa, what sort of a beetle is he? No one was ever interested in that. But I wanted to know what sort of a beetle it was, until I got the idea that he clearly meant it to be a cockroach, from the way it eats to the way it hides under chests and beds. What's all this talk about a beetle? The prototype of this beetle is a cockroach. The only thing I don't know is whether it's the Asiatic, American, or French species; according to the dictionary, there are three species.

But that doesn't mean anything . . .

To me it means a tremendous amount, that it has to be a cockroach. If it were some nice sort of beetle, a ladybug or a stag beetle—the word "beetle" brings a lot of things to mind—but, so to speak, the "lowest" insect in human eyes is really the cockroach, and the fact that this beetle is a cockroach is to me very important. That point is just enough for me to understand the joke. So I have noticed precision in Kafka's work, in the way he goes about things. It's not for nothing that he sets so much store by the description of the beetle's circumstances. Basically, he wanted people to decode the message that his beetle was a cockroach. That might be a very important feature of the metamorphosis; it is for me at any rate.

Do you think that many GDR writers misconstrued the objectives of their art?

GDR literature was never bedside reading for me. I always had a very critical, even contemptuous attitude toward it. People like Heiner Müller were of course potentially important for me, because he really did go into the cellar every day, perhaps out of a literary necrophilia, and brushed the corpses' teeth and combed their hair. But he was the only one who went regularly into the cellar. I would say that he did a lot of our historical dirty work: he represented us. And it's no excuse for all the people who didn't do it to say, "We had Heiner Müller; he did it for us."

Christa Wolf was not as important?

She's such a conscience of the nation, something that, for a long time, I've regarded as questionable. To my mind, the most interesting book she wrote is really *Kindheitsmuster* [Patterns of childhood]; it's the only attempt she made to come to terms honestly with *her* subjective history. All the rest, even *Kassandra,* were, as far as I am concerned, an attempt to express seven unimportant truths in order to leave an important lie covered up.

Is your problem with *Kassandra* the quasiallegorical mode of the book?

It's a Protestant way of doing things, this "verily, I say unto you" literature, like the Sermon on the Mount; it gets on my nerves, I don't like it. It's too solemn and, at the same time, too polemical for me. It's too pathetic, and it seems as though all it does is to help people to discover that their main enemy is within themselves and nowhere else.

In *Kindheitsmuster* she makes an attempt to come to terms with her own history, and for this reason, as I see it, *Kindheitsmuster* is, from the literary point of view, her best book and the one where one really senses the difficulty of writing. You notice the struggle with herself. And this is the book in which her confrontation with herself—her own person, her development, her compromises, her type of dishonesty—goes farthest. She's Protestant in this book too, has a pietistic claim to good and evil, to what is simple and just. But, after all, that's her way of thinking about things, and if she's consistent about it then I can accept it; if she isn't, then I find it totally uninteresting or just annoying.

Do you think that she is inconsistent?

Yes, I have nothing against personal inconsistency, but literary inconsistency, where I come across it, leads to worse literature than would be possible without it.

Exactly what inconsistency do you mean?

I can't say exactly. Simply through her precise grammatical structures she creates unbelievably complicated entanglements that, as a reader, I am forced to follow only, at the end, for her to tell me that trees are green. I knew that already, without the complicated entanglement, and that annoys me because then I notice how evasive she is. She displays her effort to be just in her narrative, and I think that doesn't work. I consider the goal of a narrative justice in prose as an illusion. All right, I'm unjust, and I'm suspicious from the outset of everyone who pretends to be just, and when they try to do it in literature, then, at best, it merely leads to boredom.

Have you read *Was bleibt?*

Yes. It too is still naive, in spite of everything, it's still terribly naive. I'm sorry. I also don't understand how anyone could go on living in such circumstances for so long, how anyone could have written all those books and then write one like that. It's like a relapse into some early stage of consciousness.

But she experienced the GDR as an enlightened land of reading, and the book's about her being rescued by this young poet, or by her readership. I find that sentimental.

Yes, it is. Sentimentality can be forgiven. It's not something bad. But, first of all, this form of sacrificial strategy doesn't appeal to me. For me, victims are potential corpses, and the true victims, that is, people who are really destined to be victims, are those who resist most strenuously. All true victims know that if they assume a sacrificial position they are finished. And if one sells oneself as a victim, as Christa Wolf does, then I find myself unable to believe it. I simply doubt it.

Do you find her books dubious?

That varies from book to book, but increasingly she substitutes pathos for consistency; it grows stronger in each book. Pathos and polemics. And that's, if you like, the material that ideology is made of, and for that reason I simply find it suspect.

On the subject of feminism. Does a book like *Kassandra* have a special significance?

Not for me. As far as feminism is concerned, as it is presented today, I'm unique—except for a few Italian women—because I'm working on some material about Medea, the only real female culprit in mythology. I think that women will only advance if their status as victims—and this always seems to be the terminus—is overcome. I'm interested in culprits. I'm all for culprits. The culprit who was formerly a victim is, so to speak, not a culprit. As far as I'm concerned, that all comes from Protestantism. The culprit is good *and* evil, not just good *or* evil. It's nonsense always to separate the culprit and the victim: they consist of two parts. A lot of social factors help determine what is dominant in the interim result or in the final result, being a victim or being a culprit. But since victims are so incapable of action, I find this insistence on being fatally wounded or abandoned leads nowhere, achieves nothing, ends up only in repetition.

And Medea does not seem to be a victim.

Well, from my point of view, she really is a culprit. Then there's the story that Jason doesn't grow old, whereas she does grow old, and then he doesn't sleep with her any more—Medea is cunning enough, she knew she could handle that. She wouldn't have needed to put him or herself into this position: it was in her control, it was her gift. What she did was to provide herself with a motive to go on doing it. When she commits the next murders—the king, her own sons, and her husband— every judge, and especially every male judge, is naturally inclined to say, vainly, that she did it because she was crossed in love. But it has to be proved that that really was the case. So you see, you can confront mythology and what has come of it, in exactly the same way that you can confront all other circumstantial evidence—criminally. That's what is interesting. Victims are simply boring, but culprits are interesting to us. This is apparently leading us away from *Kassandra,* but I never liked Cassandra, and I was never sorry for her. I can't do much with the figure, and I don't like the way Wolf treated her one bit. The Cassandra who, so to speak, points her finger out of the apocalypse and says, "I told you so," as though she didn't belong to the human species, is simply too silly. The isolated woman giving her warnings—it's too dumb. A lonely old woman whom no one wants to listen to. And yet she is the only one who possesses the truth, and that's really too stupid, it's daft. If someone possesses the truth and no one else does, then the "truth" is not true.

The idea of "magic" belongs to both figures: both have special abilities because their knowledge is unearthly in nature.

Yes, except that in the case of Cassandra it's a sort of ability that she has brought on herself, as a curse, because of her refusal, her rejection. She is condemned to it. In the case of Medea, it's not clear. She acts much more of her own free will. No one has forced her to fall in love with Jason, leave her home, tear her brother to pieces, needle her father, and shit on her sister. She thought that all out for herself, and it is not at all clear whether she has really fallen in love, or whether Jason was only an excuse for her desire to be evil. I think we won't get any further at all if we go on separating good and evil and making evil the opposite of good. This East German–West German back-and-forth doesn't interest me at the moment at all—or no more than is necessary. There are more crucial things to ponder and think about.

Have you considered the effects of the revolution on you?

Yes, I completed the revolution for myself years ago—and voluntarily. For me it is truly a repetition, even if it is much larger and affects a far, far greater number of people. Besides, both things are in a state of dissolution—the place I came from, and the place I went to. So that soon neither will exist in the form in which I left it, or in which I found it. That's a good point to leave.

Have you already asked yourself the question about your livelihood, or was that not a problem for you? For most people in the GDR it is one of their main concerns.

Look, I reject people—especially writers—who say they don't know anything besides the alphabet. I think that's what brought the profession—if you can call it a profession—into such disrepute. It took me a long time to get to the point where I could accept the fact that it was my profession and, now and again, I make a conscious effort to do something else. That's to say, I really do go and work in a hospital from time to time, because I need to, for the sake of the different experience. And if what I write's not enough, or if no one wants to publish it, then it's quite clear that, at that point in time, I am not an author, and I have to look around to see how I'm going to earn my living. I think that's perfectly normal, and to moan or get upset about it is idiotic. If you produce goods that nobody wants, you simply have to look around and find another way of earning your living. As far as I'm concerned, there are no polemics to be made, and I'm not sorry about it. The idea of sitting down somewhere and saying, "I can't go on living any longer because no one wants my things any more" is, in my opinion, narrow-minded and spoiled. Any German should really be ashamed to argue like that. What is happening in Germany, the division between author and reader, between great literature and minor literature, between "high" literature and trivial literature, is an elitist snow job.

Have you already given readings in the GDR?

Strangely enough, I did so quite early on. Shortly after the border was opened, I gave three readings. They didn't involve literature but politics. The first question I was asked, because I'm one of the "ones who left," came from my former German teacher: "Well, Katja, is it the Promised Land?" Such a mixture of uncertainty, prejudice, and ignorance certainly wouldn't allow us to discuss literature.

Before this did you take the idea of a land of readers seriously?

People really did read a lot, and I also read a lot, especially at work [laughs]. Of course, I know why it was called a land of readers. It was because people often felt the need to escape. As a child I also read a lot when I felt desperate—every book, uncritically. Because when you're reading—just as when you're watching a film—you can take a rest from yourself. You immerse yourself in the characters and forget yourself for a time. It's also a chance to suppress things, quite normally. And I also think that it would have been even more true of video films, if we had had them. Reading is simply not occupying yourself with your own person at a technically lower stage. I have to put this prosaically because that's the way I see it.

I also think that it has a little bit to do with the fact that there really are people who find that their discomfort with reality is articulated by writers, even if only in very small measure. Theater really functioned as satire. When, for example, in a production of Büchner's *Leonce und Lena* the state council enters and consists entirely of blind people dressed in raincoats and carrying canes, that was terrific fun, because everyone understood the metaphors. Of course, literature functioned as a safety valve, but that is precisely the bad effect of literature that I'm talking about. When literature or theater relieves people of the obligation to act for themselves, it's like a group dynamic process: whatever someone does *for* you, even if it's only partially done or badly done, you don't have to do yourself; or you can, if you want to do it yourself, put it off or postpone it. It all serves to maintain the status quo, without your wishing or knowing it, because it relieves people of the necessity of tackling their own problems. If you can go to the theater and really laugh then that's the first step to seeing that you are not alone with your thoughts. Good, then you drink a couple of schnapps and go to bed.

And that's what happened?

Yes, that's what happened. Everyone liked jokes. Jokes are wonderful safety valves, but they never intensify the need for confrontation, your personal confrontation with the circumstances in which you live.

• • •

Wasn't it a surprise for you that in the first election people . . .

No, I wasn't the least bit surprised. They voted 98 percent for the SED; they always come down on the side of power, for the people who hold power, no matter who, whether it's Hitler, Honecker, or Kohl. That's part of the opportunism that's supported by the state and the people. It's a part of the dislike of being, and inability to be, independent.

Isn't that the case everywhere?

I think it's particularly true of the Germans. But because of the artificial situation of always having to be three years old that existed in the GDR, it was more widespread there than among the West Germans. Whatever you say against capitalism—and there's a lot that can be said— existence under it is much more severe, and the individual has to take care of his own life to a much larger degree. And this really leads to people seeing freedom not only as an ideal: they can comprehend freedom in all its aspects. You also have the freedom to die; you have the freedom to be a junkie; you're free to do all sorts of things. No one in the GDR would understand that. I had a recent discussion with someone who wants to force all the junkies to seek psychiatric help. No one can understand that that won't work, that the individual must be free to die of drugs if he doesn't want treatment, because it won't help him if he's forced to undergo treatment. But this is all part of the concept of freedom that is only seen idealistically, but is not understood.

Because people have had so much pressure . . .

They have also exerted pressure, not just been subjected to it. They are both culprits and victims, they really are, in the way they combine their functions. I was too. I swindled the state out of thousands and thousands of marks when I was still a typesetter. We laughed when Honecker once said at a party rally, "There's still a lot more to be gotten out of our factories." We would gladly have obeyed his injunction, but we already had everything that could be gotten out of our factory at home. Every one of us was involved in one way or another, everyone, and anyone who says differently is denying their own experiences. We were saboteurs of socialism and despots. One person exerted pressure on another within the framework of the power at his command. Most people were actively involved in things. And that really has to be understood in a therapeutic sense, own's own part in things. Emancipated from the Protestant notion of guilt.

How long is it since you realized that you are not a socialist?

I was never one. I was never in a party or a mass organization. It was easy because of my confrontation with my parents' generation, which was really in power. At puberty, I experienced my divorce from it. It wasn't a process. In that sense I was really favored by my origins.

Are you still in contact with your parents?

I haven't been in contact with my parents for many, many years, actually before I went to Outer Mongolia, not since the Biermann petition. I don't miss them, and I don't think they miss me either. We simply had little to do with each other, too few common interests. But I'm by no means the only one. I think that my whole generation, or the postwar generation as a whole, has very damaged relationships with its parents' generation.

With politics too?

With politics too, in the narrow sense of day-to-day politics. In a broader sense, I am, of course, a person who thinks completely politically. I believe in politics in the service of power, i.e., capital.

• • •

One entered the party or not, I understand, depending on one's belief in the possibility of changing society. But even without that belief, older writers have said, one could still live from one's party membership book.

I can say something quite clear about that. Of course, there were clearly both categories. There were those who really believed that they could only criticize the party from outside. That can't do much good, you've got to go into it and change it, so to speak, from within. And then of course there were those who knew precisely, "If I want a better paying position, one wage group higher, then it's very helpful if I'm a member." To separate these two categories now is the first mistake. Again it's this distinction between good and evil. I can well understand an individual with two children who was living in a two-room apartment and joined the party because he knew that then he would get a four-room apartment. Things would be better for him, and if things were better he could do more. If an individual improves his personal situation, then he also improves his chances of influencing his nonpersonal situation. I think it's stupid to divide the two up, and say, "Some were hypocrites, and others were honest but misguided sheep." It's simply not true. I think that both things played a part for anyone who joined.

Some professions traditionally recognize a duty to follow some higher or more moral course of action: clearly, a parish priest; less clearly, a scholar or a philosopher. Perhaps just as unclear is the profession of writer.

I think that, as a writer, you do not have a duty. The motives for writing have nothing to do with that. To unmask the writer when he is telling falsehoods, or to find him bad when he is bad and to say that he's bad, is the privilege of the reader, the critic, and of those who have, or want, to confront his work. Creativity and duty are, to a great extent, mutually exclusive.

You're forgetting one thing. In Greek mythology, as you know, creativity was symbolized by limping, by the club foot. Artists, i.e., writers and painters, always appeared limping in the theater of antiquity, as lame people, cripples. That is very important. Most people who begin to paint, to write, or do something similar are people who have not had therapy, people with enormous psychological difficulties. Precisely the ones who turn out to be quite good are often people who work in isolation. They are people who, in part, really do what they do for existential reasons, and not because they have a consciousness of mission. They don't want to save people; they write because there's nothing else that they can do. That puts them in a different position. They can only accept, to a limited degree, the responsibility for what they do. The person who exhibits their work, in the case of paintings, or prints it, in the case of literature, is the one who should take responsibility for it. Of course, the one who brings his things to the notice of the public has to accept questions, reproaches, and criticism, a whole lot of it.

And to say, "I simply wanted to occupy myself," is no answer.

That's no answer. It is an answer as well, but an answer that I would not accept. And since Christa Wolf, for instance, makes herself out to be a good German, as a conscientious left-wing humanist, she has to do justice to this claim. And she does not do it justice. I can only judge her on the basis of her own claims.

UWE KOLBE

February 15, 1991, Hamburg

Uwe Kolbe *(b. 1957) is a lyric poet who in 1987 received a long-term visa permitting him to live in West Germany. His father was an officer for cultural affairs in the Stasi. He has published several books of poems:* Hineingeboren *(1979),* Abschiede und andere Liebesgedichte *(1979),* Bornholm II *(1986), and* Vaterlandkanal *(1990). He took some courses at the Johannes R. Becher Institute in Leipzig in 1980–81, but he had been recognized as a freelance writer since 1976. From 1983 to 1987 he edited the journal* Mikado oder Der Kaiser ist nackt *with Lothar Trolle and Bernd Wagner. His most recent collection of poems is* Nicht wirklich platonisch *(1994). He lives in Hamburg.*

In *Vaterlandkanal*, the poems in the middle section all have dates. Why?

They are old. There are even texts from 1979 in the work. They date from the years that are printed underneath them. I didn't work any further on those texts. They are very engagé, mainly with political themes. For that reason they're labeled satirical today by the person to whom they were dedicated. I can't really go along with that very far, because I took it all much more seriously than just a satire. The other two sections are the book, and what is in between seemed to me quite important to document again. So that's how it looked, and it needn't be rated too highly, but it was an attempt to react in verse to the circumstances of the time: the poems treat concrete and biographical circumstances.

249

In the book you often deal with life in exile. You're very bitter and ironic about it, aren't you?

Yes, absolutely ironic. In the one poem that is called that, dedicated to Günter Kunert, I deal with some of Kunert's earlier figures.[1] There are small Jewish figures in his works, in earlier prose from the 1970s. What's behind the text is a notion of some people who went from the east to the west: as Wolf Biermann also put it, he'd come out of the rain into the *Mist*.[2] The notion was that you were choosing the lesser of two evils. That's not my attitude. The GDR was not only the greater evil but also a situation in which you could not go on living in the long run—the death of all social or human activity. In this connection, the exodus of GDR authors or people from the GDR also disturbed me. But there are also some nice statements by older authors. Hans Joachim Schädlich said that it can't be exile if you arrive and immediately have a publisher, money, and an apartment; and everything is wonderful, and people are speaking the same language. How is that exile? It was formulated before the union of the two German states, and I was just as disturbed by the maudlin sentimentality about that as I am today by the maudlin sentimentality of the former GDR citizens.

How does your experience in Amsterdam fit in with the exile theme?

Well, that has more to do with the travel situation—that wasn't normal. It wasn't tourism, and it wasn't an educational tour, although there were aspects of that about it. Whenever you traveled abroad as a GDR author you were in an exceptional situation. You were more tense than other people. You were a much more attentive traveler and, at the same time, one who was much more concerned with himself. It was an intense time for me in Amsterdam, and important, because I became more familiar with certain everyday forms of living or, rather, I got to know them at once in their otherness and their normality.

I realized a lot of sociopsychological things there. Seventeen million people, whether grown up or not, are completely incapacitated, like small children, so that they themselves are not in the position to take a step, buy a loaf of bread, or order a glass of beer, because Big Brother is there, or someone is there to do it for you. Or, for example, filling out a certain form: you can't do it, because someone does it for you. This principle of delegation is part of socialist bureaucracy, or, I suppose, of every bureaucracy. But the bureaucracy in Western countries tends to delegate a lot to the individual who is looking for something from it, while the eastern bureaucracy functioned so as to take everything away from you.

Many GDR writers looked on themselves as utopians, idealists who hoped that a better society would evolve from a socialist society and economy.

Well, that's something I can only laugh at. And my laughter isn't even bitter any more. Now I just find it ridiculous when grown people say things like that. It goes on in the mentality and tearful sentimentality of the whole of the former GDR population. The Hungarian György Konrad in *Intelligenz auf dem Wege zum Klassenkampf* [1978] describes the road to power for the Communist Party, especially the Bolsheviks.[3] Long stretches of the book are devoted to the marginal intellectuals, that is, the critics of the system who are, however, basically involved in power play; and in the GDR that was a very important element. The writers' power could easily be seen in people like Stefan Hermlin. There was a rumor that he used to play chess regularly with Honecker.

This game—I called it "ring-around-the-rosey with power"—this was something which, as a younger author, you could experience, if you published. As quick as lightning you could get power, that is, influence, fame. That came cheaply, it didn't cost much in the GDR. You would stand in a church, say a few simple sentences—something about the cynicism of power and things like that, that everybody knew, but that they would not have formulated so harshly, or were too cowardly to formulate themselves, or to admit to themselves—and you could already wield an enormous influence, be important, a guru. You could get into it in all innocence. By deviating just a little you could achieve enormous effects. That was connected with the fact that the whole of socialism was merely a linguistic, mental edifice.

Was it dangerous for writers to be so effective?

I think it's very healthy that they aren't any longer. Now they're sitting there in the Writers' Union, which they are still trying to keep going. But it's all a game; those are things that I find ridiculous. From 1976 onwards, the union was a disreputable organization. The fact that they are still trying to keep it going now, with Rainer Kirsch of all people—with a snob, if you like—as its head, is of course curious. He's a brilliant author, but I use the word "brilliant" consciously. An expert, someone who works very finely—but at the head of the former political and ideological instrument and organ of the party! That's where the pure artists are working.

I have been told that verse forms in the GDR were kept more conservative than in the FRG.

For the older people, the generation of Adolf Endler, Karl Mickel, Volker Braun, Rainer and Sarah Kirsch, et al., that's right. It's really astonishing. Different sorts of poems were created—modern ones too—but fundamentally a large number of these poets were classicists. It's not by chance that ancient mythology was pressed into service by so many writers. It would be interesting to compile an anthology of Sisyphus poems that were only written in the GDR—or Prometheus poems. It was the form as well; it wasn't just a topos.

Is the writing of parables part of this?

That was very widespread. Terrible. The pinnacle of the wretched parable-writing is not a poem, but Christa Wolf's *Kassandra,* which can be read as a pure roman à clef. She describes her role at court. Even less necessary were the things that were published about it afterwards. You can see the same thing in Volker Braun, the constant metaphors—it's terrible. There was no satire. And the rulers were taboo, just as themes of state were taboo. For this reason, a novel like Stefan Heym's *Collin* was an enormous violation of the taboo, because the novel was set within the inner circles of power. The rulers were simply taboo, and, for this reason, people took refuge in ridiculous trivialities, until finally Christoph Hein used King Arthur's Round Table as a metaphor for the Politburo. It's ludicrous that people still needed a metaphor like that as late as 1988 or 1989.

All the lovely authors in the GDR were . . . I always like to say quickly, "cowardly"; but we were all cowards, and to be a coward is to be human. I'm very quick to use it as a reproach; but that's nonsense, for then I have to reproach myself as well. Fortunately my generation is the first genuine group of GDR authors and also the last. The first genuine ones dug the grave most easily. I'm very happy with that. The earlier, the middle, generation of lyric poets is enormously strong, the ones who started publishing their poems in the mid 1960s, among them Günter Kunert and Biermann, Sarah Kirsch, Rainer Kirsch, Volker Braun, Karl Mickel, Adolf Endler, Elke Erb. It's a huge group, and then there are marginal figures, such as Czechowski and Kito Lorenc.[4] There are endless names, and all of them significant authors. But they all suffered from one thing: they began by identifying with the socialist model, and that—

especially after the Wall was built in 1961—was the perverse situation. They were particularly impassioned and joyful participants in the buildup of socialism. Their motto was, "Now we're isolated; now we're on our own." It was the Stalinist idea of isolation, of autarchy. They accepted the claim that, isolated behind the Iron Curtain, you could do something, build a healthy world. As Biermann says, "Then they would all come to us." But unfortunately that didn't happen.

Was the promotion of "humanism" and literary translation part of the monumentalization of socialist culture?

Of course; they decked themselves out with every imaginable sort of thing. The whole complex of humanism belongs to the center of the argument. The idea that the home of the true humanist heritage was the GDR was part of the constant struggle with West Germany. Earlier, people had formulated the "heritage" in a much more reduced way, when emphasis was placed almost exclusively on the values of the labor movement. I think that "generally human" and "humanistic" were blurred in the period of the great verdicts and the Lukács discussions.[5] At that time it was given a harsh and reduced formulation, so that only the "progressive" heritage of history was taken over, not everything that was humanistic. Sartre and much later even Sigmund Freud were absorbed as part of "humanism." They had the greatest difficulties with modernism. Gradually, over the past ten years, many of the gaps of literary history were eliminated, but always accompanied by the statement that we were still interested in the humanist heritage. At one point, even Stefan George had to be published because he belonged to the tradition, and the GDR was after all a German state. Towards the end, the tendency became more and more "national," because "GDR" did not function as a means of identification, nor did socialism. And so you had need of the old national tradition, and humanism suited that.

• • •

How big were the editions of your books in the GDR?

At the end they were gigantic. I think all three books ran to over ten thousand copies in their various editions, which is a lot for a volume of poems. One of them ran to thirteen or fourteen thousand, in three editions. Compared with West German or, now, pan-German editions of volumes of poems, that's gigantic. Of course this derives from misunderstanding, because they contained forbidden material, and even poems could substitute for journalism. The poems mentioned the taboos, even if they didn't actually attack them.

That leads back a bit to the authors who now sit at home in the GDR and are desperate because their existence as professional writers is threatened there. Their professional existence wasn't normal; it was hypertrophic, the whole thing. Every text, no matter how small, even when it only contained a minute pointer in a really fair direction, politically, went straight through, even if it was a bad text. That deformed everything. I already know the situation here, and perhaps I'm suffering under it. For example, my editions are now perhaps a tenth of what they were. But I'm not really suffering, only in material ways. At the moment I'm not interested in that.

Literature, as a marginal thing, is very normal in Central Europe and is, in any case, marginal in America. Included in it were a lot of popular forms of art. Literature, and especially poetry, only has a chance to enter the social context in its essential form as a trace element. And at the same time that's what I consider its real chance. I think that the idea of developing yourself on the margins of things has more to offer when you compare it with the situation in which everyone is hanging on to your words and you are obliged to behave in this way or that, the way they actually want you to. I mean being manipulated by the censor into a certain direction, so that you . . .

Conform?

. . . no, no perverse conformity, but that I personally had a bad conscience when I published a volume containing love poems . . . that is perverse. Looking at it today, I would say, "What else? Only love poems!" I think this was a terrible deformation, where I constantly had the feeling that I had to say something of social relevance. Of course it suited me, it was what I wanted, but then it assumed obsessive forms.

By "deformation" do you also mean that if you read a love poem out loud, it was interpreted as though it had political content?

Yes, of course: revolting.

In America we long for a literary culture where poems are as effective as they are in Ireland or Poland.

This was the way West German writers looked at East German ones. They were envious; it was the same thing. Envious! Because by virtue of the censor we had so many readers . . . really perverse. To the point of complete inversion: "Stay there and defend yourselves, we'll go on suffering in the west, because we are ineffective. In compensation we'll go to Tuscany in the summer. You don't have to do that, because you have to suffer."

You spoke about someone imprisoned because of poems, and how no one took any notice. When people talk about the Stasi they seldom mention jail.

The intellectuals really weren't threatened all that much. Now that we read all this stuff in the newspapers and see it all on television—what really happened—you can get frightened retroactively and ask whether you had really played often enough with the thought, "actually it really ought to be otherwise." Like the stinging nettle on Adolf Endler's desk. There's a poem ("Nadelkissen" [1980]) by him where the nettle stays on his desk so that he can sting his finger from time to time. We also played around a bit with the Stasi theme as though it were only a stinging nettle. You could make jokes about it, but actually you didn't really know . . .

. . . how strong it actually was?

Yes, and how much they despised people, and how brutally they went about things, and with what detail, how perfectly organized and glassy everything was. But for intellectuals, especially authors, who somehow or other already had a name—a small publication was enough—the Stasi was not so threatening. That's why I always come back to calling the lot of us cowards. Only others more so than myself, and a lot of them especially so.

Why did so few intellectuals oppose the state?

It was the compromise of living; it was something that was simply human. It functioned. There were little advantages and a little bit of life. As an author you could arrange for that just like anybody else, perhaps a bit better. Perhaps you could have a vacation home somewhere simply because of such institutions as the union. How cheap that was actually! And at the same time you always operated with a good conscience because, on the one hand, you were kicking against the pricks, had produced your criticism and written something and, on the other, you had a critical idea about the reform of the whole thing. You were subjectively upright about the whole project "Socialism," to which there was no alternative.

West Germany couldn't be the alternative. In that way you were in agreement with the left-wing German authors whom you met. The Writers' Union is an organization that was completely involved with the German Communist Party in West Germany. That's also normal. The problem was merely that a particular viewpoint was communicated as being mutually positive and projected onto both the GDR and Federal Republic, always alternating: "You (in the east) must be a bit critical, and we (in the west) have to be fundamentally critical; you (in the west) have to do something against imperialism, and we have to do something about the harmful outgrowths of what is actually right." The common picture was—I don't know—a world freed from exploitation?

That was common to both; they could both have a clear conscience. You were disturbed by the fact that you always had to make more and more small compromises, had to cross something out. You couldn't say something quite as loud if you wanted to travel somewhere later on. It was unpleasant. I'm glad that at the end I saw everything from outside.

Do you think that the authors are questioning each other among themselves?

That's hard to say. Apparently a lot of them are still not doing so, at least not publicly. I've gotten to the point where it really doesn't interest me any longer, these agonies. All right, I'm younger; I have the advantage of belonging to another generation. I have the peace of mind to wait. I think it will happen sometime. But not in the form of the campaigns that are being fought by today's feuilleton writers; they themselves have difficulties, apparently. They could have found out earlier that one or another of the GDR writers was not to be valued so highly as a literary person, but they did value them highly because they came from the GDR and were a bit critical politically. Even to the point where they were going to propose Christa Wolf for the Nobel Prize.

Also, at the moment, the atmosphere is wrong. No one's interested any more in any case. The public in the former GDR isn't in the least interested any more about what happened there and what writers still have to say. The decisive appearance was when Christa Wolf cosigned the famous appeal, "For Our Country." That was, I think, the last public act by writers in the old style. That was partly instrumental in bringing about the situation that, after that, only derisive laughter—or election results—answered.

SASCHA ANDERSON, I

September 4, 1990, West Berlin

Sascha Anderson (b. 1953) is a lyric poet, editor, and publisher. He was trained as a printer and then, in the 1970s, studied filmmaking for three years. In the late 1970s he was imprisoned for writing bad checks. After his release he moved from Dresden to Berlin, where he was known as the impresario of the avant-garde scene in Prenzlauer Berg during the 1980s. He edited the important anthology Berührung ist nur eine Randerscheinung *(1985). His collections of poems include* jeder satellit hat einen killersatelliten *(1981),* Ich fühle mich in Grenzen wohl *(with Bert Papenfuss and Stefan Döring, 1985),* brunnen, randvoll *(1988), and* jewish jetset *(1991). He translated a selection of the poems of the beat poet Bob Kaufman (1990). In 1986 he left the GDR to live in West Berlin. In 1991 he was exposed as an important informant for the Stasi.*

Hermann Kant told me that the past forty years have been a good time for literature.

I can't imagine that a state that functions feudally and uses fascist methods to boot can, in any sense of the word, be a basis for literature. All right, everything is a basis for literature—the table, Africa, New York—so why not the GDR? But why *more so* than other places—that's what I don't understand.

Because you could survive there as a freelance.

The writer's profession is so diversified. The journalist is a writer, the lyric poet; anyone who writes, why shouldn't they call themselves

257

writers? But what calling yourself a writer contributes to literature I simply wouldn't know. It does provide a certain social security that, at the present moment, I consider anachronistic, and it raises the consciousness that when we stick together we are strong, but who are we to be strong against? That's the question: why do we need this strength? It comes from the working class tradition: united we are strong. But now we're in a period in which everything has become senseless. It is the senselessness of strength.

How did you live in the GDR? Did you have a job like other people?

Yes, I didn't like it, but I did. Everybody had some sort of job or some spurious appointment. You had to work in the GDR. If I hadn't worked I would have been regarded as asocial. You didn't need all that much money in the GDR. If you had about four hundred to five hundred marks a month—as a young person—or even less, three hundred marks, then you had enough to live on. Rent was about twenty marks, living was very cheap. On this basis everyone was able to live, or some older writer or other gave you some money every now and again, or we produced something together and then sold it, and we managed. For instance, I did a lot of music, but I did it under a pseudonym, I worked for rock groups. Money wasn't a problem at all.

When did you decide not to join the Writers' Union?

It was a principled decision on my part not to belong to anything, to be able to say, "I'm not in any party, not in any organization, and I'm not in the Writers' Union either," that's perfectly clear.

Here in West Berlin, would you also not join PEN?

I don't think so. Actually, not founding an autonomous Writers' Union proved to be more useful than founding it, because if we had founded it, they'd have been able to get hold of us more easily. We sat down together in 1984 with forty or fifty writers of our own generation and didn't found a union. Nonfounding of the union protected us more, kept us together more, than its founding could have.

There was a time, at the beginning of the eighties, when the West Germans said we were in a period of new inwardness. What is happening politically is exactly the opposite: there is no longer a society in which there are different niches. People opened up their own apartments for social events, for social life. People held readings in their apartments—

not that it started then. Biermann sang in apartments too. But then it got to the point where everyone could come, and it was completely open. There were no more conspiracies, as there had been in the sixties. In the sixties, what happened was that twenty people were invited, and the event took place. It was a conspiratorial circle, or at least not everyone had access to it, whereas in the eighties it was advertised, this or that is taking place, at this or that time, in an apartment, and anyone who wanted to could come. It started with exhibitions held by painters in their own studios, because the galleries didn't accept them, then readings took place in the studios, and then people opened up their apartments. This is placing your own space at the disposal of the public. That means a great deal. When people open up their apartments they've opened up themselves, they've placed themselves at other people's disposal, they have become very social individuals.

Why did the authorities allow apartments to be opened up?

Well, I don't really know. Apparently it's something that comes from English law. I'm really puzzled why the Germans didn't just say: "Your apartment belongs to the state. It's true that you rent the apartment, but we'll decide what you do in there." Somehow or other there is a traditional law that you are master of your own dwelling and the family is sacred; that's German, and it happens to play a big part in the working-class tradition. "You've got to work, you produce, you dig everything out of the bowels of the earth and then you go home, and that's your home." Apparently the people who ruled the GDR and who came from the working class grew up with precisely this tradition, this petit bourgeois tradition that emerges from the labor movement. It's possible that they cling much more to the old things than is imagined.

But surely they sent Stasi informants along to the meetings?

Of course. Everything was possible, and they did that too. But if the Stasi informants are sitting down with you, it's better than if they're slinking around outside the door or threatening you at night. The possibility that the Stasi would always be there reassured them. They actually only became aggressive if they were kept out. If something conspiratorial was going on, then they started to sit up and take notice. But without conspiracies there was no violent Stasi action of that sort.

We knew that. We also knew some of them, and we used to drink together. We all drank a lot, and after we'd had a few they would tell us their side of the story as well. They weren't permanent employees, they were all just informants. They needed some human warmth, and they found more of it with us than they did with their employers. It was all OK. They were young people, women too—the whole range was there.

You said that artists started this system. How did you come to collaborate with artists?

Perhaps it's easier to live with people who do not work in the same medium as yourself. And then again, I simply grew up with art. We had impressionists at home. I come from Weimar. I saw my first impressionist painting in the museum—Beckmann's *Youths Bathing*, painted in 1904 or thereabouts—and then I went to Dresden and came into contact with Dresden expressionism. That was a great break. In Dresden there were mainly artists and no writers. I didn't know anyone in Dresden who had anything to say to me. I simply wanted to produce something together with the people I met there. But it didn't do much for me, when we sat down at a table and everybody explained his system, how he did things, and afterwards we'd all break up. I'm not a reflective type, so that didn't have any effect on my work. I needed to make something out of all this sitting down together, and then I simply thought, "I'm a poet, and I know a whole lot of poets in Berlin, these people were all Dresden artists; now let's try it with books." Then in the GDR we needed a permit to publish, first of all a permit to set the text in type, and a permit to print the text, and then you needed a thousand other permits. It's not just one office that gives the permits, but ten. And that's a long, long road till you reach your goal.

However, an artist was allowed to make up to one hundred prints of a work, and if there was a written text within the picture that was his business. That was the loophole in the law, and we placed ourselves in that gap and exploited it both formally and aesthetically. That was the whole trick with the art books and the fact that afterwards you had something in your hand that documented the communal way in which people lived or thought. From 1980–85, when I was there, about thirty art books were produced in the scene, and they were widely distributed.

There were also periodicals with editions of one hundred, where the painter made a different jacket each time. The fact of the jacket made the work into a unique volume, and they didn't require printing permits. It was all so stupid. But in this way an aesthetics of the periodical developed. People copied their own texts. We had authors whom we liked, who were perhaps in the union or the party, but that didn't matter at all. We liked their texts and included them. There were no boundaries: "You're in the party, I'm not in the party." They sat down and copied out twenty copies of one text, and in one volume there were nineteen authors. Then the whole thing was bound together, and there was one copy left, and that was published; or everyone passed around the copy they had received. Then for the first time ever, people had a chance to read what the others were writing.

Were you so aware in 1980 that your literary life would be constantly involved with struggles against legal obstacles?

At a certain point, becoming involved with the official publishing houses would have been death, and for some authors it was death; there was no rapprochement afterwards. And then there was still another way open to us: to publish in West Germany. Having a publisher in the west was also very good for one's image in the east.

Frauke Meyer-Gosau wrote recently that the "scene" is over now. It's one thing to create a scene, she says, but writing poems is another. What are the consequences of that difference?

As far as I'm concerned that's not crucial. But for literary studies, of course, the poem is more valuable than the scene. But perhaps not even for that; sometimes you prefer the scene, sometimes literature. The funny thing is that they are placed in opposition to one another. Literature was produced only because there was a "scene." That's a fact. The rest just doesn't matter. How the individual thinks of himself, what standards he or she applies, that's a personal decision. The scene isn't over, it's just assumed another form. While the state is disintegrating, the scene is cohering. The whole society is disintegrating in fear, in hope, and all sorts of concepts like that. And in the east, our publishing house is collaborating with the west. That's another form of scene. But that probably doesn't have all that much effect on literature. We're too postpubescent for that.

Perhaps you can explain how you worked.

When I was young, fifteen to seventeen, I played jazz. That was at the end of the sixties, and jazz was what was important for me then. It was a bit more aggressive then than previously, but it was always somewhat aggressive. Later I played rock music—that was at the end of the seventies, actually in the mid eighties too—but the reason for that was not that I was a great fan of rock. I really prefer classical music. I made music because it helped me get to know completely different people. At that time we held a lot of readings in a very small circle—the clubs or private circles—and at some point you always end up saying the same thing; you always meet up with the same sort of questions, the same people, the same sort of intellect. For me, then, rock music was a different sort of stage—different public, different people, and a different sort of work. I wrote my own texts, and I sang them myself.

How did it go?

For the GDR, spectacularly, but it was otherwise quite normal music. If I were to make a comparison, the sort of music we made was like Captain Beefheart, a very highly constructed, but very aggressive kind of rock. As far as I'm concerned that was really a side issue: something I needed in order to be what I was, but not something that was fulfilling.

Was it attractive reading the poems to music?

Not in the least, as far as I was concerned. The way the public reacted to them was interesting when, for example, in the middle of a rock concert I switched off the music and read a poem or a story. What does a rock audience do—they're used to breaking the chairs up. That's what interested me. The rest didn't interest me at all. The effect of rock music is so familiar to me. That's what we grew up with in school. People explained to us what rock was and how it affected people. We knew all that.

You have no great ambition to present your poems to an audience?

None at all. If I do readings at all, then the thing I like best is to have other people there who read with me, and I'm much more interested in the dialogue with the audience than in reading poems. When I do readings, I usually read texts for a quarter of an hour—that is at most ten poems—and then I ask the audience to engage in a dialogue, or we leave it at that. The average length of my readings is ten to twenty minutes.

In the States, readings are a significant form of publication, because more people listen to readings than actually read books of poetry.

And I think it's right, too. It was exactly the same in our case. Because of the many readings that we held, in the east, we had a much larger audience and were much better known than the people who had only written a book and were never read. But I never felt any pressure to publish, that's the difference. Books are a very lofty form of publication mainly because they insist on the individual. But as far as I'm concerned, my own person is not in the least important. My person plays no part in my writing at all; it is of no interest to me when I write. Perhaps it does play a part, but it doesn't interest me.

You said that, for you, personal life was politically important.

If we want to do something communally, and we discuss the form that we will do it in, then we can quickly reach agreement. That's the really simple possibility inherent in the decision to do something: this way or that. In politics that's not possible. I consider private life more politically effective than the politics of public life. I think pluralism is a tremendous experience: everything is possible, and everything is shit. But it's OK for it to be that way. Everybody is an artist. For me that's the basic situation I accept. Then we can begin to talk to one another about whether one artist should give up making art and another should go on. But in the east, in a society dominated by ideology, it was completely different: this person was an artist, this one a worker, and the other a politician. It was quite clear. That's the way it was, but the recent trend is different. And this trend is noticeable in the most private sector. It has fatal consequences, because if my neighbor starts telling me things about poems, I want to throw up. But I know that the possibilities—that is, the social possibilities—lie in just that situation.

What sort of effect did French literary theory have on your colleagues?

Here in West Berlin there was a small publisher, the Merve Verlag, and their books were read very closely in the eastern scene. The books were mainly about Foucault, Baudrillard, and Barthes, as well. The publisher had published translations of the works of this whole circle, which was very important for the scene.

You have to realize that everybody wrote poems. That's OK. They wrote poems every day. And then people noticed that there was a huge mountain of these productions. I'm telling you this from today's perspective. At the time, I was not really clear about it. And this overproduction had to be stopped somehow. Otherwise the scene would have burst. In a society that was functioning normally, even a literary society, it would not have reached that stage, because there is a reflective level in such a society. That's to say, the text that reaches the public has been reflected upon. This is how the poet decides whether to write or not, or to write differently, or to go on writing in the same way. It regulates itself. But because it was a very homogeneous situation—so many artists—they all wrote texts without stopping. The reflective level had to be introduced from outside.

You could remain an artist even if you worked as an essayist. This was a quite direct effect of the interest in theory. We had to stop production. And we did stop it by, for example, founding a periodical, called *Ariadnefabrik,* that only published essays by artists. The idea that you could divert production into reflection in this way was something quite new and helpful for our generation. Production declined rapidly, and after the event, I would say that that was probably the start that should have had a much much greater effect. The scene should have reflected upon itself, because that's something that also happens in society.

The east was hell-bent on production. Whether it was effective or not didn't matter; they produced like maniacs. That's their tradition, or else their consciousness of themselves depends upon production. In the west there are contrary trends. When I look at artists' studios in the east now, they're full of pictures, crammed with pictures, not because they can't exhibit them, but because they go to their studios every day and paint three pictures. If they'd had to pay ten marks rent per square meter, they wouldn't have painted a picture every day, because they wouldn't have known how they were going to pay for the space to store the pictures. Then there's the fact that there's paint on the picture, and paint comes from the earth, and they pour their turpentine down the drain. Something should have been done, so that at the point where we reflected upon ourselves, someone would have also reflected on the question of why it had all taken place. But we couldn't manage to do that. It was simply too early. The artist's ethos is satisfied by production. That's something really fatal. Those little books from Merve Verlag, the essays by Baudrillard, Lyotard, Foucault, and Barthes began to introduce a critical perspective on the scene.

RAINER
SCHEDLINSKI

September 12, 1990, East Berlin

Rainer Schedlinski *(b. 1956) is a lyric poet, essayist, and editor who greatly influenced the absorption of French theory by writers of the Prenzlauer Berg group. Like Sascha Anderson, he was exposed in 1991 as an informant for the Stasi. Since 1982 he has been a freelance literary critic. In 1986 he founded the journal* Ariadnefabrik, *for which he received a regular subvention from the Stasi. This essayistic journal was intended to theorize the literary and artistic practice of the Prenzlauer Berg scene. He has published two collections of poems,* die rationen des ja und des nein *(1988) and* die männer/der frauen *(1991); and a collection of essays,* die arroganz der ohnmacht *(1990).*

Was your generation of poets less attracted to the SED than previous generations had been?

Among the older generation there was always a critical ambition to change society from within. There was scarcely any of that among my generation, because the conditions were already clear. They were inflexible and unchangeable, so reform seemed impossible from the outset. Earlier the most important dissidents came from within the party, like Bahro and Havemann and Biermann and Stephan Krawczyk.[1] In the sixties and seventies, the whole of art, the DEFA [Deutsche Film AG] films, and literature had fought to extend the limits imposed by censorship, and to change society through party discussions. But I think that in the mid seventies it became clear that it couldn't happen here, because of the party's inflexibility.

That is, after Biermann?

Yes, after Biermann the party's cultural policy became retrogressive. This made the older people resigned, but perhaps it actually opened up opportunities for the younger ones. The blackmailing attitude of the regime became clearer and clearer. For example, the director of a gallery would be visited by the Stasi and forbidden to hold certain events. Then the Stasi would come to an artist and say: "Don't go to the gallery. You don't want your friend, the gallery director, to be dismissed." Then the point comes when you can't go along with it any longer, you have to make a decision. You can't stick to such agreements. People worked in a lot of fields thinking that if they made concessions at one point they could achieve something somewhere else— make something possible, change things. When we were published by the Aufbau Verlag in 1988, not one line was corrected, or changed, or censored. The people who made cultural policy knew that we wouldn't stand for having so much as a word altered.

Your generation developed a third possibility, in addition to joining the party or expatriating. How would you describe that?

Of course, an actor can hardly work without a theater, but a painter can exhibit his works without a gallery; he can organize things himself. We publishers knew how to organize things ourselves; we did our own printing. For the older generation that wasn't possible. To that extent we did have a third possibility. If you weren't published you didn't have to conform or go to the west. You could print your stuff here. You simply had to take the risks into account, but there never actually were any. For as long as I can remember, no one was convicted of illegal publishing or holding illegal exhibitions. There was always a bit of harassment, but it was always tolerable. In part we looked on it as funny. But this possibility didn't come about until the eighties; before that, no one would have dared to print anything without permission. I'm sure it was connected with the new technology: people had laser printers, computers, copiers. Of course, that was also illegal, but the technology was so advanced that the state could no longer stop people from exchanging information.

Then it wasn't a question of the older generation's being too cowardly to try it. They didn't have the technological possibilities at their disposal—plus the previous political climate was different.

The idea first had to mature—or the independence. You first had to be conscious of autonomy. That calls for certain historical premises, and these probably weren't shared until the eighties. It wasn't only the young ones, there were older ones too—Gert Neumann, Adolf Endler, and Elke Erb—who worked on the periodicals that we were producing.[1]

And the older ones were members of the Writers' Union?

Yes, some of them. Endler wasn't. Some of them had resigned, and if they were still members it was only a matter of habit. The difference wasn't who was official and who wasn't. You can't draw such a distinct line. Of course, there were authors in the GDR who had been publishing for years and yet were still some of the leading enemies of the state, and then there were those who were never published but who had never had anything against the authorities. You can't infer opportunism from the fact that someone was a member of the union, or from the fact that they were published here. There are a lot of other criteria that go to make up such a judgment.

What were the new enabling political conditions in the eighties?

The asocial statutes that declared that everyone had to work, like it or not—or they would be hounded by the taxman—weren't strictly enforced.

Since when?

Since the beginning of the eighties. From then on you didn't necessarily have to be in the union. The social premises for collective work were there. You could move to Berlin and live in a house; you could work together. A lot was done with bands. You could form a band and have your texts taken round by them. I did it less, but in the beginning Bert Papenfuss and Sascha Anderson did it that way. You weren't dependent on being an informant in order to make a living, simply because the social pressure was off in the GDR. Perhaps the Stasi accepted the fact. It was decided simply to accept such things, because there were always people who ran their own galleries or did their own printing. Perhaps it was the result of an order from above or happened by way of a process of softening up. You can't really say.

· · ·

Hermann Kant and Rainer Kirsch spoke fondly of a "land of reading" because of the very large editions that were published.

There's a big question about this much-quoted "land of books." The figures are merely statistics. Books were sold to firms, to libraries; the

editions were in part complimentary copies of these books published
by the state. When, on the other hand, I see what there is in West Berlin
alone—how many publishing houses, how many literary periodicals,
how many fellowships, readings, literary cafés, societies for the promotion of literature, etc.—then all this about the GDR as "the land of reading" is obviously a lie. My readings in the west—since 1987 I've been
able to travel—were always well attended. I was always more read and
better known in the west, and it was the same with other authors. What
sold well here was, of course, state literature, but the fact that it sold
doesn't mean that it was also read. They were compulsory sales, just as
the work teams got complimentary movie tickets. Whether they went or
not didn't matter. Those are rotten statistics, behind the "land of reading." Overall, it was pretty much the exact opposite.

**Do you see any concrete differences between the authors who
were in the Writers' Union and those who were not?**

Well, authors like Christa Wolf and Christoph Hein work with completely different assumptions. They hold to the traditional concept of the
public, the traditional concept of the subject. As far as I'm concerned,
there is not *a* public. So the question that is now often asked—whether
GDR writers failed—doesn't affect me either, because it again implies
that a social demand is made upon literature. I think that's unhealthy.
The sociocritical taking up of themes is the exact reverse of a state
commission. It was in America that graffiti was invented; that's where
they breakdance, without anyone having to ask what it means, or what
people are trying to express by it. Either people feel that it's our feeling
for the age, or they don't. It's quite a simple decision, no one has to
formulate a social demand. Of course that's a German syndrome.

It's not only the state that demands something from literature, but
also vice versa: the critical authors have formulated a very dubious critical social mission for themselves. We are in an age when the public is
parceled out by the media. People are divided up among all the genres.
There are people who listen to jazz, and those who listen to pop music.
Why should it be any different in literature? As far as I'm concerned,
people should be equally accepting of literature and not always be demanding everything for everybody. And this has consequences for political thought and for writing itself. In a traditional way, people still talk of
the subjective view of the author if something is especially enigmatic,
but I consider that rather as an objectivization, if you are speaking with

things and not *about* them. The French, of course, distinguish between speaking and language. Speaking actually becomes clearer the more individual it becomes, because it is only when it breaks with convention that it stands out. The more stereotypical it becomes, the more it belongs to language and the less it belongs to speaking. These aren't theories that I've used to derive a way of writing; they rather arise out of the logic of the writing itself.

I think a particular social climate will always invent its own cultural signs. In school, in the army, you develop your own peculiar jargon, your own hairdo. These are signs, they are agreed upon, and they are right for a certain group. I think it is healthier, instead of laying claim to universality, to relate to a microclimate like that, and then communication is also right. Before we were published, I had the experience of holding readings in churches, and they were full. There were two thousand people there, and after I had been published by the Aufbau Verlag we went into the provinces and read poems to fifteen old women in Hoyerswerda, in some little town or other, and it was pointless. There was absolutely no contact. It was then that I realized that the effect of literature does not increase with the size of the edition, but with the friendliness, the harmony, and the natural social communication of the environment in which you live, and this is what you relate to in your writing. I don't write for myself, but for my friends.

Is harmony a sort of urban art?

Yes, I mean, here in Prenzlauer Berg it wasn't a Bohemia. There weren't only artists; there was a perfectly normal social structure. There were alcoholics, asocial types, also some who made a lot of money dealing in automobiles, and barkeepers. Yet, in spite of that, it was a group that was united by one thing: namely, that you could live here with the smallest possible amount of social control. It was by no means only painters and poets who isolated themselves here.

Why were the lyric poets of Prenzlauer Berg particularly intent on a critical scrutiny of linguistic structures?

I always start with the spoken sentence, even if it is syntactically distanced and broken up. But Papenfuss writes in thieves' cant—that's an old argot—or in Yiddish, or Hebrew, or English, or Old Celtic, in order to uncover the actual meanings of the words. He was once asked in the Academy of the Arts, on the occasion of his first reading in the GDR—that was 1986 or 1987—how he came to be a writer. Erik Neutsch, the state poet, asked him.[3] And Bert said, "We went to school every morning in the bus, and read the newspaper, and started laughing as soon as we saw the headlines." Of course, it's a question of mentality, a consciousness of language like that. You have to feel the words quite differently, or see them more acutely, then you can write something like that. For me that is a perfectly plausible explanation. The linguistic situation that was predominant here was extreme: extremely normalized and meaningless, senseless and involuntarily comical. When you develop a sense for this involuntary comicality, then it is an ideal country in which to play games with words.

I assume that your generation does not have to come to terms with the question of shared blame?

Yes, that's right. Yet when we got passports, in 1987 or 1988, we were breaking off from our readership, because we suddenly had privileges. It's difficult when you're holding a reading in front of a lot of eighteen-year-olds and you start reading a poem from the cafés of Amsterdam: that's pure cynicism. To that extent, a breach did take place—because of the privileges. But that's a difficult situation. Are you to give up a journey just so as not to have more than all the others? If that's shared guilt, OK. But that was the effect it created. Uwe Kolbe and a lot of other authors were discredited in this way, although apart from that, they had done nothing reprehensible. That was a clever move on the part of the state.

What was the procedure for getting a passport? Were you told that you could now simply collect your passport, or did you apply for it?

We had been getting invitations for a long time to poetry festivals in Belgium, Holland, and West Germany every year, for ten years. We applied from time to time, but we were always refused. The people in the Ministry of Culture who refused us always acted very helpfully and considerately. They said, "I would like to let you go, but I can't get anything approved." Then one day they simply said, "Now it's OK, now we can put it through." At some point, it all worked out. For some reason they got the green light from above.

Can you formulate a political perspective for the writers of Prenzlauer Berg?

We are very political, but simply in a different way. You see, the generation of authors that wanted to change society from within demanded that censorship be eliminated, publishing houses and periodicals be allowed to set themselves up, and other authors be published who weren't allowed to be published. We didn't ask these questions any more. As soon as we noticed that our words were falling on deaf ears, that we were up against a wall, we simply went ahead, and, to that extent, we were political because we acted. We didn't ask anybody, we did it, and that's the difference. We understand politics as action and not as complaint or demand.

But we were always a bit suspicious of the Protestant will for change. Somehow I sensed that what has happened would happen. We were a minority then, and we're in the minority again now. I was an enemy of the state before, and now I'm an enemy of the people. What has changed? Well, 98 percent of the people voted for Honecker. If the polls were rigged, they weren't rigged by more than 1 or 2 percent: they would have voted 96 percent for Honecker. They did that voluntarily. Why should I get politically involved for people like that? In the mid-eighties, there was the question of travel abroad. People came streaming into the churches because they wanted to support their travel applications in this way. Then I saw them coming with their white patent leather shoes and their big cars from the west. And I'm to get politically involved for people like that? I thought the whole thing was nonsense. In general I found it all very dubious. That doesn't mean that I agreed with the system. It was simply clear to me that the people would always be the usual ones, what is called the majority. You can't force them to be happy. Everyone has the government they deserve, and you're as free as you choose to be.

Were you in jail?

Yes, for a short time, three or four days, for interrogation and detention, but I was never sentenced.

Why were you there?

No particular reason. Previously they didn't need a particular reason. Every six months you were brought in again and interrogated. That was standard.

Didn't that scare you?

No, actually it didn't. You weren't beaten. The cops beat you sometimes, but the Stasi didn't. They always acted correctly, and you saw the funny side of it a bit. We always laughed about whose tail [Stasi agent] was outside, yours or mine, and we made a joke of it. That was how we played with the authorities. There are authors like Detlev Opitz, who created a literary form out of it.[4] He was always bringing cases to court that he was constantly reducing to absurdity, so much so that nothing happened to him when he did so. It wasn't all that serious. No one who was critical of the state was in prison for long. He was shot off to the west. That was the worst that could happen to you; that was the weak point of the system. They were, as Nietzsche would say, frustrated in their instincts: quite different from the Nazis, or the Stalinists. Here even the most stubborn of the bigwigs made a moral claim to want to be better.

BERT
PAPENFUSS-GOREK
February 14, 1991, East Berlin

Bert Papenfuss-Gorek (b. 1956) has been a freelance writer in Berlin since 1980, though he has had difficulty publishing his poetry in the GDR. A first book of poems, harm, *appeared in 1985. Since 1989 a number of his poetry manuscripts have been published:* Dreizehntanz *(1989),* Vorwärts im Zorn *(1990),* Tiske *(1990),* Soja *(1990),* Led Sadaus *(1991), and* Nunft *(1992).*

Literature does not have an important function in American society. Since 1941 literature was supposed to be strongly integrated into the GDR society. Writers gained considerably in prestige through the support of the state.

The generation before mine, people like Christa Wolf and Heiner Müller, was really involved with the system. They entered the system in the fifties and tried to work in politics as well as literature, apparently on the basis of a tradition that also embraced Brecht and others. Many personalities in cultural politics in the fifties were writers who like Brecht had emigrated to America or the Soviet Union or Mexico. They then returned and started to work at the social experiment, the actually existing socialism. The first generation died off fairly quickly. Then the new generation established itself: Christa Wolf and Heiner Müller. They entered the system and tried to achieve something from within. One part of the people became corrupted and adjusted to the system. Christa

273

Wolf became something like the "conscience of the nation." As early as the 1960s Heiner Müller took up a critical stance, as did Biermann.

In the fifties, in Christa Wolf's generation, they had a fairly concrete social scheme. They dreamed of the new socialist being and wanted to create it, just as fascism wanted to breed a new type of being. There was a final break with this tradition of social schemes and new beings in the seventies. Not by everyone of course. Perhaps you can see this—and this sounds a bit bold and impudent—but we wrote scarcely any children's books, for example, or very few. A lot of people made adaptations of material for children's books to earn money or wrote radio plays, but there was no serious tendency towards didactic or pedagogic projects. That is actually a pity, but I can only explain it to myself by remembering the fact that the claim to work for a social scheme was no longer present. If you have a scheme of this sort it will result in the desire to teach it to other people and to children as well. I don't find the concept "hopeless" all that bad. It is not a negative concept. Because hope is always stubbornness, an illusion to which you abandon yourself. I can live very well without hope. I can relate to the thing I'm involved with—my daily life, my constantly changing political position—that's confrontation enough for me. I don't have to fight for some hope or other.

I was born in 1956. The people with whom I work and whom I know well were also born in the 1950s. So we are yet another generation. I started writing about the beginning of the 1970s, pretty conscious of my underground position. I knew that I did not want to enter the system, and I refused the offers that I received to be culturally politically active. At the beginning I was in a very difficult position. I could scarcely hold readings.

When was that?

The first public readings were 1977–78, and then the ban was imposed. Some Stasi guys or some cultural political authority had learned of these readings, which were really official—that is, they were held in youth clubs or at gallery openings—and they did not agree either with the formal, or, especially, with the political aspect. It was clear at the first readings that my work was oppositional. I could not be politically categorized and involved. At the time, in a roundabout way, Karl Mickel got to know some texts of mine. He thought they were good and stood up for them. He tried to persuade me to join the Writers' Union. If you wanted to join the Writers' Union you needed two sponsors. I made an application not because I really wanted to join the union but because I was interested whether it would happen—or rather, I knew precisely that it wouldn't happen. In spite of Karl Mickel's recommendation, they rejected me. That seemed quite normal. I didn't regard myself as a writer who had anything to hope from a union. The union could have helped me financially in the early stages, but in principle that was all. There was certainly no prospect of publishing books. I knew the publishing program and the sort of people who worked for the publishers. My manuscript sat with the Aufbau Verlag for ten years, from 1978. It appeared in 1989.

What did the editors say in the meantime?

At the beginning I was actively involved. I went to them from time to time and spoke to people. They wanted to censor certain things: there were texts I was to remove. But I didn't want to, and at some point I simply didn't bother any more. But the manuscript was still there, until 1988, when we were quasi-rehabilitated, but now I'm getting ahead of myself. The anthology that Sascha and Elke Erb published in 1985— *Contact Is Only a Peripheral Phenomenon*—was important. Then the Aufbau Verlag had a new director, Elmar Faber, who tried to brighten things up and think in terms of market strategy.[1] He also thought that he could put us young oppositional GDR authors on the market, especially in the west. He invited all the authors who were in the GDR at that time. Half the people who had contributed to the anthology had, in the meantime, gone over to the west. We all sat down together at the press, and he offered to publish an anthology. We said that in our opinion the potential was strong enough not only for an anthology but to establish a new series of books. Then the editors retired to consult among themselves, thought about it for a few weeks, and agreed. At this time, 1986, I was invited to read at the Academy of the Arts before about fifteen people like Volker Braun, Heiner Müller, Karl Mickel, Gerhard Wolf, and others. Mickel and Wolf gave speeches, and I read a few poems. Everyone thought it was wonderful, and people said it should be published. To give a sign that I was quasi-rehabilitated, the periodical *Sinn und Form* printed a few texts from a cycle of poems that I had put together for this purpose.[2] Then I started to rework the book that appeared in the Aufbau Verlag in 1988–89.

Was this new series wholly integrated in Aufbau Verlag's program?

Well, no. Gerhard Wolf offered to publish the series, and the suggestion for the title, "Outside the Series," came from the publishers. They wanted to indicate that they were treating these authors differently from what is usual in the Aufbau Verlag, where every author becomes an author for the firm. "Outside the Series" was to be an exception.

Like a scruple.

. . . that any author can make his debut there, but there's no guarantee that he can go on publishing with them.

About your first public reading: you said that you didn't fit in with official cultural policy. Was that a question of content or of style?

The texts were difficult for people to understand. First of all, their formal aspects were not clear. There was a lot of word play, a lot of distortion, a lot of playfulness, in which, however, politics plays an important role. There was no clear authorial line and position for readers to recognize.

But from the point of view of content it was clear that the poem was intended to be political?

Yes, that was clear. But the language was different from what was usual at the time in dissident circles. It was not the language of tradition, like Wolf Biermann's. There were people who went on working with the method of clear political expression, like Lutz Rathenow or Rüdiger Rosenthal, who wrote gentle satires on conditions in the GDR in a clear political language, whereas in my texts, ambivalence played a great part.[3] It was more important for me to come to terms with ambivalence than to stand there and say: "The system makes me want to throw up."

Then the first bans on readings started to be imposed. But at the end of the seventies my manuscript was still at the Aufbau Verlag. They kept on delaying, and said, "Perhaps we'll do it next year," and the next year they said, "All right, a year later." But it never happened. In the meantime something like a scene had grown up. Sascha Anderson had come to Berlin from Dresden, and Stefan Döring was here, and a group of friends grew up.[4] You can't describe it as a group, because we never formulated ourselves as a group, but we worked together, did a lot of readings together, worked together on lyric/visual arts projects, together with musicians and painters. We were pretty active, although we were forbidden to perform. At the end we were so suspect that we weren't even allowed to make translations and adaptations. That had been our one chance to make a living.

But that was handled in different ways. There was a general ban on readings by Sascha, and none of the publishers was allowed to work with him. It wasn't as bad in Stefan Döring's case. He was banned now and again but was allowed to make adaptations. I wasn't allowed to do anything. Then we organized our own performances. For private occasions, for example, openings at private galleries or in churches. The church put space at our disposal for oppositional art and literature, although there were difficulties there. People were very scared. From time to time you'd find someone who was willing to risk his hide, like the leader of a cultural center, for example. He put on one event with us before he got thrown out. We were very active in spite of the ban on events and readings. We probably did more readings than the official authors who were reading in normal cultural centers and literary institutes at this time.

Were your readings permitted in this form?

No, they were not permitted. Most events were illegal. We could have been prosecuted. The criminal code was the same as in the previous years, but it was not enforced so strictly. In the 1960s and 1970s you might even have to show where you were working. If you weren't working, you had to reckon with the consequences: you could be given a compulsory job, or, in bad cases, you could be put into prison. That stopped in the 1970s, although the laws on asociality still existed.

· · ·

What was your relationship to the generation of Wolf and Müller when you worked with Sascha? Did you feel critical or indifferent towards them?

It varied. Sascha put together an anthology with Uwe Kolbe that was sponsored by Franz Fühmann and that appeared here in the Academy of the Arts around 1982 to 1984.[5] There were contacts with these people, and we were friends with some of them, such as Karl Mickel and Adolf Endler. We appeared with them in churches too, especially with Adolf Endler and Elke Erb. Less with Karl Mickel, but with him too sometimes. They tried to promote our activities, to make contacts with publishers, and to influence readers and publishers to take our manuscripts seriously and publish them. They helped us financially too. People who were rich like Christa Wolf or Heiner Müller financially supported us, informally, by giving us money or financing certain expensive projects, like publishing books or creating lyric/graphic arts editions or exhibitions. But that doesn't mean that I think everything these people wrote is good. There are good things by Karl Mickel and Adolf Endler in the sense that you can talk about them, whereas Christa Wolf never expected me to read her books or discuss them with her. She was more a social than a literary authority.

A social solidarity among the generations.

Yes, but that has nothing to do with the fact that you were continuing a literary tradition. That was not the case with us. The so-called GDR literature that was written between 1950 and 1980 played no part in my work.

You said that you knew from the beginning that you did not want to be involved in cultural politics. How did you make that decision so early on?

I knew that I was opposed to the system here and that I had no ambition to pick a quarrel with it, though I was in a permanent clinch with the system. People like Lutz Rathenow, Rosenthal, Fuchs, et al., who drew their literary substance from this argument with the GDR, were different.[6] For me it went without saying that I was against repressive tendencies in the system, but that was not my literary substance.

Were these repressive tendencies the worst disadvantage of the system?

No. That somehow went without saying. You dealt with repression more or less doggedly. I always tried not to be too dogged and to get a bit of humor out of the whole thing if it was possible. Of course it was often a nervous business, and you suffered because of that. For example, I had to work at night, and the Stasi waited in front of the house and took me to work. They drove slowly along behind me and waited till I was finished and then saw me home again. Then I realized that they had been asking around in my circle of acquaintances and had tried to recruit people to give them information about me or about us. I didn't think that was so bad. There are people who think quite differently. Lutz Rathenow was much more harshly affected by these procedures. He does not have as much personal distance or humor to get along with the business. Of course the Stasi drove people to suicide and murdered people and so on. That's true. But still I regarded myself more as a poet than as a political fighter.

Your father was a highly placed doctor, and in this way you got to know the authorities.

Yes, my father was a general in the army. I have no idea what he's doing now; I haven't seen him for twenty years. We separated when I was fourteen or fifteen years old. We kept in contact for a few years. Then I refused to do military service, and he had to break off his ties with me officially. His department made him do that.

I can explain a lot of things about that. My father's father had a lot to do with the Nazis and the Gestapo and worked for the secret service. After World War II he was listed as missing. Actually he was not missing but in West Germany and still working for the secret service. My father's reaction to this was to volunteer for the army at eighteen, straight from secondary school into the army, where he became an officer. He was a vehement antifascist, and the officers, of course, were Stalinist. He got into a conflict there. As a result he retired completely from political activity while he studied medicine, and then he became an army doctor. What he did exactly, I don't know. At the end he was a faculty member at the military university in Dresden.

I could have gone on playing the game and opposed my father again. But that seemed too silly. I think it would have been too schematic for my life, to bring to light again the same opposition that my father had had towards his father. Of course I was against my father because sons are against their fathers, but not so schematically and narrow-mindedly. Of course I was against the system he represented for me; but I never saw him, for example, as a personal enemy. Besides, I don't know him all that well. He plays a part for me as a representative of the superstructure, but more in a literary way. That's what I have to come to terms with in my writing, not with him personally. If I shoot off things against the system or the hierarchy, they are always aimed at my father, but really only in the abstract.

This is also Katja Lange-Müller's situation; that's why I asked you.

In my case it sounds interesting because he's a general, but this clash with him didn't play the same part as it did, for example, in Uwe Kolbe's case. His father was a member of the Stasi and a personal enemy when we confronted one another. I did a reading with Uwe in a youth club in the 1980s. The youth club was then closed, and the woman who put on the show thrown out. We traced that back to his father. His father came to the reading as a Stasi observer, listened to it, and then told his bosses that it was no good.

What his son was doing . . .

He always protected his son, so I was the bad guy. Uwe's father then became the Stasi advisor to the Aufbau Verlag. That's why for years my books were never published. The clash Uwe had with his father is much closer and more direct than it was in my case. It's the same in the Brasches' case. The distance between my father and me is too great for me to be able to look on him as a personal enemy. He is an abstract quantity to me like "the state" or "the system" or "the army."

But I only understood the psychological dimensions of this when I was in the army myself. My father also comes from a long tradition of Prussian officers. I wasn't prepared for the army. I was already very old, twenty-six when I joined up. I had a wife and a child. It tore me away from my life. Because I'd refused military service, repressive measures were still taken against me in the army. People who had refused military service were from all imaginable sects: Seventh Day Adventists, Jehovah's Witnesses, a few anarchists and neo-Nazis, and a few homosexuals. That was the mixture, but it was also nerve-wracking because the interesting experiences that were to be had came in a period of eight weeks, though I had eighteen months to get through. I've written a lot about my time in the army. The next book from the Galrev Verlag will contain the texts that confront the militancy I have within me as an inheritance of psychic ingredients. In the final analysis, rhetoric itself is militant, and the texts confront that.

I asked you before about the political significance of formal experimentation.

The formal elements were the main thing for the group of people with whom I worked. It's different in the case of "political writers" like Lutz Rathenow and Rüdiger Rosenthal. They also work more as journalists; they wrote for a lot of newspapers and periodicals in the west. Their books and poems are political in the sense that they do not attack the formal structure, but the political structure. But we worked very formally, though we also used political language. I have to write as well as possible in order to be able to live. I use any language I can. Political language in the GDR was very stimulating and penetrating. You had to confront it. It flowed into texts, mostly in satirical form, or upside down, or distorted, or totally playful. My texts were also regarded as political poems because they used this subject. But not only this subject. I had exactly the same sort of confrontation with the fossilized language of science, or the newspapers, or colloquial language, or gutter language, or underground language like thieves' cant. I really tried to confront all forms of language. Because political language happened to be one of them, my texts were seen as having a stronger political dimension than I would have wished. For me, that was only a part of speech with which I was working, but the text could be read as a political one.

Reiner Kunze said that political excitement in the GDR was so great that many poems that were not intended to be political were interpreted as such.

The process of politicizing literature in the GDR is very interesting. When we began giving readings in the 1970s, they were really communicative events. They were very long, even if only one author was reading—two hours, sometimes longer. In between there were shortish pauses in which a conversation would start. That's to say, people were there to communicate. The text was understood as a stimulus to communication. There were also a lot of political discussions that were tough, where people would say what was not permitted to be said in the GDR. Things were approached very directly, and very clear opinions were expressed. There were certainly Stasi people present on each occasion who kept an eye on the whole thing. And there were certainly also provocateurs present who asked provocative questions. The public expected patterns of identification from the writers—patterns with political relevance. That actually came from the previous generation of Heiner Müller, Christa Wolf, and Karl Mickel. We, who worked more formally, also provided patterns of identification for the public. Not to the extent that Christa Wolf did, but we did do so, and thus contributed to the political discussion that took place after and often during the readings.

Today, readings are different. There are scarcely any discussions afterwards. People are looking less for identification patterns than simply trying to take the text as text. Today's writers make more of a show of it. You go there and try to read your poems as impressively and with as much bravura as possible. Appearances are short in comparison with those days—about half an hour. But that was also our experience in the west. From 1988 on, it was possible for me to travel to the west and hold readings there. In the beginning, I was still the exotic from the GDR, and then there was always a discussion about the GDR theme. But

I also held readings where it was no longer announced; the exoticism was no longer there. There were no politically motivated questions and discussions, and instead people concentrated on the text. I actually prefer that to the paranoia that excited the public here. People found something to suspect in everything that could be seen politically. The public reacted in exactly the same way as the Stasi; it was looking for something everywhere. In the final analysis, it was a bit demeaning for poets always to have to deliver patterns of identification.

Novels come more inevitably into politics than lyric poetry.

Yes, I think you're right. The subversive tendency in lyric poetry is of course incomparably stronger than in the novel or in a large narrative work that is more suited to superstructures. Poems never have this political relevance, or for my part merely material relevance, as the novel does. When I hear poems by someone I try to imagine the attitude to life or the philosophy that is expressed in the poems as a political system. The less repressive the system, the better I find the poem, and the less it can be exploited for a repressive policy.

Irrespective of whether it is left or right?

Yes. That's not all that makes a poem good, but it plays a part for me: it ought not to be able to contribute to the build-up of a new ideology. Utopian tendencies in literature come from the great novels and not out of small volumes of poetry. I am a reactive. A large part of what I write is criticism of ideology. The only method I had to offer in a propagandistic sense was uncontrollability. In the final analysis that was what we practiced. We were constantly under observation and had to react uncontrollably for these people in order to be able to bring about certain things at all. To pull people's legs a bit, to tease them. They thought in logical sequences, whereas we were in the position to leap and move around in complete freedom. We were relatively uncontrollable as far as they were concerned. But still only relatively. I would not make a present of my writings to any party politics.

You've spoken of ambivalence about some political issues. Is your effort to try to maintain independence of thought?

Perhaps the German expression *Gleichgültigkeit* [indifference] is the right term, because it has the same duality of meaning. On the one hand, being indifferent means that everything is uninteresting, but the literal meaning is that everything is equally valid, is to be taken seriously in the same way and to the same degree, or has the same value. I make my political decisions at the polls or when I take sides in a political dispute. But my writings treat everything indifferently. For example, I can take up a political position against Saddam Hussein, but in the text Saddam Hussein is just as important as his enemies.[7] The text is a microcosm, and a microcosm should contain everything that is in the macrocosm. I wouldn't leave something out of a text because of my political convictions. I must represent the emotional complex as faithfully and truthfully as possible. Then I have the integrity of my emotionality and my surroundings. I can probably only achieve that in the text. It is much more difficult as a social being than as a literary being to be a person of integrity. But that is probably a dilemma for all writers.

GERHARD WOLF

February 17, 1991, East Berlin

Gerhard Wolf (b. 1928) is a literary critic and editor who has vigorously supported poetry in the GDR. He has been particularly active as an advocate of the poets of the Prenzlauer Berg group. He is married to Christa Wolf. His collections of essays include Der arme Hölderlin *(1972),* Im deutschen Dichtergarten *(1985), and* Wortlaut, Wortbruch, Wortlust *(1988). He edited the poetry series* Ausser der Reihe *at Aufbau Verlag, in which a number of the younger Prenzlauer Berg poets appeared.*

Do generational divisions among GDR authors correspond to large literary and political differences?

I'm someone who has kept track of several of these generations because I was always working as a reader for them. Volker Braun, Karl Mickel, Sarah and Rainer Kirsch, Berndt Jentzsch, and Heinz Czechowski were my first authors at the Mitteldeutscher Verlag.[1] That was at the beginning of the sixties. It was a favorable moment—when Khrushchev made the first move towards de-Stalinization. It extended to us too. That was the time of the gigantic lyric poetry forums in Moscow where Yevtushenko and Voznesensky read poems to umpteen thousand people.[2] In the GDR, it coincided nicely with a very large number of gifted people who were born between 1938 and 1945. Because things could get going then that had previously not been permitted, they got a chance. It was a very favorable moment. They were committed in terms of poetics and much more strongly ensconced in a traditional relationship to German literature than the present generation in the Federal Republic is.

Committed to German romanticism?

And earlier: Klopstock, the Enlightenment, Sturm und Drang; not to romanticism in the beginning, if you don't count Hölderlin as a romantic, but more Klopstock.[3] It even went as far back as the baroque period. They were very strongly oriented towards prosodic forms. Sonnets played a gigantic role: how you can handle the form, how you can break it, treat it differently, modernize it, and play with it. People knew exactly what an ode was, why the free rhythms that had been introduced by Klopstock worked this way or that, whether the rhythm was still fixed, a hexameter or not. Things that are totally unimportant to the present generation. At that time, for example, there was a connection to Brecht in Mickel's work. People were concerned with the generation of antifascist and socialist lyric poets, but on a quite different level. That's not of the least importance for the authors of today's Prenzlauer Berg connection. For them, the generation that was born in the mid fifties, the concern with their fathers' generation was completely existential. It is not played out in terms of poetics.

In the mid-seventies, few authors spoke about the role of language in literature, and yet it is precisely questions of language that are the most important thing for the younger authors like Papenfuss-Gorek.

But there was already a consciousness of that in the seventies. For example, from the very beginning, the linguistic factor was much stronger in the work of Elke Erb than the ideological or even the poetic one was, and even in the work of the older generation, it already plays a part in Christa's [Wolf] work.[4] In the lectures on *Kassandra,* the claim "I can no longer speak the way people used to speak" plays a part. But it was much more strongly ideologized then. It operates on the edge of what can be said: "What's up with language, what's the matter with me, what am I doing here?"

That's also in *Was bleibt.*

Yes, that's the mistake, because it's a really old text. The new language that she is looking for there is attempted in part in *Kassandra.* It's conditioned by this late date of publication. Nobody took the trouble to take another look at when it was published—except Elke Erb. The whole text deals with the fact that, in the final analysis, the writer is at the end of a language and is trying another, a new language.

Looking for this new language meant moving away from the ideologization of language.

Yes, completely. You can discern it in other texts more indirectly. For example, in Christoph Hein's *Der fremde Freund.* There should really be a more thorough investigation of why it is completely different from what it is in narratives with the usual realistic strata. Even within his oeuvre there would be interesting comparisons to be made. This transcends generations with very different emphases and quite different starting positions and relationships to tradition. The political point of intersection was 1968.

As early as that?

I think so, yes. For example in Christa's *Nachdenken über Christa T.,* you can see a change that makes the plot and the story appear unimportant. What is important is how you treat it, how you arrange it, how you relate to the text, whether you are involved or not involved. That's all much more important than the actual story—that's narrated afterwards. I think *Nachdenken über Christa T.* had already come out at the beginning of 1969. It was a quite conscious turning point, brought about externally by a number of events.

Did you see your activity as a reader for the young poets as a sort of political task, or did you regard it as purely literary?

You really couldn't separate the two. If you managed to get those people accepted who had not been officially published for years, that was automatically a political act. They were politically and aesthetically suspect because they were different.

The subjectivity of lyric poetry has been called into question in America for a few years now. Is that true here too?

Hm, yes. With the discovery of the "I"—that was much more true of Volker Braun and that group—it became very important that people no longer said "we," but wanted, were able, and had to say "I." That was a very important factor in their works. The discovery of the subject ran completely counter to the concept of the collective, and to the whole ideology of the GDR. It was very progressive. Certainly not a regression into inwardness—on the contrary, it was an attack on the "we" that had been used before. It all began with *Provokation für mich* (1965), Volker Braun's first book. "We" still appears in it, but they discovered that they were "self-helpers," so to speak, with a conscious reference to the Sturm und Drang and early classicism. For example, there was a huge row about a poem by Mickel, "Der See," where somebody compares himself, as creator and destroyer, with Tamburlaine [Genghis Khan]. That certainly played a big role in popular culture and music, where it was turned into something quite noble. A poem like this was the subject of massive attacks: "What does he think he's doing, putting on airs like that, this guy? What the hell does he mean by it?" It was attacked like crazy. When you read it today, you don't know why the Marxist cultural scholars launched attacks of the sort that took place here at that time.[5]

Whereas the young people now, they presume an "I." That was no longer the quarrel, distancing yourself from something; that wasn't what they came up against, what they objected to. It was taken for granted that what was now being opened up was your own ability to come to terms with everything, not only with politics, but with the world as a whole, everything. You didn't have to lay special emphasis on the "I"; it was taken for granted and was no longer a point of discussion. Lyric poetry is really not so very internalized. Through working with the spoken language, even with a language that has been falsified, it is a coming to terms with what was public. But an attitude emanating, of course, entirely from the person.

But there is a strong idea of authenticity in the background of Volker Braun and the younger poets. That's not the case in America.

Yes, well, that was the concept that Christa was using; she was trying to achieve subjective authenticity. What she finds out for herself, sees, experiences, does; but placed, at the same time, on a level of what is authentic and what should not or could not, for example, be detached. In this way it was made completely poetic. But theoretical considerations of this sort are not a point of contention for the younger generation. They have already come to terms with them. There are some very strange things happening. For example, a lyric poet whose texts we have just collected, Flanzendörfer, has a book entitled *unmöglich es leben* [impossible to live it]; that is, it is impossible to deal with "it"—life itself. He is living for death. The whole work is written and engineered to that end.[6]

There's a video in which he stages his own death. He suffered from anorexia, and besides that he jumped off an antiaircraft tower, some sort of concrete tower left over from the war. And in the video that he made, he jumps from a tall house, reappears below, and then does a gigantic funeral thing, with an oratorio, and candles. He is dead, and afterwards there is a paradisal garden landscape—horses and flowing water. If you see the film now . . . it is an anticipation, for he wrote towards this death; he lived and worked towards it, and then it actually took place. He was largely conscious of what he was doing. He was the extreme pole of this group of authors, where life wasn't worth it any more. But it was something to be staged at the same time. He was a gifted artist, who drew, painted, and held performances in his huge condemned building, something that actually produced a very creative effect, but everything was tainted with the theme of "death"—that it was impossible to live. That was certainly his way of realizing subjectivity. That is the most extreme example.

• • •

Christa Wolf said (apropos of Walter Janka's book) that "we must examine our own difficulties with the truth. . . . " I wonder whether such a self-questioning among writers should take place in public?

People are really organized in very different ways. For people like Christa it has always been a problem. For example, the consciousness of guilt in *Kindheitsmuster.* For her it was always a question of expounding the problem in this direction. This was upset by the crazy press campaign against *Was bleibt.* It would have continued quite normally. But the attempt to negate these efforts entirely was bound to interfere with the process. You can see it in a lot of cases. For example, Fritz Rudolf Fries: if you read his latest speeches—they are very beautiful—you will see that he is suddenly on the defensive.[7] He includes himself, although no one ever drew a bead on him as a target. He sees that his situation—and his existence—has also suddenly become questionable. That was not the case. His first book, *Der Weg nach Oobliadooh,* never appeared in the GDR and could scarcely appear at all until 1989, because there were such direct anti-Stalin statements in it. Because of his book he left the Academy of Sciences and was immediately forced to become a writer. He was always a translator. But suddenly he was faced with having to secure his existence—and his existence, like it or not, was in the GDR—in a completely different way. Now he simply can't accept what came rolling in, as a wave, with these West German literary supplements. People suddenly came up with unexpected statements that were not, at first, in the media's main line of fire. They had to include things like that, what was happening as a process. It was going on everywhere.

The terms of this questioning ought to be much more widely developed and differentiated than they are now: "privileged," "not privileged"; "guilt," "nonguilt"; "state writer," "non-state writer." You don't get there with categories of this sort. I think that the internal discussion that would have begun very quickly was blocked initially by these massive, blunt, external attacks. Suddenly writers have become more formal and are defending what they shouldn't defend at all. Fries didn't have to defend himself, but suddenly he is defending himself and his life in the GDR, which he had always questioned and written against.

Why was the critical literature of the GDR, unlike that of Eastern Europe, aimed at improving rather than undermining the state?

Because of the national situation, things were different here from the way they were in Poland or the Soviet Union. That was also the problem that underground literature faced: it was far from having the same standing in the GDR that it did in Czechoslovakia. There are individual authors who can stand as examples—Jan Faktor is one. He's a writer who came to the GDR for purely personal reasons and then felt at home here in the literary scene and was able to work, something that would not have been possible for him in Prague. There his work would have immediately been political dissidence—something that was certainly kept under observation here, but the unofficial periodicals were left alone. If you like, you can say that there was a rich samizdat culture here. Not—as in the Soviet Union—with a "Chronicle of Current Events" about camps and things like that, but still *different* literature, quite consciously different from what prevailed otherwise. Because of the German situation, there was scarcely any direct persecution.

But what do we mean by "improve"? The younger writers no longer wanted to improve. They lived in another world. A number of different models were in vogue for the older generation, saying that they wanted to change—I won't even use the word "improve"—to democratize. Strangely enough, it was precisely the opposition—which was formed in the course of 1989 and always worked on the premise that a democratic form of state would arise here—that failed to recognize the national problems. Whether that could be called socialist was a matter of hot dispute; whether you could use the word at all, even if you had socialist ideas, was questionable. But they always worked on the premise that here—in contrast to the democracies structured by capitalism—a more social form of democracy might be possible. This determined the whole opposition—the "New Forum," the new social democratic party that was formed at that time. But 1968 was probably the last time that the socialist system could have been saved, if there had been some democratization. The west's economic, scientific, and technological advantage was probably not as great at that point, and had not yet created differences so great that they could hardly be overcome any longer. But I could already see the difference when East Europeans would talk about "undermining" the state, because in other Eastern European countries, nationalism was immediately involved as well. The Poles finally want to become Poles, to be free. The Germans have a different relationship to nationalism.

What was the most difficult fact of life that had to be accepted in order to work with socialism? In *Was bleibt* it's the Stasi. No one else has said that to me. Was the Stasi pressure aimed directly at the intellectuals?

Perhaps the effect of habituation played a big part in that. I was disappointed that the literary scholars so seldom showed any independence. Now I have to start with my own experiences. When I had finished at the university, I could have become a Germanist, but I could not have fitted in at all with the ideas they were teaching. Our brand of German studies often did nothing but swear oaths of disclosure. They weren't literary judgments any longer, but the scholars knew exactly what was at stake. If they were clever, they saw to it that they didn't harm their "object"—their author. But there was scarcely a single Germanist who gave up his position. That always surprised me. There were real punishments that were again connected with literature. I know that because they affected Christa. There were two female Germanists at the Humboldt University who defended the book when *Christa T.* was the subject of controversy and attack. They were just thrown out. One of them had to go into a factory as a suspended sentence—as it was called here. That was Inge Diersen, a Germanist who has done a lot of work on Thomas Mann.[8] She defended the book when it was attacked, and she had to do cultural work for years in Bitterfeld [an industrial center]. The other one left the university and became a reader at the Aufbau Verlag: Sigrid Töpelmann. She could not be kept at the university. That's an example of a couple of people who stuck to their opinion that a direct literary object was not a bad, and not a nonsocialist, book. But there are hardly any examples of people resigning. They often practiced solidarity, as in the case of Frank Hörnigk, who supported Heiner Müller and was then heavily attacked by party functionaries. His department defended him, and he was able to keep his job.

But to survive in this structure would have been more than I could have done. You had to find other places in order to be yourself. I had interrupted my university career to work for radio, and when I was finished at the university I went back to radio. That was in the mid fifties. At that time we still had the Deutschlandsender [German station], and people here still had an eye on the unity of Germany. That lasted till 1961, and then it was over, and I was in charge of cultural policy. I could have made a successful career of that. But of course, after 1956, I knew that was finished, with the suits against Harich and Janka.[9] Harich was actually a cult figure who had been a professor; I'd heard him lecture at the university. When I saw that the whole cultural policy was making a 180-degree turn, as far as I was concerned, there was no question of my making a career there.

Then the young poets came, and that was another job. I wouldn't characterize my work as "undermining" the state, but I wouldn't call it "improving" either. You looked for other areas of expression where people had a different understanding of socialism from that of the state. You looked for allies. Then came 1968, and that was all past; it was clear to everyone then that you couldn't do that politically. Once again, you began to look for other areas of expression. It always astonished me that the Germanists, with permanent civil service status, managed to put up with so much the whole time—they had to internalize much of the Marxism that was demanded of them—even if they were able to do something in individual cases. Of course, there were bound to be a lot of variations from case to case, but you were certainly very constrained within the hierarchy.

In the institutions, people knew the rules of the game and the code of what you could and could not do. There are certainly very interesting works by Dieter Schlenstedt, who was always a very accurate worker, and who also made advances that bordered on the tactical. The process of approving a book for publication entailed getting an expert opinion. Two expert opinions came from the publishers themselves, and then you needed an external evaluator. You had to look for someone who knew the rules of the game and would go along with you in order to get the book through. Schlenstedt did this for Volker Braun. And when the discussion started, it was even said that the real "ideological brains" were not the author's but the expert's. For example, Schlenstedt wrote a foreword to Volker Braun's *Hinze und Kunze Roman*. And in this way he acted as a lightning rod. He fully recognized his potential, and he used it quite coldly and skeptically, but he was the exception. There are certainly quite blatant examples to the contrary.

Did the Germanists' conformity, or restraint, have to do with the fact that their profession was structured by the academy?

A lot of them looked for areas that were not so embarrassing; you could veer off into the past with projects. But there wasn't one of the tenured civil service Germanists who took on the generation of authors of the "other" literature. Wait a minute! There was Peter Böthig, an assistant at the Humboldt University; he left.[10] No one defended him or could defend him. He was actually one of the new recruits to the party's Germanistic cadre, but at the same time he participated in the alternative artistic scene. That was his offense; he wasn't viable as a scholar. At the same time he was one of the theoretical brains behind the "scene"—the scene had its own theoreticians. Another one was Michael Thulin (Klaus Michael), who is just completing his Ph.D. in another area, but he also wrote poetry and essays and published the unofficial periodical, *Liane*.[11] And Böthig wrote for him under a pseudonym—P. V. Poltry. It was a second existence, and when his dual identity was eventually disclosed, it led to an action to remove him from the university. Thulin managed to hang on: at the academy there were more liberal working conditions than at the university.

But Böthig's dual identity was secret?

Well, yes. Böthig appeared in the church and held readings there. At one of these unofficial events, in 1986, all the unofficial periodicals were presented. Nobody took any action, none of the periodicals was forbidden. That never happened here, and for that reason it wasn't a proper samizdat. People knew that the Stasi had its observers there, but in Böthig's case it became known at the university, and he had to go.

PART FOUR

After the
Surprising Revelations

SASCHA
ANDERSON, II

March 18, 1992, West Berlin

This conversation took place several months after Sascha's fifteen-year coopera-
tion with the Stasi had been exposed.

What significance did the Stasi have for your generation?

To me it meant nothing. For a particular group of people it was not
that influential; its influence is not perceptible in the way it was for
another generation twenty years earlier. We ignored it, but that's not to
say everyone could have ignored it. The specific case was that a particular
cultural scene was not ready to indulge a particular paranoia.

**I would have thought that it would be easier for someone who
had never been in jail to get away from such a paranoia.**

I lost my paranoia after I'd been in jail. I knew how bad it could be.
For me, it was a fundamental and decisive turning point in my life, and
everything led up to it. The whole of the 1970s led up to the fact that at
some time or another I would end up in jail, that at some time I would
feel the extremity of this society. Afterwards I was completely—not free,
but no longer afraid. I knew where my fear was; I could place it exactly.
That's a dangerous condition, not being afraid any more; but that's the
way it is with people who live in jail all the time, who constantly return
to jail. They are completely indifferent. I was completely indifferent in

the 1980s as to what society did with me. I knew nothing more could happen to me. I knew the margin of society, and that is jail.

Weren't you afraid that your conversations with the Stasi would become public, that you could once again become an outsider?

No, that was a taboo and, in retrospect, I say it was a senseless and idiotic taboo. From today's perspective, contacts with the Stasi were completely idiotic, really, for me.

And did you sometimes think that you would sever your links with the Stasi?

No, I couldn't sever them myself. I didn't seek contact with the state security forces; it was the Stasi who made contact with me, in a way that was very humiliating for me. They were always tough, always knew what they were talking about, or at least pretended to. In conversations with them, I was regularly reminded of all the breaches of law that I'd been guilty of or might possibly soon be guilty of.

I was not in the Writers' Union; that was probably my misfortune. If I had had sufficient self-assurance to say, "But I am a writer—you can't do anything to me." But I was an outsider in my relations to official cultural policy, not one but one of many, and I was always considered illegal by them. So their argument towards me was: "Herr Anderson, you are an illegal. You give illegal readings, you have no license as a writer. So what shall we say now, what shall we do with you now? You have appeared here and there, have persuaded musicians to start a rock band with you." You needed a license to do that in the GDR. So my whole attempt to find some sort of mid position in higher literature, not to write less or not to write less complicated things, but to do something side by side with literature, that permitted me to have relationships with people whom I would otherwise not touch directly by literature. That was illegal in the GDR, what I was doing then: organizing readings, doing performances, organizing exhibitions, printing books and publishing them—that was all illegal. Not absolutely contrary to the law, but in an emergency you could not appeal to the law. You can make the appeal, but it's no use. The laws are always there for people who are legitimized by an identity card or by relatives. I was never in any association. Well, one day I was supposed to be admitted to the Writers' Union as a candidate, and I was thrown out again at once. I'm neither suited to an association nor in any way suited to accommodate myself legally to the state. But in the final analysis that may have been—in a certain way—

something that was forced on me by the state security people, to leave me outside the law.

Did the Stasi also know that you took manuscripts to West German publishers.

I don't think so. No, then they would have said it directly to my face. My own [manuscripts]—yes, they knew about that, that's obvious. They knew of my association with Gabi Dietze at Rotbuch; I hadn't concealed it from them. It wasn't a question of becoming famous, but I was happy that I had a publisher whom I liked. Rotbuch is a publisher that in the 1970s seemed exactly right to me. It was a political publisher for whom I did not have to write politically. I wouldn't have let the Stasi impede my dealings with Rotbuch. The manuscripts that I got over to the west for other people—if they'd known about that, they could have found them. They didn't know, otherwise they would have stopped it; they'd have turned our place upside down. I don't think that they really knew.

Did the Stasi ask about those manuscripts?

Yes, they did ask if I was smuggling texts, whether I was giving diplomats texts to take along. I said, "Oh, that's nothing, a few things of mine for Rotbuch." Or, "I've written a newspaper article for someone."

If they had asked you more directly, would you have admitted it then?

Possibly. I answered their concrete questions concretely. You notice in conversation very precisely how much the other person knows and whether his information is only speculative. Especially in an interrogation, where they ask an incredibly long question that you can finally answer by "yes" or "no." Then you notice very precisely what they know and what they only pretend to know, or where they're just poking about in the haystack to see what comes out. You can distinguish all that.

But you were frightened that you'd land up in jail again?

Yes, of course. I actually only felt afraid at the moment it happened. I knew I would not survive a second and a third time.

Did you have a guilty conscience when you were talking to the Stasi?

Yes, of course you have a conscience. You're thinking all the time, "How am I going to get out of this? What more can I say so that it won't go too far and yet I can still get away quickly?" But I can't say that I had great conflicts of conscience.

Didn't you think that there were some moral problems caused by your speaking freely to the Stasi?

No, I had no moral problems. I certainly had some strong self-doubts, some dark moments when I simply didn't know any more what I was to do, how I'd get a grip on it at all. To exist like that but not as any sort of split personality, rather in the linearity in which I have tried to live . . . that was a total block, and because of it, of course, I was plunged into the worst of mental situations. I just tried to get through the affair somehow.

You say that you did not suffer "great conflicts of conscience," and yet you haven't discussed your Stasi involvement with anybody?

I have told people, in general terms, that I was constantly being hauled in as an author. But the pressure that was on me was drawn off my milieu. The people I lived with were aware of that. We told anyone who came to us and started whispering, "We are not a conspiratorial association. There's nothing to hide. Anyone who has something to hide has to go to another society." We spoke openly about everything. At home in our private rooms—which were very public—we talked a lot. That was a very fruitful source for the Stasi, but there was nothing that could have been used to ruin anybody. All the people who went to the west used our phone to talk to people in the east again. All day long people were coming to us and saying that they had to call the west, had to talk to a friend who had just left. There was nearly twenty-four-hour telephoning. Everything was open, and I had no more to say elsewhere than I had to say at home.

It's been said that you did things with a particular aim in mind; that you were told, "Take a photograph, here," or something of the sort.

They could never have done that with me; my psyche is simply not capable of taking an order like that. I have always failed, when working as a writer, if I was under orders to do something. If I do something, then I do it of my own accord. No, I think they have professionals for that sort of thing.

You didn't previously take an ironic attitude towards the Stasi.

Well, I had an attitude. I knew the sort of fellows who were sitting opposite me. I knew that they had no idea about art; nor had they surveyed what actually took place there in front of their eyes. And when you see what was done by them, concretely: someone chasing someone else or someone being shadowed, when hearses were parked in front of my door so that I wouldn't dare appear at a particular reading. That is very existential. On the other hand it's like something out of a bad play, and then you can laugh about it. At the moment I can't be so amused, because I know what else was done.

Did you think at the time that you could talk freely with the Stasi without that having serious effects?

No, rather the opposite. I always tried to explain, to seize the opportunity to pour out generalized explanations as to how harmless everything was. The bad thing was that I couldn't see what effect what I was saying was having, because the material in question was worked over in a hierarchy that I had no way of observing. Finally I saw the noneffect that my argumentation had. What I probably never understood was the incredible pressure from above that they were under; that they were in a hierarchy that functions so tightly that they simply had no other chance. I never talked to the same person for more than a year. Otherwise I would have turned to someone as a sort of father figure. I probably would not have been so averse to always having the same man to talk to, but the danger would have been that I would have spelled everything out, that I would convert him. That could have happened. And they probably knew that too. They couldn't afford to have me convert the man I was talking to. They themselves had a very firmly structured hierarchy that had to give strict account of itself to the higher powers, and I couldn't get a clear view of how much people were trapped, how much they were committed to this hierarchy.

How do you get on with your circle of friends?

It's not me and a circle of friends. There are twenty different people, and each of them reacts to the whole thing in his own way. The one thing that is expected of me, on the part of Lutz Rathenow or Jürgen Fuchs, is that I make a public confession—that I scourge myself in public in some way, as far as possible in linguistic form, as a confession, and apologize for something they reproach me with, and I can't do that. I never have the feeling myself that I could apologize for something, or should or have to. Perhaps that's going a bit far, but I would sooner say that I feel no remorse. I cannot in any way introduce the concept of remorse at this point. I regret nothing.

Do you mean in general, always, or in this case?

I simply could not have acted differently from the way I did then. I did what it was possible for me to do and never for myself but, on principle, always for some project or other, or for something else. I wouldn't know how to live differently. If I put myself back ten years, I would act in exactly the same way today. Everything was so inevitable in my twenty years of life in the GDR. There's no way that I can fulfill all that is expected of me now.

I don't really understand your motivation.

I don't have a motive, that's the point. If you take it all back to motives, if there were any motive, then it would all be very simple. It's like a criminal case that has to be solved. If you have a motive and the weapon, then it's all very simple.

I compensate for my literary self-doubt with a sort of organizational permanent stress. I can't use every poem to express my self-doubts. That would be really dreadful, therapeutic literature. Ninety percent of literature is therapeutic in one way or another, and I accept that. But that's not what I want to lay upon literature. I don't have to burden my literature, or literature in general, with that. This very, very active organizational part of my life, this book fetishism, is a sort of compensation for the self-doubt that I have about literature. I can't make literature simpler than it is. And yet I see in the great mass of people who from some sort of concept of themselves, or through their education, live with literature that they put pressure on poets or writers to make it easy for them. This corresponds to what they expect from life. They all live on an unbelievably complicated basis, and yet they make things as simple as possible in order to be able to exist there at all. That is the great contradiction: they have this craving for simplicity, for clarity, or dialectic; it is a sort of pubescent craving for the simplicity of life. Biermann is for me an absolutely clear example, a brilliant master of dialectic form, but he compensates by making things, basically, as simple as possible for people. This corresponds to what they themselves want from their own lives: to have things as simple as possible when they leave work. There's the TV, there's the beer, and there are your slippers. That's the craving for simplicity and manageability, and that's what they demand from literature too.

But literature is tremendously congruent with life, rhizomatically connected with life. And if I know anything about literature then I am daily on the point of failure, somehow or other. I cannot write more simply than the material itself actually is. A poem is a very complicated case. I write the poem: TV, slippers, beer. The text may perhaps be gigantic and complicated, but I filter out the three words and make it simple so as to be able in some fashion to bear the complexity. I simply do not go along with this in literature, but I can of course compensate for complexity in completely practical things. When I publish a book, I make things fairly simple for myself, although the book may not show this when the material is complex. The book is a form that is very simple but very tangible, into which you can place quite a lot. I want to remove something—a book, or a few poems—from the complexity or from the really incredible failure that I constantly have in literature.

The simple thing you said in the interview with *Die Zeit* is that you had talked with the Stasi. Is that the main thing?

The fact is that, by all reckonings, I talked to them hundreds of times in the fifteen years from the beginning of the 1970s until the mid 1980s. I was ordered to appear, almost always, before them, to go to some office. In the *Zeit* interview I acknowledged that I said a great deal. I said almost everything I knew. I could not have said more. And there's no more I can say now about the whole business. It's certainly worth looking at the details to see what effect my talk had. I'm ready for that, but never ready for self-chastisement.

You were never taken in by the Stasi after 1986, when you moved to West Berlin?

I was completely free for the first time in my life, not under pressure. I felt an incredible relief. I still feel it today on occasion when I travel to the east and come back to the west. It's as though I have been liberated, even if I don't like this society. Perhaps I do like the society, but I don't always like the system. I had lived for thirty or thirty-five years in the east, and I can never get rid of those years. I have to live with the pressure that the east imposes.

For example, I can remember the situation in 1983, when Allen Ginsberg came to see me in East Berlin. If the Stasi had known, they wouldn't have admitted him. I knew about it two or three days beforehand. Gabi Dietze called me and said, "You're getting a visitor; stay at home tomorrow morning." I had read all his books and had written a few things about them. I rushed out and told people that Ginsberg was coming. I knew at once what was meant. We collected about a hundred people for the evening. If I had said anything about it beforehand, they wouldn't have let him cross the border. Then we'd have all been in jail. Had I been a real collaborator, I would have been duty-bound to tell them, "So-and-so's coming at such-and-such a time." This visit had a great effect on the consciousness of freedom of people living in the GDR. Even the fact, for example, that human contacts are possible, in spite of a dictatorship; in spite of the Wall and everything, it's possible to live actively. That was the effect.

It's true that early on you admitted having talked with the Stasi, and that you said then that the whole issue was not that simple. But on the TV program for Channel 2, it looked as if you were emphatically denying Stasi involvement.

Yes, the bad thing about the TV program was that Biermann knew that we were to be talking together, and he acted as though he didn't know. Channel 2 had asked him, "Would you talk to Herr Anderson about the affair?" and he agreed. Then Channel 2 came to me and told me that Biermann would be ready to talk with me. I said, "OK, if he's ready, then of course I am." Biermann gave the date of his concert in the Maxim Gorki Theater, and I went there and met him backstage. But he had already made a sound check, so we agreed to meet in the cafeteria. I'd been sitting in the cafeteria for about half an hour when he arrived and acted surprised. Then I exploded, and I noticed that a part of my youthful illusions collapsed.

It's only true in a complicated sense that I went to prison because of Biermann. I was held for interrogation once because I had printed some of his poems and then sold them. But a part of my life, from, say, 1970 to 1980, or until Biermann left [1976]—perhaps shortly afterwards—was given its character by the Biermann phenomenon. I got to know his songs very early on. They were very important for me, even if they weren't the sort of literature that I write. That all fell apart in this one second, and that's why I screamed. The bad thing for me was that of course the camera simply fixed on this. It was American-style TV, at the scene of the crime, or the accident, and taking pictures as the blood was flowing.

What was so disappointing was that Biermann was playing for the cameras?

Yes, he was putting on a gigantic act. True, he became very insecure, but I didn't see it until afterwards. I sat opposite him and saw that he was one of the most narrow-minded dandies of contemporary light theater. I sat on the stage, was introduced (he wasn't introduced), and I exploded, nothing more. I could have saved myself that. I could simply not have gone. It's very important to me that I never appear in Germany again— not even in connection with this whole affair. Doing this interview here and now has nothing to do with Germany. There will never be any more publishing rights of mine in Germany.

ADOLF ENDLER
AND
GABRIELE DIETZE

March 15, 1992, East Berlin

Adolf Endler *(b. 1930) is a poet and essayist who was born in Düsseldorf and moved to the east in 1955. He studied at the Johannes R. Becher Institute from 1955 to 1959. His collections of poems include* Die Kinder der Nibelungen *(1954),* Erwacht ohne Furcht *(1960),* Das Sandkorn *(1974),* Nackt mit Brille *(1975),* Verwirrte klare Botschaften *(1979), and* Akte Endler *(1981). In 1966 he coedited with Karl Mickel an anthology of "poems for the GDR,"* In diesem besseren Land. *He has translated the Russian poet Esenin (1982). Among his collections of prose are* Zwei Versuche über Georgien zu erzählen *(1976);* Ohne Nennung von Gründen *(1985);* Schichtenflotz *(1987);* Den Tiger Reiten *(1990), on GDR lyric poetry;* Vorbildlich Schleimlösend *(1990); and* Tarzan an Prenzlauer Berg.

Gabriele Dietze *(b. 1951) studied Germanistics at the University of Frankfurt. In 1979 she edited a collection of essays of the women's movement,* Die Überwindung der Sprachlosigkeit. *She was an editor at Rotbuch Verlag in West Berlin from 1980 until 1990. She was responsible for the western publication of many GDR writers. Currently she is completing a Ph.D. thesis on American popular culture.*

How different does the Prenzlauer Berg scene look after the exposé of Sascha's and Schedlinski's work for the Stasi?

G.D. The thesis that the writers there contributed to the dissolution of the power structures by ignoring them. . . . It's questionable whether this can be maintained in the light of the ongoing discussion of these informers.

A.E. But Frank Schirrmacher's idea that the Stasi officers read Baudrillard and then simulated something of the sort is fantastic.

Is there a connection between the cases of Anderson and Christa Wolf?

G.D. What links the Wolf and Anderson debates is the introduction of moral categories into the aesthetic discussion. That's what Schirrmacher and Ulrich Greiner, for example, accomplished with their claim that Christa Wolf, in their eyes, was a state poet.

A.E. The introduction of moral positions in aesthetics took place ten or twenty years ago with reference to Christa Wolf. She was built up as a great figure, and the moral aspect contributed to it. Only in Anderson's case, and in the whole debate about the Prenzlauer Berg scene that had begun four or five years earlier, morality never played such an important part. Biermann is completely clear: these writers are not only low-grade bunglers and dadaist windbags, as he always knew; they are also—small wonder—Stasi agents. Or as the old fox always said, "delayed avant-garde poets." Everything that is emotionally opposed to modernism or postmodernism quite clearly—in Stalinism and elsewhere as well, among the petite bourgeoisie or wherever—was suddenly politically activated. You can immediately set Biermann's statements on aesthetics side by side with any statements on aesthetics by Free German Youth (FDJ) functionaries.[1] You could make a collage; the statements would not differ from one another in the least. It's different in the case of the Christa Wolf debate.

Why did the Stasi put up with the scene for ten years?

A.E. The Stasi not only put up with the scene, the Stasi, or the state, or GDR cultural politics, put up with the publication of sometimes tough political literature, sharp political poems, or satirical political belles lettres, political articles in West Germany and in the Western world, *without* that having any consequences for the authors, and some of those authors were in the Writers' Union too. The Stasi left the whole field more or less unmown, not just the Prenzlauer Berg.

Now you can of course come up with all sorts of thoughts about this phenomenon. It occurred to me that the great expansion of the Stasi started about the beginning of the seventies—in fact, shortly after the eighth, so-called liberalizing, party conference of the SED.[2] It was announced in 1971 that there were to be no more taboos for literature. Of course that was a lot of nonsense, but no more taboos as long as literature was loyal to the party, yes! But there were taboos: the Stasi was taboo. The Stasi didn't appear in realistic literature. The fact that people were constantly fleeing did not appear. There was a whole host of taboos. But many writers understood the policy to mean "now we can talk freely," and if they had any difficulties, they insisted that there were no longer any taboos. And in connection with this suggestion of liberalization, there was an order from the Central Committee to the State Security forces, to Mielke, to double the size of the Stasi force, or as we should call it, "the Stasi collaborator force." I think the connection is fairly clear. If we are now going to start liberalizing, then of course we must take countermeasures. We have a very cunning dialectic! Very cunning. Of course we must have twice the number of police, secret police, to squash any possible deviations. It's a bureaucratic thing too: they are a law unto themselves. When you set something like that rolling it never stops. And then in the 1980s you *always* had the feeling, every three days or so, that this person or that person was a member of the Stasi. There was a constant flicker of Stasi and suspicions.

G.D. The agents were also very visible.

A.E. There was the famous phenomenon of demonstrative shadowing.

G.D. I hated that.

A.E. Yes! I experienced that once, twice, three times. There were three or four guys *demonstratively* visible, right? And in such a way that you were forced to notice them. Of course it was a signal: all right, stop. All right, now you must pay attention. All right, we're here. The people they must have used, the money they must have spent! There is a theory that this was what ruined the GDR.

A lot of people connect liberalization with the fact that the GDR for international reasons didn't want to have any trouble. The GDR wanted to be thought of in the international community as something very decent, without blemish. That was something we went along with. Our only means of power was to threaten to make an international fuss. If a book had been published in the west, and then the author had been sent to jail, there would have been a fuss. There must have been five hundred of us who had written letters or who had collected signatures. There weren't three hundred thousand people, but there were always ten or twenty thousand refractory people who as a rule wanted to stay in the GDR, but who, out of some sort of defiance or whatever, weren't ready to put up with it. They weren't the people who had left because they were fed up to the teeth.

What sort of censorship was there in the period of liberalization?

A.E. There were rows, for example, in connection with the anthology that Elke Erb and Sascha published, *Contact Is Only a Peripheral Phenomenon* [1985], where twenty people suddenly came up from the underground who had simply not been there before. There was a paper on strategy, which we got from Höpcke. No, it was found in the copyright office; right next door to Höpcke. Every manuscript was actually supposed to pass through the copyright office. Höpcke only acted as though he had nothing to do with it. The copyright office oversaw questions of currency. Some criminal proceedings were considered against Elke Erb, as the editor-in-chief, but only she appeared in this paper on strategy, not a word about Sascha. That only occurred to me afterwards. What appeared in the paper on strategy was: "In the anthology *Leyle Anastasia* we are dealing with first publications of twenty GDR authors, together with further authors who have, in the meantime, emigrated to the FRG. The manuscript is in the hands of Kiepenhauer and Witsch, Cologne. The editor is Elke Erb. The manuscript contains texts that display the position of an outsider, or of someone who is getting out of our socialist society. An awareness of life is articulated in which resignatory and nihilistic characteristics predominate. Elegiac and bitter feelings of being imprisoned are expressed. Suicide and death are privileged motifs." That's true, too. "There is no question of the manuscript being published by a GDR publisher for this reason and because of the combination of authors. This was expressly stated to the editor, Elke Erb, in several conversations with the director of the Aufbau publishing firm to whom the manuscript was presented." I experienced that. "In the same way . . .

G.D. Faber, eh?

A.E. Faber, yes. "In the same way she was called upon to cease her activities with a view to having the anthology published in the FRG, as it contravenes the legal requirements of the GDR." This is the point at which you were reminded of the law. Incidentally, nothing happened for six months; it appeared that that was what they had in mind.

"A. As the behavior of Elke Erb is in contravention of the statutes of the Writers' Union of the GDR, of which she is a member, it can be assumed that the expulsion of Elke Erb—which has already been considered—will now be implemented by the council of the Writer's Union, as well as by the secretariat of the Central Committee."

G.D. Didn't it happen?

A.E. No. But "will now be implemented" was a threat that she always had to consider.

"B. Manuscripts that Elke Erb has presented to the Aufbau firm to be read will now be sent back to her without comment. There is also no question of another GDR firm publishing them.

"C. The juridical means that can be used for the opening of proceedings for a breach of the order of awareness . . . to the introduction of an investigation for the purpose of ascertaining breaches of Paragraph 219 of the Criminal Code of the GDR." We have all offended against this particular paragraph, but it has almost never been used for prosecution. "The decision as to the appropriateness or nonappropriateness of using these juridical means must be taken on the basis of *political aspects*." Well, it's a six-page strategy paper dated January 7, 1985, and it presumably comes from the BfU.[3] Presumably, Stasi, don't you think? Paragraph 219, "Illegal Contacts." We all contravened this paragraph. Sascha constantly contravened this paragraph.

G.D. Ten times a day.

A.E. Yes, you have to state that. "Whoever has contact with organizations, institutions, or persons who have as their goal any activity that is against the laws of the GDR." We all did that, didn't we? "Whoever enters into such an association, having knowledge of this aim or activity, will be condemned to a suspended sentence of imprisonment of up to five years, or fined. Secondly, in the same way, the following will be punished":

First: "Any citizen of the GDR who spreads or causes to be spread abroad information that is able to harm the interests of the GDR, or who makes statements with this aim in mind, or causes such statements to be made . . ." Statements! That's pretty broad, isn't it? An autumn poem, a sad autumn poem, can, so to speak, be harmful—can communicate a harmful impression.

Second: "Anyone who hands over to organizations, institutions, or persons abroad, writings, manuscripts, or other materials, within the purview of legal regulations, that are in a position to harm the interests of the GDR."

Third: "The attempt is punishable in the case of paragraph 2, number 2." The attempt. Three times a day, Anderson made those attempts.

G.D. Especially Anderson.

A.E. But here it is, we've found it now: they had prosecution in mind. But still nothing happened. The anthology was a spectacular thing, because it suddenly embraced a whole generation. There were perhaps thirty people altogether. After a year and a half, there were only ten of them left in the GDR. Some had been blackmailed into leaving immediately: "We don't need you any more." Schulze, for example.[4] He'd been to see me the day before and said, "Write me a letter to the director of the ministry or something." I've still got the letter half written. The next day he was already in the west; they threw him out. Franz Fühmann accompanied him over the border because they were afraid that he would disappear when he crossed the border. Things like that actually happened. People also helped who were not directly connected with Prenzlauer Berg: Heiner Müller; Christa Wolf, it has to be admitted; and Fühmann was particularly involved; and now and again, for a bit, Stefan Hermlin.

Do you think that the Prenzlauer Berg scene was really oppositional, in spite of the Stasi spying?
A.E. Yes. First of all, they had developed certain artistic characteristics that were generational in nature, and they are connected with the fact that people had observed very similar movements abroad—in America, for example. Incidentally, music played a big role: punk music, rock music, which was under attack for a long time in the GDR, just as jazz was for a long while as good as banned. Anyone who took up jazz as an art did it as a protest. And there had always been this aesthetic opposition in the area of music. The young poets actually had something to do with musical groups. Or they got together with them. And it was from this opposition to the FDJ, against state youth, etc., that almost a whole generation was formed.

I don't think that other utopias, so to speak, or let's say an improved utopia, were set up by these artists in opposition. It was more that a Pynchon-like weakness towards the world prevailed. There's little optimism to be seen; that's an international situation in literature. This oppositional standpoint comes less from the church than, so to speak, from the FDJ. The Poppes were functionaries in the FDJ, and Bärbel Bohley—I once talked to her about it, as we both wept over President Pieck's death in 1960.[5] And now we know what a pretense that was! Thank God I never wrote a poem about Stalin; I might have. There you are, a naive business.

That is a chapter in world literature. Some of these civil rights campaigners actually wanted a better GDR. These Prenzlauer Berg poets were apparently clear about the fact, or at least sensed, that socialism is dead for the time being. That's something that still plays a part today in conversation, particularly in the case of Bärbel Bohley. She didn't want this hideous capitalism; she wanted "a more beautiful GDR." That was a strange illusion—from the time before the Soviet Union started to collapse. No, I think the poets were cleverer. But people today still reproach the poets, namely, that we could perhaps have created this more beautiful GDR. Didn't you publish the paper on radical change?

G.D. Yes, I organized that. It was a paper about reorganization.

A.E. So there was a small group of papers on reorganization, by SED members who wanted to change the GDR into a more beautiful GDR.

G.D. Yes, we assumed in October 1989 that Schabowski and Krenz would get the whole thing into their own hands.[6]

A.E. If I understand it correctly, some of these papers have been exposed as the work of Stasi officers. Rotbuch only published Stasi people on principle.

G.D. But of course.

A.E. At the beginning of 1990 it could still seem revolutionary for a small group of SED people to say, "All right, shit on the old, we are going to make a really new GDR!" But socialist, that was in the air too. From the beginning, I and all the Prenzlauer Berg people . . .

G.D. Absolutely idiotic.

A.E. . . . illusionary and childish view.

Sascha said recently that the scene is continuing, that the Galrev publishing firm is continuing, and that the people who are now sending their manuscripts to Galrev are younger authors for whom the Stasi affair is not important.

A.E. Yes, I notice that too, that a few of them don't take it so seriously. But it is conspicuous, in any case, whenever there's a reading in the Cafe Kiryl, which is operated by the [Galrev] publishers. It's chock-full every time, almost demonstratively full. People really demonstrate their attachment to the firm. Of course this irritates the other publisher, the civil rights publisher, BasisDruck, ten houses farther down in the Lychener Strasse. That's the artists' and civil rights corner. And that must be irritating . . .

Still?

A.E. Yes, still. There was a reading a few days ago. I went . . . we went to demonstrate support. Because they're simply good publishers, aren't they? Of all the new publishing houses founded in the east, it was the only really interesting one. It has its own complexion, a Stasi one! Well, not really. But is there, in the whole of Germany, anything else that is so consistent?

JAN FAKTOR

March 19, 1992, East Berlin

Jan Faktor *(b. 1951 in Prague) immigrated to the GDR in 1978. He published in unofficial magazines. In 1990 he published* Georgs Versuche an einem Gedicht und andere positive Texte aus dem Dichtergarten des Grauens *and in 1991* Henry's Jupitergestik in der Blutlach Nr. 3 und andere positive Texte aus Georgs Besudelungs- und Selbstbesudelungskabinett.

I am trying to determine what Sascha Anderson regards as false in the newspapers and what he admits.

He's terribly shrewd and such a good liar. I've seen a document or two, and even [Gerd] Poppe's files.[1] In 1981, I held a reading at the Poppes', and Anderson was there too, and had his Walkman with him. At that time that was something so unusual that I assume he got it from the Stasi. He always put his Walkman on the table and left it running. Now I've read his report about the reading. He was recording for the Stasi. The original tape was for them. He handed it over. So what else is there to say? After the reading I was summoned to the police station. The other person who was reading was dismissed from the university.

He admitted that he spoke openly to the Stasi and that when he was asked concrete questions, he gave concrete answers.

That's a tactic that's over and done with. He could do that last fall because we believed a lot of things at that time. But now that we have the documents it's a different story. Of course, he's waiting to see what documents will surface. He is still trying to maneuver. He's trying to react carefully to individual things that turn up, but of course he'll only *311* admit to the things that do turn up and probably won't even admit to things that are there for all to see. He's hoping that as little as possible will come out. But he was so hard-working that documents are turning up all over the place. The point has come where he can't escape, and I've no desire whatsoever to talk to him about it. I've given it up. He just goes on lying.

Had you previously heard that he was suspect?

No, no. Only Schedlinski—there were rumors about him. As for Sascha, well, people thought that there were some pretty ridiculous stories about him, that he'd pinched a shirt and some other things from Eberhard Häfner, and books, etc., from other people—years ago.[2] It was all so silly. People thought, "Oh, well, he's a bit crazy, a kleptomaniac," but they tried to put a good construction on it, as something childish. As to having anything to do with the Stasi—that would have been absurd, because that was also something we were concerned about. "The Stasi? The Stasi isn't a matter of concern any longer. We're not interested in that." Those were his words. At the same time he said—and this is a direct quotation—"I have no morals." But people didn't see how consistently amoral he was. At the same time, it was this amorality in him that fascinated people. That's why most people didn't distance themselves from him. Somehow or other he always had a wallet stuffed with money, was very clever—a perfect organizer. He facilitated a tremendous amount. Fundamentally this unscrupulousness fascinated most people. Just as evil is always fascinating, so something like that was attractive in him. He was always a leader. People who didn't want to invest so much time and energy in organizing things naturally left that to him, and in a lot of cases that misfired. Valuable pictures were stolen and smuggled out. He withheld my share of a graphics collection we did, but I got them back—because I threatened to make it public. Well, I wasn't going to have them stolen from me, but a lot of people were reticent, didn't want to attack him because he was an authority, and didn't want to cause a break.

• • •

You publish with BasisDruck, don't you?

Yes, I was involved with *Neues Forum,* the periodical. We produced the first numbers on my computer here in my apartment in the fall of 1989.[3] And then, through the periodical and my contacts with Neues

Forum, I got into the newspaper—that was *Die Andere* [The other], published by BasisDruck. I was already integrated into the citizens' rights movement. As far as I was concerned, communal life in the Prenzlauer Berg scene had basically been over and done with for a long time. There was something artificial about the attempt to resurrect it after the revolution.

When did it end, in your opinion?

The really intensive period was already over by 1984. There were no more regular readings, and some people were also excluded, and that really splintered the "scene." The end really started in 1984, and then the first contacts with West Germany began to take shape: radio programs, publications, and so on. These were all things that Sascha organized, and people he didn't like, or those he obviously had orders to exclude, weren't part of it. That was something that ruined a lot of people. Emotionally I felt an increasing distance from the whole group. In 1987, I wrote an attack on the group and published it in Schedlinski's *Ariadnefabrik.* I was violently attacked by Schedlinski, which is really funny from today's point of view. After that there was a complete break: I was the one who had fouled the nest. Nobody expressed solidarity with me.

Did the break have political significance?

No, it was more that I found whatever they were writing terribly questionable from an artistic point of view. There were a lot of shows put on that I found totally without artistic merit, phony and superficial. And personal relations were not really open. Everything was hidden, nothing was said straight out: no direct quarrels, no open disagreements, everything went on behind your back. It was all dishonest, and I wanted to provoke discussion in *Ariadnefabrik,* but nothing came of it. Schedlinski attacked me vehemently and said that I had no right to make judgments of that sort. Everything was simply fine, and I was left hanging with my criticism. There was no place for argument in the scene. You really didn't have the courage to criticize people openly, because there'd be severe consequences—which I experienced firsthand. People are finally starting to be able to quarrel, through the papers, and they're pretty brutal. I think that's important now.

You were the exception in participating in Neues Forum?

Yes, the Prenzlauer Berg writers all avoided taking part in political things. It was part of the ideology not to become involved in politics, and I was part of that too for a long time, until 1989. In the 1970s I was very politically involved. I had experienced 1968 in Prague. I was very politicized and wrote political things. But I didn't think that politicization was the right thing artistically. I wanted to get away from political writing, to be apolitical. This fit in with the movement that was already here in Berlin and that I felt very close to from the very beginning.

Did the superficiality of the scene after 1984 have anything to do with the Stasi affair?

It was really a historical coincidence. The time had come when you really couldn't rail against the state as Biermann did. That had all been said, and all of it was terribly simple—the political prose, political songs—it was all old hat. The more radical step was to ignore the state and involve yourself with things that the state simply didn't understand. That impulse really came from within, from aesthetics, and was, so to speak, opposed to the Stasi. The fact that then, and now too, there were people who said that of course it was all directed from outside, or supported by the state, is all nonsense. And the fact that later on it was so phony, so preserved, that there was a certain stagnation in the second half of the 1980s, was, I think, due to the indirect influence of Sascha and the Stasi. The Stasi had absolutely no interest in the scene developing further, perhaps becoming politicized again—that could have happened. That had an effect on the scene.

Can you say that at that point a decision was made collectively not to politicize the scene? Is there a point where a political possibility clearly existed?

The point where I felt that it could actually become more political, or more genuine, was in 1988. That was when they held the memorial vigil in the Zion church, when there was the Stasi business about the environmental library.[4] I don't know whether you've heard anything about that. In the church, there were magazines and environmental groups. The whole thing was investigated by the Stasi. The magazines were confiscated, and people were arrested. The atmosphere in the parish was much more political. I felt that somehow that was what was missing in the Prenzlauer circle: suddenly there it was, this radicalization, this politicization, in a direct confrontation. But as far as my own work is concerned, I didn't allow myself, I think, to be influenced by Sascha, nor by the mood surrounding him—at least I hope I didn't.

When did you come to the GDR?

In 1978. In 1968, I was already seventeen years old, and the experience of the Russian occupation of my country was unbelievably decisive for me. I became a radical and wanted nothing at all to do with the official culture. There was a much sharper division in Czechoslovakia. There was absolutely no question of decent people publishing: the most important writers did not publish. In the GDR a great deal was fundamentally more liberal. When I came here, it was a piece of real freedom for me. The readings, illegal concerts, exhibitions—all that was hardly possible in Prague. I'm really thankful for a lot of things. I would not have experienced in Prague what was possible here in the GDR. I was able to develop as a writer much better here without the really strong political pressure there was in Prague. Basically there was a sort of aestheticism present, and that wasn't bad either. Of course now people reproach you: that you were blind and didn't want to see. That's true too, in part. I don't try to idealize the time. That's what the Galrev people do. They really try to preserve a lot, and I don't think that's good.[5]

How do you explain the Stasi's intentions in tolerating the scene, and why did they let East German authors smuggle out manuscripts?

Smuggling to the west was a safety valve. When you published something over there, no attempt was made here to organize large editions. At the same time—this was also clear to me—from the psychological point of view, publications in the west managed to ground the fear of the Stasi. They let it all happen, let their people—their informers—do everything, because this produced an illusion of security by showing all the others what sort of activities were possible. Basically the Stasi kept a lid on things: that was their influence, and that was basically their clear intention. The Stasi tactics were not to interfere, not to arrest people, not to put pressure on all the people. The Stasi actually prevented the scene from radicalizing itself. Fundamentally, that actually quieted the whole thing down, and we were left to do our own thing, which from a production point of view was very pleasant. You didn't have to bother with courts and police, and you didn't have to defend friends or organize campaigns in their support, because nothing of importance happened. So the Stasi tactics were really fairly good—from the Stasi's point of view, I mean, of course.

Do you think that the Stasi intentionally depoliticized the scene in this manner.

Yes, but again you have to differentiate: the aesthetic element was truly present; they couldn't influence that. But they exploited it because it suited them. If there had been another more adversarial aesthetic, there would have been even more conflicts. By not intervening, they prevented us from radicalizing ourselves.

Conclusion

Outsiders are the bane of the police as of other professions.
Joseph Conrad, *The Secret Agent*

What produces intellectual conformity? Surely enthusiasm, a sense of mission, though a malaise might as effectively produce the same; fear of notoriety leads to timidity, but so too does a hunger for legitimation. Intellectual conformity has no single cause, and the issues it raises are certainly complicated. But the answer to the question that repeatedly arose in the interviews here is the not at all obvious but nonetheless true proposition that professional organization encourages conformity among intellectuals. One might think that in a totalitarian society fear of the police would back up the directives and suggestions received by intellectuals, but nothing of the sort seems to have occurred in the GDR. GDR intellectuals—not just literary intellectuals—now often say: "In fact, we could have done a lot more."[1] The reason they did not do more was rarely the threat of imprisonment or torture but, rather, fear of professional obstacles. My claim is not simply that certain professional structures, such as the Writers' Union or the Central Institute for Literary History, enforced particular kinds of conformity. The more interesting phenomenon is that the elaborateness of GDR professional organizations seemed to have rendered intellectual life devastatingly predictable: one knew that one would indeed be read carefully, if only by censorious authorities; one thought one knew what would happen if something in particular were said. Even when the organization itself produced no pressure to write or repress something in particular, colleagues with whom one collaborated closely were assiduous in warning of repercussions and asking for revisions in anticipation of what—often wrongly— they thought would be the authorities' response. "In fact, we could have done a lot more": but they didn't because they spoke often with their colleagues, who thought that the intellectual world was systematically organized and therefore predictable. In addition, the sense of consequence given intellectuals, partly by their organization, was something no one was willing to sacrifice or even place in jeopardy. These considerations are making me an antagonist of intellectual cooperation, which can't be right.

There is a sense in which a professionalized literary culture *reduces* dispute: professionals have a stake in keeping the peace. And they do so by encouraging conformity necessary for processes of accreditation, and dividing the literary culture into specialized sectors that supplement each other without directly competing. The professionalization of literary culture in the GDR fits very nicely with Foucault's notion that power is thoroughly dispersed throughout modern societies: "Resistance is never in a position of exteriority in relation to power. . . . There is no single locus of great Refusal, no soul of revolt, source of all rebellions, or pure law of the revolutionary."[2] The professional, by definition, is an insider, and confrontation is not the insider's way. Peter Böthig has remarked that "one finds the entire misery of the intellectual culture of the GDR reflected in this lack of a culture of arguing."[3] Professionalism, according to Durkheim, inevitably produces consensus: "The more closely the [professional] group coheres, [i.e.] the closer and more frequent the contact of the individuals, and the more frequent and intimate these contacts and the more exchange there is of ideas and sentiments, the more does a public opinion spread to cover a greater number of things."[4] Of course, we want close cooperation with our colleagues, a sense of common endeavor for ourselves and our students, and yet we should not be hurt by realizing that this sense of community carries with it the risk of inappropriate intellectual conformity and mediocrity. The very instruments we create for working with one another—departmental structures, methodological collectives, critical journals, conferences—carry not only the promise of intellectual refinement of issues through critical exchange but also the threat of inhibiting dissent and independence, precisely because they promote conventionality and predictable intellectual discourse.

My misgivings about professionalism in the literary culture inevitably sound nostalgic for a time when critics were not installed, one and all, in university departments of literature. I should acknowledge as much here, even though my own entry to literary criticism came exclusively through the most professionalized channels of the discipline of literary studies. I have benefited directly from the professionalism of literary studies, and there were times when I wished it had been still greater. I remember, for instance, the vestiges in the mid-1960s of a rapprochement with the nonprofessionalized parts of the literary culture, the annoyingly pretentious and misleading claims of some of my teachers at Berkeley to be looking for "insights" and "literary sensitivity" among their students. Inquiring into the nature of these then-mystifying terms left one open to the judgment that one was "wrongheaded." My nostalgic impulse is not so great that I would like to return to those classrooms, and a historical reversal is not possible. There is a sense, as Samuel Weber has said, in which the university since the mid-nineteenth century has become "the institutional expression and articulation of the culture of professionalism. It was [then] and remains the gateway to the professions."[5] But formerly the term *profession* had a narrower sense, medicine or law, whereas now the culture of professionalism has swallowed up what were not long ago known as arts. Academic literary criticism has a doubly vexed relation to arts as distinguished from scholarly disciplines. Obviously it justifies itself as a service industry to an undisputed art. But it is itself traditionally more an art than a science. Insofar as literary critics have recently recognized their work as an art, they have likewise seen themselves in competition with the more recognized practitioners of the literary arts, with poets and novelists. At least since the inception of the New Criticism in America, we have seen explicit competition between professional literary criticism and the arts of writing. John Crowe Ransom and others wanted to establish rules and standards that would professionalize literary criticism, excluding amateur men and women of letters; the university was the place for literary criticism. Ransom's effort has been extraordinarily successful: academics do not even acknowledge the critical labors of nonaffiliated American intellectuals; the critical writings of poets and novelists have a doubtful status in the academic literary culture. I would like to encourage my colleagues in the university literary culture to develop greater skepticism regarding the academic hegemony over the art of literary criticism, not only because the split between writers and professors has high costs for the antagonists, but also because the professionalization of literary criticism necessarily encourages intellectual conformity, and we need to protect our sources of difference and diversity, even those that simply qualify our own credentials without providing us with that now familiar aura of political progressiveness.

The stories told in these interviews don't reduce to a single moral. But a number of them, particularly those told by people born before 1950, elaborate the dangers of politically engaged writing, and still others, told by younger intellectuals, show how hard it is to achieve any sort of position one can call autonomous. That the ideal of autonomy was precious to the writers of Prenzlauer Berg is well known, but it was not obvious just how elusive autonomy was; the state's effort was constantly to manage these young writers, though we do not yet know how effective that effort was. The present climate of opinion in the United States holds suspect any aspiration to autonomy. Adorno claims that autonomous art is merely that which has lived on past its critical moment: "Neutralization is the social price art pays for its autonomy."[6] The more widespread Anglo-American view is that artists who assert the autonomy of their work are either masking or misunderstanding their own agendas.[7] The story of Prenzlauer Berg might well be used to confirm the view that there are always agendas, even when not self-imposed, behind aspirations to autonomy. Yet one sees that the most compromised authors are not those who wrongly thought that their work was free from its political context. The most compromised are in fact those who responded enthusiastically to the state's encouragement of social and political engagement.

The conversations collected here renew some old doubts about the political engagement of literary intellectuals and encourage, I hope, a renewed respect for the idea of an autonomous literary culture or, rather, for those corners of the literary edifice where degrees of autonomy can be achieved; there are moments when intellectuals need to be protected from their own desire for consequence. A number of the intellectuals with whom I spoke were too ready, in their own retrospective accounts, to suspend skepticism in order to preserve their ability to function within a particular institutional context. And there were hazardous byproducts of an engaged literature, such as an audience that always wishes not only for critically engaged writing, as Christoph Hein remarks, but for the most extreme expression of political commitment. "That's a danger for literature. A Proust would have no chance in the GDR."[8] Better Proust than Dreiser, it is easy now to say, but the choice between autonomy on the one hand and engagement on the other is obviously false. Autonomy and engagement are blunt terms easily dismissed when they are asserted absolutely. Measurements of relative engagement and distance can be made, however, and we may be quite wrong to think that the disregard suffered by writers and critics in America is without consolation.

Two weeks before the Wall opened, the French sociologist Pierre Bourdieu, in a lecture at the Humboldt University, reminded East German intellectuals that the needs for autonomy and for engagement derive from the paradoxical nature of intellectuals. His point then was that the first need for intellectuals is to guard the conditions necessary for intellectual autonomy.[9] On the following day he told an audience at the Central Committee's Academy for the Social Sciences to consider what the party apparatus had made of those who had been all too ready to give everything to the apparatus that had given them all.[10] He was not a popular guest, but he told them what they needed to hear: that there can be no elimination of the intellectual's need for autonomy or for engagement. His notion that the intellectual's need for autonomy is logically prior to all else makes sense, because it is the intellectual's disengagement from partisan politics that holds out a promise of a fresh and independent perspective, once intellectuals become engaged on any particular topic. The challenge to intellectuals is always to think differently. There are ways to preserve opportunities for engagement without sacrificing independence or cultivating bluntness and impatience: one must answer the lay challenge to speak from a perspective that is not avowed by any party. What one wants from intellectuals is not that they be unwilling or unable to speak to political, economic, or social issues but, rather, that what they do say about such issues will be irreducible to a familiar interest or partisan perspective.[11] By this account, autonomy is a precondition, as Bourdieu implies, to a proper engagement.

American literary intellectuals routinely accept the claim that ideology is very comprehensive: that literary texts are inevitably ideological, that literary history and criticism are likewise ideological. There is certainly abundant evidence to support these claims; problems come, though, from our seeing no limits to the ideological dimensions of literature, nor any to those of our own scholarly efforts. Many writers have sought in novels and poems alternatives to the public discourses that dominate one or another sociopolitical context. To many writers, literary genres seem to resist the conventional categories of thinking and belief. The effort to locate, in our own scholarly and critical efforts, areas of inquiry that are relatively free of ideological burdens may encourage intellectual independence or even provide a foothold in some fresh terrain.

The intellectuals I spoke with in this book felt, as most of my colleagues do, that ideology is the overriding determinant in literary activity; one merely chooses a particular ideology to promote. None of these people had participated in the civil rights groups much before October

1989, though Heinz-Uwe Haus presented himself in 1990 as a political candidate for Democratic Awakening. Ludwig Mehlhorn, one of the founders of Democracy Now, claims it is no accident that literary critics and writers did not participate in the organized opposition:

> Many opposition activists in the fall [of 1989] came out of the realm of the church. The study of theology was the only thing you could engage in that was free of party ideology. . . . Just look at the opposition intellectuals in Poland. There you find literary critics, philosophers, historians, and so on. And who are these people here [in the GDR]? Either they are Protestant ministers, or they are natural scientists. In other words, they came out of those sectors in which ideology was not as important, where you did not have to be a member of the party. This is true almost across the board.[12]

The willing acceptance by the GDR literary culture of its ideological burdens left writers and critics standing at the margins when historical changes came. Not many writers or literary critics tried to occupy those parts of their professions where ideological pressure was not strong. They were seduced by the sense of consequence that ideological engagement offered them, and who can blame them? How uninviting is the counsel I propose: cultivate inconsequence! But there is a connection between intellectual independence and marginality, as no one in literary studies now needs to be reminded. But where are the real margins now? A guideline, perhaps severe, might be that any topic or perspective commanding two sessions at the annual MLA conference is no longer marginal. The capacious center of academic literary culture has absorbed many recently marginal perspectives, and it does so now proudly in the name of political progress. The criticism of contemporary poets and novelists, however, has not been well integrated, or we might speak of stylistic criticism as marginal. For the time being, these are sources of difference within academic literary studies. But the lasting issue is the cultivation of skepticism toward propositions and perspectives that enjoy consensus at any particular time.

We need to listen at the margins not only to those excluded by an earlier generation of scholar-critics because of race, class, or gender; that sort of attentiveness is easy now and goes without saying. The more difficult thing is to listen to those whose views we have excluded because we thought that professional academics could do the job of criticism better than writers or journalists could, or to those who seem just wrong (or retrograde) to us. Are we sufficiently interested in the voices at the margins to listen closely to those whose views seem to us mistaken, ill-intentioned, or merely retrograde? This is the sort of listening that can produce doubt about the academic hegemony in literary criticism, doubt about the ambitions and importance of this group of professional intellectuals. The East German dissident Ulrike Poppe notes that "the Stasi like[d] to use ambition as a hook for ambitious people. . . . The sense of being taken seriously . . . could be compensating for a damaged sense of self-worth, which in this paternalistic state was produced as if programmed. . . . Thus in a report [on] the state of party cadres in the field of nuclear technology of 1957: 'It is generally true for all professors that it is important to them to be recognized for their work by the party and the government. We should show them from time to time that our party is paying close attention to their research and development work. When such recognition takes place, professors are very impressed and willing to use all their energies even more emphatically for the development of science and the application of their experience.'"[13] The Stasi knew their targets, and here we can see how cynically and easily intellectuals were manipulated by their own sense of engagement and importance.

What possible relevance does the example of the GDR have for American literary intellectuals? We have no writers' unions, no single institute for literary history, no party structure to parallel our professional structures. Those differences might well lead us to regard the stories told here with the curiosity we have for other people's problems. While I am sure that their problems are not exactly our own, I do think we can establish sufficient common ground between the two literary cultures to enable us to benefit from a critical examination of the GDR experience. We have our own institutions for establishing professional consensus—journals, departments, associations based on fields, the overall structure of the Modern Language Association, and creative writing programs. Although I have emphasized the institutional structures supporting and organizing the literary culture of the GDR, the scholars and writers with whom I spoke tended rather to emphasize certain idioms and ready-made arguments that codified ideological intentions. Indeed many poets and novelists praised the extraordinary sensitivity of GDR nonprofessional readers: a single phrase could trigger a train of thought "between the lines," as was often said. Although our institutional structures are less elaborate than those of the GDR, our critical idioms are also codified and often aimed at easy agreement between writer and reader. The danger is not that we become too institutionalized but rather that we inhibit our own thinking by agreeing with one another.

There is one area of close resemblance between the two literary cultures. In the 1970s and 1980s, both the GDR and the American scholarly cultures saw greater professional structuring accompanied by a noticeable weakening of the connections between scholars and the poets, novelists, and dramatists of the time. In both countries the academic culture cut itself off from contemporary writers and, at the same time, granted more degrees in creative writing to young writers. The only creative writing program in Europe was at the Johannes R. Becher Institute in Leipzig. In Europe only the East Germans believed, as Americans do, that the writing of literature can profitably be taught. However, contact with contemporary writing outside the professional structures could be difficult. Klaus Michael was known to participate in the Prenzlauer Berg scene, though he was a doctoral student in modern German literature and a staff member at the Central Institute. He acknowledged and respected the separation of these two activities by using (nonconspiratorially) a pseudonym, Michael Thulin, for his activities in the Prenzlauer Berg magazines. Peter Böthig studied modern German literature at the Humboldt University until he was expelled for participating in a church exhibition on the alternative literary scene. The rift between these two sectors of the literary culture in America is frequently discussed in terms of prose style: academics have only an attenuated faith in the capacity of a plain style of exposition. The issue is not just style, of course: the idioms of academic literary criticism assert a professional's exclusive claim to credibility in this discipline or, as amateurs might call it, art. The marginalization of nonacademic criticism is an altogether predictable chapter in the history of the professionalization of literary studies in America. In the GDR the suppression of critical commentary on the Prenzlauer Berg scene expressed an effort by professional literary scholars to protect themselves against the critique of engagement and complicity articulated by the young writers of the 1980s. What is suppressed in both cases is a critical perspective on professionalized academic literary culture. Professions come into existence by discrediting rival practitioners; they maintain hegemony by controlling accreditation. But they can renew themselves by listening attentively to their vanquished rivals, the outsiders.

I have spoken of the criticism of poets and novelists as an alternative to the professional academic literary criticism that advances careers in the universities, but it would be quite mistaken to suggest that the nonacademic literary sector is itself not professionalized as well. In the literary culture one speaks of as outside academia, there has also been an increase in the professionalization of writing. In the past half-century creative writing programs have proliferated across the country. Poets too are professionals, though their guilds and accreditation procedures are different from those of literary academics. Creative writing is taught in most universities, and several small colleges offer programs that are based principally on correspondence courses with well-known writers. A number of poets are able to hold down full-time regular appointments while supplementing their income by teaching in these correspondence programs. There is real demand for instruction in the writing of poems, plays, and narratives. But what are the intellectual effects of the professionalization of creative writing in the United States? Three of those effects are worth discussing here. One is an enormous productivity among poets, which is now regarded as normal; one new book every three years or so is pretty common. Poets, like their scholarly colleagues in the English Department at the University of X or Y, need to be productive too in order to qualify for promotions and pay increases at institutions dominated by professional scholars. A second consequence of the professionalization of poets has been an institutionalized conformity of style: critics commonly refer to the "workshop style" of recent poetry as the product of such writing programs as that of the University of Iowa. The collaboration of the poets who inaugurated the confessional style in the late 1950s and early 1960s—Robert Lowell, John Berryman, W. D. Snodgrass, Sylvia Plath, and Anne Sexton—took place in creative writing seminars at Iowa, Princeton, and Boston Universities.[14] The third consequence I have in mind comes from the desire of professionals to reach consensus. When poets and novelists take their places in professional literary institutions they begin to reach agreement more easily than they might otherwise do; even when they fail to agree, they tend to fend off issues that are divisive. During the period when the creative writing programs proliferated, the reviewing of poetry declined.

It is unusual now to find poets willing to review other poets critically. Most reviews of poetry are admiring: they are one way poets have of networking like other professionals. The professionalization of contemporary American writing has softened criticism. Often a young poet's work is offered for review by an editor of a literary supplement. The reviewer is a mature, well-recognized poet who has long held a tenured position at University X. The young poet also has a teaching job, according to the jacket copy of the book sent for review. The reviewer judges the book jejune but is unwilling to say as much in print, for fear that a critical review could cost this young poet his or her livelihood. The professional stakes are too high: one hesitates to write skeptically about young poets, and in the end one simply hesitates to accept any reviewing assignments. What is lost to the literary culture is a forum where new books of poems and stories are taken seriously and reviewed critically, especially by other writers. Not surprisingly, poets continue to be very critical of the work of their contemporaries. But one cannot read much of this criticism now, because it is more often heard in private conversation than read in the public sphere of print. Where intellectuals gather frequently to discuss their work, the enlightenment notion of intellectual skepticism is in some peril.

I have moved away from the topic of the GDR here in order to think generally about the adverse consequences of professionalization in American letters and to speculate about some local antidotes. The particular problems of German intellectuals are quite different from those of American literary intellectuals, but the overall issues of professionalization and conformity touch both communities. The GDR experience has led me to construct a sharply critical perspective on the professionalization of literary intellectuals, though I have no illusion of some general alternative to a professionalized literary culture in America at this point. But I do hope for a greater range of difference among literary academics, specifically differences not subsumed by identity politics. I also hope to see poets and fiction writers commit more energy to the construction of a public discourse about contemporary writing outside of the apparatus for professional promotion. The experience of German intellectuals after 1989 has shown that the publics that fund universities and buy books of poetry and fiction are not so complacent as many literary intellectuals have become about the superannuation of certain obligations traditionally attached to the vocations of writers and intellectuals. Looking at the record of constrained dissent among German literary intellectuals, many of them a lot like us, we can ask if we are really entitled to the sort of derisive irony current in academia when the idea of a nonprofessional literary culture is raised. Are rolled eyes an appropriate response to the aspirations designated by the term *belletristic,* or even *literary*? Aren't these words that, in our circumstances, express hope for a literary culture produced at the margins, not at the institution-alized, disciplined, and subsidized centers like my own university, and for a public that expects writers to transcend the ethos and conventions of professions and corporations?

Notes

Introduction

1. Stephen Brockmann, "Introduction: The Reunification Debate," *New German Critique* 52 (winter 1991): 4. *New German Critique* is hereafter abbreviated as *NGC*.

2. Martin Walser, *Über Deutschland reden* (Frankfurt: Suhrkamp, 1989), 92. The translations from German in this Introduction, unless otherwise indicated, are my own.

3. In 1987 John Ardagh referred to the goal of reunification as "a kind of official myth in the Federal Republic" (*Germany and the Germans* [New York: Harper and Row, 1987], 383).

4. Quoted in Dirk Philipsen, *We Were the People* (Durham, N.C.: Duke University Press, 1993), 199, n. 5.

5. Walser, *Über Deutschland reden*, 117.

6. Christa Wolf, *Im Dialog* (Frankfurt: Luchterhand, 1990), 171. In ways that do her credit by focusing on the issue of complicity, Wolf has often said that she has trouble saying "we." In *Cassandra* (trans. Jan Van Heurck [New York: Farrar, Straus, Giroux, 1984]) the narrator observes that "it is so much easier to say 'Achilles the brute' than to say this 'we'" (118). At Alexanderplatz, on November 4, 1989, however, Wolf had no difficulty uttering her claim to identity with the founders of the GDR (and blaming the leadership of the party for imposing Stalinism on the country) in a statement written by Stefan Heym. Three months later she would use the "we" to identify herself with those who began the revolution that ended the GDR: "Does all this mean that what we began in autumn of 1989 has already failed? I hesitate to say that, I refuse to give in to that suggestion. I want to remember the conditions which we decided were no longer acceptable" (Wolf, *The Author's Dimension,* trans. Jan Van Heurck [New York: Farrar, Straus, Giroux, 1993], 326). Was Wolf really present at the creation of the GDR revolution? She was not a member of any of the citizens' rights committees that organized demonstrations in Leipzig; she was rather a member of the SED. Reform-minded socialists did not initiate the demonstrations. Instead, it seems that the pressure for peace prayers and demonstrations in Leipzig originated with would-be émigrés who had applied for exit visas and been kept waiting too long. (See the comments of Klaus Kaden in Philipsen, *We Were the People,* 143.) Wolf's sincerity or at least thoughtfulness is at issue here. Of course

as a political orator she is loose in her use of the first-person plural. In November she was with the founders of the state, and in January with its disrupters. There are admittedly ways of sorting out this contradiction, provided one's actions sort with one's claims. But the writer Wolf seems to have known all along that life in the GDR called into question the integrity of anyone who participated in its self-representations, though in the fiction the fraudulence of all self-representation is the overt theme: "The ingenuous open heart," she wrote in 1968, "preserves one's ability to say 'I' to a stranger, until a moment comes when this strange 'I' returns and enters into 'me' again. Then at one blow the heart is captive, one is prepossessed; that much can be foretold" (Wolf, *The Quest for Christa T.*, trans. Christopher Middleton [New York: Farrar, Straus, Giroux, 1970], 14).

7. Robert Darnton quoted the latest polls on March 3, 1990, predicting 53 percent for the SPD and 13 percent for the CDU (*Berlin Journal, 1989–1990* [New York: Norton, 1991], 248.

See too Stephen Brockmann's account of earlier polls indicating a majority against reunification ("Introduction," 15).

8. Günter de Bruyn, "Der Riss und die Literatur," *Frankfurter Allgemeine Zeitung* (hereafter abbreviated as *FAZ*), Oct. 23, 1991. The failure of GDR intellectuals to foresee the outcome of the balloting in March 1990 suggests that the representation of GDR society as unstratified was seriously misleading. It was common to hear before 1989 about how people who in the west would be divided by class boundaries were able to maintain closer contact in the east. John Ardagh was told by a West German journalist stationed in the east that GDR society was characterized by groups of twenty to thirty people held together by discussion and friendship. These were said to be "multiprofessional" mutual-help societies. This is part of the myth of the GDR as a friendlier place than the FRG. Ardagh drew the mistaken conclusion that in the GDR "professional people tend to be much less career-minded than in the West" (*Germany and the Germans,* 340). The interviews collected in this book show that GDR writers and scholars were highly professionalized and career-minded, though affluence was not the measure of professional effectiveness in the east.

9. Christoph Hein, *Texte, Daten, Bilder,* ed. Lothar Baier (Frankfurt: Luchterhand, 1990), 40.

10. Christoph Hein, *Als Kind habe ich Stalin gesehen* (Berlin: Aufbau, 1990), 162.

11. Fritz Rudolf Fries, "Braucht die neue Republik neue Autoren?" in *"Die Geschichte ist offen,"* ed. Michael Naumann (Reinbek bei Hamburg: Rowohlt, 1990), 55.

12. *Bild-Zeitung,* Nov. 9, 1990; cited in *FAZ* 22–23 (Dec. 1990): 14.

13. Andreas Huyssen, "After the Wall: The Failure of German Intellectuals," *NGC* 52 (winter 1991): 144.

14. Stefan Heym, "Ash Wednesday in the GDR," *NGC* 32; originally published in *Die Zeit* (Nov. 17, 1989).

15. Peter Schneider, *The German Comedy,* trans. Philip Boehm and Leigh Hafrey (New York: Farrar, Straus, Giroux, 1991), 89.

16. Walser, *Über Deutschland reden,* 119.

17. Jürgen Habermas, *Die nachholende Revolution* (Frankfurt: Suhrkamp, 1990), 181; quoted in Klaus Hartung, *Neunzehnhundertneunundachtzig* (Frankfurt: Luchterhand, 1990), 67.

18. Hartung, *Neunzehnhundertneunundachtzig,* 50.

19. Ibid., 60. Poppe is quoted by Dirk Philipsen, *We Were the People,* 317; see also the comments of Ludwig Mehlhorn in Philipsen, 370–72.

20. Hartung, *Neunzehnhundertneunundachtzig,* 60.

21. Thomas Rietzschel, "Revolution im Leseland," *FAZ* (Feb. 10, 1990): pars. 5–7.

22. Günter Kunert, "Weltfremd und blind," *FAZ* 149 (June 30, 1990): 27, par. 4.

23. Helga Schütz, "Ein Stück der täglichen Wahrheit zur Sprache bringen," in *Mein Deutschland findet sich in keinem Atlas,* ed. Françoise Barthélemy and Lutz Winkler (Frankfurt: Luchterhand, 1990), 22.

24. Hans Joachim Schädlich has characterized this view of the role of writers: "The gentle mediators between the dictatorship and the reading public who tried to educate the dictatorship, and who because of unnatural causes enjoyed an artificially high regard as quasi-priests, quasi-psychiatrists, and quasi-journalists—they too have lost the dictatorship that they wanted to educate and that they at the same time effectively stabilized" ("Tanz in Ketten," *FAZ* [June 28, 1990]: 33, par. 15).

25. It is important to understand that a moralistic and didactic understanding of the German writer's function prevailed not only in the east. In 1972 a survey determined that 62 percent of West German writers saw themselves as the "conscience of the nation" (*Der Autorenreport* [Reinbek: Rowohlt, 1972], 357, cited in Dietger Pforte, "Schriftsteller," *Handbuch zur deutsch-deutschen Wirklichkeit,* ed. W. R. Langenbucher et al. [Stuttgart: J. B. Metzler, 1988], 629).

26. Hein, *Texte,* 40.

27. Katie Hafner, "A Nation of Readers Dumps Its Writers," *New York Times Magazine* (Jan. 10, 1993): 25.

28. Fritz J. Raddatz, "Ich weiss, dass wir keine Chance haben," *Die Zeit* (Feb. 2, 1990): 18.

29. Rolf Schneider, *Frühling im Herbst* (Göttingen: Steidl, 1991), 81.

30. Helga Königsdorf, "Der Schmerz über das eigene Versagen," *Die Zeit* 23 (June 1, 1990): 64, par. 6.

31. Monika Maron, "Writers and the People," *NGC* 39; originally published in *Der Spiegel* 7 (1990).

32. Philippe Sollers, "Berührung," *Die Zeit* 42 (Oct. 13, 1989): 2.

33. Ardagh, *Germany and the Germans,* 340.

34. Wolf, *Author's Dimension,* 291.

35. Schneider, *Frühling im Herbst,* 77.

36. This distinction corresponds to Gramsci's "traditional" and "organic intellectuals." See Antonio Gramsci, *The Modern Prince and Other Writings,* trans. Louis Marks (New York: International Publishers, 1957), 118–25. I prefer my own terms because Gramsci's account of the class origins of organic intellectuals does not fit many of the cases of the East German literary intellectuals with whom I spoke. I do not want to suggest that the strife over intellectuals in Germany derives in any straightforward sense from a single class struggle, as Gramsci's use of these terms suggests.

37. Julien Benda, *The Treason of the Intellectuals,* trans. Richard Aldington (New York: Norton, 1969), 158; hereafter abbreviated as *TI.*

38. On page 154 Benda refers to play as "the perfect type of disinterested activity"; see T. S. Eliot, *The Sacred Wood* (1920; reprint, London: Methuen, 1969), 45, on Benda's relation to Arnold.

39. Edward Said, *The World, the Text, the Critic* (Cambridge, Mass.: Harvard University Press, 1983), 171.

40. Ibid., 175.

41. Emile Durkheim, *Professional Ethics and Civic Morals,* trans. Cornelia Brookfield (London: Routledge, 1992), 4.

42. Bruce Robbins, *Secular Vocations* (London: Verso, 1993).

43. Stanley Fish, *Doing What Comes Naturally* (Durham, N.C.: Duke University Press, 1989), 215; hereafter abbreviated as *D.*

44. Schütz, "Ein Stück," 21.

45. Günter Grass, *Two States—One Nation,* trans. Krishna Winston with A. S. Wensinger (San Diego: Harcourt, Brace, Jovanovich, 1990), 2, 6, 122.

46. The debate about whether to incorporate the GDR under Article 23 of the Basic Law or to convene a constitutional debate under the auspices of Article 146 is examined by Micha Brumlik, "Basic Aspects of an Imaginary Debate," *NGC* 52 (winter 1991): 102–8.

47. Before 1989 it was customary to hear that the GDR came to terms with fascism and the FRG tried to cover over its Nazi past. It was the case that former Nazis survived in positions of power and authority in the FRG. But writers like Hans Joachim Schädlich, who believe rather that the GDR has not yet begun its engagement with the German past, have gained a new hearing (Hans Joachim Schädlich, *Aktenkundig* [Berlin: Rowohlt, 1992], 9).

48. For an excellent discussion of the right-wing violence in East and West Germany, see Michael Schmidt, *The New Reich,* trans. Daniel Horch (New York: Pantheon, 1993). Peter Schneider has written well about the racism of the former GDR in *German Comedy,* especially 92–109.

49. See Hellmuth Karasek and Rolf Becker in conversation with Günter Grass, "Nötige Kritik oder Hinrichtung," *Der Spiegel* 29 (July 16, 1990): 141.

50. Ulrich Greiner, "Mangel an Feingefühl," *Die Zeit* 23 (June 1, 1990): 63.

51. Ibid. Thomas Anz shows how the charges against Wolf originated in Marcel Reich Ranicki's claim that she had capitulated and withdrawn her signature from the 1976 petition protesting the expatriation of Wolf Biermann (*"Es geht nicht um Christa Wolf,"* ed. Thomas Anz [Munich: Spangenberg, 1991], 30 ff.).

52. Hellmuth Karasek, "Selbstgemachte Konfitüre," *Der Spiegel* (June 25, 1990): 162.

53. Wolf, *Cassandra*, 62–63, 69.

54. Christa Wolf, *Patterns of Childhood*, trans. Ursula Molinaro and Hedwig Rappolt (New York: Farrar, Straus, Giroux, 1980), 43, 171.

55. Ibid., 171.

56. *The Fourth Dimension: Interviews with Christa Wolf*, trans. Hilary Pilkington (London: Verso, 1988), 83; hereafter abbreviated as *FD*.

57. See the commentary of Thomas Anz on the background of the 1990 campaign in *"Es geht nicht um Christa Wolf,"* 30–31; and Marcel Reich-Ranicki's allegation on page 35. Wolf explains that she found in her Stasi files evidence of the Stasi having initiated the rumor that she had privately withdrawn her support for the petition ("Eine Auskunft," *Berliner Zeitung*, Jan. 21, 1993).

58. Frank Schirrmacher, "'Dem Druck des härteren, strengeren Lebens standhalten," *FAZ* 127 (June 2, 1990), 47, par. 5.

59. Christa Wolf, "Das haben wir nicht gelernt," *taz* (Oct. 31, 1989): 11, par. 4.

60. Wolf, *Im Dialog*, 76.

61. Thomas Rietzschel, "Revolution im Leseland," *FAZ*, Feb. 10, 1990.

62. Christa Wolf, *Was bleibt* (Frankfurt/Main: Luchterhand, 1990), 21; cf. also 28.

63. Karasek, "Selbstgemachte Konfitüre," 165.

64. Ibid., 162.

65. Wolf, *Author's Dimension*, 329–30.

66. Iris Radisch, "Das ist nicht so einfach: Ein ZEIT-Gespräch mit Sascha Anderson," *Die Zeit* 45 (Nov. 1, 1991): 65.

67. Ibid., 66.

68. Anthony Giddens, *The Consequences of Modernity* (Stanford: Stanford University Press, 1990), 57–58.

69. Ulf Christian Hasenfelder, "Waghalsiges Spiel im Wirbel der Phrasen," *FAZ* 122 (May 29, 1991): N4. For an account of some of the dubious ways in which poststructuralist thought was used in the Prenzlauer Berg scene, see Friederike Eigler, "The Responsibility of the Intellectual: The Case of the East Berlin 'Counter-Culture,'" in *Cultural Transformations in the New Germany*, ed. Friederike Eigler and Peter C. Pfeiffer (Columbia, S.C.: Camden House, 1993), 157–71.

70. Wolf Biermann, "Ein öffentliches Geschwür," *Der Spiegel* 3 (Jan. 13, 1992): 162.

71. Ibid., 167.

334 Notes to pages 26–30

72. Frank Schirrmacher, "Verdacht und Verrat," *FAZ* (Nov. 5, 1991): 33.

73. Iris Radisch, "Warten auf Montag," *Die Zeit* 48 (Nov. 29, 1991): 63.

74. I learned in 1992 of the case of one of the academics I interviewed who, under duress, had signed an agreement in the last year of the GDR to cooperate with the Stasi. However, it seems that no information was ever provided to the Stasi. Nonetheless this scholar's academic position was lost, less because of the Stasi connection than because of the scholar's effort to conceal the matter.

I would have liked to examine this case in detail, but in order to retain this literary historian's permission to publish the interview we did before he/she was exposed, I have had to agree not to reveal his/her identity. There is, however, one conclusion to this case that I do want to mention. Writers who collaborated with the Stasi have been publicly exposed, and in time we will know whether they lost all or only some credibility as a result of their exposure. Scholars who have been revealed as collaborators, however, have been less publicly exposed. This particular scholar is no longer employed directly in teaching or research, but he/she does hold a position in a cultural institution. It appears that the professional structures in place in the scholarly sector are considerably more forgiving than those in the literary sector.

75. Sascha Anderson, "Ein hoffentlich schöner und lang anhaltender Amoklauf," *FAZ* (Oct. 30, 1991): 35.

76. Ibid. Holger Kulick, "Grautöne: Der Amoklauf Sascha Andersons," in *MachtSpiele,* ed. Peter Böthig and Klaus Michael (Leipzig: Reklam, 1993), 194.

77. Sascha Anderson, "Strategy Paper on the Prenzlauer Berg Writers," in *MachtSpiele,* 255.

78. Christoph Hein, *The Distant Lover,* trans. Krishna Winston (New York: Pantheon, 1989), 87.

79. Bärbel Bohley, "Die Macht wird entzaubert," in *Aktenkundig,* 42.

80. Anderson, "Strategy Paper," 271.

81. Richard Stern, *The Chaleur Network* [formerly *In Any Case*] (1962; reprint, Sagaponock, N.Y.: Second Chance Press, 1981), 138.

82. Harold Perkin says that "professional people, rightly or wrongly, see themselves as above the main economic battle, at once privileged observers and benevolent neutrals since, whichever side wins, they believe that their services will still be necessary and properly rewarded" (*The Rise of Professional Society* [London: Routledge, 1989], 117). This is quite suggestive. Perkin also notes that professionals seek to generalize the conditions they as a group enjoy. This means that there is a natural affinity between professional society and any party that proposes, as socialists do, the transcendence of economic struggle. (Perkin speaks of the welfare state where I refer to socialism [9]).

83. On the subject of writers excusing Sascha, see Andrea Kühne in *Süddeutsche Zeitung* [hereafter abbreviated as *SZ*] (Apr. 21, 1992), cited by Uwe Kolbe: "His small betrayal—to the extent it even was one—does not weigh very

heavily when compared to the achievement of having actually internalized the maxims of the postmodernists" (Kolbe, paper presented at conference, University of Chicago, May 2, 1992, 2).

84. Peter Böthig, "leib eigen & fremd," *Die Zeit* 13 (Mar. 20, 1992): 81.

85. Kulick, "Grautöne," 192.

86. Sascha Anderson, "In dem das Aufwachen nichts bedeutet" [1986], in *Vogel oder Käfig sein,* ed. Klaus Michael and Thomas Wohlfahrt (Berlin: Galrev, 1992), 108.

87. Anderson, "Strategy Paper," 271.

88. See memos by Major Heimann and Oberst Reuter, Sept. 27, 1985, in *MachtSpiele,* 244, 245.

89. Christa Wolf, interview with the *Wochenpost,* vol. 24 (Jan. 1993): 2.

90. Volker Hage, "Wir müssen uns dem Schicksal stellen," *Der Spiegel* (Feb. 8, 1993): 198.

91. "Hannes," quoted in "Die ängstliche Margarete," *Der Spiegel* (Jan. 25, 1993): 160.

92. Robin Detje, "Heiner Müller und die Stasi," *Die Zeit* (Jan. 22, 1993): 13.

93. Schirrmacher, "Verdacht," 33.

94. See Otto Köhler, "Vom Neuen Denken der Deutschen," *Die Zeit* 52 (Dec. 27, 1991): 16.

95. Walter Janka, *Schwierigkeiten mit der Wahrheit* (Reinbek: Rowohlt, 1989). Peter Huchel, founding editor of *Sinn und Form,* wrote: "People of my generation like Arnold Zweig, Anna Seghers, Johannes R. Becher, whom I considered friends, from one day to the next didn't know me anymore, didn't visit me" (quoted in Hans Dieter Zimmermann, "Der Traum im Tellereisen," *Die Zeit* 2 [Jan. 11, 1991]: 17).

96. Quoted in Gerwin Zohlen, "Wider die Chimaere," *SZ* 228 (Oct. 4, 1990): 55.

97. "Nötige Kritik oder Hinrichtung," 141.

98. See, for example, Brigitte Haberer, "Literaturkitik als Trojanisches Pferd," *SZ* 213 (Sept. 15–16, 1990): 16: "Without doubt the crucial question runs: what is the status of aesthetic criteria in GDR literary criticism? It has to do with the *how* of writing, not so much with the *what*." This new emphasis on formalist, idealist aesthetic judgment is plainly a reaction against GDR engaged art. The same issue is under discussion in painting, too. See Wieland Schmied, "Zur Moderne keine Alternative," *SZ* 176 (Aug. 2, 1990): 14.

99. Ernest Gellner, *Nations and Nationalism* (Ithaca: Cornell University Press, 1983), 55. *Literaturstreit* (literature strife) is the term that refers to the controversies set off originally by the critical attacks on Wolf's *Was bleibt.*

100. Rüdiger Schaper, "Der deutsche Frühschoppen," *SZ* 238 (Oct. 16, 1990): 36.

Norbert Krenzlin

1. Günter Grass argued strenuously for a confederation of the GDR and the FRG and an experiment in "democratic socialism" (*Two States*).

2. Günter Mittag (b. 1926) became a member of the Central Committee of the SED in 1962; in 1966 he joined the Politburo; and in 1976 he became the secretary for economy.

Erich Mielke (b. 1907) headed the Ministry for State Security (popularly known as the Stasi, from Staatssicherheitsdienst, State Security Service) from 1957 until 1989. Upon his return from Soviet exile to Germany in 1945, he became actively engaged in organizing a political police force in the Soviet occupation zone. After the founding of the GDR he was in charge of establishing the Stasi, which became a powerful instrument of party control and oppression in all spheres of cultural, economic, and social life. From 1959 to 1989 Mielke was a full member of the Central Committee of the SED. In 1989 he was arrested on charges of corruption, abuse of power, and murder of a policeman before the war.

Willi Stoph (b. 1914) became a member of the Central Committee in 1950 and of the Politburo in 1953.

Heinz-Uwe Haus

1. Heinz Knobloch (b. 1926) is a journalist and, since 1953, editor-in-chief of the popular weekly magazine *Wochenpost*. He was awarded the prestigious Heinrich Heine Prize (1965) and the National Prize of the GDR (1986). He has never been a member of a political party. In 1990 he was elected president of the GDR PEN Club.

2. Rudolf Bahro (b. 1935) is a philosopher who served as deputy editor-in-chief of the magazine *Forum* in the 1960s. He was part of the Marxist opposition to the GDR regime and an outspoken critic of the concept of "real existing socialism." In 1979 he was released from prison and expelled from the GDR. His major theoretical work, *Die Alternative: Zur Kritik des realexistierenden Sozialismus* (1977), was published only in the Federal Republic. Upon moving to West Germany, he became actively involved in various peace initiatives and the Green movement. His publications include *European Nuclear Disarmament* (1981), *Elemente einer neuen Politik* (1982), *Wahnsinn der Methode: Über die Logik der Blockkonfrontation* (1982), *Building the Green Movement* (1986), and *Rückkehr*.

Hermann von Berg (b. 1933) became professor in political economy at the Humboldt University in 1972. He spent many years in the Federal Republic as a special envoy of the GDR government.

Marianne Streisand

1. Dieter Schlenstedt (b. 1932) is a highly regarded scholar-critic, formerly at the Central Institute, who concentrates particularly on contemporary GDR literature. His publications include *Wirkungsanalysen: Poetologie und Prosa in der neueren DDR Literatur* (1979), *Die neuere DDR Literatur und ihr Leser* (1980), *Egon Erwin Kisch: Leben und Werk* (1985), and contributions to a number of collaborative projects.

2. Bruno Apitz (1900–79) was a writer who became very popular with his novel depicting the persecution of Jews by the Nazis, *Nackt unter Wölfen* (1958). He had been a member of the Communist Party since 1927 and spent nine years in the concentration camp at Buchenwald (1936–45). He became a freelance writer in Leipzig in 1955. His works include *Ester* (1959), *Der Regenbogen* (1976), and *Schwelbrand* (1983).

3. Inge Münz Koenen was editor of the collection of essays *Werke und Wirkungen: DDR Literatur in der Diskussion* (Leipzig: Philipp Reclam, 1987).

4. Steffi Spira is a popular GDR actress.

5. In East Berlin, the Gethsemane Church became a center for protest in the summer and fall of 1989, with sermons on such apparently innocuous texts as Jesus' treatment of the Pharisees gaining intense current political significance, and with peaceful candlelight vigils for reform. Some demonstrators embarked on fasts, remaining in the church for days without food; others came for short periods to talk and demonstrate their solidarity. Young women at the Gethsemane Church approached members of the militia with flowers and invited policemen to change out of uniform and join them in demanding democratization.

6. *Sinn und Form* is a bimonthly publication of the Academy of the Arts founded in 1949. The most prestigious academic literary journal of the GDR, it has been subjected to temporary suspensions for publishing authors like Kafka and Sartre, whose books were banned in the GDR.

7. *Sonntag* was a wide-circulation weekly publication of the Cultural League of the GDR.

8. Joachim Herrmann (b. 1928) was a full member of the Politburo and secretary for agitation and propaganda from 1978.

He had previously been editor-in-chief of the FDJ newspaper *Junge Welt* (1954–60), *Berliner Zeitung* (1962–65), and *Neues Deutschland* (1971–78).

Frank and Therese Hörnigk

1. Werner Mittenzwei (b. 1927), literary critic and editor, directed the Central Institute for Literary History from 1969 to 1973. Later he held the chair for art and literature at the Central Committee's Academy of the Social Sciences. He is well known as an editor of Brecht.

2. Theodor Fontane (1819–98) was a prolific German novelist whose works portray the social scene of his time, particularly in Berlin, with subtle and delicate

irony. His most popular prose works include *Irrungen, Wirrungen* (1888), *Frau Jenny Treibel* (1892), *Effi Briest* (1895), and *Der Stechlin* (1898).

3. Willi Bredel (1901–64) was a member of the Association of Revolutionary Proletariat Writers. He was imprisoned in a concentration camp for two years, then released. He fled to Moscow, where he edited the journal *Das Wort* with Brecht and Lion Feuchtwanger. From 1937 until 1939 he fought in the International Brigade in Spain. In 1945 he returned to the Soviet-occupied zone and served as a functionary.

4. Klaus Hermsdorf (b. 1929) has been professor of modern German literature at the Humboldt University since 1959. He defended his dissertation on Kafka, whose works initiated heated debates and controversies in the GDR in the 1960s. In 1961 he published his first book, *Kafka: Weltbild und Roman.* His most recent critical book is *Literarisches Leben in Berlin* (1987). He recently edited Kafka's *Amtliche Schriften* (1991).

5. The conference, organized by Eduard Goldstücker, took place in May 1963 at the Liblice Castle near Prague. Party officials regarded the conference as a provocation, because Kafka had formerly been regarded as decadent. Goldstücker, Garaudy, and Fischer advanced the thesis that alienation was relevant to socialist society. The lectures from the conference were collected in *Franz Kafka: Aus Prager Sicht* (Prague, 1965; Berlin, 1966). Alfred Kurella was one of the cultural politicians who strongly opposed Goldstücker's thesis.

6. The Petöfi circle played a role in the anti-Russian insurrection in Hungary in 1956. Georg Lukács was one of its leaders.

7. The Twentieth Congress of the Communist Party took place in February 1956. East German intellectuals had hoped for a change of political direction after Khrushchev's secret speech about Stalin's crimes. Instead the party stiffened in response. For alleged conspiracy, intellectuals who had collaborated on the *Deutsche Zeitschrift für Philosophie;* Walter Janka, director of the Aufbau Verlag; and later Erich Loest were all sentenced to prison. Many other intellectuals, such as Heiner Kipphardt, Uwe Johnson, and Helge Novak, evaded punishment by escaping to West Germany between 1956 and 1969. After the Hungarian uprising in 1956, Lukács was condemned as revisionist. Ernst Bloch's works were officially banned in 1957, also as revisionist. Hans Mayer, professor of German at Leipzig; and Peter Huchel, editor of *Sinn und Form,* were repeatedly attacked for alleged revisionism and elitism.

8. Christa Wolf, Heiner Müller, and Volker Braun were among the original twelve signatories of the petition protesting the expatriation of Wolf Biermann in 1976.

9. Robert Havemann (1910–82) was a Marxist philosopher and scientist (chemist). A party member since 1949 and member of the GDR parliament (Volkskammer), he was a staunch opponent of the dogmatic ideological positions of the party leadership towards literature and science. In 1964 he was banned from teaching at the Academy of Sciences, dismissed from academia, and expelled from the party. In 1979, he was given a 10,000-DM fine for "violating

some currency regulations," that is, for publishing in West German periodicals (*Die Zeit*) and receiving honoraria in West German currency. His membership in the Academy of Sciences was posthumously restored in November 1989.

10. Sarah Kirsch (b. 1935) was one of the original twelve signatories of the petition protesting the expatriation of Wolf Biermann in 1976. In 1977 she left the GDR to live in the FRG.

11. Erich Loest (b. 1926) originally left the GDR in 1981 with a three-year visa. Karl-Heinz Jacobs (b. 1929) studied at the Johannes R. Becher Institute in Leipzig. Because of his protest of the expatriation of the writer-performer Wolf Biermann, he was expelled from the party in 1976. After the publication of his novel *Wilhelmsburg* in West Germany in 1979, Jakobs was expelled from the Writers' Union. He left the GDR in 1981.

12. Andrey Dmitriyevich Sakharov (1921–89) was a Soviet nuclear physicist and civil rights activist. He had participated directly in the development of Soviet nuclear weapons. In the late 1960s he became a spokesman for the civil rights movement in the Soviet Union. In 1980 he was exiled to Gorky without court trial. In 1986 he was permitted to return to Moscow, where he became a board member of the Soviet Academy.

Simone and Karlheinz Barck

1. Hans Koch (1927–87) held the chair in theory and history of literature and art at the Central Committee's Academy of Social Sciences from 1969 until his death. In addition to editing the works of Franz Mehring, Koch edited *Marx, Engels, Lenin: On Culture, Aesthetics, and Literature* (1958) and *On the Theory of Socialist Realism* (1974), and wrote *Marx, Engels, and Aesthetics* (1983).

2. Franz Mehring (1846–19) was a social democrat and the leading Marxist historian before World War I. During the war he was part of the circle around Rosa Luxemburg and Karl Liebknecht.

3. In the Katyn forest near Smolensk, Russia, the mass graves of 4,443 Polish officers were first found by the Germans and investigated in 1943. It was the largest execution of officers—prisoners of war—during World War II committed by the Soviet security service. The mass executions included 15,000 captured Polish military, intelligence, police, and territorial officers by the Soviets, who acted on Stalin's orders in the spring of 1940. The Soviet Union denied the accusations and contended that the Poles were executed by the Germans. Fifty years later, in April 1990, USSR President Mikhail Gorbachev admitted the NKVD's (the Soviet secret service) responsibility for the killing of the Polish POWs.

4. Ernst Nolte (b. 1923), professor of history at the Free University of Berlin since 1973, triggered the Battle of the Historians in 1986 with an essay challenging the notion that the Holocaust was a unique event. During the debate, which lasted until 1988, Nolte drew structural and functional parallels between Nazi Germany and the Soviet Union.

Irene Selle

1. Jurek Becker (b. 1937), fiction writer, is the author of *Jakob der Lügner* (1970), *Der Boxer* (1976), *Aller Welt Freund* (1982), and *Bronsteins Kinder* (1986). He was expelled from the party in 1976, after the protest of Wolf Biermann's expatriation, and resigned from the Writers' Union in 1977. Since the end of 1977 he has lived in West Berlin on an extended visa.

Dorothea Dornhof

1. Alfred Kurella (1895–1975) became a member of the German Communist Party in 1919. He was a close friend of Johannes R. Becher and Georg Lukács. From 1955 to 1957 he was director of the Institute for Literature in Leipzig. In 1957 he joined the Politburo, where he remained until 1963.

2. Alexander Abusch (1902–82), like Kurella, joined the German Communist Party in 1919. He was an orthodox theoretician of socialist realism. From 1958 to 1961 he was the vice minister of culture of the GDR (under Johannes R. Becher). He is the author of *Humanismus und Realismus in der Literatur* (1957) and *Literatur im Zeitalter des Sozialismus* (1967).

3. Hermann August Korff (1882–1963) was professor of the history of German literature at Leipzig from 1925 until 1957.

He also taught as a visiting professor at Harvard (1935) and Columbia (1938). He was the author of *Humanismus und Romantik* (1924) and *Geist der Goethezeit* (1923–66).

Werner Krauss (1900–76) was a highly regarded Romanist who directed the Institute for Romance Languages and Culture at the Academy of Sciences until 1966. His particular specialty was the French Enlightenment.

Walter Markov (b. 1909), a historian, took his doctorate at the University of Bonn in 1934. He began to devote his energy to the antifascist movement in 1935, editing an underground magazine, *Sozialistische Republik*. He was arrested for his activities and spent twelve years in prison. In 1946 he came to Leipzig and became professor of history there in 1949, where he remained until his retirement in 1979.

4. Die Rote Kapelle (Red Orchestra) was a term coined by the Gestapo for the largest spy and opposition organization during the Second World War. In 1938 the Polish communist Leopold Trepper received a commission from the Soviet secret service to build up an information network for keeping Moscow informed about Nazi Germany's war preparation. As a cover, Trepper founded a trading firm in Brussels, which later was moved to Paris. Politically diverse leftist intellectuals, writers, artists, and journalists formed a group around Harro Schulze-Boysen and Arvid Harnack and made contact with Trepper's Red Orchestra. They edited illegal pamphlets and maintained radio contact with the outside. In August 1942 the Gestapo arrested over one hundred members of the organization, and many of them were sentenced to death.

Arvid Harnack (1901–42) was an economist. In the late 1920s he was appointed to the Economics Ministry. From 1931 on he belonged to the "Working Group for the Study of the Soviet Planned Economy," where he later had access to the most secret plans of German heavy industry, including armament plans. When the Nazis seized power he became involved in different oppositional activities. In 1936 he made contacts with the Soviet secret service, and in 1939 he formed an alliance with Schulze-Boysen. Harnack was arrested in 1942, tortured by the Gestapo, and executed for "high treason."

Harro Schulze-Boysen (1909–42) was an officer and opposition fighter. He received a post in the Reich Air Ministry as a lieutenant colonel in the Intelligence Division. From 1935 on he gathered around himself opponents of the Nazis for such actions as distribution of illegal publications. In 1939 he joined forces with Harnack's resistance group. Schulze-Boysen was apprehended in 1942 and condemned to death by hanging for "high treason."

5. Krauss wrote the novel *Gracians Lebenslehre* (1947) while in prison. He was arrested by the Gestapo in 1942 and returned to prison because of his contacts with Schulze-Boysen and Harnack.

6. Ernst Bloch (1885–1977) was a philosopher who lived from 1933 to 1948 in exile in the United States. On his return to the GDR he became a professor of philosophy at Leipzig University. In 1957 he was forced to retire and left the GDR for the Federal Republic. He became a professor at Tübingen University in 1961. He was the most distinguished heir of Hegelian Marxism. His membership in the Academy of Sciences was posthumously restored in November 1989. His works include *Geist der Utopie* (1918), *Freiheit und Ordnung* (1946), *Das Prinzip Hoffnung* (1954–57), and *Verfremdungen* (1962–64).

7. Alfred Kantorowicz (1899–1979), a convinced socialist, returned from exile in 1947 and decided to stay in Berlin. In the early 1950s he lectured at the Humboldt University on German authors who were considered decadent by the official literary establishment. He was the head of the Archives Department of the German Academy of Arts and the trustee of Heinrich Mann's literary bequest. After being severely attacked by orthodox Marxist ideologists like Alexander Abusch and Alfred Kurella, Kantorowicz left the GDR and settled in Hamburg in 1957.

8. Wolf Biermann (b. 1936), poet, singer, composer, and guitarist, was forbidden to perform in the GDR from 1964 until 1976. Having been given permission to perform in the Federal Republic, he was deprived of his citizenship on November 17, 1976, after a spectacular success at a concert in Cologne. It was made impossible for him to return to the GDR. The event divided the GDR writers into opposite camps. On the same day a group of twelve GDR writers (Sarah Kirsch, Christa Wolf, Volker Braun, Franz Fühmann, Stefan Hermlin, Stefan Heym, Günter Kunert, Heiner Müller, Rolf Schneider, Gerhard Wolf, Jurek Becker, and Erich Arendt) sent an open letter of protest against the decision of the authorities. Soon the list of the protesting intellectuals grew to 150. At the same time, Biermann's expulsion was endorsed by some prominent GDR authors like Anna Seghers, Hermann Kant, Erik Neutsch, Paul Wiens, Peter Hacks, and others. The Biermann affair had long-lasting effects on the GDR literary scene and entailed the exodus of many talented writers: Thomas Brasch, Berndt

Jentzsch, Sarah Kirsch, Reiner Kunze, Günter Kunert, Rudolf Bahro, Erich Loest, and others.

Petra Boden

1. Manfred Naumann (b. 1925), scholar of Romance languages and literatures, entered the Academy of the Sciences in 1969.

Along with Karlheinz Barck, he was very influential in orienting GDR scholarship on reception history. He coauthored *Gesellschaft—Literatur—Lesen* with Barck in 1973.

2. Marxism-Leninism was a common core curriculum at the universities. The courses were staffed by a large faculty with their appointments in that particular area.

Brigitte Burmeister

1. Antoine Saint-Exupéry (1900–1944) was a French aviator and writer whose works are the testimony of a pilot and warrior seeking romance and danger. His works include *Courrier-Sud* (Southern mail), 1929; *Vol de nuit* (Night flight), 1931; *Terre de hommes* (Wind, sand, and stars), 1939; *Pilote de guerre* (Flight to Arras), 1942; *Lettre à un otage* (Letter to a hostage), 1943; and, most famous, *Le petit prince* (The little prince), 1943.

Klaus Michael

1. Robert Weimann (b. 1928), a scholar of English literature and literary theory, is well known in the United States for his work on Shakespeare, but in the GDR he also contributed importantly to the rehabilitation of the concepts of modernism and the avant-garde. He was a member of the Academy of the Arts and the Central Institute for Literary History at the Academy of the Sciences.

Sylvia Schlenstedt, a scholar of modern German literature, has written critical works on modern German poetry and a book on the GDR author Stefan Hermlin.

2. Christoph Martin Wieland (1733–1813) was a prominent, versatile man of letters in the second half of the eighteenth century. He wrote sentimental and pietistic poetry in hexameters (*Lobgesand auf die Liebe,* 1751; *Briefe von Verstorbenen an hinterlasse Freude,* 1753); translated twenty-two plays of Shakespeare; and wrote one of the most perfect enlightenment novels, *Geschichte des Agathon* (1766–67), in which a young man, after his time of trial, reaches rationalism. Beginning in 1968 the Akademie Verlag published Wieland's correspondence in a major modern edition of twenty projected volumes under the editorship of Siegfried Scheibe.

Johann Gottfried Herder (1744–1803), a contemporary and close friend of Goethe, studied theology at Königsberg, where Kant taught. He made major contributions to German literary and historical thought, aesthetics, and theology. He was also a collector of folk songs (*Stimmen der Völker in Liedern,* 2 vols.,

1778–79). His other major works were *Über den Ursprung der Sprache* (1772), *Auch eine Philosophie der Geschichte zur Bildung der Menschheit* (1774), *Ideen zur Philosophie und Geschichte der Menschheit* (1784–91), and *Briefe zur Beförderung der Humanität* (1793–97). A fifteen-volume comprehensive edition of Herder's correspondence began to appear in 1984 from Aufbau Verlag, and in 1985 the same publisher began to issue an ambitious edition of his works, *Ausgewählte Werke in Einzelausgaben.*

Georg Büchner (1813–37) was known as a talented playwright (*Dantons Tod,* 1835; *Leonce und Lena,* first performed in 1895; *Woyzeck,* published in 1879) and for his revolutionary activities. He became keenly interested in the ideas of organized movements against authoritarian government and political oppression, and aimed at a peasants' revolt in his native Hesse. His deep sympathy with social misery was the mainspring of inspiration for the political pamphlet *Der Hessische Landbote* (1834). His works were published in a GDR edition in 1964, and his letters followed in 1967.

Georg Herwegh (1817–75) had a gift for vigorous denunciatory poetry in simple forms and was famous for his straightforwardly socialist and anticlerical opinions. Two volumes of his revolutionary poetry are *Gedichte eines Lebendigen* (1841–43) and *Einundzwanzig Bogen aus der Schweiz* (1843). The Nationale Forschungs- und Gedenkstätten der Klassischen Literatur in Weimar brought out a one-volume edition of Herwegh's works in 1967.

Werner Mittenzwei of the Central Institute edited the well-known five-volume Brecht edition (*Werke* [Berlin/Weimar: Aufbau, 1973]).

3. Ursula Ragwitz, director of the Central Committee Secretariat for Culture, was responsible for overseeing censorship in the GDR.

4. Stefan Döring, Leonhard Lorek, and Andreas Koziol emerged on the GDR literary scene in the mid 1970s.

Stefan Döring (b. 1954) is a poet who published mostly in the small independent and semiofficial literary journal *Der Kaiser ist nackt* (The emperor has no clothes), founded by Uwe Kolbe, Bernd Wagner, and Lothar Trolle in 1981. In 1983 the journal was renamed *Mikado* and continued until 1987. Döring has recently published two books: *Heutmorgestern* (1989) and *Zehn* (1990).

In 1982 Leonhard Lorek (b. 1958 in Poland) was expelled from the Humboldt University just before graduation. In 1988 he emigrated to West Berlin.

Andreas Koziol (b. 1957), a poet who published in the underground magazines of the Prenzlauer Berg scene, coedited *Ariadnefabrik* with Rainer Schedlinski. He published two books in 1991: *Bestiarium literaricum* (with Cornelia Schleime) and *Mehr über Rauten und Türme.*

Thomas Rösler (b. 1960; pseud. Thom di Roes), writer and performance artist, studied at the theatrical school in Berlin and emigrated to West Berlin.

Hermann Kant

1. Anna Seghers (1900–1983) had been a member of the German Communist Party since 1928 and member of the Proletarian Writers' Union (Bund Proletar-

344 Notes to pages 146–147

ischer Schriftsteller) since 1929. She returned from exile to the GDR in 1947, where she became prominent as an author politically committed to and unswervingly supportive of the official organs of the regime. From 1952 to 1978 she was the president of the German Writers' Union. She was honored with numerous awards. A particularly skillful writer of novellas and short narratives, she became known for *Das siebte Kreuz* (1942), *Transit* (1944), *Die Toten bleiben jung* (1947), *Der Ausflug der toten Mädchen* (1948), and *Sonderbare Begegnungen* (1973).

Arnold Zweig (1887–1968), after living in exile and working as a journalist in Palestine, moved to East Berlin in 1948 and lived there until his death. From 1950 to 1953 he was the president of the Academy of the Arts of the GDR. He was also the recipient of various prizes for literature. His works include *Der Streit um den Sergeanten Grischa* (1927), *Junge Frau von 1914* (1931), *Erziehung vor Verdun* (1935), *Einsetzung eines Königs* (1937), *Feuerpause* (1954), and *Traum ist teuer* (1962).

Ludwig Renn (1889–1979) became very popular with his pacifistic novel *Krieg* (1928), written in the wake of World War I. Renn became a member of the German Communist Party in 1928 and secretary of the Proletarian Writers' Union (Bund Proletarischer Schriftsteller) from 1928 to 1932. He returned from exile to Dresden in 1947 and became a professor in Berlin and Dresden. From 1952 on he was a freelance writer. He was honored with numerous awards in the GDR. His works include *Russlandfahrten* (1932), *Adel im Untergang* (1944), *Krieg ohne Schlacht* (1957), and *Auf den Trümmern des Kaiserreiches* (1961).

2. Paul Rilla (1896–1954) was a Marxist literary scholar, critic, and editor of Lessing's *Collected Works* (1954–58). With Becher, he was an early critic of "l'art pour l'art," formal "deviations," and nonrealistic art. However, he was not as dogmatic as Alexander Abusch and others.

Paul Reimann was a Marxist literary scholar and critic.

Ernst Bloch (1885–1977) was a professor of philosophy at Leipzig from 1948 until 1957. His work was carefully scrutinized by party officials. After publication of his *Subjekt-Objekt: Erläuterungen zu Hegel* and *Avicenna und die Aristotelische Linke* in 1951, Bloch became editor of the *Deutsche Zeitschrift für Philosophie* from 1953 to 1956. The journal's relative independence led to arrests and trials of its contributors in 1956–57. Although Bloch was only indirectly involved, he was forbidden to publish. In 1957 he retired, and his work was officially condemned. Although he was finally permitted to publish the third volume of his *Das Prinzip Hoffnung* in 1959, Bloch asked for political asylum during a visit to the FRG in 1961.

Georg Lukács (1885–1971) was the leading voice of Marxist literary criticism in the GDR. He was professor of aesthetics at the University of Budapest from 1947 until 1956. He was a leader of the Petöfi circle in 1956. He was Minister of Culture of the short-lived Imre Nagy government, which led to his work being officially condemned as revisionist. Nonetheless his work had immense impact in the GDR.

3. Joachim Seyppel (b. 1919) moved from West to East Germany in 1973,

after Honecker announced a liberalization of cultural policy; but because of his engagement on behalf of the dissidents Robert Havemann, Biermann, and then Heym, he became an unwanted character in the GDR, was expelled from the Writers' Union in 1979, and returned to West Germany in 1982.

4. Kurt Hager, a member of the Politburo, was responsible for cultural affairs and the chief ideologist of the Central Committee. His response to *glasnost* and *perestroika* was: "I see no reason to change the wallpaper in my house, just because my neighbor does so."

Rainer Kirsch

1. Friedrich Dieckmann (b. 1937) is a playwright, critic, and fiction writer. In 1983 he was awarded the Heinrich Mann Prize of the Academy of the Arts. His books include *Bühnenbilder der DDR* (1977), *Orpheus, eingeweiht* (1983), and *Richard Wagner in Venedig* (1983).

2. Andrey Zhdanov (1896–1948) was a Soviet government and Communist Party official, a close associate of Stalin. He reached the peak of his career after World War II, when, as a full member of the Politburo since 1939, he severely tightened the ideological guidelines for postwar cultural activities. This period (1946–53) in cultural policy, commonly known as the years of Zhdanovism, established strict governmental control of art and promoted an extreme nationalist, anti-Western bias. The policy was initiated by a resolution of the Central Committee of the Communist Party of the Soviet Union that was formulated and signed by Zhdanov, the party cultural boss.

Karl Mickel

1. *Kolkhoz:* Russian, *kol(lektivnoe) khoz(yastvo)*. *Kolkhozy* were state-run collective farms founded in Soviet Russia after the expropriation of land from private farm owners.

Renate Feyl

1. Gerhard Henninger became the first secretary of the Central Board of the East German Writers' Union in 1966.

2. Hoechst AG is a German chemical concern founded in 1863 in the Hoechst quarter of Frankfurt am Main. By the late twentieth century it became one of the world's largest producers of pharmaceuticals. It is also known for sponsoring various cultural exhibitions and book publications in Germany.

3. Klaus Höpcke (b. 1933), the acting minister for culture, served as deputy to Hans Joachim Hoffmann, the minister of culture of the GDR after 1973.

4. Günter de Bruyn (b. 1926), novelist, poet, and essayist, was a member of the Central Board of the Writers' Union from 1965 until 1978. Heinz Czechowski (b. 1935) is a poet who worked in the theater in the early 1970s before becoming a freelance writer. Juri Koch (b. 1936), Sorbian novelist, poet, playwright, and

translator, and chairman of the Sorbian Writers' Union, was a pioneer in the ecology movement. Erich Loest (b. 1926) was arrested in 1957 and sentenced to seven and a half years in prison. He withdrew from the Writers' Union in 1979, after he and others signed an open letter protesting censorship in the GDR. In 1981 he was given a three-year visa that permitted him to resettle in the FRG.

5. Lutz Rathenow (b. 1952), who participated in the Prenzlauer Berg scene of the 1980s, contributed to alternative journals and anthologies. He moved gradually closer to the civil rights movement and was persecuted by the Stasi. He was first arrested by the Stasi in 1976. In 1977 he was compelled to leave the university for political reasons. He was arrested in 1980 (but then soon released because of protests) for publishing a book in the west.

6. The Cheka was the Soviet secret police agency, established in 1917.

7. Kurt Hager (b. 1912) was secretary of science and culture in the Central Committee from 1955 until 1989 and a member of the Politburo from 1963 to 1989. Under Honecker, Hager was the most powerful cultural politician. Joachim Herrmann (b. 1928) was secretary of agitation and propaganda in the Central Committee and a member of the Politburo from 1978 to 1989.

Helga Schubert

1. Stefan Heym (b. 1913) signed the petition protesting Wolf Biermann's expatriation in 1976 and, consequently, was not permitted to publish in the GDR. In 1979 he was sued because of his violation of the foreign exchange law (he had published *Collin* with West German publishers without permission from the GDR government) and expelled from the Writers' Union. The proceedings against Heym led other writers, such as Jurek Becker, Adolf Endler, Klaus Schlesinger, and Erich Loest, to write a letter to Erich Honecker protesting the use of criminal law to censor writers. As a consequence of this letter, these writers too were expelled from the Writers' Union in 1979.

Rolf Schneider (b. 1932), after signing the petition protesting Biermann's expatriation, was expelled from the Writers' Union in 1979. He held a visa that permitted him to work in the FRG. Klaus Schlesinger (b. 1937) moved to West Berlin in 1980.

2. Ingeborg Bachmann (1926–73), one of the most accomplished Austrian poets and prose writers, received many prestigious prizes for literature. Among her works are *Der gute Gott von Manhattan* (1958); *Das dreissigste Jahr* (1961); *Simultan* (1972); and a cycle of three novels: *Todesarten—Malina* (1971), *Der Fall Franza,* and *Requiem für Fanny Goldmann* (fragments, published posthumously in 1978). She committed suicide in 1973.

Max Frisch (1911–91) was a famous Swiss prose writer and playwright. Some of his works are *Blätter aus dem Brotsack* (1939), *Tagebuch 1946–1949* (1950), *Stiller* (1954), *Homo Faber* (1957), *Biermann und die Brandstifter* (1957), *Andorra* (1961), *Mein Name sei Gantenbein* (1964), *Montauk* (1978), *Der Mensch erscheint in Holozän* (1979), and *Blaubart* (1982).

From 1958 to 1963 Ingeborg Bachmann and Max Frisch lived together in

Zurich and Rome. Some entries in Frisch's literary diary, *Tagebuch 1966–1971,* refer to their relationship. In *Montauk* (1978) one finds unidentified quotations from Bachmann's poetry, references to the radio play *Der gute Gott von Manhattan* (1958), and variations of passages from her short fiction, *Das dreissigste Jahr* (1961).

Christoph Hein

1. Wenceslas Square (Václavski Namesti), in the center of Prague, is named after Wenceslas I, king of Bohemia (1228–30), who since 1860 has been the symbol of Bohemia's sovereignty.

2. Mikhail Afanasevich Bulgakov (1891–1940) was a Russian writer whose work was harshly suppressed by state censorship. His most important play, *Dni Turbinych,* was banned shortly after its successful premier in Moscow in 1926 until Stalin's death in 1956. *D'javoliada* (1929) was the only book he was permitted to publish during his lifetime. His application for an exit visa in 1930 was denied.

Kerstin Hensel

1. Franz Fühmann (1922–84), a poet and freelance writer in Berlin since 1950, was renowned for his generous help of young writers, particularly those associated with the Prenzlauer Berg group. He sponsored Wolfgang Hilbig (b. 1941), Frank Wolf Matthies (b. 1951), and Uwe Kolbe (b. 1957) for membership in the Writers' Union. Georg Maurer (1907–71), poet and (after 1961) professor, taught the poetry seminar at the Becher Institute from 1955 to 1971. His students included Sarah and Rainer Kirsch, Karl Mickel, Adolf Endler, Kurt Bartsch, Heinz Czechowski, Volker Braun, Andreas Reimann, and Walter Werner.

2. Hans Magnus Enzensberger (b. 1929), West German poet and essayist, is a sharp critic of the media. In the 1960s he founded the journal *Kursbuch* and helped initiate the extraparliamentary opposition. As an essayist he has written in particular of the relations between poetry and politics. Günter Grass (b. 1927) is a West German writer who began as a sculptor, graphic artist, poet, and playwright, but since *Blechtrommel* (1959) he has been known principally as a fiction writer.

3. The Luddites were organized bands of English handicraftsmen who from 1811 to 1816 rioted and destroyed textile machinery that was displacing them. They are named for Ned Ludd, who thirty years earlier had destroyed knitting machines. They eschewed violence against persons and often enjoyed local support.

Hans Joachim Schädlich

1. The League of Revolutionary Proletarian Writers (Bund Proletarisch-Revolutionärer Schriftsteller) was founded in 1928 and included authors commit-

ted to the Marxist-Leninist ideology like Johannes R. Becher (its first president), Anna Seghers, Andor Gábor, Alexander Abusch, Ludwig Renn (its secretary from 1929 to 1932), Erich Weinert, and others. The majority of the members of the league were also members of the German Communist Party. The league was given large financial support directly by the Soviet Union. It also published a journal, *Linkskurve,* edited by Ludwig Renn. The organization dissolved in 1932–33, when most of its members went into exile.

2. Willi Bredel (1901–64) was a member of the Central Committee of the party. From 1962 to 1964 he was president of the Academy of the Arts. He wrote a novel trilogy, *Verwandte und Bekannte* (1941, 1949, 1953), about three generations in the proletarian family of Hans Marchwitza (1890–1965), one of the antifascist novelists of the founding generation. Marchwitza's major work was the Kumiak trilogy (*Die Kumiaks,* 1934; *Die Heimkehr der Kumiaks,* 1952; and *Die Kumiaks und ihre Kinder,* 1959), which examines the development of a family, originally of miners, from 1920 until the first years of the GDR.

3. Fritz Rudolf Fries (b. 1935) studied Romance and Germanic languages and literatures in Leipzig. From 1961 to 1966, he worked at the Academy of the Sciences, and in 1966 he became a freelance writer and translator. His first novel, *Der Weg nach Oobliadooh* (1966), was published only in West Germany. Other works include *Der Felsenkrieg* (1969), *See-Stücke* (1973), *Der Luft-Schiff* (1974), *Alexanders neue Welten* (1983), and *Verlegung eines mittleren Reiches* (1984).

4. Karel Capek (1890–1938) was an internationally renowned Czech novelist, short-story writer, playwright, and essayist. Among his most famous books are the play *R.U.R.* (1920); the novels *The War with the Newts* (1937) and *The Absolute at Large* (1944); and his short-story collection, *Tales from the Two Pockets* (1932).

5. Frank Wolf Matthies (b. 1951) is a writer who was arrested and imprisoned by the Stasi in 1980. He was permitted to move to West Berlin in 1981.

6. Egon Krenz (b. 1937) was a functionary in the Socialist Unity Party (SED). From 1961 to 1964 and from 1967 to 1974 he was a secretary in the Central Board of Free German Youth (Freie Deutsche Jugend, FDJ), a Communist youth organization. From 1974 until 1983 he was first secretary of FDJ, and in the same period he was a member of the Central Committee of the SED and in charge of security and personnel policy. From 1983 to 1989 he was a member of the Politburo. Upon Honecker's resignation as the general secretary of the SED and the chairman of the Council of State on October 18, 1989, Krenz was chosen as his successor. Under Krenz the Politburo sought to eliminate the embarrassment caused by the flow of refugees to the west through Hungary, Czechoslovakia, and Poland in the summer and fall of 1989. On the evening of November 9, 1989, the Communist authorities announced new travel regulations intended to enable those who wished to travel to the west. This was widely interpreted as a decision to open the Berlin Wall and the borders to the Federal Republic. Large crowds demanded to pass into West Berlin, and the guards let them go. Krenz was forced to resign on December 3, 1989, and was expelled from the Politburo in January 1990.

Reiner Kunze

1. The Tatras are a mountain group in northern Slovakia and southern Poland, where GDR citizens often vacationed.

2. Wulf Kirsten (b. 1934) is a poet particularly interested in ecology. In 1965 he became a reader at the Aufbau Verlag in Weimar. His books include *Poesiealbum 4* (1968), *satzanfang* (1970), *der bleibaum* (1977), *die erden bei Meissen* (1986), and *Stimmenschotter* (1993).

3. Günter de Bruyn (b. 1926) has been a freelance writer since 1963. From 1965 until 1978 he was a member of the Central Board (Zentralvorstand) of the Writers' Union. In 1989 he refused the National Prize for Literature. His works include *Buridans Esel* (1968), *Preisverleihung* (1972), *Leben des Jean Paul Richter* (1975), *Märkische Forschung* (1978), *Neue Herrlichkeit* (1984), and the autobiographical *Zwischenbilanz* (1992).

Katja Lange-Müller

1. Thomas Brasch (b. 1945), poet, playwright, scriptwriter, and film director, was the son of Jewish emigrants in England. Upon his return to Berlin, Brasch's father became a high-ranking party functionary. Thomas Brasch was expelled from the university for "defamation of prominent citizens of the GDR" and his "existentialist views." In 1968 he wrote pamphlets against the invasion of the Warsaw Pact army in Czechoslovakia and was sentenced to two and a half years in prison. He left the GDR in 1976. His works include *Poesiealbum 89* (1975), *Vor den Vätern sterben die Söhne* (1977), and *Frauen-Krieg* (1989).

Monika Maron's (b. 1941) stepfather, Karl Maron, was minister of the interior (1955–63). She worked as an assistant director in television and a journalist for the weekly "Wochenschau" until 1976, when she became a freelance writer. Since 1988 she has lived in Hamburg. None of her novels was published in the GDR until 1989. Her works include *Flugasche* (1981), *Das Missverständnis* (1982), and *Die Überläuferin* (1986).

Uwe Kolbe

1. Günter Kunert's (b. 1929) partly Jewish descent excluded him from secondary education but saved him from military service. He has written poems, film scenarios, plays for radio and television, travelogues, essays, and short prose-fictions. After supporting the protest against the expatriation of Wolf Biermann, he moved to the Federal Republic in 1979.

His works include *Im Namen der Hüte* (1967 in the FRG, 1976 in the GDR), *Notizen in Kreide* (1970), *Ortsangaben* (1971), *Die geheime Bibliothek* (1973), *Der andere Planet* (1974), *O Warum schreiben?* (1976), *Verspätete Monologe* (1981), *Dieseits des Erinnerns* (1982), *Zurück ins Paradies* (1984), *Vor der Sint-*

flut: Das Gedicht als Arche Noah (1985, Frankfurter Vorlesung), and *Berlin beizeiten* (1987). His most recent book is *Baum, Stein, Beton* (1994).

2. Pun in German on *Mist,* bullshit.

3. György Konrad (b. 1933) is a Hungarian writer and Marxist philosopher on social and political problems of socialist societies. His works include *Der Besucher* (1969), *Der Stadtgründer* (1975), *Der Komplize* (1980), *Aussenpolitik: Meditations Mitteleuropa* (1985), *Geisterfest* (1986), and *Europa im Krieg* (1992).

4. Kito Lorenc (b. 1938) is a poet and translator. His poetry volumes include *Struga—Bild einer Landschaft* (1967), *Flurbereinigung* (1973), *Poesiealbum 143* (1979), and *Wortland: Gedichte aus 20 Jahren* (1984).

5. During the revisionism debate in 1956–57, Lukács, who had been the leading voice in literary criticism in the GDR, was judged to be a counterrevolutionist. His involvement with the Hungarian revolt of 1956 allowed others to denounce him as having been on the wrong side since 1931. Lukács had supported the idea of a "third way." He was condemned too for despising the literature of the working class and favoring instead bourgeois realism. These familiar charges were renewed during the revisionism debate.

Rainer Schedlinski

1. Stephan Krawczyk (b. 1955), songwriter, studied guitar in Weimer in 1978–82. With the well-known group Liedehrlich, he made one record in the GDR in 1982 and two years later moved to Berlin and made contact with oppositional groups in Prenzlauer Berg. In 1985 he was forced out of the party and forbidden to practice his profession. He nonetheless performed in private venues. In 1987 he worked with the one illegal radio broadcaster in the GDR and wrote an open letter to Kurt Hager in support of independent art and protesting infringements on human rights. He was arrested the following year on his way to the now-famous Luxemburg-Liebknecht demonstration and compelled to resettle in West Berlin.

2. Gert Neumann (b. 1942), is a prose writer who in the early 1960s became a member of the party and was admitted to study at the Becher Institute in Leipzig. In 1969 he was expelled from the party and the institute for his nonconformist views. He was permitted to leave the GDR in 1989. His works include *Die Schuld der Worte* (1979, in West Germany only), *Die Stimme des Schweigens* (1987, Selbstverlag), *Elf Uhr* (1981, in West Germany), and *Die Klandestinität der Kesselreiniger* (1989).

3. Erik Neutsch (b. 1931), a prominent GDR novelist and journalist, became a party member in 1949. His novel *Spur der Steine* (1964) became one of the most popular books in the GDR (five hundred thousand copies sold). Frank Bayer made a film based on Neutsch's book, and the film was banned in 1966. Other works include *Am Fluss* (1974), *Frühling mit Gewalt* (1978), *Wenn die Feuer verlöschen* (1985), *Nahe der Grenze* (1987), and *Claus und Claudia* (1989).

4. Detlev Opitz (b. 1956) is a poet who published mostly in the independent journal *Mikado*. He was an active member of various GDR dissident peace movements, and he was often arrested. With Sascha Anderson, Rüdiger Rosenthal, and Lutz Rathenow he published an anthology of peace poetry.

Bert Papenfuss-Gorek

1. Elmar Faber became the director of the largest GDR publishing house, Aufbau Verlag, in 1983. Among his works are *DDR: Geschichte und Kunst von der Romantik bis zur Gegenwart* (1977, with Gerd Baier and Eckhardt Hollmann), *Allein mit den Lebensmittelkarten ist es nicht auszuhalten: Autoren- und Verlegerbriefe 1945–1949* (1991, with Carsten Wurm), and *Und ein leiser Jubel zöge ein: Autoren- und Verlegerbriefe 1950–1959* (1992, with Carsten Wurm).

2. *Sinn und Form,* edited at the Academy of the Arts, is a very prestigious literary journal.

3. Lutz Rathenow (b. 1952) studied German and history in Jena. He lived as a freelance writer in East Berlin beginning in 1977. In 1980 he published *Mit dem Schlimmsten wurde schon gerechnet* in Munich. *Zangengeburt* (1982) and *Boden 411* (1989) were likewise published in the west.

Rüdiger Rosenthal (b. 1952) studied physics and engineering. In 1975 he became active in the peace movement and ecology groups. He published a volume of poems in 1984 called *Polnische Reise*. In 1987 he emigrated to West Berlin, but in 1990 he returned to East Berlin.

4. Stefan Döring (b. 1954) studied electronics and engineering in Dresden, then worked in Berlin as a building superintendent. In 1985 he collaborated with Sascha Anderson and Bert Papenfuss-Gorek in a volume of poems and graphics called *ich fühle mich in grenzen wohl*.

5. Franz Fühmann (1922–84) was a Soviet prisoner of war from 1945 to 1949. He came to Berlin in 1950. He was well known and highly regarded as an encourager of younger writers. His books include *22 Tage oder die Hälfte des Lebens* (1973) and *Der Sturz des Engels: Erfahrung mit Dichtung* (1982).

6. Jurgen Fuchs (b. 1950) studied social psychology in Jena beginning in 1971. He joined the party in 1973 but was expelled from it and from the university in 1975. He then moved in with the dissident Robert Havemann. He joined the protest of the expatriation of Wolf Biermann in 1976 and was held under arrest for nine months as a result. He was expatriated in 1977 and lived thereafter in West Berlin as a freelance author. His works include *Fassonschnitt* (1984) and *Einmischung in eigene Angelegenheiten* (1984).

7. Saddam Hussein, the Iraqi head of state, came to mind because the conversation took place during the Gulf War, but also because the West German poet Hans Magnus Enzensberger had recently published an essay in defense of the American actions against Iraq. Enzensberger claimed that Hussein could properly be compared to Hitler ("Im Fremden das Eigene hassen," *Der Spiegel* 34 [Aug. 17, 1992]: 170–79).

Gerhard Wolf

1. Volker Braun (b. 1939) studied philosophy in Leipzig, then worked as dramaturge at the Berliner Ensemble. In 1965 Mitteldeutscher Verlag published his first volume of poems, *Provokation für mich.* Two years earlier, Gerhard Wolf had brought out Karl Mickel's first volume, *Lobverse und Beschimpfungen,* with Mitteldeutscher Verlag.

Sarah Kirsch (b. 1935) studied at the Johannes R. Becher Institute in Leipzig from 1963 to 1965. Her former husband, Rainer Kirsch, also studied at the Becher Institute then, and Wolf brought out some of his early poems in a collection with other young poets, *Bekanntschaft mit uns selbst* (1961), again with Mitteldeutscher Verlag.

Berndt Jentzsch (b. 1940) published his first collection of poems, *Asphalt des Morgens,* with Mitteldeutscher Verlag in 1961.

In 1976, after he had protested the expatriation of Wolf Biermann and the expulsion of Reiner Kunze from the Writers' Union, Jentzsch did not return to the GDR from a study trip in Switzerland. The Stasi had threatened to put him on trial for his "disparagement of the GDR."

Heinz Czechowski (b. 1935) also studied at the Becher Institute, from 1958 until 1961, when he began to work as an editor at the Mitteldeutscher Verlag. His first book of poems, *Nachmittag eines Liebespaares,* appeared from Mitteldeutscher Verlag in 1962.

2. The Soviet poets Yevgeny Yevtushenko (b. 1933) and Andrey Voznesensky (b. 1933) were two of the most prominent of the generation of writers that emerged after the Stalinist era. During the late 1950s and early 1960s, Soviet poets staged a creative renaissance. Poetry readings became so popular that they sometimes were held in sports arenas to accommodate thousands of listeners. Voznesensky and Yevtushenko were charismatic performers who became star attractions at these events. The readings came to a sudden halt in 1963, when Soviet artists and writers working in "excessively experimental" styles were subjected to an official campaign of condemnation. After several months of official criticism they returned to partial favor. Charges of obscurity, experimentation, and "ideological immaturity" continued to be periodically leveled against them in the 1960s and 1970s. Voznesensky's best-known poems are: "Goya" (1960), "My Achilles Heart" (1964), "Self-Portrait" (1964), "Anti-worlds" (1964), and "Soblazn" (Temptation) (1978). Yevtushenko was allowed to travel and hold poetry readings abroad, even in the United States and Western Europe, but he fell into disfavor at home when he published his *Precocious Autobiography* in Paris in 1963. He was recalled, and his privileges were withdrawn, but he was restored to favor when he published his most ambitious cycle of poems, *Bratsk Station* (1966). Other works include *Baby Yar* (1961), *Under the Skin of the Statue of Liberty* (1972), and *Wild Berries* (1982).

3. Friedrich Gottlob Klopstock's (1724–1803) *Oden* (1771) and religious epic *Der Messias* (1748), written in classical hexameters, marked the culmination of German baroque and strongly influenced the younger generation of the time, especially the circle around young Goethe.

4. Elke Erb (b. 1938) is a poet who contributed to the alternative journals of the Prenzlauer Berg scene. She collaborated with Sascha Anderson in the selection of writers for the anthology *Berührung ist nur eine Randerscheinung* (1985). She is one of the figures of connection between generations of writers in the Prenzlauer Berg scene.

5. Karl Mickel published an anthology, *In diesem besseren Land: Gedichte der Deutschen Demokratischen Republik seit 1945* (Halle: Mitteldeutscher Verlag, 1966) that touched off a vehement debate about poetry. In the Socialist Youth Organization journal, *Forum,* the controversy led to a critical examination of Mickel's work generally. "Der See" (1966) was one of Mickel's poems that received particularly critical attention. Professor Hans Koch had the last word in the debate when he judged "Der See" a sick poem full of ambiguity and condemned it as an affront to the socialist concept of humanity.

6. Frank Lanzendörfer (pseud. Flanzendörfer), born in 1962, committed suicide in 1988. He published texts and prints in unofficial journals and through his own publishing house, Selbstverlag. He also helped edit *Schaden.*

7. Fritz Rudolf Fries (b. 1935) was not permitted to publish his first novel, *Der Weg nach Obliadooh.* Through the intervention of Uwe Johnson, a former fellow student of Fries, it was published in the FRG in 1966.

8. Inge Diersen, *Thomas Mann. Episches Werk. Weltanschauung. Leben* (Berlin: Aufbau, 1975).

9. Wolfgang Harich (b. 1921), a follower of Lukács and Ernst Bloch, taught at the Party College. He was also editor-in-chief of the journal *Deutsche Zeitschrift für Philosophie.* The journal's relative independence led to arrests and trials. In 1957 Harich was sentenced to ten years imprisonment for allegedly forming a conspiratorial group hostile to the socialist state.

Walter Janka (b. 1914), head of the Aufbau Verlag since 1952, was sentenced to five years imprisonment for his alleged connections to the Harich group and alleged counterrevolutionary conspiracy against the Ulbricht government. In 1989 Janka published his own account of the charges against him and the process of his trial, *Schwierigkeiten mit der Wahrheit.* It became a bestseller.

10. Peter Böthig (b. 1958; pseud. P. V. Poltry) was assistant at the Institute for German Studies at the Humboldt University. He was expelled from the university in 1986 for participating in readings at the Samariter Church. He wrote essays about the Prenzlauer Berg writers in unofficial journals. He moved to West Berlin in 1989.

11. Five issues of the journal *Liane,* edited by Michael Thulin, appeared in 1988–89.

Adolf Endler and Gabriele Dietze

1. Free German Youth was a mass organization of people as young as fourteen. It was founded in 1946 in the Soviet occupation zone and later used as a major tool by the Socialist Unity Party to train whole generations of young people

in faithfulness and supportiveness to the political regime of the GDR. Among its leaders was Erich Honecker, who served as the first secretary of FDJ from 1946 until 1955.

2. At the Eighth Party Congress, in 1971, the hard-line Stalinist Walter Ulbricht stepped down as first secretary of the SED to be succeeded by Erich Honecker. In his keynote address to the Party Congress, Honecker proposed a greater degree of autonomy for literature and encouraged a "creative debate." This period of liberalization of cultural policies came to an end with the expulsion of Kunze, Havemann, and Biermann in 1976.

3. The BfU (Büro für Urheberrecht) was the state-run copyright agency, founded in 1956, whose official role was to protect the copyrights of GDR writers. But in fact it exercised tight control over the contacts and financial transactions of GDR intellectuals with publishing houses in the FRG and Austria.

4. Hans Joachim Schulze (b. 1951), a painter, studied in Leipzig, participated in a number of the journals associated with Prenzlauer Berg, and moved to West Berlin in 1986.

5. Bärbel Bohley is a prominent GDR artist, who with the writer Jens Reich founded the New Forum (Neues Forum) on September 10, 1989. It was the first citizens' initiative and opposition organization that was not associated with the church. In its founding petition, the New Forum appealed to the government for dialogue rather than power while looking for solutions to the current social and political conflicts.

Wilhelm Pieck (1876–1960) was the president of the GDR from its founding in 1949 until 1960. He had been a member of the German Communist Party since 1919 and became its leader in Soviet exile. From 1938 to 1943 Pieck was general secretary of the Kommintern. He returned to Germany with the Red Army in 1945 and worked actively for the union of the Social Democrat Party and the Communist Party in the Socialist Unity Party (SED) in 1946. From 1946 until 1954 he shared the office of the chairman of the SED with Otto Grotewohl, the leader of the former Social Democrats.

6. Günter Schabowski (b. 1929), a journalist and high-ranking party function-ary, has been the deputy editor-in-chief (since 1968) and the editor-in-chief of the official SED newspaper *Neues Deutschland* (since 1978). He was a Politburo member, the highest party leader of the Berlin region, and a government spokes-man when Honecker's short-lived successor, Egon Krenz, took over. At a press conference on November 9, 1989, it was Schabowski who announced the new, liberal regulations for GDR citizens to travel to the west.

Jan Faktor

1. Ulrike Poppe was one of the founders of Women for Peace. She and her husband, Gerd, were active in the civic movement. Their apartment in Prenzlauer Berg was a routine meeting place for many people, and they often held poetry readings there. In the autumn of 1989 Ulrike participated in the Central Round

Table discussions, which were broadcast on television. Gerd Poppe ran and was elected as a candidate for Bündnis 90 for the German parliament.

2. Eberhard Häfner is a poet who contributed to the underground journals of the Prenzlauer Berg.

3. Neues Forum, founded by thirty people on September 11, 1989, is the largest of the opposition groups of the civic movement in the former GDR. Its members decided not to become a party, but instead, to be an umbrella organization for other groups. Neues Forum was recognized by the party on November 8, 1989, the day the Politburo resigned, and the day before the announcement of an open border. At that time there were about two hundred thousand members of the group.

4. The Zionskirche, in Prenzlauer Berg, maintained a library for environmental issues. An illegal publication, *Umwelt Blätter,* was generated there. In 1987 the Stasi searched the library and arrested seven young people there.

5. See, for example, the anthologies published by Galrev: *Vogel oder Käfig Sein: Kunst und Literatur aus unabhängigen Zeitschriften in der DDR 1979– 1989,* ed. Klaus Michael and Thomas Wohlfahrt (Berlin: Galrev, 1992) and *Abriss der Ariadnefabrik,* ed. Andreas Koziol and Rainer Schedlinski (Berlin: Galrev, 1990).

Conclusion

1. These are the words of Werner Bramke, chairman of the History Department at the Karl Marx University in Leipzig, quoted in Philipsen, *We Were the People,* 106. Many of the people I spoke with said exactly the same thing.

2. Michel Foucault, *The History of Sexuality: An Introduction,* vol. I, trans. Robert Hurley (New York: Random House, 1978), 95–96.

3. Peter Böthig, "Interrogation and the Autonomy," Responsibility of Intellectuals Conference, University of Chicago, 2 May 1992, 6.

4. Emile Durkheim, *Professional Ethics and Civic Morals,* trans. Cornelia Brookfield (London: Routledge, 1992), 7–8.

5. Samuel Weber, *Institution and Interpretation* (Minneapolis: University of Minnesota Press, 1987), 31.

6. Theodor Adorno, *Aesthetic Theory,* trans. C. Lenhardt (London: Routledge & Kegan Paul, 1984), 325.

7. See, e.g., Terry Eagleton, *The Ideology of the Aesthetic* (Oxford: Blackwell, 1990).

8. Christoph Hein, *Texte, Daten, Bilder,* ed. Lothar Baier (Frankfurt: Luchterhand, 1990), 44.

9. Pierre Bourdieu, *Die Intellektuellen und die Macht,* ed. Irene Dölling (Hamburg: VSA Verlag, 1991), 49–50.

10. Ibid., 39.

11. Here I am in complete agreement with Edward W. Said's recent effort

"to speak about intellectuals as precisely those figures whose public performances can neither be predicted nor compelled into some slogan, orthodox party line, or fixed dogma." Said, *Representations of the Intellectual* (New York: Pantheon, 1994), xii.

12. Quoted in Philipsen, *We Were the People,* 377–78.

13. Ulrike Poppe, "The humiliated elite of the political system," Responsibility of Intellectuals Conference, University of Chicago, 2 May 1992, unpublished paper, 7–8.

14. For analyses of the workshop style, see Robert Pinsky, *The Situation of Poetry* (Princeton: Princeton University Press, 1976), esp. 162–69; and Paul Breslin, *The Psychoanalytic Muse* (Chicago: University of Chicago Press, 1987). Ian Hamilton's *Robert Lowell* (New York: Random House, 1982) tells the story of Lowell's interaction with the other confessional poets. See also Jeffrey Myers's *Manic Power* (New York: Arbor House, 1987) for a less reliable account of the formation of confessional poetry.

Photo Credits

The photographs on pages 125, 180, and 249 are reproduced courtesy of Renate von Mangoldt; those on pages 134 and 265, courtesy of Susanne Schleyer; those on pages 143, 155, 164, 186, 200, and 311 courtesy of Ullstein Bilderdienst; that on page 170 courtesy of Manfred Gößinger; and that on page 208 courtesy of Marion Wenzel.

Index

Abusch, Alexander 102, 340–341n, 344n, 348n
Adorno, Theodor 42, 320, 355n
Aldington, Richard 332n
Anderson, Sascha 24–33, 35, 134, 138, 265, 267, 275–277, 295–296, 304–305, 307–308, 310–314, 333–335n, 351n, 353n; and Stasi scandal 24–32, 35, 257, 267, 275, 276, 295, 302, 311–312
antifascism 5, 59, 88, 90, 96–97, 102, 143, 152–153, 218, 220–222, 228, 279, 285
Anz, Thomas 333n
Aptiz, Bruno 63, 337n
Aragon, Louis 94
Arendt, Erich 341n
Ardagh, John 11, 329n, 330–331n
Arnold, Matthew 15, 18, 332n
audience 42–43, 244–245, 262
autonomy: intellectual 321; literary 216–217, 266, 320; political 189

Bachmann, Ingeborg 192, 346–347n
Bahro, Rudolf 47, 129, 265, 336n, 342n
Baier, Gerd 351n
Baier, Lothar 330n, 355n
Balzac, Honoré de 162
Barck, Karlheinz 41, 84, 132, 342n
Barck, Simone 84
Baring, Arnulf 33
Bartenschlager, Klaus ix
Barthélemy, Françoise 331n

Barthes, Roland 25, 263–264
Bartsch, Kurt 347n
Bataille, Georges 25
Baudrillard, Jean 263–264, 304
Bayer, Frank 350n
Beauvoir, Simone de 95
Becher, Johannes R. 34, 84, 143, 335n, 340n, 344n, 348n
Becker, Jurek 97, 147, 188, 230, 340–341n, 346n
Becker, Rolf 332n
Benda, Julien 14–17, 34, 332n
Benjamin, Walter 68–69
Berg, Hermann von 47, 336n
Bergounioux, Pierre 125
Berryman, John 325
Bierce, Ambrose 239
Biermann, Wolf 22, 24–27, 35, 80, 86, 106, 147–149, 180, 213, 230, 246, 250, 252–253, 259, 265–267, 274, 276, 300, 302, 305, 314, 333n, 338–341n, 345–346n, 349–350n, 352n, 354n
Bloch, Ernst 103, 146, 338–339n, 341n, 344n, 351n, 353n
Boden, Petra 99, 110
Bodi, Leslie 222–223
Boehm, Philip 331n
Bohley, Bärbel 7, 28, 309, 334n, 354n
Böll, Heinrich Theodor 212
Böthig, Peter (P.V. Poltry) 31–32, 134, 292, 318, 324, 334–335n, 353n, 355n

Bourdieu, Pierre 320–321, 355n
Bramke, Werner 355n
Brasch, Thomas 195, 237, 280, 341n, 349n
Braun, Volker 4–5, 8, 10, 24, 80, 129, 139–140, 188, 252, 275, 284, 286–287, 291, 338n, 341n, 347n, 352n
Brecht, Bertolt 45–46, 68, 71, 74, 89–90, 102, 135, 139, 143, 207, 209, 273, 285, 337–338n, 343n
Bredel, Willi 72, 213, 338n, 348n
Breslin, Paul 356n
Brockmann, Stephen 3, 329–330n
Brookfield, Cornelia 332n, 355n
Bruyn, Günter de 5, 103, 174, 185, 217, 230, 330n, 345n, 349n
Brumlik, Micha 332n
Bukowski, Charles 56
Bulgakov, Mikhail Afanasevich 204, 347n
Burmeister, Brigitte 125
Büchner, Georg 135, 244, 343n

Camus, Albert 94
Capek, Karel 217, 348n
censorship 10, 14, 41, 61–64, 68–69, 72–73, 75, 86, 95, 97, 105, 119–121, 128–129, 136, 170, 172–173, 175–177, 198, 200–202, 204, 218, 237–238, 254–255, 265–266, 275, 307, 309; acceptance of 55, 74–75, 97, 100, 105, 128, 132–133, 162–163, 177–178, 189–190, 209, 275, 317
Cervantes (Saavedra), Miguel de 41
CIA 27
circumlocution 41–42, 68, 73, 97, 127, 132, 200–202, 208, 229, 252
Claudius 234
communism 5, 58–59, 62, 74, 94, 178, 184, 188, 215, 217–218, 220, 251, 256
conformity: intellectual 317–319; professional 11, 14, 73, 80, 85–88, 105, 108–109, 121, 130–131, 136–137, 149, 187–188, 254–256, 292, 326

Conrad, Joseph 317
Corbin, Alain 125
Cramer, Karen ix
cummings, e.e 56
Czechowski, Heinz 174, 252, 284, 345n, 347n, 352n

Dante (Alighieri) 4, 159
Darnton, Robert 330n
Davie, Donald 18
Deleuze, Gilles 25
Detje, Robin 335n
di Roes, Thom (Thomas Rösler) 138, 343n
Dickens, Charles 184, 238
Diderot, Denis 109
Diersen, Inge 290, 353n
Dietze, Gabriele 26–27, 297, 301, 304
Dornhof, Dorothea 99, 110
Dölling, Irene 355n
Döring, Stefan 138, 257, 276–277, 343n, 351n
Dreiser, Theodore 55, 320
Drescher, Horst 174
Durkheim, Emile 16, 318, 332n, 355n

Eagleton, Terry 355n
Ebert, Christa 118
education 10–11, 13, 47, 52–53, 57–60, 68, 71, 73, 76, 78, 94–95, 104, 112, 126–127, 151, 154, 157, 165, 168–169, 184, 194, 197, 214, 217–218, 229, 238, 250, 274, 324–325; failure of 9, 103, 129
Eigler, Friederike 333n
elections, of March 18, 1990 3, 5, 12, 107, 245, 256
Eliot, T.S. 55–56, 159, 332n
emigration 5, 7–10, 21, 23, 65, 81–82, 102–103, 113, 127, 147, 159, 180, 191, 193, 217–220, 220, 222–223, 231–232, 236–237, 244, 246, 249, 273, 298, 301, 306–309, 315

Endler, Adolf 27, 139, 164, 190, 214, 223, 252, 255, 267, 277–278, 304, 346n, 347n

Engels, Friedrich 339n

Enzensberger, Hans Magnus 99, 209, 347n, 351n

Erb, Elke 140, 214, 217, 252, 267, 275, 277, 285, 307–308, 353n

Esenin, Sergei Aleksandrovich 304

Faber, Elmar 275, 307, 351n

Faktor, Jan 138, 289, 311

FBI 28–29

Falkner, Gerhard ix

Feuchtwanger, Lion 338n

Feyl, Renate 170

Fish, Stanley 17–18, 332n

Flanzendörfer, Frank (Frank Lanzen-dörfer) 31, 287, 353n

Fontane, Theodor 72, 337n

Foucault, Michel 24–25, 263–264, 318, 355n

Freud, Sigmund 253

Frisch, Max 192, 346–347n

Fries, Fritz Rudolf 5, 217, 288–289, 330n, 348n, 353n

Frings, Theodor 102

Fuchs, Jürgen 33, 278, 299, 351n

Fühmann, Franz 209, 217, 219, 230, 277, 309, 341n, 347n, 351n

Gábor, Andor 348n

Gellner, Ernest 35, 335n

generations, conflict between 24–28, 39–40, 42, 47, 78, 79, 82, 98, 100, 113, 135, 137, 139–140, 147, 169, 188–189, 195–196, 225–229, 237, 246, 252, 258, 264–266, 270, 273–274, 277, 280–281, 284–287, 289, 295, 308–309, 322

George, Stefan 253

Giddens, Anthony 24, 333n

Gide, André 94

Ginsberg, Allen 119, 301–302; his popularity 56

Goethe, Johann Wolfgang von 130, 164–165, 168, 205, 342n, 352n

Goldstücker, Eduard 73, 338n

Gorbachev, Mikhail 78, 106, 112–113, 131, 203, 339n

Gramsci, Antonio 15–17, 332n

Grass, Günter 19, 34, 42, 209, 212, 332n, 336n, 347n

Gratian (Flavius Gratianus) 102

Greiner, Ulrich 21, 33, 305, 332n

Grotewohl, Otto 354n

Guattari, Felix 25

Haberer, Brigitte 335n

Habermas, Jürgen 6, 331n

Hachs, Peter 341n

Hafrey, Leigh 331n

Hafner, Katie 331n

Hage, Volker 335n

Hager, Kurt 14, 41, 148–149, 176, 345–346n, 350n

Hamilton, Ian 356n

Hansen, Miriam ix

Harich, Wolfgang 291, 353n

Harnack, Arvid 340–341n

Hartung, Klaus 6–7, 331n

Hasenfelder, Ulf Christian 333n

Haus, Heinz-Uwe 45, 322

Havel, Vaclav 91, 145

Havemann, Robert 80, 265, 338n, 345n, 351n, 354n

Häfner, Eberhard 312, 355n

Hegel, Georg Wilhelm Friedrich 112, 166, 234

Hein, Christoph 4–5, 8–10, 28, 185, 200, 252, 268, 285, 320, 330–331n, 334n, 355n

Helms, Jesse 75

Henninger, Gerhard 170, 345n

Hensel, Kerstin 208

Herder, Johann Gottfried 135, 342–343n

Hermann, Joachim 69, 176, 337n

Hermlin, Stefan 194, 230, 251, 309, 341–342n

Hermsdorf, Klaus 72, 338n

Herwegh, Georg 135, 343n
Heym, Stefan 4–6, 8, 46, 64, 190, 200, 230, 252, 329n, 341n, 345–346n
Hilbig, Wolfgang 347n
Hitler, Adolf 107, 166, 218, 221, 245, 330n
Hoffmann, E.T.A. 167
Hoffmann, Hans Joachim 345n
Hollmann, Eckhardt 351n
Homer 41, 207
Honecker, Erich 3, 23, 44, 58, 152, 158, 194, 197, 245–246, 271, 345–346n, 348n, 354n
Honecker, Frau 58
Horch, Daniel 332n
Höfele, Andreas ix
Hölderlin, Friedrich 234, 284
Höpke, Klaus 46, 172, 175, 307, 345n
Hörnigk, Frank 71, 290
Hörnigk, Therese 71
Huchel, Peter 34, 335n, 338n
Hurley, Robert 355n
Hussein, Saddam 283, 351n
Huyssen, Andreas 6, 330n
Huxley, Aldous 188

Ickstadt, Heinz ix
intellectuals: role of ix-x, 4–6, 8, 36; in government 7; types of 14–18

Janka, Walter 34, 288, 291, 335n, 338n, 353n
Jannings, Emil 168
Jacobs, Karl-Heinz 82, 339n
Jentzsch, Berndt 284, 341–342n, 352n
Johnson, Uwe 338n, 353n
journalism 7–8, 33–35, 98, 144, 146, 148, 161, 170, 177, 186, 197–198, 200, 205, 227, 229, 254–255, 322
Joyce, James 102

Kaden, Klaus 329n
Kafka, Franz 23, 71–74, 102, 167, 207, 239–240, 337–338n
Kant, Immanuel 234, 342n
Kant, Hermann 46, 62, 140, 143, 155, 171, 194, 230, 257, 267, 341n
Kantorowicz, Alfred 103, 341n
Karasek, Hellmuth 21, 23, 332–333n
Kaufman, Bob 257
Keller, Dietmar 9
Kerouac, Jack 56
Kirsch, Rainer 155, 164, 251–252, 267, 284, 347n, 352n
Kirsch, Sarah 81–82, 139, 186, 252, 284, 339n, 341–342n, 347n, 352n
Kirsten, Wulf 230, 349n
Kleist, Heinrich Wilhelm von 239
Klopstock, Friedrich Gottlob 284–285, 352n
Knobloch, Heinz 46, 336n
Koch, Hans 87–88, 339n, 353n
Koch, Juri 174, 345–346n
Kohl, Helmut 3, 245
Kolbe, Uwe 30, 195, 249, 270, 277, 279–280, 334–335n, 343n, 347n
Konrad, György 251, 350n
Korff, Hermann August 102, 340n
Koziol, Andreas 138, 343n, 355n
Köhler, Otto 335n
Königsdorff, Helga 10, 331n
Kracauer, Siegfried 134
Kraus, Werner 84, 90, 102, 125–126, 340–341n
Krawczyk, Stephan 265, 350n
Krenz, Egon 220, 310, 348n, 354n
Krenzlin, Norbert 39
Khrushchev, Nikita 284, 338n
Kipphardt, Heiner 338n
Kulik, Holger 334–335n
Kunert, Günter 139, 250, 252, 331n, 341–342n, 349n
Kunze, Elisabeth 234
Kunze, Reiner 220, 227, 234, 281, 342n, 352n, 354n
Kühne, Andrea 334n
Kurella, Alfred 102, 338n, 340n, 341n

Lange, Ingeburg 196, 236
Lange-Müller, Katja 196, 236, 279
Langenbucher, W. R. 331n
Lanzendörfer, Frank (Frank Flanzen-
    dörfer) 31, 287, 353n
Lenhardt, C. 355n
Lenin, Nikolai 22, 139, 215, 339n; Le-
    ninism 25, 39–40, 42–44, 46–47,
    54, 116
Liebknecht, Karl 339n
literary criticism, function of 7,
    9–10, 56, 58, 74, 76–77, 89–92,
    103–104, 109, 111–114, 116, 120,
    122–123, 132, 162, 166, 215, 319,
    321, 323–325
literary theory 24–25, 31–32, 39,
    68, 72, 79, 99, 100–104, 123–124,
    132, 136, 140, 166, 198, 214,
    263–265
literature 6, 8, 33, 35, 40–42, 68–69,
    71–73, 75, 80–82, 86–87, 97, 99,
    100, 104, 110, 116, 118–119, 121–
    122, 132, 134, 143–144, 152, 154,
    156, 158–160, 172–173, 187, 193–
    194, 197, 200–201, 204–205, 209,
    211–213, 229, 239–240, 248, 257–
    258, 261, 268, 284–285, 290, 296,
    302, 305, 309, 318, 324; function of
    ix, 22, 55–56, 64, 73–74, 76–77,
    88, 91, 103–104, 111, 135–136,
    139, 149, 151, 156–161, 165, 177,
    179, 182–184, 204, 213–217, 229–
    231, 237–238, 241, 244–245, 254,
    268–269, 273, 281–282, 289, 290,
    300–301, 320
Loest, Erich 3, 82, 147, 174, 218–219,
    338–339n, 342n, 346n
Lorek, Leonhard 138, 343n
Lorenc, Kito 252, 350n
Lowell, Robert 325, 356n
Ludd, Ned 211, 347n
Lukács, Georg 72, 74, 76, 84–85, 90,
    102, 146, 253, 338n, 340n, 344n,
    350n, 353n
Luxemburg, Rosa 339n
Lyotard, Jean-François 25, 264

Mafia 48
Malraux, André 94
Mandelstam, Osip 155
Mann, Heinrich 72
Mann, Thomas 72, 290, 353n
Manske, Eva 53
Mao, Tse-tung 139
Marchwitza, Hans 213, 348n
Markov, Walter 102, 340n
Marks, Louis 332n
Maron, Karl 349n
Maron, Monika 10, 188–189, 191,
    196, 237, 331, 349n
Marx, Karl 41, 43, 113, 139, 164, 169,
    339n, 355n; Marxism 11, 25, 39–40,
    42–44, 46–47, 54, 74, 79–80, 88,
    100, 102–103, 112, 116, 123–124,
    126, 128, 132, 162, 164–165, 291
Matthies, Frank Wolf 219, 347n, 348n
Maurer, Georg 209, 347n
Maurras, Charles 14
Mayer, Hans 103, 338n
Mehlhorn, Ludwig 322, 331n
Mehring, Franz 87, 339n
Meyer-Gosau, Frauke 261
Michael, Klaus (Michael
    Thulin) 30–31, 134, 292, 324,
    334–335n, 353n, 355n
Mickel, Karl 139, 157, 164, 252, 274–
    275, 277–278, 281, 284–286, 304,
    347n, 352–353n
Middleton, Christopher 330n
Mielke, Erich 44, 175, 306, 336n
Miller, Henry 57
Mittag, Günter 44, 336n
Mittenzwei, Werner 71, 78, 84, 135,
    337n, 343n
Modern Language Associ-
    ation 322–323
Molinaro, Ursula 333n
Münz (Koenen), Inge 64, 87, 337n
Müller, Heiner 8, 32–34, 49–50, 61–
    62, 64, 68–69, 71, 80, 240, 273–275,
    277, 281, 290, 309, 335, 338n, 341n;
    involvement with the Stasi 32–33
Myers, Jeffrey 356n

Nagy, Imre 344n
national identity 7, 12, 15, 18–21, 34–36, 74, 102, 157, 160, 173, 193, 204–205, 228, 253, 289–290
Naumann, Manfred 94, 113, 135, 342n
Naumann, Michael 330n
Nazism 19, 30, 48, 74, 76, 98, 107, 169, 186, 193–194, 221, 223, 272, 279–280
Neumann, Gert 267, 350n
Neutsch, Erik 269–270, 341n, 350n
Nietzsche, Friedrich Wilhelm 272
Nixon, Richard 4
Nolte, Ernst 93, 339n
Novak, Helge 28, 338n

Opitz, Detlev 272, 351n
opposition: intellectual, 67–69, 85, 89, 190, 112–114, 222, 255, 274, 309; political 79–80, 97, 150–152, 190, 222, 275, 279, 309, 314
Ortega y Gasset, José 84
Orwell, George 188

Papenfuss-Gorek, Bert 25, 138, 140, 195, 257, 267, 269–270, 273, 285, 351n
Pascal, Blaise 157, 163, 168–169
Perkin, Harold 334n
Petersen, Julius 110
Pfeiffer, Peter C. 333n
Pfister, Manfred ix
Pforte, Dietger 331n
Philipsen, Dirk 329n, 331n, 355–356n
Pieck, Wilhelm 309, 354n
Pietrass, Richard 180
Pilkington, Hilary 333n
Pinsky, Robert 356n
Plath, Sylvia 325
Poltry, P.V. (Peter Böthig) 31–32, 134, 292, 318, 324, 334–335n, 353n, 355n
Poppe, Gerd 311, 354n

Poppe, Ulrike 7, 309, 323, 331n, 354–356n
Pound, Ezra 55–56
Prenzlauer Berg scene 24–27, 29–32, 34, 88, 122, 137–138, 147, 195–196, 226, 233, 257, 261, 263–265, 269–271, 284–285, 304–306, 309–310, 312–316, 320, 324
professors 39, 47–48, 70, 102; role of 13, 16, 46, 59–60, 82, 86, 110, 224, 227, 236, 290, 323, 326
Proust, Marcel 320
publishing: procedures for 13, 55–56, 61–63, 86, 94, 100, 129, 132–133, 138, 146, 156, 187, 189, 193, 291, 297, 307- 308; scholarly 35, 87, 104–105, 121, 125–127, 130; economics of 5–6, 20, 27, 58, 86, 127, 144, 153–154, 171, 174–175, 189, 209, 211, 232, 243–244, 253–254, 260, 267–268, 315, 325
Pynchon, Thomas 309

Raddatz, Fritz J. 331n
Radisch, Iris 26–27, 333–334n
Ragwitz, Ursula 135, 343n
Ransom, John Crowe 319
Rappolt, Hedwig 333n
Rathenow, Lutz 174, 276, 278, 280, 299, 346n, 351n
Reich, Jens 354n
Reich-Ranicki, Marcel 22, 333n
Reimann, Andreas 347n
Reimann, Paul 146, 344n
Rein, Gerhard 1
Renn, Ludwig 143, 344n, 348n
reunification, of the two Germanies ix, 3, 6, 19–20, 36, 39, 47, 67, 131, 134, 243
Reuter, Oberst 335n
Rietzschel, Thomas 7, 23, 331n, 333n
Rilla, Paul 146, 344n
Rimbaud, Arthur 85, 140
Robbins, Bruce 17, 332n
Rosenberg, Rainer 110

Rosenthal, Rüdiger 276, 278, 280, 351n
Rösler, Thomas (Thom di Roes) 138, 343n

Said, Edward 15–16, 332n, 355–356n
Saint-Exupéry, Antoine 132, 342n
Sakharov, Andrey Dmitriyevich 82, 339n
Salinger, J. D. 56
Sartre, Jean-Paul 94, 253, 337n
Schabowski, Günter 310, 354n
Schaper, Rüdiger 35, 336n
Schädlich, Hans Joachim 9, 46, 82, 191, 213, 250, 331–332n, 334n
Schedlinski, Rainer 24, 27–32, 134, 265, 304, 312–313, 355n
Scheibe, Siegfried 342n
Schirrmacher, Frank 23, 26, 33, 35, 304–305, 333–335n
Schlenstedt, Dieter 63, 111, 291, 337n
Schlenstedt, Sylvia 135, 342n
Schleime, Cornelia 343n
Schlesinger, Klaus 190, 346n
Schmidt, Michael 332n
Schmied, Wieland 335n
Schneider, Peter 6, 331–332n
Schneider, Rolf 3, 10, 13, 190, 331–332n, 341n, 346n
Schottländer, Rudolf 94, 96
Schubert, Helga 186
Schütz, Helga 8, 19, 331–332n
Schulze, Hans Joachim 309, 354n
Schulze-Boysen, Harro 340–341n
SED (Sozialistische Einheitspartei Deutschlands) 3, 8, 10, 14, 40, 47–48, 51–52, 59, 66, 87, 96–97, 106–107, 120, 135–137, 182, 190–192, 197, 227, 245, 305, 310; benefits of membership 25, 40, 47, 51–52, 66, 113, 171, 305; attractions of 77–79, 265
Seghers, Anna 34, 143, 219–220, 335n, 341n, 343–344n, 348n

self-examination 60, 105, 107, 131, 205, 128, 163, 168, 194, 201, 205, 209, 232, 288, 300–301
Selle, Irene 94
Seyppel, Joachim 147, 190, 344–345n
Sexton, Anne 325
Shakespeare, William 55, 201, 205, 342n
Snodgrass, W.D. 325
socialism x, 4–6, 11–12, 16, 19–20, 23, 42–44, 47, 50, 59, 64–65, 68, 73–74, 77, 80, 90–92, 98, 102–104, 114–115, 123, 128, 131, 139, 144–145, 148–149, 153, 156, 161, 166, 173, 178, 183, 202–203, 209, 213, 217, 228, 246, 251–253, 255, 285, 289–291, 307, 309–310; its unpopularity 5–6, 8–10, 12, 42, 65, 175–177, 179, 196, 221, 273, 290
Sollers, Philippe 11, 331n
Solzhenitsyn, Aleksandr Isayevich 233
Sontag, Susan 55
Spinoza, Baruch 96
Spira, Steffi 64, 337n
Stalin, Joseph 156, 215, 288, 309, 338n, 347n; Stalinism 24, 34, 47–48, 73–74, 88, 90, 92, 94, 136, 175, 194, 196, 253, 272, 279, 284, 288, 305
Stasi 9, 13, 14, 20–21, 24–34, 45, 48, 95–96, 115, 117, 122, 129, 131, 133, 135–137, 181, 190, 201, 204, 209–210, 220, 223, 227–228, 230–231, 233, 249, 255, 257, 259, 265–267, 271, 274, 278–282, 290, 292, 295–298, 301–302, 304–306, 308–312, 314–315, 323, 333n, 334–336n, 346n, 352n; collaboration with 9, 21, 24–26, 28–29, 31, 107, 117, 143, 149, 227, 234, 249, 257, 259–260, 265, 295–302, 306, 309, 312
Stern, Richard 29–30, 334n
Stoph, Willi 44, 336n

Streisand, Marianne 61, 74, 86, 104–105
Strittmatter, Erwin 62
surveillance 41, 129, 133, 183, 147–149, 299

Thierse, Wolfgang 40–41
Thulin, Michael (Klaus Michael) 30–31, 134, 292, 324, 334–335n, 353n, 355n
Töpelmann, Sigrid 290
travel, foreign 7–8, 52, 59, 95–96, 98, 104, 113, 136–137, 140, 147, 170–172, 176, 181–182, 186–188, 191–192, 198, 212, 218, 250, 270, 281, 301
Trepper, Leopold 340n
Trolle, Lothar 249, 343n

Ulbricht, Walter 44, 168, 219, 354n
utopia 11, 41–42, 45, 50, 64–65, 80, 90, 98, 114, 121–122, 165, 175, 202–203, 251, 282, 309; as alibi 7, 10, 50, 165, 22

Van Heurck, Jan 329n
Voznesensky, Andrey 284, 352n

Wagner, Bernd 249, 343n
Walser, Martin 3–4, 6, 329n, 331n
Walther von der Vogelweide 130
Weber, Samuel 319, 355n
Weimann, Robert 85, 135, 342n
Weinert, Erich 348n
Weiss, Peter 39, 41
Wenceslas I 203, 347n
Wensinger, A. S. 332n
Werke und Wirkungen 71, 74–75, 85–87, 104–105, 136
Werner, Walter 346n
Whitman, Walt 53
Wieland, Christoph Martin 135, 342n
Wiens, Paul 341n
Winkler, Lutz 331n
Winston, Krishna 332n, 334n
Wohlfahrt, Thomas 335n, 355n

Wolf, Christa ix, 4–5, 8–12, 20–23, 26, 31–35, 42, 62, 64, 71, 78, 80, 82, 89, 97, 103, 106, 109, 129, 140, 151–152, 159, 161, 192, 196–198, 200–201, 205–206, 217–218, 238–242, 248, 252, 256, 268, 273–274, 277–278, 281, 284–288, 290, 305, 309, 329–330n, 332–333n, 335n, 338n, 341n; as conscience of nation 9, 12, 20–22, 109, 205, 238–243, 248, 256, 274, 288; her effort to stem emigration 5, 21, 23; debate about *Was bleibt* 9, 20–23, 26, 33–35, 89, 106–107, 151, 160–162, 190, 205–206, 217–218, 238, 241, 288–290; involvement with the Stasi 9, 20, 32–33, 106, 196–197, 205–206; on conformity 21–22
Wolf, Gerhard 22, 137, 192, 275, 284, 341n, 352n
women's rights 21, 57–58, 95, 176–178, 242
women's movement 95, 99, 100–101, 170, 178, 186, 198, 212, 236, 242, 304
writers, conformity of 14, 66–67, 69, 74–75, 77, 82, 86, 91, 108, 152, 229, 243; role of 6–7, 43, 64–65, 90–91, 97, 138–140, 150, 185, 191, 247–248, 251, 256–258, 283, 325
Writers' Union 13–14, 25, 62, 140, 143–150, 153, 155–156, 161, 170–172, 178, 180–182, 186–188, 190, 192, 197, 200, 212, 227, 230, 251–252, 256, 258, 260, 267–268, 274–275, 296, 305, 307, 317
Wurm, Carsten 351n

Yevtushenko, Yevnegy 284, 352n

Zhdanov, Andrei Aleksandrovich 161–162
Zimmermann, Dieter 335n
Zohlen, Gerwin 335n
Zweig, Arnold 34, 143, 335n, 344n